P9-BVG-481

Caring on the Clock

Families in Focus

Series Editors
Anita Ilta Garey, University of Connecticut
Naomi R. Gerstel, University of Massachusetts, Amherst
Karen V. Hansen, Brandeis University
Rosanna Hertz, Wellesley College
Margaret K. Nelson, Middlebury College

Katie L. Acosta, *Amigas y Amantes: Sexually Nonconforming Latinas Negotiate Family*

Ann V. Bell, *Misconception: Social Class and Infertility in America*

Anita Ilta Garey and Karen V. Hansen, eds., *At the Heart of Work and Family: Engaging the Ideas of Arlie Hochschild*

Katrina Kimport, *Queering Marriage: Challenging Family Formation in the United States*

Mary Ann Mason, Nicholas H. Wolfinger, and Marc Goulden, *Do Babies Matter? Gender and Family in the Ivory Tower*

Jamie L. Mullaney and Janet Hinson Shope, *Paid to Party: Working Time and Emotion in Direct Home Sales*

Markella B. Rutherford, *Adult Supervision Required: Private Freedom and Public Constraints for Parents and Children*

Barbara Wells, *Daughters and Granddaughters of Farmworkers: Emerging from the Long Shadow of Farm Labor*

Caring on the Clock

• •

The Complexities and Contradictions of Paid Care Work

EDITED BY MIGNON DUFFY, AMY ARMENIA,
AND CLARE L. STACEY

NO LONGER PROPERTY OF DBRL

Daniel Boone
Regional Library

Rutgers University Press
New Brunswick, New Jersey, and London

NO LONGER PROPERTY OF DBRL

Library of Congress Cataloging-in-Publication Data

Caring on the clock : the complexities and contradictions of paid care work / edited by Mignon Duffy, Amy Armenia, and Clare L. Stacey.
    pages   cm. — (Families in focus)
  Includes bibliographical references and index.
  ISBN 978-0-8135-6312-1 (hardback) — ISBN 978-0-8135-6311-4 (pbk.) —
ISBN 978-0-8135-6313-8 (e-book)
    1. Service industries workers. 2. Caregivers. 3. Household employees. 4. Social service.
I. Duffy, Mignon. II. Armenia, Amy, 1972– III. Stacey, Clare L. (Clare Louise), 1973–
  HD8039.S45C37 2015
  331.7′61361—dc23

                                        2014014274

A British Cataloging-in-Publication record for this book is available from the British Library.

This collection copyright © 2015 by Rutgers, The State University
Individual chapters copyright © 2015 in the names of their authors
All rights reserved

No part of this book may be reproduced or utilized in any form or by any means, electronic or mechanical, or by any information storage and retrieval system, without written permission from the publisher. Please contact Rutgers University Press, 106 Somerset Street, New Brunswick, NJ 08901. The only exception to this prohibition is "fair use" as defined by U.S. copyright law.

Visit our website: http://rutgerspress.rutgers.edu

Manufactured in the United States of America

Contents

Figures

Tables

Foreword

MARGARET K. NELSON

In writing here, I have the privilege and honor of wearing two hats. The first hat, and the reason I initially volunteered to write a foreword for *Caring on the Clock*, was so that I could reflect, at least briefly, on the many changes in the study of care work since my sister Emily K. Abel and I edited one of the first collections on this topic almost twenty-five years ago.

To be sure, as we brought together the fifteen chapters of *Circles of Care: Work and Identity in Women's Lives* (1990), we were attentive to a range of the varied issues raised in this wonderful new anthology. We addressed the fact that caregiving was a practice associated overwhelmingly with women, and we theorized about how feminist reformulations could help capture the meaning and nature of caregiving. We reflected on the constellation of events that were transforming the nature of caregiving in our society, such as the growing number of women in the labor force, the expanding size of the service sector, cutbacks in public funding for human services, and the aging of the population. And, well aware that context mattered, we organized the chapters around different domains in which the provision of care occurs.

Of course we had no way of knowing then how the scholarship on caregiving would expand over the next two decades. But it did. The initial theoretical foray of Berenice Fisher and Joan Tronto (1990) developed into full-blown books and essays. Some of this development is both reviewed and brilliantly expanded by the editors of this new collection in the first chapter about how to define and analyze care work.[1] The substantive work on a range of caregiving occupations and activities has exploded to include separate studies of a wide range of different occupations. This research also finds a home in this collection in the essays about occupations as diverse as nannies through hospice workers and nurses.

In addition, a whole new field has emerged in the scholarship of care—that which concerns itself with history—represented by the unique scholarship of Emily Abel on informal care (2002, 2013), the excellent writing of Eileen Boris and Jennifer Klein on the history of homecare workers (2012), a burgeoning history of the nursing industry centered at the University of Pennsylvania, Ellen More's (2001) complex history of women doctors, and Mignon Duffy's (2011) astute overview of paid care in the twentieth century. Some of that development is included here in Duffy's chapter on "Beyond Outsourcing: Understanding the History of Paid Care." Finally, the collection explores whole new sets of issues—violence in the workplace, the experiences of migrant care workers, and paths to social change for caregiving occupations—that were barely understood (or foreseen) a quarter of a century ago.

As a result of this expansion, the tentative hypotheses Emily and I put forth have now been subject to empirical test: in some cases our guesses were substantiated, in others they were refuted, and in still other cases they have now been shown to be too simple and too narrow. Take just one example. We acknowledged that care work was rewarding; we insisted as well that it was hard work. Likewise, the essays in this book acknowledge the rewarding nature of care work in its many manifestations. But these essays also show concretely how variations in rewards depend on the context in which the work occurs. And by taking an unflinching look at just how hard the work is, the authors document the physical, emotional, and financial consequences of that work for the individual worker as well as the ways those consequences radiate out from the individual worker to the broader network in which she (or sometimes he) is embedded both in the workplace and at home.

The mention of the spillover of care work into the home provides the occasion for me to replace my first hat with my second one, as an editor (along with my dear friends and colleagues Rosanna Hertz, Naomi Gerstel, Karen Hansen, and Anita Garey) of the Families in Focus series at Rutgers University Press. When this book was first presented to us in proposal form, we were both wildly enthusiastic and a wee bit hesitant. We were enthusiastic because we were well aware of the marvelous scholarship each of the three editors had already produced. I have mentioned Duffy's historical work; I would add here Armenia's work on family day care providers (2009) and Stacey's work on home care aides (2011). We also were enthusiastic because the proposal contained a rich range of essays that touched on such critical points as pay, hours, and the bodily impact of the labor of care; we also appreciated how the collection as a whole represented the interdisciplinary approach of so much of the preexisting scholarship on care. Even so, we edit a series on the family. Would a book on paid care adequately make explicit the links to the issues that are the topic of our series?

We need not have worried. The marvelous introductory chapter—indeed the introductory paragraph of the introductory chapter—states explicitly that paid care workers "embody the complex intersections between families and work," not least because families today rely on "growing numbers of paid workers [who] are important partners in the provision of care across the life course." If the introductory chapter lays out a key link between paid care work and families, many other terrific essays expand on that theme. One chapter talks about what happens when care workers are viewed like members of the family; another focuses on the time dimension of paid care and the resulting type of family life workers in different occupations can sustain; still another shows how workers move between institutional and home environments and how the "home" remains an ideal for many. In short, although the links to family are most explicit in the section titled "Work and Family," the real relevance of paid care for family life is a theme throughout the chapters.

Running short on steam (and maybe imagination), Emily Abel and I wrote a brief acknowledgments section to our collection. It read: "Author's prefaces are generally testaments to caring. We hope this book as a whole serves such a purpose." Brief as it was, we were thinking, as we wrote that, about our own relationship and the care we already took of each other as we supported our simultaneous engagement in motherhood and scholarship; we were also thinking about the support we gave to the authors of the separate chapters as they struggled to find voice in a new field of scholarship. Shortly after the book was published, when first our parents, then Emily, and then our series editor, Joan Smith, fell ill, we learned at first hand even more about the satisfactions and demands (the rewards and the hard work) of caregiving in personal relationships. Watching the editors of this cutting-edge anthology interact with each other and with the many different authors included here, it is obvious that this next generation "gets it." Reading this superb collection of essays, we know for sure that the scholarship on care is both alive and very well indeed.

Note

1   Some of these ideas are even more fully developed in a recent article by Duffy, Albelda, and Hammonds (2013).

Acknowledgments

The editors wish to acknowledge the many individuals, organizations, and institutions that helped bring *Caring on the Clock* to fruition. First and foremost, we would like to thank the contributing authors for their patience and perseverance, and for producing what we think are some of the best pieces around on paid care. We are so grateful that you embarked on this journey with us.

There are several people who read drafts of the volume and provided invaluable feedback. For countless hours of editorial work, we express our sincere gratitude to Hannah Tello, who patiently combed through the chapters and generally kept us on track. Without her diligence and keen eye for detail, we would have never met our deadlines. We thank Mignon's writing group—Karen Hansen and Debi Osnowitz—for their close read of our introductory chapters and section essays. Their insightful feedback helped us refine the framing of the book. The reviewers and editors at Rutgers University Press—including the fantastic group of Families in Focus editors—made the review process as seamless as possible, carefully reading every chapter of the volume and making intelligent and insightful suggestions along the way. Peggy Nelson, Mary Tuominen, and Karen Hansen also helped improve the book immeasurably by serving as discussants at the *Caring on the Clock* mini-conference in March 2013. This interactive forum proved a very effective way to move our ideas forward and we were so lucky have such esteemed scholars commenting on our work in progress. Thanks to the Eastern Sociological Society for supporting and promoting the mini-conference and to the Carework Network for providing a forum through which we were able to solicit contributions for the volume.

The Center for Women and Work at the University of Massachusetts–Lowell served as an intellectual and practical home base for this project, and was instrumental in supporting the mini-conference. For logistical and travel support, we wish to acknowledge the Department of Sociology at Kent State University, the Creative Economy Initiative of the President's Office of the University of Massachusetts, the Sociology Department at the University of Massachusetts–Lowell, and the Sociology and Anthropology Department at Randolph-Macon College. Support also came from the Walter Williams Craigie Teaching Endowment at Randolph-Macon College and Rollins College.

Our ability to see this project through to completion is, in part, the result of the paid and unpaid caring labor of many people who helped tend to our children and parents while we worked. A special "shout out" to our partners Scott Englehart, Gary Jorgensen, and Zach Schiller, who all contributed extra hours at home so we could write and revise. And a final thank-you is owed to the little (and not so little) people in our lives, Maxwell, Lillian, Elena, Ben, and Rebecca. In many ways, you are the inspiration for this book and the reason the three of us are passionate about improving the lives and working conditions of paid caregivers.

Part I

Paid Care Work

• •

1

On the Clock,
Off the Radar

• •

Paid Care Work in
the United States

MIGNON DUFFY, AMY ARMENIA,

AND CLARE L. STACEY

A nurse inserts an I.V. A teacher helps a child with his math. A social worker visits a new mother. A personal care attendant helps a quadriplegic bathe and get dressed. A nursing assistant feeds an elderly resident of a nursing home, the meal prepared by a dietary aide. A nanny reads a bedtime story to soothe a child to sleep. Every day workers like these provide critical support to some of the most vulnerable members of our society. *Caring on the Clock* is about these workers and others like them who perform the essential labor of taking care of people's most fundamental needs. Across the occupational landscape of health care, education, child care, mental health, and social services, paid care workers embody the complex intersections between families and work, challenging the ideological division between private and public through their very existence.

The goal of this volume is to bring together cutting-edge empirical research about paid care workers into a comprehensive frame. We believe that collectively, these disparate occupations represent a critical sector of our economic and social activity. Not only is care for the young, the old, and those who are ill and disabled one of the basic ethical obligations of a society, but it is also labor that undergirds the successful participation of many members of society in the labor market, in families, and in communities. This group of occupations is also linked by a tendency to be devalued relative to other similarly situated workers. Because care is labor intensive and dependent on interpersonal relationship, it is less responsive to the supply and demand mechanisms of the market, leading to shortages in both the quality and quantity of care provided by paid workers. In addition, many paid care occupations in the United States have been historically constructed as extensions of women's unpaid roles in the home, contributing to the lack of economic and social recognition of paid care work. Within paid care, some jobs have been disproportionately relegated to groups of women who are further marginalized by their class, race, ethnicity, or citizenship. Our current social organization of care depends on paid care workers to meet some of the most critical needs of American families. The challenges facing paid care workers undermine the ability of the sector to provide adequate, quality care to those families who need it.

By bringing together studies of a range of different paid care occupations, we aim to better understand the challenges faced by this group of workers as well as illuminate the potential strengths of the sector. A comprehensive frame allows for a comparative approach that identifies both common threads and fractures within the paid care sector. While these issues have significant intellectual and theoretical import, our ultimate interest is in advancing knowledge that can inform policy and social change with an eye to closing the gap between the inadequacy of our current system of care provision and the care needs that are so fundamental to our society. In this chapter, we explain our definition of paid care work as well as describe a number of ideas that are central to our conceptualization of care. We also present the reasons why understanding paid care work is important—to care scholars, to scholars of families, work, and inequalities, to students, to policymakers, and really to anyone who lives in the United States today.

What Is Paid Care Work?

Care is a slippery concept at best, frequently used in a range of both scholarly and popular contexts. For the purposes of this volume, we have adopted a set of definitional criteria borrowed from the earlier work of Mignon Duffy, Randy Albelda, and Clare Hammonds (2013) to draw boundaries around paid care work organizations and industries:

1 the activity [of the industry] contributes to physical, mental, social, and/or emotional well-being;
2 the primary labor process [in the industry] involves face-to-face relationship with those cared for;

3 those receiving care are members of groups that by normal social standards cannot provide for all of their own care because of age, illness, or disability; and

4 care work builds and maintains human infrastructure that cannot be adequately produced through unpaid work or unsubsidized markets, necessitating public investment (147).

In practice, this conceptualization of paid care includes those who work in the industries of health care, education and child care, mental health, and social services.

Within this broad classification of industries, specific jobs can be further categorized into nurturant and non-nurturant occupations (Duffy 2005). Nurturant care includes workers whose jobs are typically understood to involve a significant amount of face-to-face interaction and relationship with those being cared for. These are nurses, social workers, teachers, childcare workers, psychologists, home care aides, and other related workers. Non-nurturant occupations include hospital janitors, school cafeteria workers, nursing home administrative workers, and many other groups of workers who work in homes and care institutions to support the direct provision of care. While the paid care sector as a whole is dominated by women, there are important cleavages within the sector based on class, race, ethnicity, and citizenship. In general, those jobs identified as non-nurturant (often lower paid) tend to have a higher proportion of women of color and immigrant women than nurturant care occupations (Duffy 2005, 2007).

Because an exclusive focus on nurturant care obscures some of these most significant racial, ethnic, and citizenship-based inequalities, we have chosen to include both nurturant and non-nurturant care workers in the current volume. That said, the explosion of job growth (and a significant amount of empirical research) in the paid care sector has been driven by nurturant care (Duffy 2011). The volume also reflects this emphasis on nurturant occupations.

Why Care about Paid Care Work?

All of us need care as young children, most of us will need care again as we near the end of our lives, and many of us will need care of varying levels of intensity for longer or shorter periods in between. Although an enormous amount of these care needs are met by the unpaid labor of friends and family members, growing numbers of paid workers are important partners in the provision of care across the life course. In the broadest sense, then, paid care literally affects all of us—both as recipients and as partners with paid care workers in caring for friends and family members. And all of us have a stake in developing knowledge that will advance efforts to improve our current approach to care provision.

Beyond its broad social importance, paid care work is particularly significant to scholars and students studying families in the United States today. Families with means have always relied on paid workers to support, supplement, or substitute for the unpaid family labor of care. However, the nature of care provision and the role of paid care workers have changed dramatically in the past one hundred years (see chapter 2). Once dominated by domestic servants, the market for paid care has expanded outward to include specialized healthcare providers, a range of workers engaged in care of the elderly and chronically ill, distinct groups of childcare workers, and a growing number of mental health and social services personnel. As a society, we entrust our health, our children, our bodies, and our lives to these workers. Given this central role, our understanding of contemporary family life requires attention to those who do "family" work for pay.

Similarly, we cannot understand work and occupations in the United States today without attention to paid care workers. Nationally, it is estimated that 24 percent of all employment is in care industries, and that 15 percent of all workers are nurturant care workers (Folbre 2012, 66).[1] Between 1950 and 2007, the number of nurturant care workers grew sixfold, far outpacing the overall expansion rate of the labor market (Duffy 2011, 78). Home health care and home care are the industries with the first- and second-fastest rate of employment growth in the United States, and long-term care employment in nursing homes and private residences, currently about 3 percent of the total labor force, is expected to account for 10 percent of all new jobs between 2010 and 2020 (Folbre 2012, 82). In addition, a high-functioning organization of care provision creates a "human infrastructure" that supports other types of economic activity. And some of the most innovative examples of unionization and worker organizing in recent decades have been in the care sector. Paid care work is therefore both quantitatively and qualitatively central to the study of work, labor, and occupations in the United States.

Within the scholarship of care, a comprehensive focus on paid care occupations is important at this moment in the development of this active interdisciplinary field. In recent years, care scholars have developed a rich body of empirical research about individual care occupations. This volume brings together some of these specialized empirical studies within the frame of the broad theoretical reach of the more conceptual work in the field. The emphasis on paid care work is not intended to diminish the importance of unpaid care, nor to deny the overlaps, connections, synergies, and conflicts between paid and unpaid care. Rather, by examining paid care work across a range of contexts, we hope to contribute a more nuanced view of paid care, free from the shadow of a comparison to a sometimes idealized view of unpaid family care. This is a timely contribution to a field that at the same time must continue to wrestle with how to conceptualize and study the dynamic interplay between paid and unpaid care both theoretically and empirically.

Finally, paid care work is a critical area of inquiry for scholars and students who want to better understand the intersections of systems of inequalities based on gender, race, ethnicity, citizenship, disability, and class. The division of caring labor in the United States is linked to these inequalities and serves to both reflect and reinforce broader social patterns. The division of caring labor has been identified as a linchpin of gender inequality (Chafetz 1988) and the stratification of paid care workers is heavily implicated in reproducing inequalities among groups of women (Duffy 2005; Glenn 1992).

Conceptualizing Paid Care Work

As an interdisciplinary field, care scholarship draws on both theoretical and empirical research in sociology, economics, philosophy, political science, and history. Below we will address some of the major concepts in the field, both as a way of explaining our definitional choices and as a framework for understanding the empirical chapters that follow.

Reproductive Labor and Human Infrastructure

The concept of reproductive labor was introduced by Friedrich Engels to refer to activities involved in maintaining and reproducing the labor force (Engels [1884] 1972), including cooking, cleaning, and child rearing. This reproductive labor is necessary to raise, care for, and maintain a functioning and productive work force. Much of this work has been done for free by women, rendering it invisible in the economy and obscuring the dependence of men and the larger society on these activities. Feminist scholars and activists in the 1970s argued that domestic activities should be recognized as labor worthy of societal recognition and even economic rewards (for summaries, see Hansen and Philipson 1990; Laslett and Brenner 1989). Later scholars have expanded their focus from unpaid reproductive labor to include both paid and unpaid work under the conceptual umbrella. For example, Barbara Laslett and Johanna Brenner (1989) emphasize that the responsibility for reproductive labor (which they call "social reproduction") can be organized in a variety of ways and distributed among families, markets, communities, and the state. The defining characteristic of reproductive labor across the paid and unpaid spheres is its foundational role in maintaining and reproducing the basic social and economic well-being of a society.

More recently, some scholars have used the language of human infrastructure to capture this fundamental idea (Duffy, Albelda, and Hammonds 2013). Physical infrastructure, such as roads, bridges, and broadband connections, is seen as an essential prerequisite to healthy and productive economic activity in any society. It is also widely recognized that investment in physical infrastructure has benefits that reach far beyond any individual or even single company, but are broadly shared and often publicly supported. A human infrastructure that adequately addresses the range of care needs of American families is equally important to supporting our economic, social, and civic lives. Like physical infrastructure, a strong system of care provision has benefits that extend to many members of society. We take as a starting premise of our examination of paid care work that it is a critical part of human infrastructure and should be understood both as a collective responsibility and a societal contribution.

Emotional Labor and Relationality

One of the goals of this volume is to explore the macro-institutional implications of paid care work (as per our discussion of human infrastructure above) as well as the micro-interactional realities of being a care worker. With respect to the latter, several chapters in *Caring on the Clock* explore the role of interpersonal relationships and emotional labor in nurturant care. These pieces ask important questions about relations of care, including, How do paid care workers experience and understand their emotional labor? What are the consequences of this emotional labor, both psychosocially and in terms of pay and recognition? How do the boundaries of family and work blur for paid caregivers. in ways that make them unique from other interactive service workers? Focusing on the relational quality of paid care work in this way allows us to place caregivers and care recipients at the center of analysis, where we can learn more about both the constraints and rewards of caring for another person's needs.

The concept of emotional labor refers to a worker being required to "induce or suppress feeling" to produce a certain state of mind or feeling in another person, that is, a customer (Hochschild 1983). Implicit in this original definition is that when emotion management is required of a worker as a condition of employment, the results are exploitative and deleterious to the worker's well-being and sense of self (Garey and Hansen 2011; Hochschild 1983). Relationality—as a broader concept—refers to a sustained emotional connection that may or may not take place in the context of paid work and that does not necessarily result in negative outcomes for the person(s) engaged in the emotional exchange.

What does it mean to say that paid care work is relational in nature? The term, which has roots in both the feminist psychoanalytic and care work literatures (see Chodorow 1978; Parks 2003; Tronto 1993), generally refers to "sustained, reciprocal emotional connections between two people" (Parks 2003). Relationality is what makes paid care work different from other types of interactive service work (which we consciously have excluded from this volume). While a manicurist, a bank teller, or a telemarketer all engage in emotional labor as a condition of their employment—and may in fact have genuine relationships with customers—they do not generally have reciprocal emotional connections with people. By contrast, a home care aide will probably know her patient for weeks and possibly months or years. She might be privy to intimate details about her client's life and experiences; may accompany her client to appointments, family gatherings, or other outings; and may feel at times more like family than employee (see chapter 16; Stacey 2011). She may work uncompensated hours, talk to her client on the phone "off the clock," or provide groceries or medicines for her client when money is tight. As this hypothetical illustrates, the bond that can form between caregiver and care recipient is at once meaningful, personally rewarding, exhausting and—at times—exploitive. For this reason, the idea of relationality is central to understanding how paid care work can be both personally fulfilling and also make workers vulnerable to burnout, emotional fatigue, or wage exploitation.

The point we wish to emphasize here is that emotional labor in nurturant care work contexts looks very different from emotional labor in other interactive service jobs, precisely because of the sustained, relational nature of caregiving (Erickson and Stacey 2012). An example may help illustrate our point. Returning to the case of home care aides, the relational demands of the job (emoting, listening, companionship) mean that the boundaries of family and work are sometimes blurred. Aides often feel conflicted, as if they are unsure whether their client is friend, family, or employer. As such, feeling rules—norms about how one should feel/display feelings vis-à-vis others—are also confused. If an elderly client asks an aide to stay a few hours longer because she is scared of being alone, that aide may feel conflicted about whether the feeling rules of work or family/friendship apply. This confusion, we suggest, has implications for the way that care workers understand their labor but can also affect the ability of workers to avoid exploitive arrangements and engage in public advocacy (via unions or other outlets). Several chapters in this volume directly explore what happens when the boundaries of home/family/work blur, furthering our understanding of emotional labor, relationality, and caring occupations.

The Question of Dependency

The notion of dependency has a central, but controversial, position within care scholarship. A number of scholars have argued that labeling people as dependent on paid and unpaid caregivers obscures the reciprocal nature of many of these relationships and unfairly characterizes care recipients as objects rather than as actors in their own care. In addition, in the highly individualized culture of the United States, being dependent, particularly when it involves the support of the state, is highly stigmatized (Fine and Glendinning 2005). On the other hand, the notion of dependency is also used to invoke social and ethical responsibility. Some dependencies have been identified as "inevitable," as they are rooted in biological conditions of childhood, age, illness, or disability (Fineman 2000; Kittay 1999). Philosophers have argued that caring for these groups is one of the basic ethical obligations of a society, and it is considered by some to be the "field of caring that most clearly is a concern both for social policy and for feminists" (Waerness 1996, 235).

As described in the discussion of relationality above, we understand microlevel care relationships to be much more complex and reciprocal than implied by a characterization as dependent. However, at a macro level, we do believe that the concept of inevitable dependencies illuminates a key reason to focus on care of children and youth as well as those who are elderly, ill, or disabled. Our commitment to the care of these groups as a collective responsibility is not only an economic necessity (as described in the earlier section on human infrastructure) but also an ethical imperative.

Devaluation and Inequalities

Understanding the position of paid care as an employment sector requires a dual perspective. First, we have to examine the ways that the paid care sector, in all its diversity, is subject to a unique set of dynamics that leads to devaluation of workers in this sector relative to similarly situated workers in other industries. Second, we must interrogate stratification *within* the paid care sector, which is linked to the intersecting inequalities of class, gender, race, ethnicity, citizenship, and disability. This dual perspective illuminates the range of challenges facing workers in the paid care sector, issues that affect many families (including the families of the workers) by impacting the availability, quality, and cost of care.

Paid care workers are overwhelmingly women, and research shows that the gender wage gap has persisted well into the twenty-first century. In 2012, among full-time, year-round workers, women earned 80.9 cents to every dollar earned by men (Hegewisch, Williams, and Edwards 2013). This economy-wide gender wage gap disproportionately impacts the care sector, where so many women workers are concentrated. In addition to the overall gender wage gap, nurturant care workers suffer from an additional 5 to 6 percent hourly wage penalty (England, Budig, and Folbre 2002). Importantly, the researchers in this study controlled for gender, education, experience, and a number of other occupational and industrial characteristics, demonstrating that all else being equal, jobs that involve nurturant care pay less. Although the process behind this wage penalty is harder to demonstrate, the researchers conclude that at least part of this penalty is due to a gendered process of devaluation related to the cultural association of nurturance with the feminine.

Feminist economists have also identified a number of specific characteristics of care work that undermine the functioning of the market in the paid care sector. First, care is what economists consider a public good; that is, done well, it has benefits far beyond the individual directly receiving care (England and Folbre 1999; Folbre 1994). For example, a child who attends a high-quality preschool certainly receives an individual benefit. But that benefit also extends to the child's parents, her future teachers, her employers as an adult, her future partner or spouse, the community that child lives in, and so forth. Supply and demand models of wage- and price-setting depend on the consumers making a rational choice about the value of the product they are purchasing. When benefits spill over to others, this mechanism is distorted, and the market undervalues the good in question through lower production or lower price (which in this case means wages to care workers). This distortion is recognized in overwhelming support for the idea of publicly funding physical infrastructure, which is similarly a public good that benefits many.

The second reason that markets do not function very well to set employment, wage, and price levels in the paid care sector is because of the intensive relational nature of nurturant care. Market models assume that consumers can easily measure and assess the quality of the good or service they are purchasing, a challenging proposition when relationship is so central to the product itself. Some scholars have found that relational connection can make paid care workers particularly vulnerable to exploitation as they may work more hours or accept less pay because of their personal attachment to the human beings they care for (see chapter 16; Diamond 1992; Stone 2000). The centrality of relationship in nurturant care also makes achieving increases in productivity much more difficult than in other industries in which technological advances regularly lead to increases in output or efficiency and cost savings. Increasing class size or nurses' caseloads may increase the "productivity" of a teacher or a nurse but past a certain point is also likely to lessen the quality of teaching and nursing (Duffy, Albelda, and Hammonds 2013).

As a whole, then, paid care work is vulnerable to a number of mechanisms of devaluation that hold down wages in the sector as a whole and create less-than-ideal conditions for meeting care needs. Within this general context, paid care is very polarized, including some relatively well-paid professions and semi-professions (doctors, occupational therapists, nurses, teachers) and some of the lowest-paid jobs in the economy (childcare workers, home care aides, nursing assistants). The distribution of workers in these jobs is linked to class, race, ethnicity, and citizenship. One of the more important advances in the scholarship on care is the attention given to the way that social location shapes the division of caring labor (see Duffy 2011; Ehrenreich and Hochschild 2002; Glenn 1992; Zimmerman, Litt, and Bose 2006). The current volume continues in this vein, as many of the chapters consider—either directly or indirectly—how the experiences of providing paid care are anything but universal and vary considerably depending on who is providing care, where, and under what conditions.

Paid Care Work and Labor Law

For all the challenges that paid care workers face, their position as workers and employees gives them access to support and resources that unpaid family caregivers do not have. This gives them the potential to improve their jobs, to increase their ability to care for their own families, and to use these avenues to improve the quality of care they can provide for others. On the other hand, law and social policy around care has also helped make these jobs worse—through reduced budgets for the public services that fund these sectors (see chapters 9 and 10) and also through the explicit exclusion of many care workers from labor protection regulations (Boris and Klein 2012).

The most central piece of labor law that American workers draw on is the Fair Labor Standards Act (FLSA), which establishes a federal minimum wage and requires overtime pay for many workers. In addition to the FLSA, care workers have access to other protective legislation like state-level minimum wage laws, the National Labor Relations Act, the Occupational Safety and Health Act, and the Family and Medical Leave Act. These laws provide some level of resources and recognition for paid workers that are unavailable to unpaid caregivers. But care workers occupy a unique position in that many of their jobs exist outside of standard employment relationships, and therefore fall into categories that are exempt or excluded from protection by these regulations. For example, live-in childcare workers are excluded from overtime pay regulation under the FLSA, and from basic protections under most of the other laws listed above (Macdonald 2010). Even as the FLSA was expanded in 1974 to cover many other types of domestic workers, Congress maintained an exemption for "elder companions," which continues to exclude home care aides from FLSA regulation (Boris and Klein 2012). This exemption was finally overturned in 2013, with changes to take effect on January 1, 2015 (Becker 2013). Other care workers in sectors dominated by self-employment (family day care workers, for example) are also excluded from labor protections.

Even when their labor rights are protected by federal and state legislation, care workers often have a difficult time asserting their rights and needs vis-à-vis a dependent clientele. As noted above, these jobs are rooted in relationality that can result in workers placing consumers' needs above their own, even in terms of their own safety, health, and economic well-being. Because of this tension, the efforts to improve conditions that have gained the most traction have been ones that draw on public support or state intervention for caregiving (as opposed to targeting clients or consumers for redress). These efforts include unionization efforts that treat the state as the employer of record for the purposes of bargaining, like the effort that successfully organized home health aides in California in 1999 (Delp and Quan 2002) and several successful statewide efforts for family day care workers (Howes, Leana, and Smith 2012). These organizing efforts aim to create quality jobs for paid care workers and their families, and also hold the potential to revitalize the labor movement with the incorporation of new and growing populations of workers (Cobble 2010).

The tenuous position of care jobs in our economy has translated to a similarly precarious position vis-à-vis labor law and protections. If recent history is to be a guide, care workers may be best served by grassroots organizing and collective movements that agitate for more recognition and remuneration, both within their workplaces and via state action and policy.

Caring on the Clock

This volume begins with a historic overview of the paid care sector in the United States. In the second part of the book, "Contexts of Care," authors consider the impact of both organizational and locational context on paid care workers and explore commonalities and contrasts between care work in homes and institutions, organizational and self-employment, and other contexts. The third part, "Hazards of Care," explores the physical and psychological risks faced by these workers, drawing particularly on the considerable body of research in this area by occupational health scholars. The subjective meanings of care work are the focus of the fourth part, "Identities and Meaning Making." These chapters explore emotional labor and relationality from workers' perspectives, and interpretations of skill and professional status as they are crafted and experienced by workers and employers. The fifth section, "Work and Family," examines not only the material interactions between work and family for care workers, but also the impact of ideologies of work and family on the experiences of these workers. And finally, the last section, "Paths to Change," describes innovative and exciting ideas for social change, including top-down and grassroots efforts to improve recognition, remuneration, and mobility for care workers.

Note

1 Note that the authors of the source use different labels for the categories and slightly different definitions, but in practice the industries and occupations included are a very close match with those included by our definition.

2

Beyond Outsourcing

• •

Paid Care Work in
Historical Perspective

MIGNON DUFFY

> "Since we believe that it is not nature but
> society which is responsible for gender,
> race, and class hierarchies, we look to
> society's past, not to biology, for an
> understanding of the forces for
> continuity and change."
> —Teresa Amott and Julie Matthaei
> (1996, 5)

> "Without a history, public policy follows
> the path of social myth."
> —Alice Kessler-Harris (1990, 488)

These quotations from feminist scholars who have come before me capture perfectly the two reasons for the critical need for an accurate and nuanced understanding of the history of paid care work. First, we have in the United States a particular social organization of care, a way of defining and dividing up the labor of taking care of people. Importantly, our contemporary landscape of care is neither inevitable nor universal, but rather is the result of specific historical processes. Without an examination of the historical actors and events that led to an organization that links paid care work with women, with low wages, with immigration, and with racial and ethnic minority groups, those links are too easily interpreted as natural outcomes of essential differences based on gender, race, class, ability, or national origin.

The second reason that developing a strong base of historical knowledge about paid care is important is to guide public policy. A wide range of important public policy issues today involve paid care work: Should we expand public schooling to include younger groups of children? How should Medicare and Medicaid reimbursement deal with home care options? What are the implications of welfare reform efforts encouraging low-income women to enter paid care jobs like home health and family day care? How can we best provide accessible and quality care to an aging population? How can we attract quality teachers to the classroom? Are government-mandated nursing ratios good for patients? These are just a few examples of the maze of government policy around care in the United States today. Without a strong understanding of the historical and contemporary context of the paid care sector, these policy decisions are guided by nostalgia or myth.

The way that we organize care today is different from how we organized it in the past, and we have developed a number of shorthand terms to capture what we think is important about that change. We call it marketization, commodification, or outsourcing—terms that tell a story that care has moved from being an unpaid labor of love performed by friends and family members to being a commodity exchanged for money in the market. Among those who lament the decline of the "traditional" family, the marketization of care is held up as another symptom of that decline. This interpretation of history is not limited to those with a particular political agenda. Among care scholars, there is a significant amount of scholarship that is premised on this understanding of the historical trajectory of care. We frame the movement of care from family to market as the response to the "care crisis" created by women's large-scale entrance into the labor market; we analyze the impact of monetary exchange on care relationships; and we study the impact of breaking up care into easily saleable parts (for some examples, see Hochschild 2003a and 2012).

Deborah Stone's characterization provides an illustrative example of how the marketization story is presented in the care literature: "Caring comes from the private world of love, intimacy, families, and friendship, but much of it is now done in the public world of work, organizations, markets, and governments. Just as farm and craft labor were once wrenched out of the family and brought into a system of work controlled from outside, caring work is increasingly separated from the personal relationships in which it naturally arises and is performed instead in a system of managed and waged labor" (Stone 2000). While this statement points to some important questions about care in the contemporary

United States, and it captures our feeling that something big has happened, I would argue that the marketization narrative at once underestimates and overstates the transformation in care work in the twentieth century, thereby impeding our ability to truly understand the contemporary situation.

The notion that care has been outsourced emphasizes a shift in the *where* of care—from private homes to public institutions—and a change in the *who* of care—from unpaid family members to paid workers. What often gets left out of this story is the enormous transformation in the *what* of care during the twentieth century. That is, the reality is not that a constant set of tasks of care got moved from home to market and divided up among different people. Rather, the twentieth century was a time of enormous transformation in the very nature of child care, education, health care, social services, and mental health provision. These profound changes in the definition and content of care have driven many of the shifts in the location and organization of labor. In this sense, framing the primary change as one of movement from family to market understates the real revolution in care work.

At the same time, the dominant narrative of marketization also obscures the long history of paid workers performing care and their complex relationships to the unpaid family members and friends who have always and continue to play critical roles. It is difficult to overestimate the importance of domestic service in the United States during the second half of the 1800s. During this time period, nearly every middle- and upper-class family employed at least one domestic servant, and some wealthier families employed an entire staff to carry out the daily functions of their households. These domestic servants did many arduous chores of the backbreaking work of keeping house in the nineteenth century, and they also performed many more relational tasks like caring for new babies and sitting with the sick (Dudden 1983). Even as late as 1940, almost 2.5 million women worked as domestic servants, comprising just under 5 percent of the labor force (Duffy 2011). During the twentieth century, while the numbers of teachers, childcare workers, nurses, home health aides, and social workers increased dramatically, the number of domestic servants declined precipitously. By 1990, only about 500,000 workers—less than 0.5 percent of the labor force—were employed as domestic servants (Duffy 2011). There is no question that the occupational range of paid care workers has expanded, in large part due to the redefinition of care needs and the appropriate training and skills needed to meet them. But paid care work is not itself new, a fact that is perhaps obvious but is often overlooked in the debate about "outsourcing."

In addition, family members continue to contribute an enormous amount of unpaid care (Folbre 2012). The shifting roles of family members and paid workers have much more to do with a redefinition of the process of care rather than with a simple transfer of labor. Importantly, a number of scholars have made strong arguments that the very dichotomization of care into the private world of love and the public world of money oversimplifies and obscures the complex

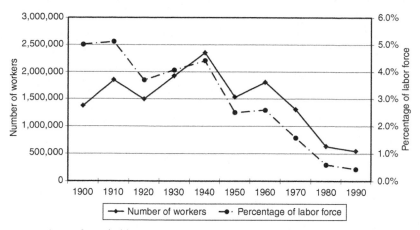

FIG. 2.1 Private household workers in the United States, 1900–1990. (Source: Duffy 2011)

webs of relationship, reciprocity, obligation, and motivations for care in the real world, both historical and contemporary (Folbre 2012; Zelizer 2005). Paid and unpaid care workers have had a long history of working in related ways to provide care, and the boundaries between labor and love as experienced by caregivers and care receivers are fuzzy and overlapping.

In this chapter, I will briefly outline the historical development during the twentieth century of four major arenas of nurturant care (see chapter 1 for conceptualization and definition of care work): physical health, long-term care of those who are elderly or disabled, child care and education, and mental health and social services. Although each story is unique in some ways, they are all stories of economic and material changes combining with shifting cultural values to transform what it means to provide care. They are stories of groups of workers constructing boundaries that have allowed them to stake occupational claims to particular pieces of paid care. And they are stories of how our assumptions based on gender, race, class, citizenship, and disability have shaped these historical processes.

From Sitting to Surgery

For most of the nineteenth century, people who became ill or disabled were cared for at home. While families may have sought advice from a local healer, the bulk of the care work fell to female relatives and friends, neighbors, and domestic servants. Where hospitals existed, they functioned not as centers of medical care but as institutional warehouses for the indigent, where ambulatory patients often provided the care for others. Occasionally, domestic servants would profess their occupation as a nurse, and hire themselves out to families specifically to care for the sick. These nurses, along with the mothers, daughters, and wives they assisted, were responsible for tasks as varied as changing bandages, applying leeches or plasters, preparing special foods or tonics, and "sitting" with patients to monitor their condition and to provide emotional support (Reverby 1987; Starr 1984).

Toward the end of the nineteenth century, a number of trends converged to alter dramatically the landscape of health care in the United States. First, the communication and transportation infrastructure was transformed by the introduction of the telephone in the 1870s and of the automobile in the 1890s, making treatment by physician a much more accessible option for a much wider range of patients. At the same time, the judgment of physicians came to be increasingly valued in a society becoming more specialized and scientifically oriented. Advances in medical science and technology, including understandings of the role of bacteria in infection and the development of new diagnostic instruments like the stethoscope, widened the gap between lay knowledge and "expert" knowledge of medicine (Starr 1984).

Physicians capitalized upon these cultural and material shifts to stake a claim to the position of expert in the diagnosing and curing of illness. In perhaps the most successful professionalization project in U.S. history, doctors introduced formal educational requirements and licensing laws that limited who could practice medicine (Larson 1977). The increasing exclusivity of the occupation raised its social and economic value, leading to the rewards as well as the professional authority enjoyed by physicians (Starr 1984). The professionalization of medicine was a male-dominated process that pushed women to the margins of the care work that had once been almost exclusively their realm (Ehrenreich and English 1979). At the same time, female reformers worked to carve out a niche in this new landscape of healing work. The need for sanitary environments and access to diagnostic tools made homes an increasingly difficult place to practice emergent curative methods, and hospitals were looked to more and more as the sites for care of acute illness and injury (Reverby 1987). Since the Civil War, reformers had been advocating that hospitals should provide their patients with moral guidance and a clean, orderly environment—a description that could not have been further from the hospitals of the mid-nineteenth century. Activists had a dual agenda: to improve conditions in hospitals and to provide respectable employment opportunities for the daughters of the new middle class. The guardians of this new hospital morality were to be trained nurses, women of strong character, honed by training and practice (Reverby 1987).

Throughout the twentieth century, many other types of workers joined physicians and nurses in administering health care in hospitals and doctors' offices—surgeons, radiologists, laboratory technicians, nursing aides, and orderlies. Today almost 10 million workers in a wide range of occupational groups are employed in healthcare industries (Duffy 2011). The explosion of specialized roles among healthcare workers has been in part a response to the continued rapid development of medical science and technology. Since the

1980s, health care has also been organized in the context of enormous pressures toward cost containment, a fact that has impacted workers' experiences of their jobs in the sector as well as the overall organization of the healthcare labor force (Gordon 2006). Within these constraints, physicians and nurses have continued to fight to define their jobs as professional roles. The combination of powerful economic interests in lowering labor costs with professional organizations distancing nurses in particular from some of the more physical tasks of care (changing bedpans and so forth) has contributed to the dramatic growth of low-wage support occupations in health care. These jobs—orderlies, nursing assistants, cleaners, dietary workers, and the like—are held disproportionately by Black women and immigrant women, and have been constructed as requiring less skilled care than that provided by (still largely white) registered nurses (Duffy 2011; Glazer 1991).

The complex diagnostic and treatment processes in health care today are far removed from the days of family and domestic servants "sitting" with the sick. There is no doubt that demographic changes, including higher rates of geographic mobility, lower birth rates, and increased female labor force participation, contributed to the shift away from family homes as the locus of care (Starr 1982). But the changes in the content and social organization of health care have been much more fundamental, driven by scientific and technological advances, a shifting cultural emphasis on expert knowledge, and the deliberate construction of exclusive domains by groups seeking occupational legitimacy and rewards. Interestingly, at the dawn of the twenty-first century, some tasks that were once considered the exclusive domain of a skilled nurse are now being delegated to nursing aides, home health aides, and even friends and family members, and the trend is toward moving the ill out of hospitals and into homes as soon as possible (Guberman et al. 2005). Changing material and cultural forces continue to shift not only where we believe care is most appropriately located but also what we think care should consist of and who should do it.

Creating Long-Term Care

As Robert Moroney (1998) points out, most families in the past did not face the kinds of institutionalization decisions faced by families today caring for aging relatives, because many more people today survive to much older ages. Due largely to the development of the modern healthcare system, life expectancy in the United States increased from an average of forty-seven years in 1900 to seventy-eight years in 2004 (Arias 2007), and the number of people aged ninety and over has tripled in the past thirty years (He and Muenchrath 2011). In addition, advances in treatment and adaptive technology now allow more people to live with chronic illness and all levels of disabilities. As a result, long-term care of those with chronic illness or severe disability and of the frail elderly emerged in the second half of the twentieth century as a new large-scale care need. Moroney's point highlights the qualitative difference between an extended family caring for a sixty-five-year-old grandmother who may also be able to help out with child care, and that same family caring for a debilitated ninety-five-year-old with significant medical challenges and needs for assistance with personal care.

The exploding need for long-term care—defined specifically as distinct from the kind of acute care provided in hospitals—has led to the development of a fast-growing set of low-wage care occupations, including home health aides, personal care attendants, and nursing assistants. Long-term care occupations in institutions like nursing homes and private homes, currently about 3 percent of the total labor force, are expected to account for 10 percent of all new jobs between 2010 and 2020 (Folbre 2012, 82). Home health care and home care (the provision of services not defined as health care to the elderly and disabled) are the industries with the first- and second-fastest rate of employment growth in the United States (Folbre 2012, 82).

Eileen Boris and Jennifer Klein (2012) have shown that the particular construction of home care work in the United States, its low-wage status, chronic underfunding by the state, and the heavy representation of women of color in the field, is the result of a complex interplay between care policy and welfare policy. From the healthcare side, policymakers faced with increasing cost pressures and rising needs saw home care as a cost-saving mechanism that would allow patients to leave hospitals more quickly. As welfare policy became more focused on quickly moving former welfare recipients into jobs, a number of programs encouraged women who received welfare to take home care jobs. The combination of these policy goals required that the job of home care have a low threshold to entry and therefore be defined as low-skilled work quite distinct from the skilled work of professional healthcare workers like nurses. The result was a series of underfunded state programs to support home care, which has become a stigmatized occupation with low wages, poor working conditions, and little opportunity for mobility. While individual care workers may find their work very meaningful (Stacey 2011), the systematic weaknesses in the provision of long-term care make this one of the most pressing policy issues of our time.

In the case of care of the frail elderly and those who are disabled, the expansion of paid care represents less a direct transfer of labor from unpaid family caregivers and more an exponential quantitative increase in the amount of care needed as well as a profound qualitative change in the type of care required. Our response to this shift has been shaped by a set of policy interests that have resulted in a particular division of labor among paid and unpaid care workers. It is also interesting that in this case, while there has been some growth in institutions to care for the elderly and disabled, there has been a strong movement to care for these individuals at home.

Caring for the "Priceless" Child

The years 1870 to 1930, the years during which health care in the United States underwent its most dramatic transformation, also saw a profound redefinition of childhood and what it means to care for a child. The "economically useful" child of the eighteenth and nineteenth centuries gave way to what Viviana Zelizer (1985) has called the "sacred" child, "economically useless but emotionally priceless." In an agricultural economy, children were indispensable contributors to the labor of running a farm and household, and during the beginning stages of industrialization many children worked alongside their parents in mills and factories. For most of the 1800s, children attended formal schooling sporadically if at all. By 1876 this had begun to change, and 60 percent of school-age children were enrolled in public schools for at least some months of the year (Carnoy and Levin 1985). The ethos of schools also began to change, from an emphasis on intellectual rigor, discipline, and corporal control of students to one in which teachers were to provide moral guidance, nurturance, and even affection (Carnoy and Levin 1985). At the same time, reformers began to fight for—and win—prohibitions against child labor and special safety and health protections for children. Children, once indispensable members of the household economy and contributors to its labor, gradually came to be seen primarily as the recipients of that labor, in need of nurturance and protection (Zelizer 1985). Although this process happened in different ways and on different timetables for children in different socioeconomic and cultural contexts, the overall trend was undeniable.

During the first three decades of the twentieth century, medical and sanitation advances drove infant and child mortality rates down dramatically. Industrialization also lowered birth rates, as children became more of an economic liability than an asset. Having fewer children, along with the higher probability that they would live to adulthood, set the stage for parents' attachment to their children to grow more emotionally charged. The sentimentalization of childhood, the expulsion of children from the labor force, and the need for an industrial work force with formal training drove the expansion of schools until, by 1920, schooling was compulsory in almost all states (Carnoy and Levin 1985).

By the time schools became the dominant form of care for children over six, teaching was firmly established as a female occupation. While teachers in the early history of the United States had been almost exclusively men, in 1900 women made up over 75 percent of the growing teaching work force (Rury 1989). The feminization of teaching was driven by two contemporary social movements of the nineteenth century and by a simultaneous redefinition of the qualities needed to be a good teacher. Male reformers advocating for the expansion of public education saw an opportunity to take advantage of the lower wages offered to female teachers to more rapidly grow the number of schools at a lower cost. At the same time, female activists looked to teaching (as they would later look to nursing) as an occupation that could provide opportunities for middle-class women. Both groups argued that women possessed the "female qualities of emotionality, maternal love, gentleness, and moral superiority" necessary to be good teachers (Preston 1993, 532). The language about women's appropriateness for the job implied a changed understanding of what children needed, one that was compatible with the ongoing process of the sacralization of childhood (Zelizer 1985).

Among middle- and working-class families, as many men began to leave family farms to work in factories, the idealization of the home as a domestic refuge and the gendered division of labor elevated women's role as manager and maintainer of the household and family. The general emphasis on the nuclear family was particularly manifested in an ideology of "intensive mothering," and the voluminous advice literature of the late nineteenth century emphasized the importance of the mother-child bond and the labor-intensive process of raising children, or at least raising them right (Hays 1996). By the late twentieth century, Annette Lareau (2003) identified the set of practices that has evolved for middle-class parents as "concerted cultivation." Concerted cultivation requires the active nurturance of children's growth and development emotionally, intellectually, and physically by parents in combination with an array of paid workers who provide everything from full-time care to music classes to sports activities to academic tutoring (Lareau 2003). The relatively recent explosion of child development research, catalyzed in part by advances in neurological science, has intensified the focus on providing rich environments and support for children, particularly during the earliest years of development. Cameron Macdonald (chapter 13) has pointed out that part of the job of middle-class mothers is to know what is required by a child's developmental needs at a given age, and then hire a paid worker (or workers) to meet those needs.

While the underlying ideological shifts have followed a somewhat different trajectory for poor families, the movement was also toward child-rearing becoming a much more labor-intensive process requiring the input of a range of specialized expert workers. With few exceptions, poverty in the United States had long been viewed primarily as an individual fault rather than a systematic social problem (Kunzel 1993). The creation of Head Start and other War on Poverty programs in the 1960s was clearly premised on the notion that paid child care could be a vehicle to compensate for perceived deficits in poor families, a strategy continued throughout the process of welfare reform in the 1990s. Sherry Wexler has argued convincingly that policymakers make different assumptions about mothers—and who is best fit to care for their children—based on their class and race (Wexler 1997). However, a service-intensive approach to intervention with poor children also requires the participation of many expert workers.

Certainly the large-scale expansion of women's labor force participation has contributed to the expanding need for paid care workers for children. But fundamental economic transformation, shifting cultural values, movements for professional recognition and women's access to occupations, and scientific development have transformed the nature of caring for children such that it bears as little resemblance to the child care of 150 years ago as surgery does to sitting with the sick. The expansion of roles for paid workers in caring for both preschool and school-age children is at least in large part a result of this reconfiguration of the meaning of care.

Doing Good: Charity Becomes Work

The beginning of the twentieth century was a time of profound change not only for health care and child care, but also for taking care of the poor, mentally ill, and other groups considered in need. In the nineteenth century, the ideal of femininity that celebrated women's domesticity was extended to the sphere of "benevolence" (Kunzel 1993). Women's role as moral guardians of the family was linked to a role as moral guardians of the wider community, and middle- and upper-class women's activism and charity work reached into many arenas, including child welfare, the care of the mentally ill, and the care of unwed mothers (as well as hospital reform). Just as nursing and teaching drew upon dominant notions of femininity to describe the special fit of women in hospital and school roles, activists used the language of feminine virtue to portray benevolence as uniquely suited to the female character. In the period between 1870 and 1930, as science emerged as the basis for the treatment of physical illness, there was a strong movement to use science to treat all kinds of emotional, mental, and social dysfunction. This movement would alter the nature of social services in substance and in organization, and lead to the emergence and growth of a new group of nurturant care occupations.

At the turn of the century, most individuals considered mentally ill were placed in custodial institutions where the primary goal was social control rather than treatment. While psychoanalysis had a presence in the United States, it was an intensive type of treatment that only those who had considerable means could afford and only those with fairly serious neuroses would undertake. For the most part, individuals with mental illness were considered one of a number of groups of "dependents," which also included orphaned or abandoned children and the poor. In fact, most asylums were generalized institutions that housed all of these groups under one roof (Philipson 1993).

In the late 1800s, this catchall almshouse model was the target of a number of different movements for reform. Both child welfare and more general mental health reformers advocated for a shift from custodial care to active treatment, and by the early twentieth century, specialized systems and expert workers in these areas had begun to emerge. In the 1870s, a group of women activists founded the Charity Organization Society explicitly to bring scientific rationality to the practice of benevolent charitable work that many middle-class women engaged in as volunteers (Kunzel 1993). While nineteenth-century benevolent work had been largely based upon charitable impulses, the organization of the COS sought to bring the methods of scientific inquiry and systematic "treatment" to dealing with the poor and needy. The approach of the COS became the basis for the development of social work as a distinct profession requiring expert training and knowledge. Like similar processes in nursing and teaching, the emergence of this occupation can be understood as a labor market process of professionalization interconnected to a particular construction of care.

Simultaneous to the development of scientific approaches to alleviate poverty, reformers like Dorothea Dix led a movement to advocate for the creation of specialized institutions to treat mental illness. Although reformers succeeded in the creation of many state mental hospitals, at the beginning of the twentieth century, conditions at many of these institutions remained little better than at the poorhouses Dix had condemned. Nevertheless, these institutions did shift to a model at least rhetorically focused on treatment led by expert psychiatrists and psychologists (Philipson 1993).

During and after World War II, mental health came to be understood as a care need of large numbers of Americans rather than limited to the seriously mentally impaired. Psychiatrists gained prominence and public recognition for their role in performing much-larger-scale mental health screening of military recruits than ever before. After the war, psychotherapy came to be seen as something that could benefit not only soldiers recovering from trauma but the many other individuals who had suffered trauma or disruptions because of the war. In addition, in a time of relative prosperity, Americans could afford to spend more time and money focusing on their well-being (Kunzel 1993; Philipson 1993). Alternative models of treatment were developed that were less intensive than traditional psychoanalysis, and occupations like psychiatry and psychology entered a period of unprecedented growth. During the second half of the twentieth century, psychology was transformed from a male-dominated field to a female-dominated field, and this feminization was accompanied by a shift from a focus on traditional psychoanalysis to an emphasis on relational therapy (Philipson 1993). Simultaneously, a movement away from institutional treatment toward home- and community-based treatment was driven by a combination of problematic conditions at institutions and an attempt to limit costs (Krieg 2001).

Like health care, long-term care, and the care and education of children, the field of social services and mental health underwent a dramatic transformation in the twentieth century. A broad focus on individual intervention and treatment for children, families, the seriously mentally ill, and those with "everyday" worries led to the expansion and redefinition of the role of a range of expert paid care workers. Again, the definition of care and the organization of care work were shaped by emerging scientific knowledge and values as well as by activists seeking to define roles for particular groups of workers.

Understanding the Past, Looking to the Future

During the course of the twentieth century, paid nurturant care work—in health care, long-term care, child care and education, and mental health and social services—expanded from a barely measurable number of workers in a small number of jobs to a sector that includes over 20 million workers and makes up 14 percent of the labor force (Duffy 2011). Even a brief look at the history of these occupations reveals that this growth cannot be understood as a simple transfer of labor.

It is important to understand care needs as dynamic and socially and historically bound. From history, we see that our scientific discoveries, our cultural values, and our policy decisions have an impact on how we define the work of care and on how we choose to organize it. Moreover, the efforts of care workers themselves to gain professional legitimacy have shaped the way care has been defined, at times at the expense of other groups of care workers. A society that once relied on family members and hired help to face one set of care challenges now depends on complex collaborations between unpaid caregivers and expert care workers to face a very different set of challenges. We need to look closely at these expert care workers and at the low-wage workers whose labor has been defined as supporting them and to untangle the web of inequalities connected to the current social organization of care.

Looking toward the future, this fuller historical perspective allows us to see greater potential and possibility for change. As Amott and Matthaei remind us, our current organization of care is the result of specific historical processes and human action—so human action can also change it. It is this goal that

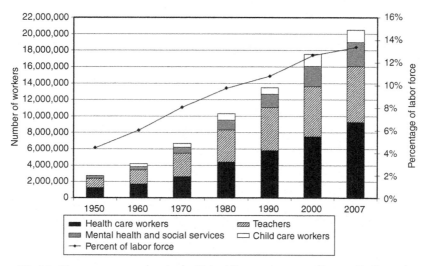

FIG. 2.2 Nurturant care workers in the United States, 1950–2007. (Source: Duffy 2011)

drives the current volume: to shine a light on the nuances of our contemporary care landscape in order to drive forward a purposeful movement for social change.

Acknowledgments

Some of the material in this chapter draws on *Making Care Count: A Century of Gender, Race, and Paid Care Work* (New Brunswick, NJ: Rutgers University Press, 2011).

Part II

Contexts of Care

• •

In the public imagination, family care represents the gold standard against which all forms of paid care work are measured. Although we know from both research and experience that families can be riddled with problems, paid care is often compared to an idealized version of family in which a loving relationship provides the basis for responsive, person-centered care. In this scenario, not surprisingly, the focus always lands on the shortcomings of care when it is performed as paid labor. However, like real family care, real paid care exists within a range of contexts. Truly understanding paid care, its potential, and its vulnerabilities requires that we examine those contexts and explore what makes care work—for workers and for care recipients.

The experiences of care workers are shaped by the institutional structures and physical spaces that define their work environments, the occupation-specific characteristics of their jobs, and their own social locations. Across the care sector—in health care, in child care, and in social services—workers find themselves in settings from hospitals to residential institutions to private homes. When scholars compare the experiences of workers in these different situations, what they see is a series of critical trade-offs. Kim Price-Glynn and Carter Rakovski find that direct care workers who work in private homes appreciate the relative autonomy and control over the pace and content of their work compared to an institutional context. They particularly value the opportunity a home setting provides to slow down, build relationships with patients and their families, and better personalize care. This ability to take more time to understand individual needs is particularly critical to the hospice workers described by Cindy Cain, and is cited as a main reason these hospice workers preferred home-based care. Given the centrality of individualized care to the mission of hospice, for these workers taking more time plays an important role in workers feeling proud that they were providing high-quality, professional care. However, relative to similar workers in institutional settings, Price-Glynn and Rakovski find that home-based workers earn significantly lower wages, often work unpaid hours in order to support the slower pace they value, and sometimes struggle to negotiate boundaries with patients in an unregulated environment. The hospice workers in Cain's study also report working off the clock to make up for the extra time they spend with patients and facing a level of unpredictability in a work environment that is someone else's home.

The experiences of the workers in both of these studies are shaped not only by the physical location of work but by the organizational structure within which they are situated. In both cases, the workers are employed by an agency rather than as independent contractors. Cain and Price-Glynn and Rakovski describe this affiliation as providing a sense of connection with other workers, mitigating the isolation that can accompany home-based work. Additionally, the structure provided by the agency was reported to give workers some protection and leverage in setting boundaries with clients. By contrast, the housecleaners and family day care providers interviewed by Nickela Anderson and Karen Hughes experienced third-party agencies as constraining their autonomy and significantly reducing their potential earnings. In these occupations, agencies have evolved differently, and these workers found self-employment to be a more profitable option that allowed them to retain more control over their work. Even organizational structures that appear similar may operate quite differently on the ground, highlighting the need for careful attention to contextual particularities.

Workers in nurturant care jobs face a unique set of constraints relative to those in occupations that involve fewer relational tasks. Like the health care workers described in the other chapters, self-employed housecleaners working in private homes reported that one of the qualities they liked about their jobs was the amount of control they could exercise over the pace and content of their work. By contrast, family day care providers—also self-employed and working in private homes—reported that their time was relatively constrained and their days were structured by an often relentless series of demands responding to the needs of children in their care. Importantly, these relationships can be a strong source of satisfaction for nurturant care workers (see Janette Dill). However, in addition to the trade-off with limited flexibility and control over one's own time, Dill also reports that these workers are lower paid and receive fewer benefits than workers in more administrative positions in health care who do not have the patient interaction.

Importantly, individuals assess these trade-offs within the contexts of their social location. As Price-Glynn and Rakovski point out, direct care workers who are younger and those who do not have another wage earner in the home may not be able to sacrifice the higher wages available in institutional settings for the benefits of home-based care. And in her comparison of hospitals to long-term care settings, Dill finds that while long-term care workers report higher levels of satisfaction with the interpersonal aspects of care, they also have heavier workloads, lower wages, and fewer opportunities for promotion than their hospital counterparts. Again, the trade-off places extra pressure on those who have less access to alternative resources, whether because of age, racial discrimination, legal vulnerability, economic insecurity, or family structure.

There is of course a larger context that is the backdrop to all of these critical distinctions among paid care workers, and that is that all of the workers described in this section are at risk for poverty because of the low level of their overall wages and benefits. As Dill points out, the intrinsic rewards that many of these workers do appreciate are not enough to compensate for low wages and inadequate benefits, as evidenced by the high levels of turnover in this work force. These chapters challenge us to examine the vulnerabilities faced by paid care workers as a group and to be sensitive to experiences of care workers in different contexts. Policy solutions to the weaknesses in our current provision of care must both strengthen the overall system as well as attend to the nuances of understanding under what conditions care works, where, and for whom.

3

The Best of Both Worlds?

• •

How Direct Care Workers
Perceive Home Health
Agencies and Long-Term-Care
Institutions

KIM PRICE-GLYNN AND

CARTER RAKOVSKI

Care for American seniors and those with extended illnesses or disabilities takes place primarily in two places: institutions and residential homes. Nearly 2 million direct care workers are employed by home health agencies and residential care facilities, and growth in the number of these workers is projected (National Occupational Research Agenda [NORA] 2009). These two settings shape the kinds of labor performed as well as the workers' subjective experiences of their labor. Similarly, the organization and location of care work influences workers' outcomes. In home agency work, caregivers' workplaces and the supervisory, organizational structure are largely independent, whereas for residential facility workers, the workplace and organization are fused. Most research on home-based labor focuses on workers hired directly by clients, either the homeowners themselves or family members. Home health workers employed by agencies are different because their supervisors and employers are part of an organization outside of the household and client.

The same job can look quite different depending on the setting. A server in an all-night roadside diner will have a different experience than a server in a luxurious downtown restaurant. Not only will pay and prestige vary, but different types of social interactions may occur. In other words, context matters. From the perspective of those needing care, home-based services are generally preferred and seen as more customized, personal, and warm compared to institutional care. However, from the perspectives of the caregivers, how are homes and institutions experienced? Could agency-based home health workers have the best of both worlds—the autonomy and customization afforded by caring for clients in their homes and the organizational support of an outside agency? Or are the risks and costs of care work greater when performed outside a controlled medical environment?

Few studies examine the same workers across different settings (Dellinger 2004). Even fewer have systematically evaluated the contexts of direct care work. Our research explores direct care workers who have the same job but perform it in different settings—institutions and private homes—using data from the National Nursing Assistant Survey (2004) and the National Nursing Assistant Home Health Survey (2007). In this study, we examine home health aides and nursing assistants employed by long-term care facilities (that is, nursing homes) or home healthcare agencies who provide hands-on assistance to clients, such as feeding, bathing, clothing, and mobility. Our study considers only caregivers who are paid and hired through an agency or institution (excluding workers hired by a family directly). We do not include nutritionists or workers with higher degrees, such as registered nurses or physical therapists. Our central question is how does organizational context shape home and facility-based work for home health aides and nursing assistants?

Caring Contexts

Direct care workers provide intense physical and emotional labor for low wages (Palmer and Eveline 2012). Reproductive labor is "defined as work that is necessary to ensure the daily maintenance and ongoing reproduction" of the current and next generations and contains both nurturant and non-nurturant tasks (Duffy 2005, 70). Direct care work is at the intersection of both aspects of reproductive labor. Nurturant reproductive labor, centered on "feelings, responsibility, responsive action, and relationship" (Duffy 2005, 69), has traditionally been privileged in studies of caring labor. Direct care workers find intrinsic value in the emotional content of their labor—understanding, connecting with and addressing their clients' particular needs (Berdes and Eckert 2007; Castle et al. 2007; Diamond 1992; Stacey 2005). Non-nurturant or "dirty work" includes day-to-day instrumental tasks like toileting, feeding, and washing (Duffy 2005; Stacey 2005). Non-nurturant reproductive tasks are less valued by society than emotional labor (Duffy 2007) and are stigmatized because they can involve "intimate, messy contact with the (frequently supine or naked) body" (Wolkowitz 2006, 147). Facility care workers' reproductive labor involves helping clients with activities of daily living (ADLs). However, home care workers' labor extends to cooking, cleaning, and grocery shopping, in addition to emotional support. In their own words, home-based direct care workers say, "We're maids plus" (Stacey 2005, 838).

Institutions that employ direct care workers create opportunities, expectations, and obligations that affect the caring labor that can be performed. As members of workplace organizations, caregivers are subject to socialization, protocols, and rules that shape their interactions with clients. Steven Lopez found that some organizations "self-consciously tried to create structural opportunities for meaningful social relationships between caregivers and clients" and termed this organized emotional labor (2006b, 134). Organizations play a role in how much of this work is available through institutional policies, practices, and norms (Lopez 2006b).

Although organizations vary, working conditions in homes and institutions are widely described as difficult. Ethnographic studies suggest that workers have little time for reproductive labor. Thomas Gass's book, *Nobody's Home,* recounts the "fifteen minutes [he had] to get each resident out of bed, toileted, dressed, coifed, and wheeled or walked to breakfast" in one midwestern nursing home (13, 2004). Similarly, Timothy Diamond's research, in *Making Grey Gold,* describes how workers in his facility rushed against the clock to finish assisting residents at mealtime before members of the kitchen staff collected trays (1992). Home health aides from California described themselves as "overworked" from chronic worker shortages, high worker turnover rates, and ineffective organizational policies regarding adequate staffing levels (Harrington et al. 2000; Stacey 2005). In facilities, workers struggle with high turnover rates, inadequate staffing, and grueling schedules that are shaped by facility size, location, and ownership (Brannon et al. 2002; Castle et al. 2007; Diamond 1992; Foner 1994; Gass 2004; Harrington et al. 2000). Since workers' time is constrained by institutional characteristics, these working conditions suggest little organizational support and time for caring relationships.

Frontline direct care workers in facilities face a host of workplace hazards, including violence, physical injuries, musculoskeletal pain, and exposure to infectious diseases (Miranda et al. 2011; Sofie, Belza, and Young 2003). They experience "toxic chemicals such as cleaning agents; heavy lifting and other types of forceful exertions; physical and verbal assault; and stressors with psychological as well as physiological effects, such as long work hours and night work" (see chapter 7). Injury and illness rates among nursing home workers are more than twice those of construction workers (see chapter 7). These risks are also present for home health workers, who encounter additional hazards such as dangerous neighborhoods and households, animal bites, and isolation, as well as other dangers that may be less well known (see chapter 8; Hasson and Arnetz 2008; Stacey 2005).

Harsh working conditions provoke dissatisfaction with salary, time for reproductive labor, and turnover (Rakovski and Price-Glynn 2010). Nevertheless, large-scale studies confirm the importance and centrality of caring to direct care workers found in smaller qualitative studies (Rakovski and Price-Glynn 2010; Rakovski and Price-Glynn 2012). Overall, direct care workers report surprisingly high job satisfaction, particularly with learning new skills, doing challenging work, and organizational support for caring labor (Rakovski and Price-Glynn 2010).

In long-term care facilities, framing direct care work as a familial rather than paid obligation can lead to employee exploitation, including doing tasks outside of the job description, working unpaid hours, and emotional stress and strain (see chapter 16). Managers of facilities justify their workers' low wages by using gendered definitions of care work as natural, women's work that is unskilled and performed for love rather than money (Palmer and Eveline 2012). Supervisors encourage workers to use family metaphors when thinking about clients. As one worker expressed, "They become like a relative, like someone in your family, to me" (Berdes and Eckert 2007, 344). Although relationships with clients are a source of satisfaction (Rakovski and Price-Glynn 2010), the obligations ultimately operate one-way with providers carrying the burden of supplying care (see chapter 16).

Family metaphors also operate in private homes and may lead to worker exploitation there as well (Solari 2006; Stacey 2005). Inside the home, norms of family prevail and obfuscate the workers' skills and labor (Solari 2006). But the home setting may add complications compared to facility-based care work. Paid domestic work is often rendered invisible and portrayed as "something other than employment" (Hondagneu-Sotelo 2007, 9). Economically, making home-based caring labor seem "effortless" justifies its low pay (Rivas 2003, 78). In part this characterization is due to normative gendered, classed, and raced assumptions that devalue household labor (Hays 1996). However, the invisibility of domestic work may serve another purpose for employers, namely, protecting their status and self-concept. For example, nannies and mothers employ various strategies to make paid care work invisible in order to protect the mother's status as the sole provider of caregiving to her children (Macdonald 2010). For people with disabilities, making personal assistants invisible protects clients' notions of self-determination and independence (Rivas 2003). In paid home-based elder care, clients may also strive to marginalize workers through invisibility and distancing.

Much of the research on direct care workers comes from ethnographic studies. While those studies provide rich ethnographic detail, they cannot fully contextualize workers' experiences. Given the small, regionally limited samples, it is difficult to know whether particular workers' experiences are representative of the broader population. Drawing from two nationally representative data sets provides an opportunity to address workers' practices across the United States and to situate their experiences relative to hundreds of others doing similar kinds of work. By also comparing direct care workers across settings, we are able to see the influence of caring contexts, something few studies have done beyond the basics of pay and demographics (Yamada 2002).

Data and Methods

This research draws upon the first nationally representative surveys of home health aides and nursing assistants in the United States: the National Home Health Aide Survey (NHHAS) and the National Nursing Assistant Study (NNAS) (Bercovitz et al. 2011; Squillace et al. 2009). The surveys were sponsored by the Department of Health and Human Services' Office of the Assistant Secretary for Planning and Evaluation (ASPE) to evaluate issues related to worker satisfaction and retention. The NNAS, conducted in two stages, was a supplement to the 2004 National Nursing Home Survey (NNHS). NHHAS was modeled after the NNAS to be its equivalent with home health aides in 2007. The first stage was the sampling of facilities and agencies, and the second stage was the sampling of workers. Both surveys were conducted by the Centers for Disease Control and Prevention's National Center for Health Statistics in conjunction with ASPE. Aides who worked in agencies that participated in the facility surveys and who provided ADL assistance (that is, direct patient care) were interviewed using computer-assisted telephone surveys in either English or Spanish. Within the two settings under study, we examined worker demographics, working conditions, satisfaction with work, pay, and benefits.

Several questions explored the time and support for reproductive labor. Time for tasks includes the following: "During a typical work week, how much time do you have to give individual attention to residents with activities of daily living (ADL) assistance?" and "During a typical work week, how much time do you have to complete other duties not directly related to residents?" Organizational support for care work was measured by items such as, "Are you assigned to care for the same residents on most days that you work?" and "In general, are you encouraged by supervisors to discuss the care and well-being of residents with their families?" Workers were also surveyed about their relationships with clients.

Differences and Similarities in Facility and Home Agency Work

In terms of individual characteristics, direct care workers were similar across both facility and home-based settings (table 3.1). Consistent with other studies, this work force is made up of women (over 90 percent) and minorities at the margins of poverty. The work force was racially and ethnically diverse, with almost half identifying as Latina/Latino, Black, or other. Nearly all (about

Table 3.1
Worker characteristics by setting

	Facility-based workers[a] % or mean	Home-based workers[b] % or mean	Significance level[c]
Individual characteristics			
Women	92.3	94.4	**
Hispanic/Latino/Latina	9.4	8.9	
Black	38.8	37.6	***
White	53.3	51.7	
Other racial group	7.9	10.8	
Not a U.S. citizen[d]	9.3	5.8	***
Age[e]	38.4	46.3	***
High school graduate	87.7	87.4	
Household characteristics			
Ever received public assistance	56.7	56.4	
Total household income			
<$20,000	37.5	23.2	***
$20,000 to $29,999	28.1	28.2	
$30,000 to $39,999	14.2	20.8	
$40,000 to $49,999	10.0	11.8	
>$50,000	10.2	16.1	
Also cares for family/friend with disability or health problem	15.3	20.0	***
Children living at home	58.7	48.0	***
Organization type and location			
For-profit facility or agency	58.5	88.9	***
Chain affiliation	54.1	51.5	
Metropolitan location	75.9	82.9	***

[a]Data source: Centers for Disease Control's National Nursing Assistant Survey (2004), n = 2,909. In this and the National Home Health Aide Survey, sample sizes for individual characteristics are sometimes smaller. The following responses were treated as missing: don't know, refused, and not ascertained. Percentages are reported for non-missing cases.
[b]Centers for Disease Control National Home Health Aide Survey (2007), n = 2,077.
[c]P-values were calculated using z-tests for differences between proportions, independent samples t-tests for differences between means, and chi-square tests for differences for categorical variables, ***$p < .001$, **$p < .01$, *$p < .05$.
[d]Citizenship status was not released in the public-use data for NHHAS. The estimate is from the NHHAS report (Bercovitz et al. 2007).
[e]Age was coded as 65 when age was 65 or greater in the NNAS data. Therefore, mean age reported here is lower than it should be.

90 percent) had a high school education and half had received public assistance at some point in their lives.

Low wages keep direct care workers at risk for poverty. Using national data on direct care workers, Yamada found that workers in both facilities and private homes were more likely to live below the poverty line than the general public, with nearly half of workers living below or near the poverty line (2002).

The majority of all workers in the NNAS and NHHAS reported total house-hold incomes of less than $30,000 per year, and over half had received public assistance. Among these low-wage workers, those employed by facilities fared better than home-based workers in terms of pay and benefits. Facility-based workers' mean hours per week (36.7) were higher than home workers (29.7) and so were their average hourly wages, an advantage that has been reported in other studies (Yamada 2002). Facility workers also were more likely to have health insurance available at work (table 3.2) and had more benefits on average than home workers (table 3.3). Nevertheless, although more than 90 percent of facility-based workers had health insurance available, 30 percent were uninsured because they could not afford it.

Other important differences between these two groups emerged in terms of age, citizenship, and unpaid caregiving responsibilities. Home-based workers were older (mean age = 46.3) and slightly more likely to be citizens than facility-based workers (mean age = 38.4). In the public-release data, age was truncated at sixty-five, and thus, the average age is likely to be higher than reported for both groups. Given that home health aides generally have lower wages and work fewer hours (table 3.3), this suggests that they have more support from a partner's income than facility-based workers.[1] Home-based workers' household incomes may also benefit from their more advanced age (that is, access to spouses' social security or retirement from another career). Though about half of all workers had children living at home, home-based workers were more likely to be caring for a dependent friend or family member than for young children, probably due to age.

Although direct care workers based in homes and institutions were gener-ally similar in terms of their individual characteristics (table 3.1), their experi-ences on the job were quite different (table 3.2). Workers in facilities were more rushed, less supported, and less respected. Home health workers felt better prepared for their jobs, had significantly more time and support for care work, were more supported by supervisors, and more highly appreciated by both cli-ents and supervisors. Even though their workplace is not being directly super-vised, 80 percent of home-based workers felt their supervisor was supportive of their career. These characteristics are related to greater reported job satisfaction among home-based workers; nearly half (47.6) of home-based workers versus less than a third (30.1) of facility-based workers were extremely satisfied with their jobs.

Having adequate time for tasks is important to the content of caring labor as well as workers' safety. Over 40 percent of facility-based workers reported a lack of time to assist patients, compared with 5 percent of home-based work-ers. In addition to direct care for clients, more than half of home-based workers were encouraged by their agencies to talk with family members about clients' health and well-being. Less than a third of facility-based workers had this kind of support for caring labor. In addition to improving reported care for clients,

Table 3.2
Working conditions by setting

	Facility-based workers[a] %	Home-based workers[b] %
Job satisfaction, injuries, and time		
Satisfaction with current job		
Extremely satisfied	30.1	47.6
Somewhat satisfied	51.5	40.4
Somewhat dissatisfied	14.6	9.9
Extremely dissatisfied	3.7	2.1
Injured in the past year	56.2	8.6
Not enough time to assist patients[c]	42.6	5.3
Not enough time for other duties[d]	43.8	12.1
Organizational support		
Encouraged to talk with family members about patient's health and well-being	28.8	55.1
Usually care for the same patients	47.1	86.7
Supervisor respects worker as part of healthcare team[e]	58.0	78.8
Supervisor tells worker doing a good job[e]	52.9	77.6
Supervisor supportive of career progress[e]	48.0	80.2
Relationships with patients		
Patients respect worker as part of healthcare team[e]	71.7	92.1
Patients tell worker doing a good job[e]	72.2	90.7
Benefits and training		
Health insurance available	89.7	71.4
Training prepared worker well for job	66.2	83.3

[a]Data are from the Centers for Disease Control (cdc.gov), specifically the National Nursing Assistant Survey (2004), n = 2,909. Sample sizes for individual characteristics are sometimes smaller. Certain responses in the NNAS and the National Home Health Aide Survey cited below were treated as missing: don't know, refused, and not ascertained. Percentages are reported for non-missing cases. All items were significantly different at the $p < .001$ level using chi-square.
[b]Centers for Disease Control National Home Health Aide Survey (2007), n = 2,077.
[c]Not enough time to assist patients with activities of daily living, such as bathing, eating, dressing, and transferring.
[d]Not enough time for other duties that do not directly involve the patients, such as food preparation, making beds, cleaning, laundry, or record keeping.
[e]Percentages are given for responses that were the most positive (a great deal, always or most of the time, and strongly agree).

having more time may have contributed to the lower injury rate for home-based workers. More than half of facility-based workers had an injury in the last year, whereas fewer than 10 percent of home-based workers reported an injury. This was counterintuitive because we expected that facility workers would have access to better lifting equipment and safety training. However, the higher injuries may be the result of assisting more dependent clients combined with the hurried pace of nursing facilities. By definition, clients receiving care in a facility

Table 3.3
Pay and benefits by setting

	Facility-based workers mean[a]	Home-based workers mean[b]	Significance level[c]
Pay, hours, time on the job			
Number of hours worked per week	36.7	29.7	***
Hourly rate of pay[d]	$11.4	$10.8	
Months worked at current job	58.1	75.4	***
Total number of benefits (0–9)	5.5	4.2	***

[a]Data are from the Centers for Disease Control's National Nursing Assistant Survey (2004), where n = 2,909.
[b]Centers for Disease Control National Home Health Aide Survey (2007), where n = 2,077.
[c]P-values are from independent samples' t-tests to test whether the means were significantly different across groups, ***$p < .001$, **$p < .01$, *$p < .05$.
[d]Wages are reported in 2007 dollars using the Consumer Price Index.

need help with at least two of the four ADLs, which would mean more lifting and help with transferring. Injuries are most likely to occur when workers are pressed for time. Under time duress, they are less likely to use lifting equipment or wait for another worker to become available to help with a lift (Sofie, Belza, and Young 2003). These results suggest that in addition to caring for vulnerable populations, direct care workers are themselves quite vulnerable.

Home Agency Work: Not Best, but Better

Historically, the family provided long-term care for dependents, the elderly, and infirm. As women entered the labor force in increasing numbers, beginning in the 1970s, caregiving shifted to others outside the family home. Nevertheless, families continue to provide the gold standard of care, despite the fact that this care is increasingly being outsourced to paid workers. Some lament the outsourcing of care as signaling a decline in families, communities, and meaningful interpersonal connections (Hochschild 2012). Such nostalgic reactions often idealize the family, which can be a place of conflict and violence; families do not always provide the best care. On a more practical note, caregiving alternatives may provide families with their only means of accomplishing care over long distances, busy schedules, and complicated relationships. To avoid a nostalgic comparison to idealized family care, we limited the scope of our study to paid direct care workers in private homes and institutional settings.

Context shapes direct care workers' perceptions of and experiences with their jobs in important ways across the NNAS and NHHAS. Despite similar tasks in both settings, institutional and home-based workplaces differ greatly in size, organization, and function. Institutionally based workers reported higher wages and greater benefits, but less time for tasks and more injuries. At first, this result seemed counterintuitive to us. How could workers in settings with more staff and better ergonomic equipment sustain more injuries than those working in private homes, which may lack all of those resources? This may be a function of the formalization, structure, and routine built into institutions that foster hectic heavy workloads as well as the greater likelihood that institutionalized care involves patients in declining health. As qualitative research makes clear, such organization can come at the expense of emotionally rewarding, physically safe worksites.

While both settings offered low pay, facility workers had higher hourly wages and more hours. This suggests that direct care workers who are younger and in need of income may be trading the emotional rewards of home health care for the pecuniary rewards of facility-based work. This has implications for their physical health as well, given that the majority of facility workers had experienced an injury on the job within the last year.

Direct care workers across settings reported good relationships with clients. Indeed, client relationships are what keep most direct care workers in their jobs (Rakovski and Price-Glynn 2010). However, the combination of home agency work may provide important benefits in terms of supervisor support, time for reproductive labor, and space for emotional labor. Due to the intimacy of home care settings, we thought workers outside of institutions would have stronger client bonds and more time for emotional labor. Qualitative researchers have found that, despite some challenges, the intimacy of the home setting engenders satisfying, emotional relationships and the expression of gratitude from clients and families (England and Dyck 2011). In our research, workers in private homes had long-lasting client relationships as well as greater time for tasks. Home-based workers also sustained fewer injuries, perhaps due to having healthier clients who are, as a result, able to stay at home. As such, home agency workers may have the best of both worlds: a setting that provides autonomy and self-determination alongside institutional support and protection. That said, there are trade-offs for home agency work in the form of lower wages.

Employment status is linked to two important outcomes for workers—individual autonomy and collective responsibility. Autonomy is highly valued by most workers and something that is often lacking in lower-wage work. For home health workers, we feared autonomy could lead to isolation, risk of exploitation, and client abuse, but this was not supported by our study. Risks may be greatest for direct care workers who are independent contractors, hired directly by clients and working by themselves. We found that agency employment mitigates these risks. As employees who are part of a collective, they have organizational support, accountability, and oversight. Employees also have benefits like Social Security, Medicare, and unemployment insurance. They may also have collective bargaining rights, if they are unionized; however, the majority of these workers are employed by for-profit chains and therefore less likely to have union representation.

Given the benefits and trade-offs in both settings, changes in workplace organization and better pay could go a long way toward improving working conditions. Steps like increasing organized emotional labor, time for tasks, support from supervisors, and pay and benefits could reduce the hardships faced by workers. Kemper and colleagues asked direct care workers across settings what could be done to improve their working conditions (2008). Coding responses to this open-ended question, the authors found the two most widely cited areas were compensation (pay and benefits) and work relationships (including respect, treatment, communication, supervision, listening, and appreciation). Compensation was cited first among home-based workers, while work relationships were cited more by facility-based workers. Our study echoes these findings.

The strength of this study is the ability to compare large samples of nationally representative workers within the same occupation but based in different settings. However, there are also weaknesses. This study is descriptive. We cannot attribute differences in working conditions solely to setting. The national surveys do not report geographic region or unionization status, which may also explain differences in working conditions and wages. Given that for-profit agencies are far less likely to be unionized than facilities, institutional workers are more likely to have and benefit from union membership. Our study also does not include direct care workers based in hospitals or in assisted living facilities. Nevertheless, our findings have implications for broader understandings of caring work. We must transform the expression "home is where the heart is," for homes have no hearts—direct care workers do. The best way to improve conditions for the frailest in our society is by supporting those who care for them. Lessons from comparing context-based outcomes provide a place to start.

Note

1   This difference may also be explained partially by the difference in the survey years (the NNAS was three years earlier).

4

The Business of Caring

• •

Women's Self-Employment and the Marketization of Care

NICKELA ANDERSON AND

KAREN D. HUGHES

Most empirical studies of care work focus on employer-employee relationships (Parrenas 2001; Spitzer, Bitar, and Kalbach 2002; Zimmerman, Litt, and Bose 2006). Little research exists on self-employed paid care workers, who hold a different legal and market status. This gap is important, given the expansion of women's self-employment in many industrialized countries (Brush et al. 2006; Budig 2006a, 2006b; Hughes 2005; McManus 2001; Minniti et al. 2005) and the significant number of self-employed workers engaged in caring labour. Theorists such as Saskia Sassen (2002) and Clare Ungerson (2005), however, highlight the growing role of self-employment in global care work, noting that the rising dependency in the global North on low-paid care workers from the global South has been accompanied by rising levels of informalization and self-employment. Likewise, Nancy Folbre (2006a) calls for a more disaggregated analysis of care, offering a typology that differentiates between the "types of market relationships" (for example, paid employment, self-employment, informal work) and "types of care" (for example, direct care involving personal and emotional engagement, and indirect care that provides support for direct care). Guided by these theoretical ideas, our goal is to direct attention to an important but understudied group: the self-employed. We draw on in-depth interviews with twenty women in Canada who provide either direct care to young children in their own homes as childcare workers or indirect care in their clients' households as domestic cleaners.

Self-Employment and Caring Work: The Literature and Comparative Framework

Research on self-employment suggests significant differences between employees and the self-employed, though among employees there is also a wide array of both self-employment and employer-employee situations. Notwithstanding such diversity, however, self-employed workers often face different circumstances from employees in terms of regulation, citizenship, and working conditions. In many countries, self-employed workers fall outside legislation governing minimum wages, working hours, and other employment standards (Cox 2005; Cranford et al. 2005; Fudge 2006). They may also lack entitlement to employment-derived social rights such as unemployment insurance, disability benefits, and parental leave. Self-employed workers tend to report longer and more atypical hours, and their incomes are more precarious and unstable (Bell and La Valle 2003; Hughes 2005; Organization for Economic Cooperation and Development [OECD] 2000). Perhaps surprisingly then, self-employed workers also report higher levels of job satisfaction than employees (Blanchflower and Oswald 1999; Blanchflower, Oswald, and Stuatzer 2001; OECD 2000). Researchers suggest the self-employed may derive satisfaction from controlling their schedules and clients, the nature of their day-to-day work, and the manner in which their work is done (Brush et al. 2006; Finnie, Rivard, and Laport 2002; Hughes 2005; OECD 2000).

Direct versus Indirect Care

Work conditions and satisfaction may vary, however, by the type of work that is done. Though not all care work can be neatly separated according to Folbre's typology of direct versus indirect care workers (2006a)—for example, live-in nannies (Hondagneu-Sotelo 2007; Parrenas 2001) and personal care assistants for the elderly (Aronson and Neysmith 1996) typically blend both types of care—many workers, including those in our study, do fall into this division. Childcare workers, for instance, spend their working day providing direct care to children, engaged in feeding, playing, and comforting that reflects "a process of personal and emotional engagement" (Folbre 2006a, 187). In contrast, domestic cleaners spend their time providing indirect care, such as vacuuming, dusting, washing, and tidying, with minimal personal interaction with clients who may be working or who prefer the cleaning to be done when they are not at home (Hondagneu-Sotelo 2007; Mendez 1998).

Studies of paid employees in child care and cleaning suggest such workers face several broad similarities in their work situations, in particular relatively low levels of pay and very high job demands (Aguiar and Herod 2006; Curbow 1990; England, Budig, and Folbre 2002; Mendez 1998; Neal 1994; Rees and Fielder 1992; Strober, Gerlach-Downie, and Yeager 1995). In one of the most comprehensive analyses to date, Paula England, Michelle Budig, and Nancy Folbre (2002) found a clear wage penalty for nurturant care workers, including childcare workers and those providing personal services (but not including cleaners). Yet while childcare workers appear to experience the greatest wage penalties of all care workers (England, Budig, and Folbre 2002), many studies find they have high job satisfaction, largely due to their emotional bonds with the children they care for (Kontos and Stremmel 1988; McClelland 1986; Mooney 2003; Rose 2003; Uttal 2002). Cleaners, by contrast, are far less likely to report these same satisfying relational aspects of work. Moreover, with the spread of large firms (such as Molly Maids) in the cleaning sector, many cleaners have experienced a significant erosion of their daily working conditions, including increased work intensity, physical health hazards, and a lack of control over equipment, supplies, and the pace of work (Aguiar 2001; Aguiar and Herod 2006; Ehrenreich 2002; Mendez 1998; Neal 1994; Seifert and Messing 2006).

While the existing literature leads us to expect both self-employed childcare providers and cleaners to fare relatively poorly in terms of economic security and extrinsic job rewards, it also raises interesting questions about the autonomy and job satisfaction they experience in their day-to-day work. Equally important are questions about potential differences between self-employed workers depending on whether they provide direct or indirect care. With these questions in mind, we focus on three issues: working conditions, levels of income and economic security, and job satisfaction and dissatisfaction.

Setting the Context: Self-Employment and the Care Deficit

Our study is situated in Canada, an ideal site for exploring these questions given recent trends in self-employment and the marketization of care. Women have moved steadily into self-employment in recent decades, working either as employers (employing others) or as solos (in a business without employees) (Hughes 2005). While still underrepresented relative to their overall labor force presence, they have nevertheless made significant gains, accounting for more than one-third of all self-employed workers. Most women workers still cluster in traditionally female fields. According to the Canadian census, nearly half of self-employed women work in just twenty occupations, many involving caring or domestic work.

Our study draws on qualitative interviews carried out in the summer of 2004 with twenty women who were working as self-employed domestic cleaners or as childcare providers in a large city in the western Canadian province of Alberta.

Alberta has one of the highest self-employment rates in Canada (Statistics Canada 1997) and one of the highest proportions of dual-earner families. Alberta also provides very low support for publicly funded daycare, with government policy supporting a flourishing private sector in day homes run by self-employed caregivers.

Daily Working Conditions

A key interest in our interviews was exploring what a typical working day was like for self-employed childcare providers and domestic cleaners. For childcare providers, one very important feature of their working conditions was that their businesses were home-based, with children being dropped off and picked up by parents. This had implications for the boundaries workers were able to maintain between paid and unpaid work as well as for their daily hours. Most of the women used only part of their home for child care as a way to ensure a safe environment, maintain non-work space, and keep order in their home. As Wendy explains, "They have only the basement to play or to sleep, they eat and do crafts in the kitchen. . . . And I have a little bathroom here for them to use, in the middle. . . . They don't need to go upstairs and they are not allowed, because there is nothing for them, all their toys are downstairs, TV is downstairs. . . . I don't want the whole house messed."

Most care providers worked over forty hours per week, and two women worked well over sixty hours. Over half currently (or had previously) also cared for their own young children while caring for others. Women cared for anywhere between one to eight children each week, with the average number falling between three and four.

Maintaining a safe, happy environment kept these women on the go throughout the day. Facing constant pressures on their time and attention, they had few opportunities for downtime or breaks. Fran describes a typical day, noting that the only slow times are during naptime or when most children have gone home: "Most days I start at 8:45 and I end at 3:30. . . . I will wait outside of the house until the lady comes with her son, pick him up, go inside, give the kids their breakfast, get them changed, play with them, and then I start preparing lunch around 11:00 and wait for them to have lunch. Whoever is finished will go outside and play if it's warm. . . . Then they go down for naps at about 1:30–2:00. And then after that I just really have the four-year-old to take care of, so it's pretty easy. It's a nice wind down from everybody screaming and vying for my attention and fighting."

Erin also notes the lack of breaks and importance of nap time when "you have that few minutes to recuperate." The need for constant vigilance often made for stressful workdays, as Kaelyn discusses, "Yeah, um sometimes I feel tears . . . if they are running around, playing around, everybody talking at the same time, um, they are complaining, if they are hungry. Sometime the difference in age is huge and sometimes some of them want to do crafts or they want to go out and play or just they want something to do with in here, playing with everything they want. And it's crazy."

While many childcare providers controlled their immediate working conditions and environment, those using a day home agency were subject to inspections and restrictions to ensure safety standards. This meant a loss of autonomy in how their work spaces were organized, as well as additional work duties in facilitating agency visits. Wendy described periodic visits to ensure safety around locks, plugs, hot water tanks, strollers, and play pens. She notes, "Every month one of them comes and visits." Erin, who had left an agency to work independently, explained, "It just made things easier so I didn't have to deal with all the other stuff, you know monthly visits and all those things. It gets to be tiring after a while. I always feel restricted."

Domestic cleaners had much greater control over their daily work, particularly in terms of setting limits on their hours and the types of work they would do. Part of this reflects the nature of the cleaning work they took on, which typically involved traveling to someone's home rather than maintaining a home-based location, and could be completed in short periods of time (three to four hours). Cleaners often combined self-employment with other paid work and, unlike many childcare providers, did housecleaning informally in unregistered businesses. Working long hours in self-employment was far less typical for this group; one in three worked fewer than twenty hours per week. Maria described a fairly typical working week including travel time, which is a key consideration for cleaners: "Well, I would probably just to round it up say five hours a day, because you have travel time and that, you know, like twenty-five, maybe thirty hours a week."

Domestic cleaners carried out difficult work with high physical demands. Grace outlines some of the occupational hazards of cleaning work: "Sore joints, yes ... hands, knees, and elbows. Yeah and the back too because of the vacuum." Others mentioned similar problems, noting the need to take care of their bodies and avoid wherever possible hazards from poor equipment or strong, chemically laden cleaning products. A few women discussed negotiating which cleaning products they would use. For example, Tricia refused anything but "100 per cent biodegradable products." Maria encouraged her clients to purchase cleaning products or equipment she preferred, in order to control her working conditions: "Well, the only concern I ever have is when somebody says you have to use bleach because ... it eats away at your skin and because I don't wear rubber gloves. I now stipulate that I bring my own cleaning supplies and they have to supply a vacuum and I strongly encourage ... a central vac."

While both childcare providers and cleaners faced heavy work demands, cleaners had more scope to negotiate and control their working conditions. Several noted how they placed limits on the days or hours they would work, or what tasks they would do. Emma, for example, listed tasks she refused to do: "I don't do the stove, I don't do the walls." Susan discussed how she placed more and more limitations on tasks she would do, or clients she would take, the longer she was in business: "You know, sometimes when you're new to the business, and you are just trying it out, you will do things that you really don't want to. [For example], we really didn't want to drive all the way out in the dead of winter . . . but we thought we'll give it a try. . . . And, you know, every single time she complained about the money. And we thought we don't need this. We have all kinds of people in the city that would love us to clean for them so she lost us."

Income and Economic Security

Just half the participants reported their detailed earnings on the survey. In the interviews, more women were willing to discuss their finances, though typically in less concrete terms. While the self-employed earn profits (revenues less expenses) rather than a fixed income, most women did not operate using a standard business model. Many women, for example, did not keep detailed records of their expenses and a number reported using personal money to cover costs for cleaning supplies, toys, gas, and food. Some participants, usually cleaners, also noted the potential to underreport revenues when cash was paid for services. Here we focus on how participants experienced their financial situation rather than on the specific dollar amounts they report.

For childcare providers, income levels varied depending on the number and ages of children and the number of hours that the children were in care. Participants cared for an average of three to four children, with a range of one to eight children per week. Higher rates of pay were received for younger children. Brenda gives a detailed breakdown of charges for an infant: "For an infant I would charge $500 a month based on twenty-two days in a month, you know, excluding weekends. . . . I think it works out to $2.79 a child, an hour. . . . I mean [the parent] can't ask for anything better. . . . And I explain that to them to when they are saying, 'Well, why are you charging $500 a month?' When you break it down into twenty-two days and so much per hour it's not a whole lot. When you are dedicating all your time and effort, you know, being a child developer, because that's what we are."

Agencies made a big difference in the level of pay received as they kept a percentage of the childcare fee to cover their costs for inspecting the homes of registered care providers. Wendy emphasized that her income was reduced by the agency and did not represent the hours a child was in her care. Kaelyn also felt she would make more money if she did not use an agency, especially for the children whose parents worked evenings and required care past 6:00 P.M.: "If I was private, I have some friends they do this too, but they are private, no agency. And they say 'OK, if you want to stay until 11:00 P.M., $20 per day.' I have this girl almost the whole month. Sometimes eight hours, sometimes nine hours, just depends on the mother, and sometimes eleven hours but almost the whole month [until 11:00 P.M.]. And it's only $40 for the baby and $40 for a ten- and eight-year-old. That's it."

Other caregivers who did not work with an agency felt their work paid well, especially compared to previous work they had done in low-paying female-dominated sectors. Hanna emphasized that she made more as a home-based caregiver than in her previous standard full-time employment, providing she had more than two children in her care: "I make good money doing a day home. If I go out to work again, like even when I was with the government, I didn't make the money that I do now. And the envelope was going around constantly, 'Well let's go for lunch,' and you know, 'Let's do this.' . . . I'm not saying that a day home doesn't pay well because it does pay well when you have more than two or three [children]."

In most cases, caregivers' payments were further reduced by expenses like food, toys, or outings not covered by the monthly fee. The lack of employment-related benefits was a concern for several women. Emily, who was with an agency, wished she could access the benefits that paid employees had through the federal government that are currently not available to the self-employed. "I'd like to work it so then, maybe I can go on unemployment [while searching for other work]. . . . But I can't . . . I'm not contributing to that." Hanna discussed how she had to rely on family in order not to lose income when she had been very ill: "[My sister] lived here at the time, which was handy and the girls helped and I think Grandma came over one day or something, you know. But that's the only time, otherwise I had to say, 'You can't bring your kids' and of course then I would not have gotten paid for it either."

Compared to childcare providers, domestic cleaners reported much higher levels of pay and had greater control over what they charged. Their economic security was also enhanced by combining their housecleaning work with either a full-time or part-time job. Many women felt they made the fullest amount possible and several compared their pay favorably to what they would receive if they worked for a cleaning company. Combining their self-employment with a formal job also provided access to health care, disability, and other benefits through their employee status.

Most domestic cleaners charged a flat rate because they did not want to be tied to a house for a set number of hours. Some did a combination of either a flat rate or an hourly rate depending on the situation, while two women charged hourly rates only. Compared to some childcare providers, domestic cleaners seemed to have far more independence in setting their rates and much more ability to contain hours and tie income directly to work effort. Susan explains how she and her partner set rates: "We go in and assess the home. So it wasn't so much per hour, it was basically we calculated how long it would take us and what we wanted to take from them and that's how we charged them."

June also visited houses first to determine the rate, then started at an hourly rate and finally adjusted it to a flat rate when she was certain of the time required: "I usually look at the house first. Then I'll say, 'Your house it's four hours for the first time. . . . I'll work four hours and see what I can do. And if

four hours is not enough, I'll let you know.' And after that it's a flat rate, that's it."
In contrast, Tammy charged by the hour, but had a sliding scale depending
on what she felt each owner was willing to pay, asking for a top hourly rate of
$16 per hour in three of her seven houses. Maria noted a minimum hourly rate
of $15 but had one client who paid her $25 an hour.

How domestic cleaners viewed their pay was often influenced by comparisons with what they would earn as an employee, as well as whether they combined self-employed work with another paid job. Discussing her income, June
noted her past employment situation working for a cleaning company, conclud-
ing that she could do better on her own: "That's right, they [cleaners who are
employees] probably get seven dollars an hour. Why would I work so bloody
hard for seven dollars an hour?"

June also combined her self-employment with a paid job, primarily for the
benefits and pension: "Ah, mostly for benefits. I am 100 percent covered with
everything. The money I am making at [my other job] and the benefits and I
have two kids, you know, their dental, their medicine and everything is covered. . . . When I get old, what am I supposed to do, I have money [a company
pension]."

Others, such as Maria, used her paid job as a buffer when cleaning income
dropped: "To have a little bit of a steadier income, to increase it a little bit more.
Some weeks you are gonna make $250 and the next week you are only going to
make $50 if people cancel on you. And that's how it is being self-employed and
doing housekeeping, that's how it fluctuates."

Job Satisfaction and Dissatisfaction

We examined job satisfaction in two ways. Firstly, the short survey that the participants completed before the interview included a series of questions on job
satisfaction. Recognizing the limitations of a global measure of satisfaction (for
example, "How satisfied are you with your job?"), we adopted a facet approach
(Spector 1997, 2–4) to probe a variety of job dimensions. Using a Likert scale
(where 1 was very dissatisfied and 5 was very satisfied), participants evaluated
both intrinsic and extrinsic dimensions, including the nature of their day-to-day
work, independence, authority, income, job security, work-family balance, ability to save for retirement, and personal fulfillment. Secondly, in the in-depth
interview we reviewed the survey responses with participants, asking them for
further details and reasoning for their satisfaction or dissatisfaction with specific job features.

Regarding childcare providers, two key factors of job satisfaction stand out.
First is the work-family balance and the ability to work from home. Over half
of caregivers currently (or had previously) cared for their own young children
while caring for others. Self-employment provided a way for women to care for
their own children while also earning valuable income. Kaelyn discussed how
her greatest satisfaction came from being able to earn money while also being at

home "with my children." Erin, who continued to work as a self-employed caregiver once her children were of school age, also valued this highly: "Being able to stay home with my kids, yeah, it made a big difference in their lives I think. I really enjoyed it while I was doing it. Yeah, that's one thing I did really enjoy."

The second area of high satisfaction was the personal fulfillment the women received from caring for children. Lisa highlighted the emotional bonds and enjoyment: "Well, as I said, I love, I like kids. And I don't think I would be doing this if I didn't like them." Fran noted that the relationships with the children made her work enjoyable: "Well, uh, it's just the kids are I think that's pretty obvious. . . . I mean they will say my name, before they could talk, um, you know when they say my name it's just like, 'Aw, that's adorable.' They come up for hugs, kisses and you know, if they fall down they will come to me. . . . You get a close bond with them. And I think that's the best part of my job or else I wouldn't do it."

For domestic cleaners, the picture of job satisfaction was very different. Cleaners were much more likely to be satisfied with their independence and autonomy in deciding how to do their work, as well as with the financial rewards they received. Tammy discussed how she liked working at her own pace and in her own way: "Because nobody can boss you . . . if somebody is going to tell you 'Do this, do that.' If somebody is watching you, I'm slow, very slow, you have to be careful. So the time is, ah, slow, you know you can't get done right away because your boss is behind you. And, you know, it's kind of that's why I like cleaning houses. Nobody's around, there's nobody around."

June's comments reflect the satisfaction of doing a good job and having that recognized by her clients, as well as satisfaction with the financial aspects of her work, tied to her ability to set rates and underreport income: "I like it when they tell me, 'June, the house really looks so clean.' It was clean in the first place, you know [but] just the satisfaction of going home, that they like what I did. That's all. And the money, it's like right now, like I said to you, it's under the table, but I pay enough taxes through my other job."

Turning to job dissatisfaction, child care providers identified issues of hours and pay. Erin was primarily dissatisfied with the long hours she had to work: "You are open sometimes twelve hours, you know, where a regular job it's usually eight." Kaelyn was also dissatisfied with the long hours she worked, noting how they affected the time she had for herself and whether she would be able to have family time in the evenings: "The long hours, yeah, I don't like it at all. Because they go to bed around 9:00 and I have to feed five children for supper, and including my husband and myself. So sometimes I have to have my supper around 9:30. And when they are here for ten or eleven hours, something like that, we can't spend time—family time—together."

For Emily, punctuality was a key problem underlying long hours and low pay. When the parents were late picking up their children her hours were extended, cutting into her own family time: "Maybe the parents say they are going to come and pick them up at 4:00 and then they come at 5:00. I don't like that. When they say 4:30, they come at 4:30. Gonna say a time, they should be at that time . . . nine hours it's OK, but ten hours is too much. It's one more hour because after your other children go home you have to cook for your family. When the children go home you have to cook for your family, so you are never finished. You go to bed maybe around 12:00."

Hanna also disliked the long hours and, while she was happy with the level of pay, she experienced frustration with getting paid on time: "You generally have to ask for your money. Like, do they have to ask for their paycheck?" Lisa also mentioned poor pay and the lack of opportunity for growth: "I dislike the pay sometimes . . . not enough . . . I just make a set amount for the month [regardless of hours]."

For domestic cleaners, the main source of dissatisfaction was with the physical demands of the work as well as its repetitive nature. Said Emma, "Sometimes I am just dead tired when I go there. And just the thought of having to clean the whole house makes me want to puke." Grace noted, "It's quite challenging, it's quite physically challenging, especially when you are an older person." Tammy also mentioned how tiring the work could be, revealing a sense of despair: "There's a part I don't like, like really sometimes you are tired and the house is dirty. Yeah, tired and I don't want to go back. Yeah, it's true. They know that you are coming, they really make a mess because I'm gonna clean it. You know, I mean, it's your house; it's your house so you have to tidy up a little bit. It's not all up to the housekeeper to do it."

Autonomy, Fulfillment, and Balance

Our study offers several insights that contribute to a differentiated analysis of paid caring work. Our central expected finding is the highly demanding nature of the work carried out by both groups of women in our study. As the interviews show, self-employed childcare providers expended a great deal of physical and emotional energy during their workdays. Most worked long hours, juggling a steady stream of demands with little downtime and the potential for erratic or expanded hours. Likewise, domestic cleaners faced high physical demands, carrying out tasks requiring significant energy and attention to detail. Fatigue, sore backs, muscle pain, and repetitive strains were recurrent themes in women's discussions, along with ongoing concerns about limiting effort and protecting their health.

In terms of unexpected findings, two key issues stand out: income and intrinsic job satisfaction. The documented wage penalty for caring workers (England, Budig, and Folbre 2002), coupled with the generally lower pay of many self-employed and routine service workers, might lead us to expect self-employed childcare providers and domestic cleaners to be especially disadvantaged in terms of pay. Yet our findings suggest important differences between the two groups. Our interviews indicated that child care providers were much more poorly paid than cleaners and that their income was a key source of dissatisfaction for them. Importantly, childcare providers' low incomes did not take into account additional costs for food, toys, outings, and other supplies. It is not surprising that satisfaction with pay was very low for childcare workers. This was particularly the case for workers who used an agency and received lower rates for children in their care. By contrast, domestic workers reported higher incomes and many felt they did better cleaning independently than cleaning for an employer. Cleaners were also more likely than child care providers to report feeling satisfied or very satisfied with their financial situation.

Key differences concerning intrinsic job satisfaction emerged between childcare providers and cleaners with respect to their autonomy and control, personal fulfillment and work-family balance. Both groups enjoyed a fair degree of independence, confirming some expected advantages accruing to self-employed status. Yet domestic cleaners seemed to have much more scope than childcare providers to limit demands and contain working time due to the nature and location of their work. Cleaners were not home-based and performed work that could more easily be assembled into short segments of time. By contrast, home-based childcare providers typically provided full-time care throughout the day or at odd hours (for example, in the evening or on weekends). Their location, the relational nature of their work, and the demand for full-time care meant that childcare providers had less scope to contain the work and create physical and temporal boundaries in the same way that cleaners were able to do (Clark 2000). This was especially true for those who worked with childcare agencies and faced additional demands in responding to agency conditions and visits.

Childcare providers did not entirely lack autonomy, nor were they less satisfied with their work. These women had significant discretion in how they provided care, deciding on daily routines, food, and outings, and how they would discipline and comfort children. Childcare workers seemed to fare better than cleaners in other aspects of intrinsic job satisfaction, not only due to the relational nature of their work and their emotional bonds with the children but more importantly because of their ability to balance work and family life. In this respect, we find, much like Michelle Budig's analysis of women's nonprofessional self-employment (2006a, 2006b), that while home-based self-employment limited women's earning and autonomy, it also delivered perceived benefits, allowing women to remain at home with their own young children while earning an income and contributing financially to the household. In contrast, while many cleaners reported a sense of personal fulfillment from their work, most gained satisfaction through the autonomy and control they had in organizing their work and from the income that they earned.

These findings suggest that employment status and the nature of care shape experiences of care workers in critical, and sometimes unexpected, ways. While it remains to be seen whether similar patterns emerge in other contexts and in larger numbers of participants, we believe it is important for future research to focus attention on self-employed caregivers in order to provide a more complete account of paid care. Beyond the questions of working conditions, economic security, and job satisfaction explored here are other questions that deserve attention, most notably concerning the self-employment situations that most benefit women and the strategies they use for raising the value of providing care. Equally important, the use of independent contracting deserves special attention, given what appears to be its limiting effect on women's autonomy, and on collective efforts to improve the economic security and status of caring work.

Acknowledgments

This chapter is a revision of "The Business of Caring: Women's Self-Employment and the Marketization of Care" published in 2010 in *Gender, Work, and Organization* 17 (4): 381–405.

5

Are Frontline Healthcare Jobs "Good" Jobs?

• • • • • • • • • • • • • • • • • • •

Examining Job Quality across Occupations and Healthcare Settings

JANETTE S. DILL

The housekeeper who empties the trash can in the hospital room. The nursing assistant who helps a nursing home resident to the bathroom. The unit clerk who organizes patient charts. The surgical technician who prepares the operating room. These workers—and others with similar skills and compensation—make up the frontline healthcare work force, an often overlooked but large and growing segment of healthcare workers. In this chapter, frontline healthcare workers are defined as those who (1) are in occupations with a low threshold to entry (typically a high school degree with little additional training), (2) provide direct care or support services, and (3) typically make under $40,000 per year (Schindel et al. 2006). Heavily dominated by women with an overrepresentation of some minority groups, these low-wage workers provide much-needed supportive tasks such as patient care, housekeeping and dietary duties, and administrative tasks. They constitute over half of the healthcare work force and are among the fastest growing occupations in the United States (Lockard and Wolf 2012).

The goal of this chapter is to provide a rich description of job quality among low-wage frontline healthcare workers in a variety of occupational categories and healthcare settings. In this chapter they are categorized into four groups: frontline care support workers (for example, housekeepers, dietary staff), frontline direct care workers (for example, nursing assistants), frontline administrative workers (for example, medical records technicians), and frontline allied health workers (for example, pharmacy technicians). The chapter also considers job quality across three different types of healthcare settings, including acute care hospitals, long-term care, and other outpatient settings.

In order to provide a well-rounded perspective on the work experiences of frontline healthcare workers, I look at a number of dimensions of job quality, including wages, health insurance benefits, workload, promotion opportunity, and overall job satisfaction. I also explore racial-ethnic and gender inequality between frontline occupations and healthcare settings. The frontline healthcare work force has been largely invisible to researchers and policymakers, who tend focus on nurses and physicians, and sometimes even to patients, who may not be aware of all of the behind-the-scenes support that these workers provide. However, the 6 million frontline healthcare workers in the United States are a large and growing segment of both the healthcare and low-wage work force.

Data and Methods

This chapter draws on two different data sources. First, I use the 2008–2010 panel of the Study for Income and Program Participation (SIPP) to examine wages and occupational transitions among frontline healthcare workers over time. The SIPP panel is a nationally representative dataset that covers eight waves of data collection over a three-year period and has extensive information on income and employment. The analytic sample includes individuals who (1) are in a frontline healthcare occupation at some point during the survey period (that is, care support, direct care, administrative, or allied health), (2) work in either a hospital, long-term care, or outpatient care setting,[1] and (3) have a starting wage of below $19 per hour (roughly $40,000 per year). I use data from the SIPP to look at the gender and racial/ethnic composition across occupations and healthcare settings, shown in table 5.1. Table 5.2 includes hourly inflation-adjusted wages (2010 dollars) and the receipt of partially or fully paid employer-based health insurance, food stamps, and welfare assistance.

I also use the SIPP data to examine wage growth during the survey period (shown in table 5.2). Individuals in the frontline healthcare worker population typically have many employment transitions and breaks, making it difficult to measure average wage growth in a particular occupation

Table 5.1

Race and gender differences by frontline ocupation type and healthcare setting

	Female (SE)	White (SE)	Black (SE)	Hispanic (SE)	Other race (SE)
Occupation					
Care support	70.1%	54.3%	26.3%	11.6%	7.7%
	(.010)	(.011)	(.010)	(.007)	(.006)
Direct care workers	88.2%	56.5%	27.5%	10.0%	6.0%
	(.004)	(.007)	(.007)	(.004)	(.004)
Administrative	88.9%	67.6%	17.4%	9.7%	5.4%
	(.007)	(.011)	(.009)	(.007)	(.005)
Frontline allied health	75.1%	71.5%	17.3%	7.2%	4.0%
	(.011)	(.012)	(.011)	(.007)	(.005)
Employer type					
Hospital	79.5%	62.3%	22.1%	9.4%	6.2%
	(.006)	(007)	(.006)	(.004)	(.003)
LTC	84.7%	57.7%	26.5%	9.6%	6.2%
	(.006)	(.008)	(.007)	(.005)	(.004)
Outpatient	85.0%	62.8%	20.5%	11.7%	5.0%
	(.010)	(.014)	(.012)	(.009)	(.006)

SOURCE: 2008 SIPP panel.

Table 5.2

Differences in wages, wage growth, benefits, and receipt of public assistance by frontline occupational type and healthcare setting

	Observations	Median wage	Mean wage (SE)	Yearly wage growth (SE)	Health insurance (SE)	Food stamps (SE)	Welfare (SE)
Occupation							
Care support	2,035	$10.53	$11.35	$0.59	56.1%	12.6%	0.5%
			(.087)	(.312)	(.011)	(.007)	(.002)
Direct care work	4,494	$11.56	$12.46	$1.03	53.1%	11.3%	0.9%
			(.066)	(.230)	(.007)	(.005)	(.001)
Administrative	1,926	$13.72	$14.25	$0.91	69.3%	4.2%	0.4%
			(.099)	(.360)	(.010)	(.005)	(.001)
Frontline allied health	1,358	$15.54	$15.36	$1.23	66.2%	4.3%	0.1%
			(.133)	(.553)	(.013)	(.005)	(.001)
Employer type							
Hospital	4,825	$13.66	$14.31	$1.41	71.1%	6.4%	0.5%
			(.075)	(.305)	(.006)	(.004)	(.001)
LTC	4,215	$10.72	$11.72	$0.59	43.6%	13.1%	1.1%
			(.062)	(.158)	(.008)	(.005)	(.002)
Outpatient	1,202	$13.47	$14.06	$0.79	66.7%	5.4%	0.0%
			(.172)	(.421)	(.013)	(.006)	(0)

SOURCE: 2008 SIPP panel
NOTES: Wages are inflation-adjusted to 2010 dollars. Yearly was calculated only for frontline healthcare workers that remained in the same occupation or employer type throughout the entire survey period. Having health insurance indicates that an individual participates in an employer-based health insurance plan that is either partially or fully paid by the employer.

or healthcare setting (Baughman and Smith 2011; Ribas, Dill, and Cohen 2012). Consequently, in looking at wage growth, I look only at individuals who stay in a given occupation or in a given healthcare setting (with no transitions) between their first and last survey observation.[2] Finally, I use the SIPP data to examine employment transitions within healthcare settings, away from healthcare settings, and to unemployment, which are shown in table 5.3.

The second source of data for this chapter is survey data collected between 2007 and 2010 from 1,006 frontline workers in twenty-five healthcare organizations across the United States. The data were collected as part of the "Jobs to Careers" initiative funded by the Robert Wood Johnson Foundation. I use this data to examine differences in job quality between occupational groups and healthcare settings. The survey includes rich data on working conditions, supervisor support, career opportunity, overall job satisfaction, and employment intentions. Table 5.4 includes measures of these job quality dimensions by occupation and healthcare setting.

Job Quality across Frontline Healthcare Occupations

Frontline Care Support Workers

Frontline care support workers provide nonclinical support services within healthcare settings, such as housekeeping or dietary services. These occupations have very low education and skill requirements, with workers typically needing a high school degree or less. Care support workers perform entry-level manual work and are not typically included in definitions of frontline health or care work. However, Mignon Duffy (2005) argues that excluding these workers ignores the important role of manual labor in care and discriminates against the experiences of minority women, who are more likely to hold reproductive labor jobs. Indeed, Blacks, Hispanics, and other minorities are the most concentrated in care support jobs as compared to other frontline healthcare occupations (see table 5.1). Care support jobs also employ a greater percentage of men in healthcare settings: approximately 30 percent of care support workers are men, as compared to just 10 percent of direct care workers or administrative workers.

Care support workers have the lowest level of compensation and wage growth among all frontline healthcare occupations; average wages are $11.35 per hour, and average yearly wage growth among continuously employed care support workers is only $0.59 per hour per year (see table 5.2). Care support workers are also worse off than other frontline healthcare workers in other measures of financial well-being: about 56 percent of individuals have partially or fully paid employer-based health insurance (compared to about 70 percent among administrative and allied health workers), and about 12 percent of individuals receive food stamps (as compared to 4 percent of administrative and allied health). Care support workers also do not experience high rates of upward mobility within the healthcare sector. About 8 percent of the sample moved into

Table 5.3
Occupational transitions among frontline healthcare workers between 2008 and 2011

	Care support (SE)	Direct care work (SE)	Administrative (SE)	Frontline allied health (SE)	Hospital (SE)	Long-term care (SE)	Outpatient (SE)
Experienced upward occupational mobility within healthcare settings[a]	8.1% (.014)	9.3% (.010)	7.7% (.014)	13.6% (.021)	8.2% (.009)	7.6% (.009)	8.4% (.018)
Experienced downward occupational mobility within healthcare settings	7.0% (.013)	7.3% (.009)	8.0% (.014)	11.7% (.020)	8.4% (.008)	6.5% (.008)	5.5% (.019)
Transitioned away from healthcare employment[b]	22.1% (.020)	22.5% (.013)	20.5% (.020)	26.3% (.025)	21.1% (.013)	23.7% (.014)	23.4% (.125)
Transitioned to unemployment	27.5% (.021)	25.0% (.013)	21.2% (.020)	17.8% (.021)	19.9% (.012)	29.2% (.014)	19.6% (.023)

SOURCE: 2008 SIPP panel.

NOTES: Percentages reported reflect the numbers of individuals that experienced the transition during the survey period. Categories indicate that individual was ever in the specified category during the survey period (e.g., individual was ever a care support worker, ever worked in a hospital, etc.). Categories for occupational groups and employment type are not mutually exclusive, as many individuals had multiple transitions throughout the survey period.

[a]Includes transitions to managerial and mid-level positions (which includes RNs), as well as upward mobility within frontline healthcare occupations (e.g., direct care work to frontline allied health).

[b]Indicates that an individual was working in a frontline health occupation in a healthcare setting and then transitioned out of healthcare employment. However, these transitions can include transitions to healthcare settings that were not included in this study, such as physician offices or home healthcare.

Table 5.4

Differences in job quality by type of occupation and healthcare setting

	Job satisfaction (1–10) (SE)	Intent to stay (0–1) (SE)	Workload (1–4)[a] (SE)	Financial rewards (1–4) (SE)	Promotion opportunity (1–4) (SE)	Supervisor support (0–2) (SE)	Interpersonal care (1–4) (SE)
Occupation							
Care support (n = 82)	7.35	0.64	2.50	2.57	2.81	1.51	3.23
	(.176)	(.055)	(.059)	(.084)	(.068)	(.058)	(.051)
Direct care work (n = 572)	7.70	0.74	2.49	2.64	2.88	1.55	3.38
	(.055)	(.018)	(.020)	(.031)	(.026)	(.021)	(.016)
Administrative (n = 205)	7.73	0.84	2.33	2.69	2.85	1.64	3.23
	(.095)	(.026)	(.036)	(.049)	(.042)	(.035)	(.026)
Allied health (n = 124)	7.86	0.79	2.30	2.61	2.91	1.63	3.27
	(.123)	(.038)	(.038)	(.061)	(.049)	(.040)	(.034)
Employer type							
Hospital (n = 495)	7.65	0.77	2.42	2.74	2.97	1.58	3.34
	(.065)	(.019)	(.023)	(.032)	(.028)	(.023)	(.017)
LTC (n = 265)	7.68	0.76	2.46	2.51	2.68	1.48	3.42
	(.074)	(.027)	(.027)	(.049)	(.034)	(.032)	(.025)
Outpatient (n = 328)	7.76	0.77	2.39	2.55	2.89	1.64	3.22
	(.073)	(.024)	(.028)	(.038)	(.030)	(.026)	(.022)

SOURCE: Jobs to Careers Frontline Healthcare Worker Survey

[a] A higher score reflects a heavier workload and, consequently, worse job quality.

healthcare occupations with higher average wages, but almost as many work-ers (7 percent) experienced downward mobility during the survey period (see table 5.3). Care support workers were also more likely to be unemployed than other frontline healthcare workers; over one-quarter of care support workers transitioned to unemployment at some point during the survey period. Finally, care support workers report poorer job quality than other frontline healthcare workers on nearly every measure, including heavier workloads, lower financial rewards, lower promotion opportunity, lower supervisor support, and lower overall job satisfaction (see table 5.4). Not surprisingly, they were also less likely to say that they intended to stay with their current employer.

Frontline Direct Care Workers

Direct care workers provide primarily nurturant care, which involves a high level of face-to-face interaction and "body work," such as helping patients with bathing, toileting, eating, and mobility (Twigg et al. 2011). Direct care work-ers (such as nursing assistants and patient care assistants) may perform some more technical tasks as well, such as measuring patients' vital signs. Most direct care workers have completed some training (ranging from a few weeks to a few months), but do not hold a degree. Direct care occupations are heavily domi-nated by women, who make up about 90 percent of the direct care work force (see table 5.1). African Americans—primarily African American women—are especially concentrated in direct care occupations (making up 27 percent of the direct care work force, as compared to 13 percent of the general population). Hispanics, on the other hand, are underrepresented, making up 10 percent of direct care workers but 16 percent of the general population.

Direct care workers share a similar profile of compensation with frontline care support workers; average wages are $12.46 per hour, 53 percent of indi-viduals have partially or fully paid employer-based health insurance, and about 12 percent of individuals in both groups receive food stamps (see table 5.2). A higher percentage of direct care workers receive welfare assistance (about 1 percent) as compared to care support workers (0.5 percent), which likely reflects the high percentage of women in direct care work as compared to care support work. Direct care workers also experience low levels of upward mobil-ity, and about a quarter of the sample were unemployed at some point during the survey period (see table 5.3). Further, about 22 percent of the sample left the healthcare sector at some point during the survey period for employment in a different industry. Direct care workers have notoriously high turnover (Donoghue 2010), although turnover appears to be high across all frontline occupations.

Direct care workers report lower levels of job quality across many different dimensions as compared to frontline administrative and allied health work-ers, including heavier workloads, lower supervisory support, and lower overall job satisfaction (see table 5.4). An exception is a measure of satisfaction with relationships with clients, which is labeled "interpersonal care"; direct care workers report higher levels of satisfaction with interpersonal care as compared to workers in all other occupations, which would be expected given their high amount of patient interaction. Building relationships with patients and interacting with clients are clearly meaningful and satisfying parts of their jobs.

Frontline Administrative Workers

Frontline administrative workers fill clerical positions throughout healthcare organizations, from unit clerks who prepare patient medical records for clinical staff, to medical transcriptionists who transcribe the recorded dictation of clinicians, to medical records technicians who organize and review patient records. Frontline administrative workers usually hold a certificate or associate's degree, which may take one or two years to complete. About 90 percent of administrative workers are female, and there are lower numbers of minorities in these occupations as compared to care support and direct care occupations (see table 5.1).

Frontline administrative workers are better off financially than care support and direct care workers, earning average wages of $14.25 per hour (see table 5.2). Administrative workers also have higher rates of employer-based health insurance (just under 70 percent, which is above the national average) and lower rates of food stamps and welfare assistance, as compared to care support and direct care workers. Rates of upward (7 percent) and downward (8 percent) mobility among frontline administrative are similar to care support and direct care workers, but administrative workers are somewhat less likely to leave employment in the healthcare sector for another industry or unemployment as compared to lower-level workers (see table 5.3). Finally, in general, administrative workers report higher levels of job quality in terms of workload, financial rewards, supervisor support, and overall job satisfaction than care support and direct care workers, and they are the most likely of all frontline healthcare workers to say that they intend to stay in their current position (see table 5.4). However, they report lower levels of satisfaction in their relationships with clients as compared to direct care workers.

Frontline Allied Health Workers

Frontline allied health occupations include workers with some technical training resulting in a certificate or associate's degree, such as radiology technicians, surgical technicians, or licensed practical nurses (LPNs). Men fill a greater percentage of these jobs (about 25 percent) as compared to direct care and administrative workers, and these workers are more likely to be white (about 71 percent) than workers in other frontline healthcare occupations (see table 5.1).

Frontline allied health workers have the highest average compensation of the four groups, earning average wages of $15.36 per hour, and the highest yearly wage growth at $1.23 per hour per year (see table 5.2). Frontline allied health and administrative workers have a similar profile of financial well-being including higher rates of employer-based health insurance and lower rates of food stamps and welfare assistance (as compared to care support and direct care workers). Frontline allied health workers have higher rates of upward mobility during the survey period as compared to other frontline healthcare workers (14 percent), but they also experienced greater downward mobility as well (12 percent). Notably, these workers were somewhat more likely than frontline workers in other occupations to leave the healthcare industry during the survey period but less likely to transition to unemployment (see table 5.3). Finally, frontline allied health workers also generally report the highest levels of job quality; they report the highest levels of overall job satisfaction, lowest workloads, and most promotion opportunities (see table 5.4).

Job Quality across Healthcare Settings

Health care settings vary widely in the types of care they provide (and patients they treat), the workers they employ, and the structure of the organization. In this chapter, I profile workers in three types of settings: acute care hospitals (which includes psychiatric hospitals), long-term care (including skilled nursing units and assisted living facilities), and other outpatient settings (such as community health centers or ambulatory care). When we look at variation in compensation and financial well-being, hospitals and other outpatient settings clearly provide a better working environment as compared to long-term care organizations, but other measures of job quality show a more complex picture of workers' experiences across settings.

Average wages in hospitals and outpatient settings were about $14 per hour, as compared to $11.72 in long-term care settings. Not surprisingly, hospitals provided workers with the highest average yearly wage growth ($1.41), while long-term care provided workers with the lowest wage growth ($0.59). Hospitals and other outpatient settings are also far more likely to provide employer-based health insurance (71 percent and 67 percent, respectively) as compared to long-term care settings (44 percent). Finally, workers in long-term care settings have the highest percentage of the receipt of food stamps (13 percent) and welfare assistance (1.1 percent). The variation in wages and benefits across healthcare settings is due in part to the fact that long-term care organizations hire lower-skilled, lower-compensated workers as compared to hospitals, but the differences in job quality are not fully explained by human capital. For example, direct care workers in long-term care have an average wage of $11.41 per hour, as compared to $13.87 in hospitals and $13.50 in outpatient settings.

Measures of job quality and satisfaction strongly mirror measures of financial compensation and well-being when looking at different frontline occupational groups. However, when we look across healthcare settings, a slightly different scenario emerges. Hospitals and other outpatient care settings provide the highest compensation and benefits for workers as compared to long-term care, whereas workers in long-term care report heavier workloads and lower financial rewards, promotion opportunity, and supervisory support (see table 5.4). Yet workers in long-term care settings report similar levels of overall job satisfaction, and a similar percentage say that they intend to stay with their current employer. Long-term care workers also report higher levels of satisfaction with interpersonal care (likely to be due to the high level of direct care workers in long-term care), which suggests that interpersonal care substantially contributes to overall job satisfaction for these workers, a finding that is supported by past research (Dill, Morgan, and Marshall 2012).

Variety and Inequalities across Job Titles

Frontline healthcare occupations are among the fastest growing occupations in the United States due to the needs of the aging population and more women joining the labor force (thus creating a demand for paid caregivers) (Bodenheimer, Chen, and Bennett 2009; Thistle 2006). An important question to ask is whether or not these are "good jobs" for low-skill workers (Dwyer 2013; Kalleberg 2011). In other words, are these jobs that provide decent wages, employment benefits, and/or the opportunity to advance? We have constrained our sample to look specifically at the lowest-paid earners within frontline occupations (workers earning approximately $40,000 a year or less). However, even within the constrained sample, there is substantial variety in job quality between frontline occupations. Wages in care support and direct care occupations likely will not lift these workers out of poverty, particularly for parents of young children. On the other hand, there is evidence that administrative and frontline allied health occupations provide low-skill workers with a higher degree of job stability, higher compensation, and better employment benefits as compared to other low-skill service sector jobs available to workers with minimal training and education.

There are also substantial differences in job quality across health care settings. Hospitals provide workers with the highest wages, highest average yearly wage growth, and the highest rates of employer-based health insurance. The difference in compensation and benefits is due in part to the structure of the organizations: while acute care hospitals and other outpatient settings tend to be hierarchical and have many levels of specialized occupations within each organization, long-term care organizations are typically "flat" in structure, employing only a few different types of workers (for example, supervisory nurses and nursing assistants). Consequently, long-term care organizations have a higher concentration of the lowest skill occupations. On other hand, as pointed out earlier, the wage gap between long-term care and other health care settings cannot be attributed entirely to differences in human capital between settings. The wage gap also reflects the lower reimbursement rates for services that long-term care organizations receive as compared to hospitals and other outpatient care settings. As a result, long-term care organizations are more constrained in the wages that they can offer to workers.

Even though the analysis of wages, benefits, and job quality in this chapter has been limited to examining only the lowest earners within healthcare settings, there is still evidence of racial-ethnic inequality between frontline healthcare occupations. Racial-ethnic minorities are clustered in occupations and healthcare settings with the lowest levels of compensation and job quality, a finding that is consistent with previous research (Duffy 2011). Healthcare and nursing labor has been systematically organized into ranks, and enforcing the boundaries between these occupational ranks has been a central task of the professionalization of many healthcare occupations. As nurses and other allied health professionals have sought to preserve their own authority and increase their prestige, they have shifted much of the "dirty work" of their occupations to "unskilled" occupations. Today, frontline healthcare work "continues to be a specialty of racial-ethnic women" (Glenn 1992, 140), particularly in direct care and care support occupations. There are higher concentrations of whites in administrative and allied health occupations, which require less reproductive labor.

All frontline healthcare occupations are feminized occupations, but there are more men working at both the bottom (care support) and top (allied health) of frontline healthcare occupations. Janitorial work, which comprises a large proportion of care support, has traditionally been a male-dominated occupation and has only recently become more feminized (Duffy 2011). Frontline allied health occupations require more technical skills (and garner higher wages) and are less stigmatized as women's work as compared to direct care and administrative work.

Policy Implications

Approximately a quarter of workers across all frontline healthcare occupations leave employment in a health care setting during the survey period, suggesting that there is a high level of worker turnover in these occupations. While many frontline healthcare workers report that healthcare work is meaningful and satisfying to them, their low wages may induce them to leave their employer if another job offers slightly higher wages, better working conditions, or health insurance benefits. Alternatively, frontline healthcare workers may drop out of the labor market temporarily due to resource-related circumstances (for example, lack of childcare, transportation, and so forth), and when they reenter the work force, they may take a job with a different employer. In other words, the intrinsic rewards in care work cannot compensate for low wages and inadequate employment benefits. Workers in hospitals and outpatient settings, however, are far less likely to transition to unemployment, suggesting that the higher compensation and benefits provided by these healthcare settings helps to retain workers and keep them from exiting the work force.

Is it possible that frontline workers that turn over are leaving their jobs for better positions in healthcare? The findings presented in this chapter suggest that there is not a high degree of upward mobility among frontline healthcare workers, although the time period over which workers were followed is limited in length. Indeed, there are substantial structural barriers within the healthcare system that limit workers from moving into better jobs: healthcare occupations are rigidly "segmented" by credentials, which make upward vertical mobility for the lowest earners nearly "unscalable" (Duffy 2011; Glazer 1991). For example, evidence presented in this chapter suggests that there are real advantages for workers who are able to work in frontline administrative and allied health occupations, but these occupations typically require investment in an associate's degree or other certificate. Completing this additional education is difficult for many low-wage workers, who face a multitude of challenges related to their low wages, such as holding multiple jobs, transportation issues, a lack of basic literacy and math skills, or other financial constraints (see chapters 22 and 23).

Some healthcare and work force development organizations are attempting to help frontline workers in care support and direct care occupations move into frontline administrative and allied health positions through HR policies focused on support for education (see chapters 22 and 23). As Ariel Ducey (2008) argues, however, such programs may require substantial effort and sacrifice on the part of individuals for a limited increase in wages. As shown in this chapter, many of these positions pay only marginally better wages than care support or direct care occupations. The true benefit to moving into frontline administrative or allied health positions is the increased health insurance benefits associated with these occupations, but the implementation of the Affordable Care Act may make health benefits more widely available for workers at all levels.

An emphasis on moving workers into administrative or allied health positions may also further devalue direct care work, as that defines such work as merely a stepping stone to more skilled occupations. Viewing direct care work as a rung in a ladder reinforces that the technical skills required for administrative and allied health occupations are more valuable while the relational and interpersonal skills necessary for direct care work are unrecognized or overlooked. Clearly, providing opportunities for advancement for frontline healthcare workers is an important way to make these jobs into "better" jobs for low-wage workers. However, emphasizing advancement should not further devalue the workers and occupations that are already at the bottom of the healthcare hierarchy.

Notes

1 The employer categories (with NAICS codes) include: (1) hospitals (622), (2) long-term care (nursing care facilities (6,231) and residential care facilities without nursing (6,232, 6,233, 6,239), and (3) outpatient care centers (6,214). Note that frontline healthcare workers employed in physicians' offices or offices of other practitioners and frontline healthcare workers employed by home healthcare services or other healthcare services are excluded. These workers are excluded because workers in these healthcare settings were not included in the Jobs to Careers survey sample.

2 The sample selection may result in higher estimates of wage growth for individuals in frontline healthcare work. However, past research has shown that frontline healthcare workers experience minimal wage penalties for periods of unemployment or occupational changes, and minimal wage benefits related to tenure or work experience.

6

Orienting End-of-Life Care

• •

The Hidden Value of
Hospice Home Visits

CINDY L. CAIN

The location of care, especially at the end of life, is a complex issue that affects care workers as well as care recipients. While today a great deal of the most intensive care leading up to death takes place in institutional settings like hospitals, skilled nursing facilities, or nursing homes (Brown University 2004; Gruneir et al. 2007), most Americans report a desire to remain at home during their final days (Hays et al. 2001; Whittington 2011). There are many reasons this may be so: institutional settings are perceived as cold, uncomfortable, and clinical, while the home is associated with family, comfort, and peace. Hospice home-based care is one way that persons at the end of life can receive necessary care while also remaining in a comfortable home setting. This study uses the experiences of hospice workers—working primarily in the homes of patients—to understand how the location of care shapes workers' assessments of the quality of work and quality of care provided.

Hospice and Home-Based Care

Formed in critical response to institutionalized care for the dying, hospice is a type of end-of-life care that focuses on increasing quality of life instead of quantity of life. The hospice approach includes family members in the care plan, confronts social and psychological issues as well as physical health, and quite often supports home-based care as better than institutional settings (National Hospice and Palliative Care Organization [NHPCO] 2012). The National Hospice and Palliative Care Organization sees home care as one of many issues where patients' wishes should dictate care and advises workers to acknowledge the home as the site of the family and thus a unique workplace (NHPCO 2002). Given this, U.S. hospice care is ideally designed to take place in patients' homes, adult care homes, assisted living facilities, or the homes of informal caregivers (like family members).[1] For this chapter, I refer to home-based hospice care as any hospice services that take place in the care recipient's residence, and compare these home-based care experiences to workers' assessments of end-of-life care (hospice and non-hospice) in institutional settings like hospitals or skilled nursing facilities.

Home-based care has remained a central tenet of hospice care, but scholars of caring labor more generally have outlined many benefits and disadvantages of using the home as a primary site of care work (see chapters 3, 4, and 8). Proponents of home-based care argue that bringing qualified health professionals into the home allows better communication between patients and medical staff, stronger emotional support from loved ones, and improved pain management. More pessimistic accounts find that home-based care can be exploitative to workers and sometimes leads to lower quality care as patients' independence wanes and need for skilled care increases. This chapter builds on these debates about the value of home-based care by bringing hospice workers' perspectives into the conversation. Their perspectives are especially useful because the hospice philosophy strongly supports home-based care, but we currently know little about how these lofty goals actually manifest in the organization of caring work.

Location of Care

While a century ago, most Americans died in their own homes—cared for while alive and after death by family members—our most recent history includes a move toward medicalizing death, housing it in hospitals and other institutionalized settings (Krisman-Scott 2003). However, over the past several decades, we've seen an increase in home care of all kinds (Benjamin 1993; Duffy 2011; Glenn 2010), including home-based hospice (NHPCO 2012). In the case of end-of-life care, the home is assumed to be more comfortable and closer to family, and once life-saving measures have been removed, the skill and cost required for medical intervention is lowered (Benjamin 1993).

Studies of care workers of all kinds have reported advantages of home-based care for workers, especially in terms of autonomy and flexibility. Employees often determine the hours that they are willing to work and set their own schedules. This flexibility may reduce turnover through diminishing conflict between work and family time, especially for those with caregiving responsibilities in their own homes (Moen, Kelly, and Hill 2011). Care in the home also allows staff to transgress boundaries of intimacy through regular contact with patients, their family, and their natural habitat, which sometimes makes the work more rewarding (Stacey 2011). This is especially true for hospice work, which provides ample opportunities for workers to establish meaningful connections to care recipients, leading to higher levels of worker satisfaction (Cain 2012; Lopez 2006b).

Some have also posited that home-based care is better than institutionalized care for the patients and their family members. Institutionalized care at late life or the end of life can take place in hospitals, nursing homes, skilled nursing facilities, or other settings where multiple care recipients reside and the majority of care centers on medical interventions. These facilities are often experienced as uncomfortable (Diamond 1992). Their geography is hard to navigate, both for patients and their loved ones (Chambliss 1996). Institutional care at the end of life can also be very expensive, even after patients have discontinued life-saving measures. Care recipients often prefer home-based care because they are able to use decorations and pictures to personalize the space and provide a sense of familiarity (Angus et al. 2005). Additionally, because home-based care is premised on the work of unpaid familial caregivers, it is often less expensive than institutionalized care.

However, studies have also highlighted drawbacks to home-based work, especially for care workers. Working in the homes of others can be dangerous and exploitative, especially if staff cannot set boundaries in terms when and how work will take place (see chapter 8; Stacey 2011).[2] Lack of boundaries can lead to a blurring of the line between the private space of the home and the public act of work, making it very difficult for paid caregivers to negotiate their roles as workers (Folbre 2001). Because workers are in the homes of care recipients, they are sometimes isolated from their coworkers, leading to lower levels of workplace support. Home-based care providers are expected to provide companioning services in addition to medical services but are not compensated for those services (Aronson and Neysmith 1996; Duffy 2011). Working in the home can sometimes lead to surveillance by interested parties, who stop by unannounced, make body checks for bruises and marks on the care recipient, and check the home for damages (Macdonald 2010). Finally, because home-based care is associated with presumably low-skilled domestic labor, it is currently compensated at very low levels and has few labor protections (Boris and Klein 2012). These studies have been informative, but none have taken hospice as their site of study. Hospice home-based care likely includes these same drawbacks but also provides a case where home-based care is supported through institutional practices and a strong philosophy. It is possible that these supports mitigate some of the drawbacks of home-based care.

Data and Methods

The data for this chapter come from over two years of ethnographic observation of a mid-sized hospice organization in the southwestern United States and forty-one in-depth interviews with hospice workers. Ethnographic data collection included observation and participation in patient care, consultations with family members, staff meetings and trainings, and the completion of administrative paperwork. My access to observation was aided by my status as a hospice volunteer, offering a side-in approach to research (Chambliss 1996), which allowed me to gain entrée with staff more quickly than I likely would have if I had attempted to observe without becoming a hospice volunteer.

I supplemented observational data with interviews with forty-one workers from hospices in the southwestern United States. Participants included physicians, nurses, social workers, counselors, chaplains, certified nursing aides (CNAs), administrators, and volunteers. Interview topics included the daily work of hospice, emotion management in hospice, and the ways that workers balanced their work and home lives. Several workers had previously worked in more institutionalized settings and offered their assessment by comparing hospice home-based care to adult care homes, nursing homes, inpatient hospice settings, or hospitals. Through these comparisons, workers said a great deal about how location shapes workers' experiences with providing care.

This chapter uses my observations in conjunction with workers' narratives about home-based care to contribute to debates about the value of home and institutional care. I analyzed these data by coding field notes and interview transcripts for any discussion of site of care. I then inductively grouped these discussions into comments on the advantages and disadvantages of home-based care. Workers were often explicit in their discussions of the advantages of home-based care, while mentions of disadvantages were often couched within larger discussions of difficulties of hospice work more generally. The next section will elucidate these advantages and disadvantages, especially as they pertain to the experiences of hospice care workers.

Benefits of Home-Based Care for Workers

Hospice staff emphasized that home-based care had advantages above institutionalized work they had previously performed. They talked about the ways that home-based care allowed autonomy and flexibility in their schedules, as well as encouraged them to develop more personally rewarding relationships with their patients. Additionally, because these workers generally thought home-based care was more consistent with a hospice approach, they often felt that care in the home was higher quality than institutional care.

Autonomy and Flexibility

Home-based care offers several forms of flexibility and autonomy to workers. Tammy, a long-time hospice nurse, described her schedule: "What I try to do throughout the week is do most of my visits in the morning when people are more awake, more alert, and maybe feel a little bit better and then try to reserve the afternoon for some of the charting and updating the plans of care, making follow-up phone calls to the docs." Tammy likes this schedule because she can be home with her grandchildren in the afternoon. Because she works in the homes of her patients, she has a great deal of control over how her work time is structured.

Likewise, Bethany, a new hospice nurse, said, "I work Monday through Friday, 8:00 to 5:00, and that's one of the things that I really love because I'm not cooped up in a hospital for twelve hours. And because I do home care, I set my own schedule, and I can drive and then take a break, or go to my parents, or meet somebody for lunch, or do some paperwork, and then go see my next patient, or I can just bump, seeing my patients right after each other. So I have the flexibility to set my own schedule, which is something that I really need." Both of these nurses mentioned that sometimes this flexibility meant they worked over their required hours and paperwork migrated into their evenings and weekends, but overall they positively compared the flexibility of home-based care to the rigid structure of hospital nursing.

Relationships with Patients

Being in the home also permitted staff to create closer, more rewarding relationships with their patients. One CNA, Deanna, reported that she liked hospice because "of the families that I meet and the quality time, the one-on-one time I get to deal with the patients; whereas, in hospitals, you don't get to do that. Being able—even though obviously death is a big part of it, even though that's a big part of it—I'm still able to walk out of the patient's house and look back over my shoulder and see them with a smile on their face, and they're very thankful. Everybody's just thankful for everything. You don't get that much in hospitals because nobody has the time." Deanna emphasized that time in the home and encounters with family members permitted her to feel appreciated and enjoy her work.

Some staff also liked home-based care because they were able to express their feelings during interactions with patients and their family members. Bethany, a nurse, explains how the hospice philosophy allows nurses to cry along with the family: "Well, I know when we're in the home, they expect us to be put together and kept together. . . . So they expect us to withhold [sic] a certain level of professionalism but also be able to, if we feel strongly about a situation, to be able to express that, whether it's crying or laughing at a situation to break up the intensity, or just really being able to express ourselves. It's expected that we can do that. And I know many of the nurses feel comfortable enough to mourn with the family or cry or things like that." Importantly, Bethany's comment points to some limits in the extent to which crying would be considered professional, but she remarks that hospice home-based care is unique in permitting any sharing of emotions. Several staff cited this openness to expressions of emotion as a key way that hospice generally, but especially hospice home-based care, was more rewarding than other forms of end-of-life care.

Professional Satisfaction in Quality Care

Hospice workers reported that home-based care was most consistent with the hospice philosophy and regarded home as the ideal location for the end of life. Because of this, they felt professional satisfaction related to the quality of care they were able to provide. Being in the home of the care recipient pushed hospice care workers to think about patients in humanizing ways. This manifested in three main themes: home visits encouraged workers to see the person behind the illness, understand obstacles to treatment, and better advocate for the interests of the patients. It also symbolically gave control to the care recipient, while empowering workers to form meaningful connections to patients and their family members.

Seeing the Person Behind the Illness

Home-based care was often seen as furthering the hospice philosophy by encouraging workers to acknowledge the patient's life and individuality. This sometimes slowed down care, allowing patients to make informed decisions. Sarah, an administrator, worked in nursing homes before coming to hospice. She says that hospice is nice because of the slower pace: "Nursing homes can be quite fast-paced. You've got a lot of patients coming in, a lot of meds to pass. This is just kind of a step down. . . . I had to learn to just kind of slow down just a little bit because in hospice, many times—not that you drag your feet—but you kind of analyze things a little bit slower, and sometimes those things all take care of themselves." Sarah gave an example of how this slowing is related to patient autonomy during hospice home-based care:

> Prime example is we had a patient at the inpatient unit . . . a young woman with ovarian cancer. She had IV fluids. She had an NG tube. She had heparin injections. She was at the inpatient unit. We did all those things while she was there. We were able to get her home. We taught the family what needs to be done. We educated both of them. She got home and said, "I don't want to do this anymore." So we were all geared up to get the fluids there, to get all the equipment there, and she said, "I don't want to do it anymore." . . . So sometimes if you just keep educating and just slow down a little bit, it all comes into play.

Sarah's story shows that when workers were able to slow down care, fully educate family members, and let the patient take her time, she was eventually able to make her own decision to end life-prolonging treatments. Sarah considers this to be a victory in that it empowered the patient, allowing her to die in her own home. Sarah took pride in being able to provide this empowerment to the patient.

Entering into homes also permitted nonstandard care practices supported by hospice's commitment to complementary and holistic treatments. Institutional settings often had rules that limited nontraditional therapies, especially those involving pets or music. Nina, a volunteer coordinator, described her current hospice company: "We have right now eight dogs that visit so we try to give doggy visits to those that would like it. We've got a number of musicians who have come onboard with us, that go out and play for our patients." While dog visits and live music are not likely part of the care plan for most hospital-bound patients, Nina emphasizes that home care allows her to fully use the talents and interests of her volunteers. In each of these examples, hospice staff reported that performing care in patients' homes allowed them a broader perspective on the patients' life and end-of-life needs while also reducing rules and restrictions put in place in more institutional settings.

Understanding Obstacles to Treatment
In addition to facilitating individualized care, hospice workers liked home-based care because it allowed them to identify obstacles and gaps in care. Ramon, a social worker, says he likes home-based care because:

> Well, I think part of it is, honestly, seeing clients in their homes, and being more intimately involved in the social setting and the social situation and being more intimately involved in the family. . . . So I think that there's something that's really—you know, you're a guest in their home. That's how I view myself. I think the nurses think that usually as well. So, I think that stuff does become more client-centered, family-centered, and becomes less rigid, less authoritarian because you're exposed to the social situation and you have an understanding of it. And, the understanding may be of the limits of what is going to happen.

Ramon claims that home care makes the care more client-centered and less authoritarian, but that it also allows the hospice staff to understand limits in the extent to which they can intervene in patients' lives.

Likewise, Stephanie (CNA) said that she liked home-based care better than nursing home work because "I feel more comfortable going into a private home because it's their home. And you're not having a caregiver from an adult care home telling them, 'No, they have to.' Like they don't have to." According to Stephanie, caregivers in nursing homes are too attached to the things they think patients must do, while in hospice home-based care, she feels more able to understand what patients will and will not do. Bonnie, a nurse educator and former hospice nurse, added that home-based care "gives you a whole 'nother perspective as to how people choose to run their lives. And you really have to be respectful and incorporate 'this is their way and I'm a guest there.' So I love that part. And it also then helped me identify what some of the gaps in care had been before they got to that point." Hospice workers frequently used the language of being a guest in patients' homes as a way to conceptualize the difference between institutionalized care and home-based care. By thinking of themselves as guests, workers symbolically gave patients autonomy and control over care. It is noteworthy that home-based care also gave workers autonomy and flexibility over the kinds of services they were able to provide, thus fostering a sense of professionalism in the work.

Advocating for Patients

While sometimes home-based hospice care can help workers to identify types of intervention that are not possible in institutions, other times home care permits workers to see solutions to problems that patients do not know how to articulate. Daniel tells a story about a patient's family that was really struggling, but their concerns were not readily observable. He says, "[The patient] really needed a hospital bed but he didn't want one, and in questioning him and finding out that he didn't want to be back in the bedroom by himself. So I said, 'Well hey, we can put the bed out here in the living room and he can be' . . . it never even crossed their mind." In this example, Daniel was able to uncover the real concern: the patient wanted to stay with his family members. Daniel fixed the problem by putting the hospital bed in the living room. Importantly, he concluded by noting that the family members had not even known it was possible to ask for this, but through being in the home, he could identify the real problem.

In contrast, Pam described a problem she was trying to resolve at an adult care facility. Pam's patient was moved into the facility when he could no longer care for himself. After some concerns about his mobility, Pam recounts, "He's a fall risk, so they turned his bed and they turned his bed to where he can no longer look out the big sliding glass windows in his room, which overlooks a beautiful courtyard full of green grass and beautiful bushes and flowers. And he's very depressed and I have met twice now with the IDG team [Interdisciplinary Group team] and said, 'Please can we do something about turning his bed?' Because both times I've seen him since they've turned the bed, he mentions that he wishes he could see outside because right now the way he is the only thing he stares at is literally a blank, white wall, not even a picture on it." Pam said that she battles with facility staff to move his bed back, but they are concerned about liability related to falling. She thinks, however, that if the patient was in his own home, there would be no problem placing the bed in view of a window. Like Nina (above), Pam sees institutional settings as limiting the range of choices available to care workers and care recipients. Not only is this distressing to the patient, but it makes Pam feel frustrated with restrictions that prevent her from providing the highest quality care.

Barriers to Productive Home-Based Care

Although hospice staff members positively compared home-based care to more institutional settings, they were also realistic about some of the disadvantages and the barriers to keeping home-based care productive. One disadvantage for workers is the amount of time they spend driving: "So I can drive . . . up to probably sixty or eighty miles a day, not including [driving to work]" (Annie, nurse). This is especially burdensome for workers that have a heavy enough care load that they stop recording their driving time to avoid going in to overtime. Staff frequently reported that they would face disciplinary action if they reported overtime hours, so it was easier to just not report driving time. While hospice workers appreciated that the care of patients was slowed down by home-based care, this particular organization of care meant that workers' free time was sacrificed in order to provide this slowing.

Amy, a CNA, explains that going into the home also introduces some unpredictability into her daily routine. Some patients are ready for her visit and things go smoothly: "He gets up on his walker. He'll walk into the bathroom, take a shower. He gets out. I get him dressed and he assists, putting on his shirt. And then, 'Okay, well, I'm ready.' And then he'll get in his wheelchair and wheel himself to the breakfast room or to watch TV." However, other patients, especially those who are actively dying, have needs that require much more time, so it is sometimes hard to schedule visits with families more than a day or two in advance. This often results in long days and unpredictable work hours, even as she is able to schedule those hours herself.

Natalie, a hospice volunteer for the last three years, describes another problem with home-based care. She tells about a patient who was not safe at home anymore. The patient was mostly immobile and not entirely aware of her surroundings and her husband was trying to provide care, but Natalie was afraid that he was also getting too frail to protect her safety. After discussions during team meetings, the patient was moved into a skilled nursing facility. Natalie describes the new situation: "It's a good situation for her because she's in a home where there are other people around and she's getting wonderful care, and he doesn't have to worry about her." These examples show that even though hospice workers supported home-based care, they did see situations where the risks of remaining in the home outweighed the benefits.

Josephine describes another situation where patients' and workers' safety were at risk:

> There was one circumstance where I was really fearful for the patient. . . . He was starting to get real confused and he wasn't safe and he was living alone in his trailer. It was not a good situation. And he smoked. And [the social worker] and I both walked away from that situation . . . saying, oh, jeez, this is bad—real bad. We got to address this. Within an hour, fire trucks were at that house. . . . Yeah, and he wasn't going to stop the cigarette—forget it. I mean, that

was not going to happen. So we were—I know I was frightened when I drove away. I just couldn't get it off my mind. And like I say, within an hour—yeah, that was terrible. I mean, he didn't get burned. Fortunately, he was out of the house when it actually started, I believe. I can't remember all the circumstances. But that's probably the most frightened I've ever been for someone. And then after I heard what happened, it just scared the bejeebers out of me. I thought dad gum, you know, in these situations we've got to do something faster or better.

In this instance Josephine and the social worker were not able to monitor or prevent the patient from smoking around his oxygen tank, even though the patient knew it was dangerous. She mentions feeling fear for the patient, but the incident also could have injured her as well. While keeping this patient home allowed him to make his own decisions about whether to smoke, the choice he made was dangerous.

Learning from Hospice Home-Based Care

Care at the end of life can take place in a variety of settings. Some are fully institutionalized, like hospitals, nursing facilities, and some nursing homes. Others are fully home-oriented, like home-based hospice care. It is useful to think about these locations of care as residing along a continuum instead of as discrete entities. The hospice philosophy emphasizes treating patients in the places they are most comfortable, which is often patients' own homes. However, hospice workers provide care in fully home-oriented settings as well as partially institutionalized settings. Additionally, most hospice workers in this study had also worked in fully institutionalized settings in their previous jobs. Because of these experiences in diverse settings, hospice workers were able to compare the value of home-based care to institutional care, offering unique insight into how location of care affects care workers.

These findings have implications for better understanding (and reforming) home-based care. Specifically, hospice workers emphasized that home-based care suited their desire for scheduling flexibility and autonomy while also permitting them to have meaningful relationships with their charges. By locating care in the home and supporting it with a strong hospice philosophy, these workers felt a sense of professional pride they did not feel in more institutionalized settings. Additionally, hospice workers regarded home-based care as higher quality because it allowed care workers to see the whole person, instead of just the bodies or ailments of patients, and permitted workers to creatively recognize and solve problems that increase quality of life for patients. This sense of professional pride, as well as the commitment to meaningful relationships and high-quality care, meant that hospice workers in this study reported very high levels of work satisfaction and low levels of intention to leave hospice work.

Not all aspects of home-based care were good for workers, however. Implicit in their stories were accounts of undocumented driving time, unpredictable schedules, and work weeks that extended beyond paid hours. While a supportive hospice philosophy helped to justify home-based care, it did not necessarily protect workers from exploitation (Cain 2013) Stronger worker protections are needed to ensure that the benefits of home-based care will continue to exist, even as healthcare organizations are experiencing increased financial strains that increase workload. These are issues that could be confronted at the level of individual work organizations, but given that the challenges were reported in almost all interviews with hospice workers, it is clear that these concerns also exist at the level of the industry. While the benefits of home-based care may be great for persons at the end of life, these benefits should not come at a cost to care workers.

It is also important to note that some of the expected disadvantages of home-based care were not present in hospice workers' descriptions of their work. In particular, concerns over social isolation of workers and unclear boundaries between required work and nonwork activities were not strongly represented in this setting. This is likely because hospice home-based care is supported by an organization and care philosophy that explicitly defines quality care. Hospice quality care includes a team approach, which mitigates the social isolation of workers. Hospice workers reported regular contact with one another throughout the work week. Additionally, by communicating explicitly about what constitutes work and nonwork activities, the hospice organization left fewer of those activities to be negotiated by individual workers in the home. While home-based hospice care is not without problems for workers, it serves as a case to better understand how to support home-based care to improve both quality of work and quality of care.

Finally, although this study examined home-based hospice care, the findings do illuminate a few ways that institutionalized care may be improved to better serve other care workers and care recipients. Most importantly, home-based hospice workers' experiences show that slowing down care is good for everyone. It increases workers' satisfaction as they are able to fully consider all options and feel good about giving autonomy to care recipients. It gives care recipients necessary time to absorb information and make decisions. And, ultimately, at the end of life, some of those decisions involve discontinuing unnecessary treatments, thus saving money on care provided. Taking more time can allow workers to see unanticipated problems and approach them creatively. Rules and procedures of institutional settings sometimes hinder that creativity, highlighting the value of more flexibility in regulations. By integrating elements of home settings and encouraging meaningful relationships between care providers and their charges, institutional settings can improve care worker experiences and care outcomes.

Notes

1 Hospice care is usually not provided in nursing homes, skilled nursing facilities, or hospitals as Medicare (the primary payer for hospice services) will not typically pay for nursing services simultaneously with hospice care (NHPCO 2012). Most hospice services are provided on an outpatient basis, but some hospices also include an inpatient division. These inpatient units are used to provide respite for informal caregivers and to manage intense pain that cannot be controlled in the home setting. Inpatient units are used as a supplement to home-based care, not an alternative to it.

2 Many of the studies that most clearly document these kinds of concerns are of domestic workers (see Rollins 1985, for example). More recently, studies of healthcare workers have also taken up this issue.

Part III

Hazards of Care

● ●

As they care for the bodies and minds of others, care workers regularly put their own physical and psychological health at risk. While understanding the vulnerability of the individuals being cared for, it is important not to obscure the vulnerability of the workers themselves. Some of these hazards have been studied extensively by occupational safety and health researchers, but their findings have rarely crossed over into the care work literature. We bring these literatures together in this section, with chapters that explore the unique hazards encountered by care workers, strategies for reducing these risks, and obstacles to change.

Not only are the physical risks encountered by care workers immense, but they are often invisible. Because these jobs are perceived as primarily relational, the intense physical demands and dangers of many care occupations are obscured. As noted by Alicia Kurowski, Jon Boyer, and Laura Punnett, direct care workers face injury rates that are more than twice as high as those of construction workers. Direct care work involves manual lifting and moving of clients, an activity that presents high risks of musculoskeletal disorders and injury (see Kurowski, Boyer, and Punnett; and Pia Markkanen, Margaret Quinn, and Susan Sama). Lifting bodies is only one of the activities that take a toll on care workers across the sector. Pushing heavy objects like medicine carts and beds, being exposed to bodily fluids and blood-borne pathogens, and experiencing abuse and violence from clients also characterize direct care work both in institutional and home settings. And, as Jennifer Zelnick points out, these risks are not limited to health care workers. Social workers experience high rates of violence, a phenomenon that has largely stayed under the radar even in the field of occupational health. Childcare workers also lift and move (wriggling) bodies and face exposure to bodily fluids and contagious illnesses, and school teachers face physical altercations and abuse from children. These chapters make clear that care jobs are not all warm and fuzzy.

Along with physical risks, care workers face a unique set of psychological hazards. Several of the chapters highlight the long, unpredictable, and often unconventional hours required of care workers. These characteristics of care jobs not only lead to higher levels of work-family conflict and stress (see Kurowski, Boyer, and Punnett) but can inhibit connecting to larger community networks (see Ivy Bourgeault). The pace of care jobs and the emotional demands also lead to high levels of stress and burnout. Compounding these issues, many of the workers described in these chapters see their jobs through the lens of what Zelnick calls an "ethic of care," prioritizing the well-being of those for whom they care over their own health and safety. This ethic of care leads workers to dismiss the risks as "part of the job," contributing to the underreporting and invisibility of job-related illness and injury in care occupations.

These chapters also highlight the ways that other inequalities related to race, class, gender, and citizenship status shape the hazards of paid care work. Those individuals at the bottom of the occupational hierarchy face the highest risks of physical and psychological illness and injury. For example, Kurowski, Boyer, and Punnett find that nursing assistants face higher risk of injury than registered nurses, Zelnick finds that unlicensed clinical staff are more likely to be the target of violence than licensed clinical staff, and migrant care workers face what Bourgeault refers to as "double isolation." Race, class, and citizenship structure which workers are concentrated in low-wage and high-risk jobs.

Importantly, individual vulnerabilities must be considered within the context of chronic underinvestment in the care sector overall. For example, Zelnick places risks to social services workers in the context of changes in government funding and the push for agencies to "do more with less." Bourgeault shows that the underfunding of the older adult care sector has pulled more migrant workers into these occupations and contributes to their isolation once they are there. Direct care workers who must handle patient lifts alone or without assistive devices are at much higher risk for musculoskeletal injury. Cost cutting, understaffing, and worker speed-up contribute to increased risks of injury and illness for workers across the care sector.

The implication is that governments and employers have the potential to greatly reduce the hazards of care work. For example, Kurowski, Boyer, and Punnett point to the reduction in physical stress on workers if an employer changes flooring from carpet to tile or implements the use of patient-handling devices. These authors also provide evidence that worker safety is not a zero-sum game of balancing client needs against worker needs. Markannen, Quinn, and Sama note that proactive employers can institute effective safety protections, which can improve worker turnover rates and the ability of those workers to provide quality care. And Kurowski, Boyer, and Punnett report that when patients are informed about worker safety issues, they are more accepting of the use of patient-handling devices. Taken together, these chapters are the beginning of an important dialogue about the hidden risks that care workers face, the policy and practices that create and exacerbate these risks, and the untapped potential and unmet responsibility that employers and government have to reduce these risks.

7

The Health Hazards
of Health Care

• •

Physical and Psychosocial
Stressors in Paid Care Work

ALICIA KUROWSKI, JON BOYER,
AND LAURA PUNNETT

Healthcare institutions such as hospitals and nursing homes are places where many people seek and receive medical services to improve their health. Yet the workers who provide that care, including registered nurses (RNs), licensed practical nurses (LPNs), nursing assistants (NAs), and many others, are exposed to conditions on the job that threaten their own health. These hazards cover the full range of risk factors for injury and illness: biological agents such as viruses, toxic chemicals such as cleaning agents, heavy lifting and other types of forceful exertions, physical and verbal assault, and stressors with psychological as well as physiological effects such as long work hours and night work.

Because of these hazards, direct care providers have some of the highest injury rates across industries, even compared to heavy jobs traditionally considered dangerous, such as in construction. In 2011, the U.S. Bureau of Labor Statistics (BLS) reported that the rate of nonfatal occupational injuries and illnesses for employees in nursing care facilities was 10.2 per 100 workers compared to 3.9 per 100 for construction workers (2012c). Among all occupations, nursing aides, orderlies, and attendants ranked second only to laborers and freight, stock, and material movers in injuries and illnesses requiring days away from work.

The discipline of occupational ergonomics is concerned with analysis of the work environment to understand and correct discrepancies between job requirements and worker needs and abilities. Worker-job fit should encompass physical features of equipment and workstations as well as organizational features that might underlie psychologically stressful job conditions. A range of ergonomic exposures, including both physical and psychosocial aspects of the work environment, have been associated with the development of musculoskeletal disorders (Bernard 1997; Hoogendoorn et al. 1999; Institute of Medicine 2001). Musculoskeletal disorders, including back pain, tendinitis, and arthritis, are not life-threatening but have a major impact on quality of life, affecting both physical and social functional capacity. Health care has high rates of costly work-related injuries, with strain/sprain and back injury rates being particularly high (Waehrer, Leigh, and Miller 2005). For example, 56 percent of the lost-time injuries to aides and orderlies were due to overexertion, compared to 16 percent among construction workers (U.S. Department of Labor Bureau of Labor Statistics 2012d).

This chapter covers three major topics. It begins with a literature review on some common hazards faced by care workers in hospitals and nursing homes, the two major types of healthcare institutions. The second section discusses the interplay of socioeconomic status and work conditions in how these risks vary by job and location. Finally, the role of unpaid labor is addressed as another health risk factor among care workers (primarily women) that has received little attention to date.

Physical and Psychosocial Stressors in Care Work

In their day-to-day tasks, while helping others, care workers often risk injury to their own bodies. Some physical ergonomic risk factors encountered by care workers include awkward postures of the trunk, arms, and legs (figure 7.1); forceful actions like pushing, pulling, lifting, or carrying patients or equipment; repetitive motions like administering injections; and shock impact resulting from pill-crushing actions. The intensity, frequency, and duration of these factors individually or in combination with one another affect injury risk.

One especially common physical task that puts healthcare workers at risk is lifting, transferring, and repositioning patients or residents. Most adults weigh far more than the recommended weight limit for manual lifting (Waters, Putz-Anderson, and Garg 1994). In addition, lifting people is a much more complex task than lifting an object. Care workers mobilize people—who may move unexpectedly, who are often unstable on their feet or cannot walk at all, who are not standard sizes or shapes, and who may not be compliant because of difficulty

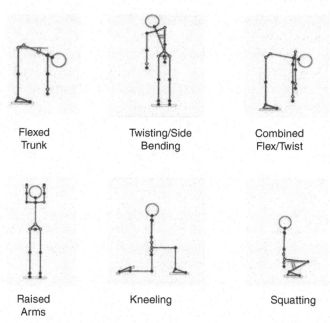

Flexed Trunk   Twisting/Side Bending   Combined Flex/Twist

Raised Arms   Kneeling   Squatting

FIG. 7.1 Examples of awkward postures. (Source: Image created using 3D SSPP software (www .engin.umich.edu/dept/ioe/3DSSPP/). Copyright the Regents of the University of Michigan)

understanding what is happening, anxiety about their medical conditions, or other reasons.

Workers who do more patient lifting have higher risk of back pain and other musculoskeletal disorders (Trinkoff et al. 2003; Waters, Nelson, and Proctor 2007). In addition to patient-handling tasks, many healthcare workers have to stand for long hours or operate equipment in awkward body postures. These activities further increase the injury risk for care workers (Boyer 2008; Janowitz et al. 2006). Nurses and medicine aides must push and pull heavy medicine carts to store, prepare, and dispense medications and supplies, which is particularly problematic on carpeted surfaces (Boyer 2008; Boyer, Lin, and Chang 2013).

Injuries to the lower extremities have not been studied as extensively as back and upper extremity problems. However, two recent studies of care workers have linked high perceived exertion at work with knee pain (Alexopoulos et al. 2011; Andersen et al. 2013). A study comparing floor surfaces in nursing homes reported care workers in a facility with a foam layer under the vinyl flooring experienced lower pain intensity in the feet than those working on traditional vinyl floors (Wählstrom, Ostman, and Leijon 2012).

Care workers' health is affected not just by physical conditions of the work-place but by excessive psychological demands (for example, high time pressure), low job control, lack of social support, low job satisfaction, and monotonous work (Hoogendoorn et al. 2000). These are all common stressors among care workers in both hospitals and nursing homes. Psychosocial stressors are well established as risk factors for cardiovascular disease, mental health problems, sleep disruption, and other chronic health issues. In care work, as well as in other sectors, they have also been associated with the development of musculoskeletal disorders, especially in combination with heavy lifting and other physical exertions (Lipscomb et al. 2002; Trinkoff et al. 2002; Yassi et al. 2004).

The distinction between physical and psychosocial stressors at work is not always clear-cut. Insufficient staffing for the workload required, highly routinized and repetitive work, lack of control over one's work schedule, and increased or unpredictable patient acuity or obesity levels may lead to increased physical as well as psychological demands, as well as perceived lack of control over the job (Aiken et al. 2002; Lipscomb et al. 2004). Low task variability implies low job control and monotonous and repetitive physical work. The combination of highly routinized work and long hours may decrease a worker's opportunity for recovery and increase risk for musculoskeletal disorders due to the effects of physical and work organization exposures.

Another important psychosocial stressor in modern life—notable in but not limited to the healthcare sector—is the potential conflict between work and personal life, referred to as work-family imbalance. This may operate in both directions and is related, at least in part, to work organization features such as long work hours and being on call; it also tends to increase with number of children, having a disabled family member at home, and being a single parent (Strazdins and Bammer 2004). While not unique to women working outside the home, work-family imbalance is especially reported as a health risk factor for women. Employment sectors such as care work, which employ a large proportion of professional women and operate on nonstandard shift schedules, may experience elevated risk of negative health outcomes as a consequence (Simon, Kummerling, and Hasselhorn 2004).

Socioeconomic Disparities in Health and the Role of Working Conditions

Low socioeconomic status is well-known to be a predictor of illness and death due to a wide range of health conditions, from heart disease to early childhood deaths. This relationship between low socioeconomic status and poor health has been observed in many countries and population samples, including in the healthcare work force. For example, blue-collar workers have significantly higher odds of nonfatal injury due to any cause (Cubbin, LeClere, and Smith 2000), and higher rates of absence from work following injury were reported among hospital employees with lower socioeconomic status (Pines et al. 1985). In general, illness and injury rates increase as socioeconomic status decreases. This is referred to as the inverse socioeconomic status gradient. Some proposed explanations of the socioeconomic status gradient include lifestyle causes and access to medical care for diagnosis and treatment. However, there has been surprisingly little attention to the contribution of working conditions to socioeconomic disparities in health.

Among the many health outcomes exhibiting this gradient, musculoskeletal disorders disproportionately impact low-socioeconomic-status individuals, in the general population and in specific economic sectors. Both the incidence and severity of low-back pain are higher in low income, low education, and blue-collar versus white-collar jobs (Broersen et al. 1996; Heistaro et al. 1998). Similar trends have been noted for neck and upper extremity disorders (Mäkelä et al. 1991), osteoarthritis of the knee (Anderson and Felson 1988), and musculoskeletal disorders in general (Badley, Rasooly, and Webster 1994).

The high physical and psychosocial exposures in care work tend to affect low-status workers such as NAs disproportionately, compared to higher-status jobs such as RNs (Lagerström, Hansson, and Hagberg 1998). Some of our research has shown that the work environment is one important mediator of socioeconomic disparities in health, because physical workload and other hazards are more prevalent in low-status jobs, and that this effect can be seen specifically in musculoskeletal disorders and injuries to healthcare workers.

In several recent studies using direct observations of care workers in hospitals and nursing homes, there were important differences in physical and psychosocial exposures between job titles, even though overall, care work jobs had high exposures to heavy manual handling and awkward postures (trunk flexion, trunk rotation, and lateral bending). In both settings, NAs spent more time engaged in manual handling of patients or residents than did LPNs and RNs (Boyer 2008). NAs spent more time with awkward back postures, more time handling the heaviest loads (above fifty pounds), and less time in seated recovery. Aides also had less task variation than other care workers, meaning that their work involved more repetition of the same basic physical activities. On the other hand, staff nurses worked overtime hours much more often than NAs (Boyer 2008). Some of these findings were later confirmed in a separate study of nursing home workers, using similar methods, where NAs (especially when handling residents) handled heavier loads and worked in more severe postures like flexion, lateral (side) bending, twisting, static standing, and with raised arms, than did nurses (Kurowski et al. 2012a). Thus the lowest-wage workers face the highest physical demands and injury risks.

We also conducted two studies of community hospitals to examine the extent to which occupational exposures explained socioeconomic differences in risk of reported injuries. One study analyzed incidents that were entered on the employers' Occupational Safety and Health Administration injury logs (d'Errico et al. 2007), and the other used workers' compensation claims (Boyer et al. 2009). Both sets of injuries included a large proportion of musculoskeletal disorders, along with falls and being cut or struck by objects.

Overall, both physical workload and psychosocial stress factors were higher in the jobs with lower socioeconomic status. In addition, several physical exposures were strongly correlated with each other, indicating that some jobs involved exposure to multiple factors simultaneously. Increasing levels of psychological demands, decision latitude, and rewards were all correlated with increasing socioeconomic status. However, some psychosocial conditions such as increasing job strain and low supervisor support were worse in high socioeconomic status jobs.

The low socioeconomic status jobs (semiskilled workers such as NAs) had higher risk of injury from both reporting sources. The Occupational Safety and Health Administration log injury reports showed a strong trend by socioeconomic status (table 7.1) (d'Errico et al. 2007). Of note, some of the jobs with highest physical exposures were not direct care occupations: cleaning and maintenance (back risk) and keyboard-intensive clerical work (upper extremity risk). Adjustment for the contributions of physical exertion, decision latitude, and supervisor support greatly reduced the socioeconomic status trend, indicating that a large part of risk is mediated by those exposures.

Similarly, for the workers' compensation claims, incidence rates for all injuries, strains and sprains, and back injuries were highest in the lowest socioeconomic status category (semiskilled workers) and lowest among administrators (Boyer et al. 2009). A large proportion of the claims were associated with physical ergonomic exposures such as manual handling—especially patient handling—as well as trunk bending and twisting and safety hazards. Increased psychological job demands, low psychological rewards, and low supervisor support increased the risk of injury claims, but more research is needed to confirm the findings. Thus, physical and psychosocial exposures accounted for an important proportion of socioeconomic status disparities in reported injuries among care workers. These findings are compatible with those of a small number of other health disparities studies in the care work sector. For example, in

Table 7.1

Numbers of hospital workers employed in two community hospitals, by socioeconomic status and average rate of lost days from work-related injuries

Socioeconomic status category	Label (sample jobs)	No. of workers	Average rate of lost days per 100 FTEs
5	Administrator (HR director)	49	0.7
4(b)	Professional (dietician)	171	43.1
4(a)	Registered nurse	336	59.6
3	Semi-professional (lab technician)	300	69.8
2	Skilled (patient care assistant, clerk)	396	28.6
1	Semi-skilled (patient/dietary aide, receptionist)	102	148.4

SOURCE: D'Errico et al. 2007. Adapted by permission from BMJ Publishing Group Limited.

U.S. hospital workers, physical workload and psychosocial working conditions explain a greater proportion of the risk for musculoskeletal symptoms and injuries than socioeconomic status does (Gillen et al. 2007).

Despite this overall trend of higher injury rates with decreasing socioeconomic status, reported injury rates were very high among RNs for all injuries, strains and sprains, and back problems. Nurses also had high exposures to physical and psychosocial risk factors, disproportionate to what might be expected for their socioeconomic status (d'Errico et al. 2007). This raises the question of why the job category of nursing emerges as an outlier on the socioeconomic status gradient. Nursing education and professional development puts a very strong emphasis on patient/resident well-being, and there is anecdotal evidence that this professional identity and work culture also serve to deemphasize the legitimacy of nurses protecting their own health and safety at work.

It has further been suggested that exposure to physical and psychosocial stressors, far above what would be expected for this relatively high-socioeconomic-status profession, and the consequent injury and disease risks, may be responsible for an important part of the high rates of nursing absenteeism (Rauhala et al. 2007), turnover, and leaving employment (Zhang et al. 2012) in many Western countries.

Differences between Hospitals and Nursing Homes

There has been little direct comparison of the job duties of care workers in different types of facilities. Our own research has shown some notable differences in physical work features between nursing homes and hospitals (table 7.2) (Boyer 2008). These differences are likely due to specific staffing patterns and policies and differences in client populations. For example, residents in nursing homes tend to stay for long periods of time, whereas hospital admissions and discharges occur on a frequent basis. However, the stable populations in nursing homes often include a higher proportion of residents with dementia who may be less compliant than average hospital patients.

In our observational studies, we recorded work organization issues such as barriers to work performance like understaffing and broken equipment, frequency of overtime, work routinization, and common safety hazards in hospitals and nursing homes. Work under high time pressure was observed more often in nursing homes than hospitals, for both nurses and NAs (Boyer 2008).

The Intersection of Paid and Unpaid Care Work

Care work does not necessarily end after punching out on the time clock. Many employees return home to the responsibility of caring for children and elderly or disabled family members. These additional responsibilities may have an additive or even multiplicative effect on physical and mental health. We have examined

Table 7.2
Differences in job duties in hospitals and nursing homes

	Hospitals	Nursing Homes
RN job duties	Hands-on direct care	Administrative duties
NA job duties		Hands-on direct care
LPN & RN physical exposures	More trunk flexion & bent trunk, more time handling loads greater than 10 lbs.	
NA physical exposures		More trunk flexion & bent trunk, more time handling loads greater than 10 lbs.
Work under high time pressure		More frequent for RNs and NAs

the influence of combined paid and unpaid care work on a few selected outcomes among nursing home care workers: mental health, perceived age, and the psychosocial stressor of work-family imbalance.

As part of an ongoing study, 1,362 nursing home workers (65 percent NAs and 35 percent nurses) completed surveys with questions related to physical and mental well-being and working conditions (Miranda et al. 2011). Two-thirds were responsible for some form of unpaid care work such as caring for a child less than eighteen years old (57 percent) or caring for an elderly or disabled relative (20 percent). These responsibilities were not mutually exclusive, with an overlap in about 12 percent of the total.

Mental health was assessed by the SF-12 Mental Health Composite Scores, comprised of responses to six survey questions (Ware, Kosinski, and Keller 1995). Scores lower than the population average of 49 were observed in 44 percent of participants. Of these care workers with lower than average scores, 70 percent were also involved with some type of unpaid care work, a significantly larger proportion than the care workers with average to high mental health composite scores (figure 7.2).

Participants were asked to report their perceived age by responding to the question, "Some people feel older or younger than they are. How old do you feel?" Actual age was calculated based on date of birth and survey date, and it was determined whether participants felt older, younger, or the same as their actual age. Older perceived age was reported by 364 care workers (29 percent). Among those participants, 71 percent also reported responsibilities for unpaid care work, a significantly larger proportion than among those who felt younger than or the same as their actual age (figure 7.2).

A work-family imbalance scale was composed of the average of participants' responses to three survey questions: (1) "After work, I come home too tired to

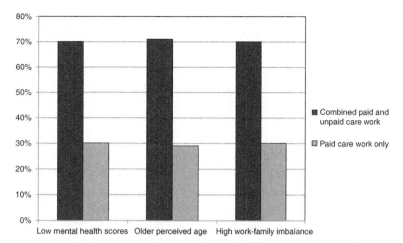

FIG. 7.2 The influence of combined paid and unpaid care work on mental health, perceived age, and work-family imbalance among nursing home workers

do some of the things I'd like to do," (2) "On the job, I have so much work to do that it takes away from my personal interests," and (3) "My family and/or friends dislike how often I am preoccupied with my work while I am at home." The score for each participant ranged from one (strongly disagree) to four (strongly agree), and the average value was 2.48. A total of 597 (45 percent) of the care workers had work-family imbalance scores higher than the average score, indicating less balance between work life and home life. Of those workers, 70 percent were also involved in unpaid care work at home, a significantly larger percentage than care workers with low to average work-family imbalance scores (figure 7.2).

Although these findings are only preliminary, without adjustment for potential confounders, they suggest that mental health scores, perceived age relative to chronological age, and work-family imbalance are disproportionately worse among care workers with additional caring responsibilities outside of their paid employment. As the larger proportion of those with unpaid caring responsibilities, NAs may be more likely to encounter poor psychosocial health outcomes due to work-family imbalance. Future studies should further address relationships between the combination of paid and unpaid care work and these outcomes as well as other important psychosocial and physical health factors.

Preventing Work-Related Injury

Care workers may not realize the full extent of the risks their work poses to their own bodies. The physical and psychosocial exposures they encounter daily often result in workplace injuries and illnesses, but are often considered to be "just part of the job." This sentiment was expressed in one of a series of focus groups of NAs conducted to better understand the risks of nursing home work as well as opportunities for improvement (Holmberg et al. 2013). One NA expressed, "I mean, it's just a job, like it comes with the job. You're going to have back problems. Even if you're working on them [residents] in bed, just changing them and rolling them and pulling them, it's the job." However, musculoskeletal disorders among care workers can be reduced if their employers take proactive health and safety measures.

Safe handling programs could reduce the highest levels of physical demands generally experienced by the lowest-wage workers. Interventions to reduce manual handling of patients/residents have been effective in reducing care workers' injuries by eliminating some exposure to heavy lifting and awkward postures (Nelson et al. 2003; Engkvist 2006). From our own observations of nursing home workers, both heavy lifting and awkward body postures were less frequent three years after the implementation of a safe resident handling program compared to the time period prior to equipment purchase and employee training (Kurowski et al. 2012a).

In the same population, nursing homes with increasing levels of equipment use and larger reductions in physical exposures were also the centers where organizational factors were more favorable. In general, low turnover and time pressure, and better teamwork, communication, and supervisory support were present in centers with increased equipment use and reduced physical workload among NAs (Kurowski et al. 2012b). Patient resistance to mechanical handling devices is a common reason for inconsistent use of equipment. However, in our experience in nursing homes, it was observed in several cases that education and consistent use of handling equipment helped reduce residents' fear of devices when they realized how much safer this type of handling was for both themselves and their caregivers.

Net cost savings due to reductions in workers' compensation claims and worker turnover were also reported for this population (Lahiri, Latif, and Punnett 2012), building a business case for improving employee health and safety. If other healthcare settings implemented similar programs, improvements in care workers' musculoskeletal and psychological health would likely follow.

In addition to the risk related to patient or resident handling, care workers may also be introduced to hazards that are not quite so obvious. For example, in a large nursing home enterprise, carpet was installed in common areas of most facilities. Informal interviews revealed that employees operating medicine carts reported musculoskeletal symptoms in the wrist, shoulder, and back, and perceived increases in physical workload that they believed could be related to cart use. A study was initiated to help answer questions around these cart handling risks (Boyer, Lin, and Chang 2013).

This study demonstrated that floor surface type (tile vs. carpet), lane congestion (hallway obstructions from people, objects, and equipment), and precision control (difficulty maneuvering the heavy and poorly designed carts) are associated with forces exerted by medicine cart operators. New evidence suggests that carpeted floors increase forces even more when combined with lane congestion during cart pushing and turning.

The combination of exposures that exist in care work settings should be explored more thoroughly in future studies, particularly among low-wage workers such as NAs, as our investigations have indicated that they tend to have high physical risks, poor psychosocial work environments, and additional caring responsibilities outside of their paid employment. Further analyses would determine if high levels of these combined exposures result in differences in musculoskeletal disorder risk and other negative health outcomes among care workers. More in-depth assessments will help epidemiologists assess risks, practitioners tailor occupational health and safety interventions, and policy makers distribute funds and regulate risks across the range of care workers and subsectors.

Acknowledgments

This data collected for this investigation was supported by Grants No. R01-OH07381 and U19-OH008857 from the U.S. National Institute of Occupational Safety and Health (NIOSH). Its contents are solely the responsibility of the authors and do not necessarily represent the official views of NIOSH.

8

When the Home
Is a Workplace

● ●

Promoting Health and Safety
for a Vulnerable Work Force

PIA MARKKANEN,

MARGARET QUINN, AND

SUSAN SAMA

According to the Bureau of Labor Statistics, the first and second fastest growing occupations in the United States are home health aides and personal and home care aides, both of which are projected to grow close to 50 percent by 2018 (U.S. Department of Labor Bureau of Labor Statistics [BLS] 2012a, 2012b). Although the home care industry is one of the fastest growing sectors in the United States, the home care work force is relatively invisible, in part because they are predominantly female, low wage, socially diverse, and often immigrants. The term "home care provider" is used to represent a range of jobs, the majority of which are aides. Home care providers perform their work in isolation over a wide range of private settings. In this chapter, we focus on the home care work force, their working conditions, and promotion of health and safety on the job.

Exposures to occupational hazards in home care have been challenging to evaluate for various reasons: the home-work environments are highly variable and not formally recognized as legitimate workplaces, and workers are typically low socioeconomic status, geographically dispersed, and transient. This overview is based on our qualitative and quantitative research conducted with home care providers since 2004 as well as on a review of the literature. We define "home care" broadly and cover working conditions of occupational groups included both in the "home healthcare" sector, employed through the healthcare system (for example, home healthcare nurses, home health aides), and the "home care" sector (for example, home care aides, homemakers, personal care attendants, companions), employed through the social assistance system. The latter assists elders and people with disabilities with activities of daily living.

The Significance of Place: Organizational Contexts of Home Care Work

Home care workers face a wide range of occupational safety and health hazards, including strenuous patient handling and transfer tasks associated with back and other musculoskeletal injuries, verbal abuse by clients and family members, violent assaults in clients' homes and neighborhoods, exposures to blood-borne pathogens from needlesticks and other sharp medical devices, accidents during long-distance driving to and from client visits, and a range of psychosocial stressors including difficult client relationships, low wages, no employee benefits, and feeling that their work is taken for granted by society in general (Bercovitz et al. 2011; National Institute for Occupational Safety and Health 2010). Though many of these hazards are characteristics of direct healthcare work regardless of setting, home care workers face a particular set of challenges and risks due to the nature of their workplaces.

While serious safety and health hazards among caregivers certainly exist in hospitals and nursing homes, it should not be assumed that the home-based care setting is safer and hence a less important work environment than the facility-based care setting. The home has particular characteristics that make workers vulnerable to adverse safety and health outcomes. The home is a less organized, less controlled, and much more variable care environment than a hospital or nursing home. Traditional inpatient settings are held to certain health and safety standards, while individual homes are not. Home care workers are at the mercy of patients and family members when it comes to monitoring or controlling safety and health concerns in the home, while hospitals and nursing homes are forced by federal regulation to provide a reasonably safe and healthy work environment. Most inpatient facilities provide employee health services with standards and written policies in the case of an employee injury whereas home care workers might be employed by an individual with no such injury standards or plan. When a home care worker suffers a serious incident or injury, a medical facility for post-exposure or post-injury care is not always nearby.

It is vital to understand the organizational context in which home-work environment hazards occur. Unlike aides in a hospital or nursing home, home care aides typically work alone without coworker support. This isolation creates especially hazardous conditions when patient lifting is needed or if, for example, a demented patient becomes disoriented and violent. The home care setting is not a priority for occupational safety and health interventions by public safety and health authorities even though the work tasks may be the same as those performed in facility-based care settings. While growing demand is placing pressure on agencies to hire more staff, the seemingly bright occupational outlook does not typically come with decent wages and benefits or safe working conditions (Bercovitz et al. 2011; Butler, Wardamasky, and Brennan-Ing 2012; Sherman et al. 2008).

Social, Economic, and Political Context of Home Care Work

The growth in home health and personal and home care aide occupations is attributed to various factors: an aging population needing support for health conditions and activities of daily living; patients' preference for receiving care at home; the availability of advanced medical and information technologies in the home allowing hospitals to discharge patients of all ages and in various health conditions sooner; and healthcare cost-saving initiatives (Committee on the Role of Human Factors in Home Health Care 2011; Markkanen et al. 2007). People with complex medical and social needs are living longer, and formerly fatal illnesses—like cancer or HIV/AIDS—are increasingly treated as chronic illnesses with care provided in the home (Committee on the Role of Human Factors in Home Health Care 2011).

Public health researchers in the United States have found strong evidence of health disparities—differences in health outcomes associated with race, ethnicity, socioeconomic status, education, and gender (Lipscomb et al. 2006). One reason for health disparities is that people in lower socioeconomic groups, immigrants, and people of color are more likely to encounter hazardous exposures in their work and living environments (Baron and Wilson 2011). All of these demographic risk factors are associated with the home care work force, as home care workers are disproportionately immigrants, minorities, females, low-income earners, and older workers. In 2006, immigrants accounted for about 20 percent of all nursing, psychiatric, and home health aides (Immigration Policy Center and Council 2009). Roughly half of the home care and personal assistance work force are nonwhite and aides are overwhelmingly female (Seavey and Marquand 2011). The average age among home health aides and home care aides is mid-forties, and it is projected that by 2018 a third of personal care aides will be fifty-five or older, up from 22 percent in 2008 (Seavey and Marquand 2011).

Through her study of home care providers in Montreal, Marguerite Cognet determined that a home care provider's job is not only associated with heavy physical risk factors and emotional burdens, but also with invisibility of their skills, which our society has molded into an easily quantifiable task list with little value (Cognet 2002). Even though their services are indispensable, these services are taken for granted by our society. Wages are notoriously low and the compensation seldom includes benefits like health insurance, paid sick leave, or holidays (Armstrong, Armstong, and Dixon 2008; Burnham and Theodore 2012). This seems particularly unfair when these workers need to provide care over evening/night shifts as well as on weekends. While home care aides' wages have received recent attention in the U.S. media—in particular due to the companionship exemption clause in Fair Labor Standards Act (FLSA) that until very recently excluded aides from the minimum wage or compensated overtime work protection—their professional knowledge and skills are largely unrecognized (Becker 2013; Boris and Klein 2012).

What Are Specific Occupational Hazards among Home Care Providers?

In 2005, we conducted five focus groups among home care nurses and home health aides as well as ten in-depth interviews with home care agency directors and managers, and union safety and health officers. All of our focus groups were audio-recorded, transcribed, and coded with NVIVO qualitative data analysis software into hierarchical themes. The results of this qualitative phase provided a foundation for a cross-sectional survey questionnaire on estimating sharps injury and other blood exposure risk among home healthcare workers. Since then, we have continued to conduct focus groups, in-depth interviews, and questionnaire surveys. Table 8.1 shows examples of occupational hazards identified in our 2005 interviews and focus groups. These hazards include but are not limited to demanding patient handling and transfer tasks, violent assaults and other personal safety issues, exposures to blood-borne pathogens and other infectious agents, long-distance driving, and hazards emerging from the home environment (Markkanen et al. 2007; Quinn et al. 2009).

Although a client visit may entail similar care tasks to those encountered in facility-based healthcare settings like hospitals and nursing homes, home visits also present unique circumstances not encountered in those institutional settings. For example, home care workers—who are usually working alone—often face environments that include inadequate work stations, a lack of assistive devices for patient handling and transfer, housekeeping and hygiene issues (for example, hoarding, bed bugs), sudden disruptions (by pets, children, family members), improperly discarded used sharp medical devices, and exposure

Table 8.1

Specific safety and health hazards experienced by home care nurses and aides

Work Hazards	

Heavy manual handling and transfer of clients and items	· moving, transfer or lifting clients to and from
	   · bed, wheelchair, or other sitting position
	   · toilet, shower

Personal safety concerns	· unsafe neighborhoods (e.g., drugs, guns, robbery, violence) · violent or unstable clients/family members · verbal abuse · home care worker out in the field alone · working during dark hours · entering an unknown place, not knowing the person who lives in the house

Blood-borne pathogens	· sharps injuries
	   · sharps disposal or management
	   · client moving during a sharp medical procedure
	   · home care aides encountering sharps when housekeeping
	   · diabetes (lancets, pens, insulin syringes), IV treatments
	 · other blood exposures
	   · wound care
	   · showering/bathing a client
	   · bleeding tumors/amputations
	   · client falls and bleeds

Long-distance driving	· accidents, rear-end collisions

Other safety concerns	· slip, trip, or fall hazards inside and outside the home
	   · snowy/ slippery walkways
	   · clutter
	   · rickety or unsafe stairs
	 · fire hazards
	   · patient on oxygen and addicted to smoking
	 · inadequate lighting
	 · pets
	   · dogs can attack/bite when sensitive to sick master

Rapid work pace	· clinicians may feel rushed to complete an assignment, even a risky procedure · dealing with uncontrollable situations in a hurry and alone
Hygiene issues	· insects (bed bugs) and rodents · hot indoor air · other indoor air quality concerns (smoking)
Home design issues	· lack of work stations · homes not designed for elderly or disabled

SOURCE: Markkanen et al. 2007.

to infectious or medical waste. In our focus groups, home care providers also described the unpredictable nature of hazards: they often must enter a home without knowing its residents, relationship dynamics between family members and friends of the residents, and the living environment inside.

Through in-depth interviews with home care agency managers, we identified the following most common underlying reasons for hazardous incidents: time constraints, rapid work pace, productivity pressures (for example, a one-hour time limit per client visit), and being out in the field alone. Time constraints may pressure an aide or nurse to conduct a risky medical procedure in haste. Aides reported spending their own, unpaid time to address a client's needs if the scheduled time wasn't enough. A major challenge for home care nurses is the detailed paperwork required for medical care insurance, billing, and reimbursement; the workday often does not end when the last patient is seen because paperwork may need to be completed at home. While working alone, difficult or uncontrolled situations may arise—for example security and safety concerns, lack of supplies, or lack of specific skills to handle an urgent situation—and backup support may not be nearby or available (Markkanen et al. 2007).

Ergonomic Hazards Leading to Back, Shoulder, and Other Musculoskeletal Injuries

Our recent interviews and focus groups clearly show that back, shoulder, and other musculoskeletal injuries are the most prevalent injuries among home care nurses and aides. These injuries occur while performing demanding client handling and transfer tasks (to and from the bed, wheelchair or other sitting position, toilet, and shower). Patient handling and transfer tasks become more strenuous with disoriented, overweight, or obese clients. A personal care homemaker shared how her back injury happened: "[Client] was like 400 pounds ... and I was the only one that was [caring for] the lady.... She had a Hoyer lift. So I had to go in the morning, put her in the Hoyer lift, wash her, and give her breakfast, everything by myself. And I wanted to be too good, and I never complained. By the time I complained three months after, my back was destroyed."

Other studies have similar findings (Faucett, Kang, and Newcomber 2013; Wipfli et al. 2012). In a study of West Virginia home care workers, overexertion injuries and falls accounted for 63 percent of all injuries (Meyer and Muntaner 1999). The authors concluded that nonadjustable beds, limited space, lack of work stations, and the absence of coworkers preclude ergonomically sound patient lifts, transfers, or other work procedures. Our 2011 focus groups and interviews indicate that while low-tech ergonomic safety tools like grab bars, shower chairs/benches, and hand-held showers in bathrooms are featured in some homes, client handling devices are rarely seen and the commercially available devices are not well suited for home use. Home care clients and their families often have limited financial resources and difficulty getting help to select and install equipment, preventing them from procuring home environment improvements or tools, including wheelchair accessible entrances, wheelchair-friendly floor plans and bathrooms, hospital beds, and high-tech client handling equipment.

Violent Assaults on Caregivers

The 2005 Bureau of Labor Statistics violence survey found that the health care and social assistance sector had the highest percentage of client-originated occupational violence compared to all other industries surveyed in the United States (2006). The threat of violence to a home care worker exists both inside a client's home and in a client's neighborhood (Geiger-Brown et al. 2007; McPhaul et al. 2010). Geiger-Brown and colleagues assessed the prevalence of violence among home care workers: 20 percent had experienced at least one abusive situation in the past six months. The most common circumstances included verbal abuse (18 percent) and criticism (12 percent) (Geiger-Brown et al. 2007). Our 2005 focus groups indicate that home care workers often visit unsafe neighborhoods where drug use is widespread, and it is not rare to see guns in homes. A home healthcare nurse reported in a focus group: "It's the people that you don't know. Because the people are not all stable and I did walk in once and see two guns sitting on the table and that was a little shocking." Our 2011 focus groups confirmed that home care aides report verbal abuse almost on a daily basis. In addition to patients and their family members, pets—especially dogs—can be aggressive and attack caregivers. While environmental design and security technologies (for example, surveillance cameras, access controls, detectors, and panic buttons) can be effective in preventing violence in healthcare facilities (McPhaul et al. 2008), these are rarely feasible in the home care setting. Most home care agencies address personal safety concerns in their mandatory in-service trainings. Our study shows that some home care agencies provide escort services for visits during night hours and in unsafe neighborhoods.

Instability in the home environment can increase other risks, as in a home visit described by one home healthcare: "The patient was very combative and the hemodialysis needle that was placed in her arm punctured through her skin into my hand." It is not unusual to have aggressive behaviors associated with blood-borne pathogen exposures in the home.

Blood-borne Pathogens

A significant occupational hazard in any healthcare setting is exposure to blood-borne pathogens (BBP)—in particular hepatitis B and C or HIV—through injuries from contaminated sharp medical devices (sharps) and other routes. Home care providers are at increasing risk of exposure to BBP as advances in technology allow more complex medical services to be performed at home (Backinger and Koustenis 1994; Friedman and Rhinehart 1999, 2000; Smith and White 1993). Our cross-sectional survey during 2006–2007 indicated that approximately

35 percent of home care nurses and 6.4 percent of home health aides had experienced at least one sharps injury during their career (Quinn et al. 2009). Annual sharps injury incidence rates were 5.1 per 100 full-time equivalent nurses (Quinn et al. 2009), which is comparable to rates seen in the hospital setting (Dement et al. 2004). Medical procedures contributing to sharps injuries were injecting medications, administering fingersticks and heelsticks, and drawing blood. Other contributing factors were sharps disposal and contact with waste (Quinn et al. 2009). Among aides, sharps injuries tended to be largely associated with improperly disposed sharps encountered during cleaning tasks.

Although home care aides' duties in nurse-supervised agencies do not include direct use of sharps for medical procedures, the reality in the home can be different. A study by Lipscomb et al. indicated that over a third (9 of 26) of personal care assistants who reported a contact with a patient's blood said that they were using a lancet or needle at the time (Lipscomb et al. 2009). Our focus groups in 2005 indicated that aides were sometimes asked by the client or client's family to assist with medical procedures, such as using a lancet for a finger stick to monitor diabetes. Personal care attendants who are hired directly by clients are known to help clients with sharp medical procedures. Despite the Occupational Safety and Health Administration's (OSHA) Bloodborne Pathogens standard requiring healthcare providers to use sharps with injury-prevention features, many of the sharps used in the home do not have these features and both nurses and aides continue to be injured by them (Quinn et al. 2009).

Exposure to blood-borne pathogens is a real and largely undocumented hazard in home care. In the United States, HIV patients are cared for more frequently in the home than in other healthcare settings. Hepatitis C–positive patients, many of whom may be unaware of their HCV status, are often receiving home care for other conditions (Haiduven and Ferrol 2004). It has been estimated that between 8 and 9 million Americans are self-injecting medication at home, and the majority of the needles used do not have injury-prevention devices and are thrown into the household trash (Gold and Schumann 2007). Needle sticks and other sharps injuries take a physical and mental toll on injured workers and their families. No data are available on how faithfully home care providers report their sharps injuries and get follow-up care, but underreporting is a well-recognized problem in other healthcare settings (Lee et al. 2005; Wilburn 2004). Sharps injuries carry a high monetary cost: it is estimated that short-term follow-up medical treatments range from $50 to $3,800 (US) and long-term treatment associated with HIV, HBV, or HCV seroconversion can reach hundreds of thousands of U.S. dollars (Lee et al. 2005).

Other Safety and Health Hazards

Getting to and from home visits can also entail risks. Home care workers drive long distances, and owning a reliable vehicle is often a condition of employment. Long-distance driving is exhausting and time-consuming, and accidents like crashes and rear-end collisions occur. Sitzman, Pett, and Bloswick (2002) reported that 25 percent of surveyed home visiting nurses had been in a motor vehicle accident during their ten-year average tenure. Nearly all of the crashes occurred while they were driving for their work. Of the 105 respondents who had been in a crash, 30 percent reported sustaining some degree of injury (Sitzman, Pett, and Bloswick 2002).

Our interviews indicate that home care agencies report to workers' compensation carriers slips, trips, and falls both inside and outside the home. These may happen because of slippery walkways, inadequate lighting, rickety stairs indoors or outdoors, badly placed cords or equipment, and clutter. A home healthcare nurse described the problem this way: "Homes can be cluttered to the point that there is no place to put even a cup. Things are boxed, boxes are piled up, you've seen it. Blankets are piled up . . . there isn't a pathway to walk. So there's no clean surface area to work from."

Solutions to Protect Home Care Providers' Safety and Health

The Department of Labor's proposed rule on eliminating the FLSA companionship exemption and providing the minimum wage and overtime protection for home care aides has only recently been finalized (Becker 2013; Boris and Klein 2012). A poorly compensated work force remains vulnerable to occupational safety and health hazards. Furthermore, poor compensation undermines the future of the home care aide occupation, as low pay makes it difficult to recruit new workers and sometimes impossible for current workers to stay in the job. Public healthcare policies must support home care aides' work as a viable career choice for younger workers. The Department of Labor's rule to extend the minimum wage and overtime protection is an urgent early step in this direction.

We have observed home care agencies with proactive safety and health committees that effectively address injury and illness hazard prevention and institute safe work practices. This is achieved through policies, initial client in-take evaluations, annual mandatory training activities, and information materials targeted to employees and clients. Home care worker safety could be addressed more broadly across the industry via comprehensive new-client intake evaluations. Examples of useful safety and health information tools include the manual *Caring for Yourself While Caring for Others* (Labor Occupational Health Program 2011) and a fifty-item household safety checklist that allows home care providers to conduct visual safety inspections in clients' homes (Gershon et al. 2012).

Installation and use of safe client handling devices in the home care setting is essential. Mechanized equipment for client handling and transfer tasks needs to be better adapted for use in homes. Our study also showed that improved home architectural design is key for protecting both workers' and clients' safety. In a National Public Radio broadcast about senior housing, Jon Pynoos, a professor of gerontology policy and planning at University of Southern California, described typical home design as "Peter Pan housing," designed for people who are never going to age (National Public Radio 2011). A novel and promising initiative for protecting workers is the U.S. National Institute for Occupational Safety and Health's (NIOSH) "Prevention through Design" model, which promotes preventing and controlling occupational injuries and illnesses by "designing them out" or minimizing hazards and risks early in the design process. The concept is defined as "addressing occupational safety and health needs in the design process to prevent or minimize the work-related hazards and risks associated with the construction, manufacture, use, maintenance, and disposal of facilities, materials, and equipment" (National Institute for Occupational Safety and Health 2012). Home care would benefit greatly from the Prevention through Design approach, as care for people with disabilities and the elderly is not systematically considered in the design of houses, home care work processes, and tools. While a few safety and health studies have been conducted in this vulnerable population during the past decade, much more research is needed to fully understand their working conditions and hazards and to develop and implement preventive interventions. The home care industry will continue to grow and remain a critical supporting pillar of the U.S. healthcare sector. Both the U.S. general population and the home care work force continue to age. To assure that the home care industry can provide high quality care services over the long term, the industry must attract a younger population. Public policy interventions must support home care work as a viable career choice for young people. Standardized training and improved wages and working conditions are important parts of this effort.

Acknowledgments

The authors' studies have been funded by the U.S. National Institute of Occupational Safety and Health (grant # 1R01 OH008229 [Project SHARRP] and grant #5R01 OH008229–06 [Safe Home Care Project]). We are grateful to the homecare agency and labor union staff who have participated in our studies over the years and to dedicated home healthcare nurses and aides everywhere. We thank all members of both Project SHARRP and Safe Home Care Project.

9

Part of the Job?

• •

Workplace Violence
and Social Services

JENNIFER ZELNICK

Sit down with a group of social service workers to discuss workplace violence, and sooner or later someone will explain that workplace violence is simply "part of the job"; around the table heads will nod in agreement. This significant workplace hazard—estimated to impact 1.7 million U.S. workers annually (U.S. Department of Labor Occupational Safety and Health Administration [OSHA] 2012)—is at best accepted, and at worst invisible, among the social service work force. What data exist suggest that, were workplace violence adequately understood, the prevalence would be daunting. A review of studies since 1990 found that 3 to 30 percent of social workers have been physically assaulted, and 42 to 82 percent have experienced verbal assault or threat (Ringstad 2009).

The relative invisibility and apparent acceptance of workplace violence in social services is best explained by the combination of two factors. First, an "ethic of care" subordinates caregiver needs to those of care recipients. Second, social service work is a relatively low-paid, low-status profession that serves many marginalized populations (the poor, prisoners, the mentally ill) in a sector where struggles for adequate funding and public support are constant (Barth 2003; Hudson 2007). In a description of health and safety challenges in the healthcare and social assistance sector, the National Institute of Occupational

Safety and Health (NIOSH) explains, "The sector is burdened by the historical and entrenched belief that patient care issues supersede the personal safety and health of workers, and that it is acceptable for healthcare and social assistance workers to have less than optimal protections against the risks of hazardous exposures or injuries" (NIOSH 2009, 4). In her analysis of the changing landscape of social service provision in Canada, Donna Baines (2005) notes that in the context of downsizing and scarce jobs in social services, "Employers can depend on workers' capacity to translate an ethic of care and sense of vulnerability in the labor market into tolerance for unsafe working conditions, including violent assault, thus relieving the employer of responsibility to enact possibly costly changes in work organization and job design" (133).

Bringing to light the obscured nature of workplace violence in social services is the first step toward creating safer working conditions for staff, clients, families, and communities who provide and are served by social services. However, workplace violence differs from many other occupational health hazards in that it occurs in the context of a relationship, and that those in need of social services are often troubled and potentially stigmatized. Protecting workers from violence and advocating for social justice for vulnerable people and disenfranchised communities (rather than scapegoating them as "perpetrators") are both important objectives in framing the issue of workplace violence.

A major tenet of care work scholarship and activism is the assertion that care work is a sector framed by universal needs of all people and communities and constitutes the human infrastructure of our society and our economy (Duffy 2011). Further, defining the issue of workplace violence in social services raises the specter of diversity among workers: Can we compare the risk of a clinician in private practice to a group home worker? Or the child welfare caseworker making home visits to a crime-ridden neighborhood to the staff in an adult day care program? Understanding workplace violence in social services within the context of the care work sector challenges us to, as Mignon Duffy describes, "sustain dialogue across all sorts of boundaries" to address the challenges of the contemporary care crisis (2011, 145). Though workplace violence risk in social services may vary according to population served, training of the provider, and environment and setting, it is best framed as a system with the goal of responding to social needs and providing quality services in an environment that prioritizes peaceful solutions and safety for workers, clients, families, and communities.

The Call to Action: Forming the Task Force on Maximizing Social Worker Safety

While there has been some research on workplace violence in the social service setting, the push for recognition of the importance of workplace violence hasn't come from the data—comprehensive surveillance of this problem is sorely lacking. It comes instead from the tragedies of individual social workers who have lost their lives on the job,[1] and this is how our research project on workplace violence in Massachusetts began as well. In February 2008, during a routine home visit, fifty-three-year-old Diruhi Mattian was stabbed to death by a nineteen-year-old client. Mattian was an extremely experienced and skilled social worker, her client had no prior history of violence, and she knew him well. Mattian was one of those special people who touched many lives, as a community member, coworker, and supervisor of new social workers and student interns.[2] In the wake of this tragedy, a summit was convened that brought together academics from schools of social work, representatives from state agencies, social service providers, and the Massachusetts chapter of the National Association of Social Workers. This summit led to the formation of the Massachusetts Task Force to Maximize Social Worker Safety (hereafter the "Task Force"). Based on the action agenda developed through a participatory process at the summit, the Task Force formed a research subcommittee.

For the next several years, the Task Force and its subcommittees met monthly to explore workplace safety best practices from other states, gather resources for a website, develop and implement a research plan, and hash out differences over how to frame workplace violence in the social service sector. One potentially divisive issue centered on the question of who "we" were. Our initial gathering was prompted by the death of a social worker and led by the state professional organization for social workers and schools of social work. Yet many who perform social service/human service activities are not trained clinical staff and do not hold an academic social work degree. This issue has deep roots in social work history and implications for framing workplace safety.

Dating back to 1915, when Abraham Flexner (1915) declared that social work was not a true profession but a handmaiden to others, social work has had what some have denounced as an unhealthy obsession with gaining professional status under the medical model. More recently, licensing has been used to carve out the professionalized skill base for social work and, some contend, ensure the provision of quality services by a well-trained professional. At the same time, the profession has a rich history of community-based approaches that draw on the experiences of community leaders and peers to address social problems that have individual, family, and community dimensions. For example, advocates of community-based treatment for mental health address housing, employment, and social and psychological well-being from the perspective of client self-determination. In many settings, entry-level social service jobs are filled by those without formal training; for example, many entry-level child welfare workers enter advanced social work training after working in the field.

The Task Force research subcommittee was committed to collecting data that included all social services workers. This commitment was based on our belief that workplace violence is an environmental risk factor, shared by all staff (and, indeed, also clients, family members, and potentially communities). We had an anecdotal understanding that those performing front-line or direct-care functions such as intake, staffing at group homes and residential facilities, and running life skills groups have frequent client contacts and are at high risk. We included all staff at social service agencies in our agency survey of workplace violence incidents, and a specific aim of our research examined the difference in workplace violence risk according to job title/education level (described in our results as "clinical" and "direct-care" staff). At the same time, we recognized the potential pitfalls in a nascent movement led by social workers claiming to speak for human service workers.

In 2011, just as we completed the data analysis of our statewide survey, twenty-five-year-old Stephanie Moulton was murdered by a client at a group home in Revere, Massachusetts. Moulton, a dedicated, skilled, unlicensed mental health worker, was the sole staff member on duty in a group home for formerly incarcerated men. Her brutal murder was a devastating blow to her family, fiancé, coworkers, and the family of the perpetrator; it also exposed systemic problems. In an environment with a predictable risk of violence, why weren't protections and preventative activities in place? This event underscored the decision to consider workplace violence in the sector overall and not just within the job title of licensed social worker.

The cases of Mattian and Moulton, though not representative of the issue of workplace violence in social services generally, are different in ways that are important to consider in the task of framing workplace violence as a policy issue. From Mattian's death, some have surmised that a job that centers on relational interactions with troubled people carries inherent risks; even a skilled clinician can never be entirely safe. The enhanced protocols adopted by the agency where Mattian worked in the wake of her death would not necessarily have prevented it. Workplace violence might indeed be "part of the job," just as injury and fatality are risks to fire fighters who are well trained to enter burning buildings. Moulton's case, on the other hand, led to an Occupational Safety and Health Administration inspection that divided the mental health/social service community over the issue of identifying a mentally ill client as an "occupational hazard," and outcry over cuts in state funding that had left group homes understaffed and workers vulnerable (Becker, Mulvihill, and Stine 2012). Workplace violence should not be considered "part of the job" when it can be avoided. Although the particular decisions around work organization and staffing at the home where Moulton worked deserve analysis, this situation is hardly unique in a sector where doing more with less is the norm.

Violence in the Social Services Sector

What Counts as Workplace Violence?

Studies of workplace violence among social workers typically include physical assault, verbal threat of assault, verbal abuse, and property damage, and some also include sexual and racial/ethnic harassment. Most collect self-reported data on the individual worker's subjective definition of "workplace violence" to account for the variation in perceptions of what is "violent" (Jayartne, Crotxton, and Mattison 2004; Newhill 1996; Rey 1996; Shields and Kiser 2003).

How Much Workplace Violence Occurs in Social Services?

In relation to other employment sectors in the United States, healthcare and social assistance is among the most dangerous. For example, according to the most recent Bureau of Labor Statistics report on workplace violence, the median number of days lost due to assault for private sector workers employed in the healthcare and social assistance sector was twice that of the private sector as a whole (9.7 compared to 4.9 per 10,000), and for state healthcare and social assistance employees the median was more than four times that of all state employees (136 compared to 30 per 10,000) (U.S. Department of Labor Bureau of Labor Statistics [BLS] 2010a). However, since government agencies that oversee health and safety—such as the Occupational Safety and Health Administration and the National Institute of Occupational Safety and Health—typically combine social services and health care into a single category, the better-studied healthcare sector dwarfs attention to workplace violence in social service settings, or limits attention to social service workers in healthcare institutions.

The most frequently used study design to estimate prevalence of workplace violence among social service workers is a survey of National Association of Social Workers (NASW) members (Jayaratne, Croxton and Mattison 2004; Newhill 1996). However, since the membership of NASW is skewed toward white, master's-level clinicians in private practice, these studies likely underrepresent minorities, those who work in nonprofit agencies, those who work in the public sector, and those in jobs requiring less education (NASW 2008). The few studies using BLS data or large samples of public sector social workers have resulted in similarly high rates of reported workplace violence, but the fact remains that there is no satisfying data set that represents the extent of the problem throughout the public, private, and nonprofit social service sector.

Why Do Social Workers Fail to Report?

Lack of data is also due to underreporting, a common practice in social services. For example, in a random sample of clinical social workers, 25 percent had experienced an incident of workplace violence that they did not report (McDonald and Sirotech 2001). Reasons for failure to report identified in the literature include not thinking the incident was serious enough, the belief that nothing would be done, fear of being blamed for the incident, and the lack of institutional reporting policies (Lowe and Korr 2008; McDonald and Sirotech 2001; Noble 2011; Rey 1996). But the most common reason for not reporting found among different studies was the perception that violence is "part of the job."

Who Is Most at Risk for Workplace Violence?

Several studies have found increased risks for male social workers compared to females (Jayaratne, Crotxton, and Mattison 2004; Newhill 2003; Ringstad 2009), though others find increased risk among women (Baines 2005; Bell, Mock, and Slutkin 2002; Flannery, Fisher, and Walker 2000). Other factors associated with increased risk have included younger age (Jayaratne, Croxton, and Mattison 2004) and urban setting (Bell, Mock, and Slutkin 2002; Shields and Kiser 2003). The only study to look at staff educational/training level found no significant relationship between risk of being the target of workplace violence and different levels of training/education (Winstanley and Hales 2008), though this study was done in the United Kingdom. The use of physical restraint has been linked to workplace assault on staff in residential psychiatric settings (Flannery, Fisher, and Walker 2000) and intellectual disability group home settings (Hawkins, Allen, and Jenkins 2004).

Where Are Incidents of Workplace Violence Most Likely to Occur?

In a study of violence against social workers, Christina Newhill (2003) identified a hierarchy of risk based on primary area of practice: criminal justice, drug and alcohol services, and child welfare were identified as "high risk" areas of practice, and healthcare services and services to the aged as "low risk." However, these categories do not reveal if elevated risk is related to the environmental setting, client population, or nature of the services/intervention. In terms of risks associated with specific settings, Robin Ringstad (2005) found increased risk of workplace violence in inpatient and correctional institutions and schools. While the dangers of providing services in the client home are frequently discussed (Rey 1996), no empirical study compares the likelihood of incidents in home-based services to other social service settings.

What the Task Force Found

"After going over the figures to complete this survey I was astounded. It seems as if the direct care workers in our agency should be receiving combat pay."
–Program director, Massachusetts Multi-Service Agency

The workplace violence leadership summit action agenda charged the Task Force with the mission of understanding the extent of workplace violence among social service agencies in Massachusetts. Based on the input of its members, the research subcommittee decided to find out "what we already knew but hadn't examined" by gathering data that was routinely collected by social service agencies. Based on a wealth of experience in social service settings, the Task Force developed a survey that asked about two types of workplace violence: physical assault and verbal threat. Since physically restraining clients (a controversial practice that occurred in some social service settings) could escalate violence, the survey classified violent incidents as either restraint-related or non-restraint-related. Departing from previous studies of workplace violence, which mainly focus on gathering self-reported data on individual experiences, the Task Force committee's goal was to aggregate agency-level data in order to better understand the hazard of workplace violence in social services as it affected different agencies across the state.

Eligible participant Massachusetts social service agencies were identified through the membership lists of two statewide coalitions (the Human Services Coalition and the Child Welfare League), public state agencies, and the attendance list for the 2008 Summit on Social Work Safety. Participating agencies were asked to designate an individual with access to human resource documents to complete an anonymous, Internet-based survey. Feedback from a pilot phase of the study indicated that without anonymity, agency leaders were reluctant to make workplace violence data public. Since a main goal of our study was to help make agency data public, we accepted that participation would be anonymous.

The survey gathered agency-level data for FY 2009 on (1) agency characteristics such as numbers of clients served, numbers of employees, populations served, services provided, settings where services were provided; (2) methods for collecting data on violent incidents; (3) reported incidents of physical assault or violent threats in the context of the use of physical restraints among those with a bachelor's level education (or below) and those with a master's level education (or above), elsewhere described as "direct care" and "clinical" staff; (4) reported incidents of physical assault or violent threats among direct care and clinical workers in a non-restraint-related context; and (5) setting of reported incidents and perceptions of risk in each setting. Participants were provided space to comment on the topic of workplace violence at their agency at the end of the survey.

In total, forty agencies participated in this study. The number of clients served in these agencies ranged from 120 to 89,000, with a median of 4,407, and the number of employees ranged from 10 to 3,500, with a median of 117. About half of the agencies who participated in this study primarily served older adults (57.5 percent), but the agencies serving populations other than older adults employed far more staff. Results of this study represent the experiences of 2,627 (29 percent) clinical and 6,395 (71 percent) direct care staff, with 9 percent of clinical staff and 17 percent of the direct care staff working primarily with older adults.

There were a total of 1,049 incidents reported of physical assault or verbal threat of violence. The incidence rate per 100 workers was high; 11.5 out of 100 had experienced an incident of physical assault or verbal threat among our sample in 2009. However, these episodes were not evenly distributed among our sample (see table 9.1). While those in older adult focused services had a comparable incidence rate to those in services that did not serve older adults (11 out of 100 compared to 12 out of 100), a far higher percentage of incidents among those working with older adults were verbal assaults (97 percent) compared to those working primarily with younger adults (40 percent). Excluding verbal threats, the rate of incidents/injuries among those serving general adult populations was significantly higher (7 per 100 per year) than that of those working with older adults (0.31 per 100). Overall, a far greater percent of incidents reported in our study occurred in non-older-adult-focused services (87 percent) than in older-adult-focused services (13 percent).

Our most striking result is the risk disparity between less-educated direct care staff and more-educated clinical staff that is evidenced by their statistically significant increased odds of nearly every type of assault or threat surveyed. Direct care staff were twice as likely as clinical staff to suffer a restraint related injury, ten times more likely to experience a restraint-related injury requiring

Table 9.1
Agency characteristics and aggregate incident data

Agency characteristics	Older-adult-focused agencies N = 21 n (%)	Non-older-adult-focused agencies N = 19 n (%)
Total number of clients served FY 2009	138,801 (36%)	245,655 (64%)
Median agency size	4,000	5,927
Total number of clinical staff	233 (9%)	2,394 (91%)
Median number of staff	10	35
Total number of direct care staff	1,071 (17%)	5,323 (83%)
Median number of direct care staff	53	126
Number of agencies using restraints	10 (42%)	14 (58%)
Number of incidents	138 (13%)	911 (87%)
Verbal threats	134	361
Physical assault	4	550
Incidence rate (incidents/100 workers per year)	11	12
Verbal threats	10	5
Physical assault	0.31	7

an ER visit, and nearly four times more likely to lose time due to their injuries. Agencies were surveyed about four types of non-restraint-related injuries: verbal threat, physical assault without injury, physical assault with injury, and death. Overall, direct care staff were twice as likely as clinical staff to be threatened verbally at work, and nearly five times more likely to be the victim of a physical assault. Since direct care staff have more contact hours with clients, their increased risk makes sense and is mirrored in health service sector data that shows higher injury rates for health support staff compared to health practitioners. Hospital support staff experienced workplace injuries at rates three times those of health practitioners (20.4 compared to 6.1 per 10,000, U.S. Department of Labor Bureau of Labor Statistics 2010a). However, this inequality in risk between staff within the same work environment is alarming (see table 9.2).

We did not collect demographic data that would allow us to evaluate patterns of risk inequity according to race/ethnicity, sexual orientation, socioeconomic status, or community background, but this is a topic that needs to be taken up in future research. For example, if members of socially disadvantaged groups are overrepresented among those in lower status social service jobs and at increased risk for workplace violence, this raises a social justice issue within the delivery of social services.

Table 9.2
Odds of physical assault and verbal threats in restraint- and non-restraint-related incidents

	Direct care workers N = 6,394	Clinical workers N = 2,627	Odds ratio (95% CI)	95% confidence interval
Restraint-related injuries/ first aid[a]	64	27	0.89	(0.55–1.44)
Restraint-related injuries/ ER visit	79	3	10.13[**]	(3.09–40.18)
Restraint-related injuries/ lost time	41	4	3.89[**]	(1.33–12.81)
Restraint-related injuries/All	143	30	2.02[*]	(1.34–3.06)
Verbal threats	443	92	2.05[**]	(1.62–2.60)
Physical assaults	266	23	4.91[**]	(3.15–7.73)
Physical assault with injury	17	4	1.75	(0.55–6.14)
Non-restraint-related incidents/All	709	114	2.75[*]	(2.23–3.39)

[*]$p \leq .05$; [**]$p \leq .01$.

[a]Since not all agencies used physical restraints, the numbers at risk for such incidents differed. In the sample, 3,301 direct care and 1,242 clinical workers were at risk for restraint-related incidents.

Patterns also emerged in terms of the settings where incidents of workplace violence took place. The majority of incidents of reported workplace violence in this study occurred in inpatient or institutional settings, versus in a client home or community setting. Most restraint-related incidents for direct care workers occurred in a group home setting (82 percent), while for clinical staff a majority occurred in the psych-inpatient hospital setting (68 percent). For non-restraint-related incidents among direct care staff, a majority of incidents occurred either in psych-inpatient hospitals (35 percent) or day rehabilitation facilities (23 percent). The vast majority of non-restraint-related incidents among clinical staff occurred in the psych-inpatient hospital setting (80 percent). Interestingly, when asked about which settings they perceived as most dangerous, those completing our surveys indicated that they found the client home to be more dangerous. It would be important to understand if incident clustering in inpatient settings is a true difference, or if this phenomenon is due to reporting differences, since reporting protocols may be more developed or better regulated in inpatient and institutional settings. It might also be the case that more volatile clients are institutionalized, or that the inpatient environment increases the likelihood of conflicts and violence. For example, the current movement to eliminate the use of physical restraints claims that the use of restraints escalates violent episodes, particularly among traumatized clients.

At the same time, many incidents of workplace violence and verbal threats occurred in settings at risk for budget cuts and restructuring over the last several decades. For example, the long-term trend of deinstitutionalization has shifted mental health patients out of costly state facilities and into group homes and other facilities often run by independent contractors. In Massachusetts, the largest component of state mental health services is community-based flexible support, which serves 14,000 clients through a multitude of independent contractors (Becker, Mulvihill, and Stine 2012). In 2011, inpatient mental health beds were cut by 25 percent, and the governor has cut spending on mental health services 10 percent since 2007 (Levenson 2011).

Recognizing that policy changes at the program level might impact both the experience of workplace violence and the potential to address it at the agency level, we spoke to a focus group composed of program managers from a statewide social service agency that provided in-home services to individuals and families. Program managers reported that contract demands meant that staff in their programs had high caseloads and were overburdened with paperwork and data entry. Exacerbating these problems was a shift in how services were billed. In order to meet contract costs, clinical social workers were employed as independent contractors who could only bill for client contact hours, thus eliminating paid time for in-service training on safety or sitting on workplace health and safety committees. Program managers saw multiple demands on billable time as obstacles to the reporting of workplace violent incidents or discussing "near misses" with coworkers and supervisors.

Program managers also reflected on the role they played as supervisors, both in creating an environment where reporting and debriefing incidents and threats were encouraged, and in not minimizing their staff's perceptions of threats. There was broad consensus among this group of managers that peer debriefing sessions were an effective and underused forum for evaluating workplace violence hazards. However, many bemoaned the lack of time for debriefing and other training and prevention activities.

Understanding Social Worker Safety

The social service workplace, and the potential for violence within it, is shaped by public social welfare policy (Karger and Stoesz 2010). Political decisions about how society responds to social needs are always at the forefront of political campaigns: spending on such services takes up a relatively large portion of federal and state budgets, and, despite the involvement of agencies and organizations in the public, private, and nonprofit sectors, the vast majority of social services are still funded by public dollars.

During the 1960s, the welfare state was expanded and reconfigured (Katz 1996). Social movements fought for expansion of individual and community social welfare policies and benefits. New policies for health, disability, mental health, and housing extended the reach of the welfare state, and amendments to the Social Security Act created the opportunity for government to contract with nonprofit agencies to deliver social services in the community (Karger and Stoesz 2011). The U.S. social service landscape, characterized by the mix of public, nonprofit, and for-profit agencies that are largely government-funded originated in this period.

Beginning in the mid-1970s, the U.S. welfare state began to come under attack (Abramovitz 2004). Economic globalization undercut the need for U.S. workers to fill the lowest tier of jobs in the labor market, and this undermined support for social welfare spending from the business and corporate sector. Politically, beginning with Ronald Reagan, the Republican Party adopted a divisive, race-based rhetoric that stigmatized welfare recipients. The government, which had represented the solution to problems of need and poverty since the Great Depression, was increasingly identified as itself the problem as the cost of social welfare programs grew. These trends have been labeled the "U-turn in social welfare policy" and associated with a return to a pre-1935 laissez-faire economic model that sought to shrink the size of government and increase the role of the private sector. These changes have had profound impacts on the social service workplace. The 1996 welfare reforms turned a federal public assistance entitlement into a state block grant, limited funding and benefit levels, and introduced work requirements. Once these changes were implemented, social service workers in New York City reported work speed-up, increased stress, and new ethical dilemmas (Abramovitz 2005).

During this period, other economic and social factors led to changes in how agencies are organized and how services are delivered. Beginning in the 1990s, "New Public Management" (a set of practices aimed at introducing efficiency and accountability into management of publicly funded programs) began to influence social service delivery, and introduced principles from private-sector business into social service management (Clarke 2009). While many embraced the need for accountability, others criticized the commodification of services and worried about the potential impact on vulnerable clients (Baines 2004a, 2004b; Soss, Fording, and Schram 2011). Regardless of how changes were viewed, agencies were getting used to doing more with less, increasing productivity in order to retain needed services for clients, often on the backs of over-stretched staff (Baines 2004b). These changes have affected work organization in social services and potentially the health, safety, and well-being of the social service work force as well as the clients they serve.

While our study of workplace violence in Massachusetts social service agencies has many limitations (see Zelnick et al. 2013 for a full discussion), our results suggest that workplace violence in social services may be a more serious problem for those in lower status, less protected jobs in settings that have borne a significant share of the cuts and restructuring. Specifically, the risk disparity between clinical social work staff and direct care social service workers and the

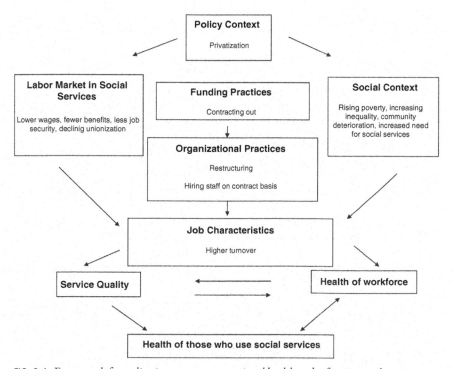

FIG. 9.1 Framework for policy impacts on occupational health and safety in social services

clustering of incidents in settings that have suffered funding cuts and restructuring (group homes and inpatient psychiatric facilities) suggests that public policy decisions may put lower-status workers and vulnerable clients at higher risk of work-related injury. Given the current environment of cuts to social service programs and the increased needs among many who use such programs, it is an important time to ignite interest in workplace safety in social services. It is also critically important that the issue of workplace violence in social services be framed from a care work perspective that focuses on the commonalities among group home workers and clinical social workers, child welfare caseworkers, and those providing services to older adults.

The policy environment that demands we do more with less pits sectors, groups, and individuals against one another as we struggle to retain needed resources for social services, or even to protect our own livelihoods. On February 15, 2013, Massachusetts governor Deval Patrick signed into law the Act to Promote the Public Health through Workplace Safety for Social Workers. This act, a direct result of the work of the Task Force, deliberately included a broad definition of social workers and has been publicized as the first ever act to protect "human service workers" (Family Continuity 2013). Although, as the title of the act suggests, we have a way to go in establishing more inclusive language, the process of framing workplace violence as a shared hazard across the social service sector can unite us in the struggle for a society that prioritizes safety for workers and those they serve.

Notes

1 Several states have introduced legislation named for a social worker killed on the job. For example, the Boni Frederick Act in Kentucky was introduced in 2007, and another in West Virginia named for Brenda Lee Yaeger was introduced in 2008. At the federal level, the Teri Zenner social work safety act was introduced in 2007 and named for a social worker who was stabbed to death in 2004 (National Association of Social Workers, Massachusetts chapter, "Workplace Safety, Policy Recommendations," http://www.naswma.org/?page=51, 2013).

2 Mattian's legacy to date includes the formation of the Task Force to Maximize Social Worker Safety, a "culture of safety" program at her former agency, and the formation of a social work library in her name in her native country, Armenia (Family Continuity, Inc., October 26, 2012, newsletter, http://www.familycontinuity.org/index.php?name=News&file=article&sid=109).

10

Double Isolation

• •

Immigrants and Older Adult Care Work in Canada

IVY BOURGEAULT

As many of our societies age, we become particularly concerned with the relative availability of care work and care workers, as well as with the appropriateness of the social organization of care for older adults either in the community
or institutional sector. Many argue that high-income Western nations have a
shortage of care workers, and this shortage is expected to become much more
acute with the aging of the population and the parallel aging of care workers
(Organization for Economic Cooperation and Development [OECD] 2010).
Together, these changes will create an even greater challenge to the sustainability of older adult care and health care more generally. One of the responses
to this concern over a shortage of care workers has been to recruit migrant
care workers or, depending on the context, to tap into the existing resources
of immigrant care workers. That is, a general trend has emerged that more and
more of the care for older adults, already generally undervalued in our society, is being undertaken by workers born in other, often less developed countries. The full extent of the roles foreign-born care workers play in the delivery
of older adult care in high-income Western countries is relatively unknown.
What draws them to work in this sector? What is specific to the sector and
what is specific to their immigration status? What are the challenges they

face? How do the changing immigration and healthcare policy contexts influence their experiences?

This chapter draws upon the insights from a comparative project carried out in Canada, the United Kingdom, Ireland, and the United States about the role of migrant or immigrant care workers in the older adult care sector (Spencer et al. 2010). We began by first undertaking an analysis of the contextual factors influencing demand for paid older adult care. This included consideration of how each of our case societies are aging, how female labor participation has increased resulting in a care deficit, and what immigration policy levers have or could be used to attend to this gap. We then undertook primary studies involving survey and in-depth interview methodologies to better understand the experiences of migrant workers, of those who employ them, and of the older people they care for across institutional (residential and nursing care homes) and home-based care settings.

One striking commonality observed across all of the country case studies was the double isolation experienced by immigrant care workers, who are isolated by their immigration status and by undertaking work in a sector that is invisible and undervalued. A number of intersecting factors lead to this double isolation. First, the undervalued nature and poor working conditions in the older adult care sector push employers to hire foreign-born workers. Second, the negative effects of the working conditions in this sector are exacerbated for immigrant workers in two ways: (1) these workers are isolated within the workplace because of their immigrant status and (2) they are isolated in their communities because of the constraints of their work. We came to see that this double isolation was due to the lack of policy attention and prioritization of the provision of care for older people and the social exclusion experienced by immigrants.

In this chapter, I describe this double isolation using data from the Canadian case, but I also highlight the similarities and differences observed in the other countries. Drawing upon an intersectionality approach, which encourages us to explicitly examine multiple layers of identity, experience, and oppression (Hankivsky 2012), I will argue that the different layers of identity of immigrant care workers of older adults may not only be additive but may have an interactive effect on their working and living conditions. Our conclusion across the country case studies is that the major challenges lie, fundamentally, in the reform of the older adult care system to meet adequately the needs of an aging population; such reforms will at the same time need to address the disproportionate role that immigrant care workers play in providing care in this sector. Before we delve into the specifics of the Canadian case study, it is important to understand some of the key tools of intersectional analysis.

A Brief Explanation of Intersectionality

Intersectionality is largely associated with a feminist perspective, which focuses on systemic inequality based on multiple, intersecting statuses combining different layers of discrimination and oppression such as sexism, racism, and classism (Collins 2000). It posits that these axes of oppression do not act independently of one another but rather interact in an interlocking matrix of discrimination. Such an approach better enables us to understand the ways that different identities relate to one another and are intricately bound together. A key feature of intersectionality is a focus on the standpoint of a "minority" or oppressed culture rather than the majority. Although intersectionality scholars typically look at gender and race or class, an examination of age and aging and how this intersects with these other societal cleavages has become increasingly common.

Applying these concepts to immigrant older adult care workers reflects the intersection of immigrant status as subordinate to Canadian-born status, as well as the subordinate status of the older adults (who are also largely women) for whom they provide care. So we see not only the marginal status of the care workers but also the status of their work reflecting the marginal status of their older adult clients. We begin with a discussion of this latter issue and then move to how the immigrant status of these care workers of older adults intersects in a unique manner.

Background to the Older Adult Care Sector in Canada

The older adult care sector in Canada, as in many countries, includes both home care and community-based services and institutional care in long-term care (LTC) facilities.[1] Neither are deemed medically necessarily services under the provincial/territorial public schemes, and thus each province has developed its own terms and conditions under which these services are provided.[2] This lack of inclusion in the package of publicly funded healthcare services can be seen as an indicator of the lack of recognition of the older adult care sector as part of the broader healthcare system.

The increasing demand for older adult care comes from multiple sources, including the aging of the Canadian population and changes within the acute care system. Specifically, health system reforms that focus on shifting the locus of care from expensive acute care institutions into less expensive long-term care facilities and community and home-based settings cause a consequent increase in the acuity and complexity of patients in older adult care. Although the provinces have rapidly increased the funding for home and long-term care, resources have not kept up with this increasing demand.

In response to the resulting deficit in funding, many home care programs have implemented cost containment strategies such as restricting the number of hours of care and/or the number of visits or services, changing eligibility criteria, and training family members to directly provide care, which is often quite complex. The institutional care sector has implemented similar cost containment strategies including higher patient-to-staff ratios and rationing of supplies.

Across both services, there has been a trend to shifting tasks from professional (and higher paid) to unregulated (and lower paid) home and institutional care workers (Sharkey, Larsen, and Mildon 2003). This has resulted in workers often working beyond their scope and carrying workloads that are unsustainable in the long term. As increasing numbers of patients with high acuity are being redirected to home and institutional care, there is a question as to whether the workers will be able to meet patient needs appropriately.

The totality of these changes has served to make a challenging sector to work within that much more challenging. Recruitment and retention of home and long-term institutional care workers has been a long-standing issue, in part because of job insecurity, low pay, lack of fringe benefits, heavy workloads, violence/abuse in the workplace, lack of career and training opportunities, and high levels of stress, burnout, and injuries at work (Aronson, Denton, and Zeytinoglu 2004; Home Care Sector Study 2003; O'Brien-Pallas 2004). Many workers are employed only part-time or casually; that is, they are paid either by the hour or by the visit and hours are not guaranteed (Canadian Association of Retired Persons [CARP] 2001).

The concerns with poor working conditions and physical resources have only been exacerbated by the increasing financial crunch experienced by the sector and rising demand. This has contributed to increasing the precarious nature of older adult care work. For example, the increasing casualization of older adult care work evidenced by many care workers being employed only part-time and without benefits means that in order to make ends meet, care workers increasingly work at more than one institution or home care service. The resulting burnout makes the retention of older adult care workers that much more difficult. Even though no national or even provincial statistics on turnover rates exist, the Ontario Community Support Association estimates that the average turnover rate for home care workers is double to triple the rate of other healthcare workers across Canada (that is, 25 to 40 percent compared to 12 percent) (OCSA 2000).

Thus, many of the challenges faced by these care workers are a result of the broader underfunding of the system of care provision, which causes this to be an often underpaid sector of employment. Indeed, the increasing reliance on immigrant care workers can be seen as a symptom of such challenges, and immigrants, while making important contributions, are not a band-aid solution to those deficiencies.

Immigrant Care Workers Fill a Need

Across all four countries, it was clear from the employers we surveyed and interviewed that they experience some difficulty in hiring workers born in their respective countries. Canadian employers noted that they do not receive as many applications from domestic care workers as they do from immigrant workers. When we asked why there is a difficulty recruiting domestic care workers, employer respondents highlighted the shortage of Canadian workers most frequently, followed by the related issue of how Canadian-born workers are not interested in this type of work because they can make more in other jobs.

Many of the employers we spoke to confirmed that they experience problems of high turnover and low retention, which creates a constant shortage in older adult care occupations. The reasons provided for these difficulties revolve around the relative underfunding of the sector and, because staffing accounts for the bulk of costs, underfunding has a negative impact on wage levels. Managers argue that this makes it difficult to attract and retain domestically trained staff.

Recognizing the difficulty of filling positions in long-term settings, in 2004, the Ministry of Health and Long-Term Care in the Canadian province of Ontario published a resource kit for long-term care (LTC) facility operators. One section of this kit focuses on targeting and recruiting new and established immigrant groups. The opening parts of that section state that immigrants represent a great recruitment opportunity for LTC facilities because (1) many immigrants are in the process of getting their qualifications recognized, therefore, by offering them an initial opportunity, the chances are great that they will stay in facility that secured them their first job, and (2) many facilities require workers with knowledge or skills relating to certain cultural groups. The kit recommends that employers (1) get in touch with settlement organizations that provide employment programs and job search workshops through which potential employees may be targeted, (2) go to ESL classes in local communities and colleges in order to meet and recruit new immigrants to their facility, (3) advertise job positions in ethnic newspapers, (4) distribute job flyers or information pamphlets at local meeting sites such as community centers, shopping centers, grocery stores, local coffee shops or restaurants, and places of worship where specific immigrant communities are located, (5) go into the community and talk with the community leaders or religious leaders about opportunities their facility can offer new immigrants, (6) offer public transportation discounts as new immigrants may lack transportation to areas where demand for workers are high, and (7) offer on-the-job training programs.

Although most employers did not cite any specific reasons for recruiting immigrant over domestic care workers, a number did note that immigrant care workers were more likely to stay in their positions because of the difficulty they had in finding other sources of employment. Indeed, some noted that immigrant care workers have strong skill sets and many are overqualified for the positions they attain in Canada. This is particularly the case with immigrant care aides who have training as nurses or physicians in their home countries. The director of one facility stated, "We have some care aides who are working as a registered care aide who actually had a nursing diploma or a nursing education in India or in the Philippines but they didn't want to write the exams here. So you get a better educated person."

Harder-to-Fill Positions Are Easier for
Immigrant Care Workers to Obtain

When we spoke to immigrant older adult care workers, there were a range of stories of how they ended up working in this sector. Some were recruited directly to do this kind of work through recruitment agencies or other organizations. Some had done this kind of work in their home country so gravitated to this sector. Others fell into these positions as it was considered an easy sector in which to get a job; that is, older adult care positions in all four countries are considered lesser-skilled jobs, thereby presenting fewer barriers to entry. This enables an accessible employment option for newly arrived foreign-born workers. The workers we spoke to in Canada noted that accessibility to this kind of work stems from the shortage of domestic workers. As one worker told us, since there was a "shortage of people in this kind of field . . . that was the easiest . . . [and] fastest way to get a job." It was also noted that job availability was related to the needs of Canada's rapidly aging population; one worker noted, "I know in Canada the older population is going up every year so the health field is the best place where you can find a job."

In many cases, immigrant care workers found their jobs through informal networks, like family and friends already living in Canada who informed them of the sources of employment or recommended them to prospective employers. As one described, "The job in which I am working now, a friend of mine who worked there said . . . they were looking for a director of care and said, 'Why don't you talk with the administrator.' [So] I went there and I was hired."

What draws foreign care workers to this sector is the availability of jobs that they are often made aware of through their social networks (if they are not directly recruited), positions that they hope to use to gain experience and skills to move onto better jobs. A number of the care workers we spoke to see their work in this sector as temporary; their time working in older adult care is seen as a stepping stone to more lucrative and challenging professional positions. Many chose to work in nursing and retirement homes because they believed that their knowledge of English was insufficient for work in a faster paced, acute care setting. As one told us, "In the beginning it was scary because I don't know if my English is good enough. . . . So my first choice I chose the nursing home. Easier? Yeah. That's my start. So after that I get used to it and I know everything about the nursing home . . . I should try the hospital."

Many use the opportunity to improve skills for credential recognition or advancement. This is particularly the case for those older adult care workers who have professional qualifications in their home countries. In Canada, the United States, the United Kingdom, and Ireland, they often must repeat training and certification while they work in lesser-skilled positions. Although this can provide them with highly coveted domestic experience necessary for advancement, managing their care work and preparations for professional licensure exams can compound their workload and social exclusion.

Working in the Older Adult Care Sector Can Be Doubly Isolating

Beyond the issue of recruitment to the sector, the general story of the workplace experiences of immigrant care workers across the four countries we studied can be described as follows: poor pay and working conditions combined with the financial implications of the obligation immigrants feel to send home remittances contributes to their precarious circumstances and overall social isolation in their host country. In Canada, for example, we found that immigrant care workers have more than one part-time job or otherwise work casually so they may work or be on call without pay for long periods of time. Although this is not specific to foreign-born workers but rather is typical of the older adult care sector more broadly (Denton et al. 2002), their preponderance in this sector makes this a key challenge for these workers.

The majority of the care workers we spoke to described a sense of isolation at work. In particular, the interviews reveal that the lack of communication with coworkers stems mostly from the short amount of time allocated for breaks and in some cases the ways in which staff are organized in LTC settings. The workload meant, in the words of one of the workers we interviewed, that "we don't have really time for chatting with the coworkers on the lunch time. No socializing." The pace of the work and having to work across more than one job exacerbated these feelings.

The isolation as a result of the social organization of care work in the older adult care sector is intensified for foreign-born care workers, particularly those who are migrant or newly arrived immigrants. Many lack strong social support networks in their new country and have responsibility for families they left behind. Thus, many immigrant care workers reported feeling a sense of isolation not only at work but also at home. Although they allocate any free time to be with their families (either in real time or virtually if their families remained in their home country), their social life is limited. Most of immigrant care workers reveal that they have few friends, and those they do have are mostly from their home countries. The problem is that they do not have enough time to spend with friends, or enough of the right time due to untraditional schedules in the older adult care sector. Since these care workers all have busy schedules, they rarely meet and often must rely on only talking on phone in order to maintain connections. For example, when prompted to tell us about his friends, one care worker responded, "I don't have too many. I have . . . really I don't have a social life. It's sad. It's not that I [don't] want it, but I hardly have any time for any of that."

Although many are aware of immigrant settlement and integration services available in their neighborhoods, immigrant care workers in our study have had limited involvement with these programs and services for lack of time. In fact, most of them state that they have been to these organizations only a few times since they arrived in Canada in order to request technical help such as translation of documents, help with filling out the applications, preparing resumés, and so on. They found these institutions generally helpful with respect to such services. Immigrant care workers reveal that in the case of more complex life problems, they tend to rely primarily on family, friends, and sometimes ethnic organizations, all of whom are scarce resources for these workers.

Opportunities for social interaction for immigrant care workers in our study were not only limited due to constraints of time but constraints of finances. Although most of the immigrant older adult care workers we spoke to indicated that they were doing better financially than they had been prior to immigrating to Canada, many have financially dependent children or family in their home countries and have obligations to send back remittances. The majority of immigrant care workers explained that by moving to Canada, they hoped to ensure not only a better life for themselves but for their families. Indeed, most of the immigrant care workers that were interviewed felt the weight of responsibility of supporting family living in their home country. Thus, the limited pay they received working in this poorly remunerated sector was that much more taxed by the responsibility of sharing these resources with family. With portions of their already-limited paycheck being sent to their family members abroad, immigrant care workers are left with few financial resources to invest in the types of social activities that could decrease their sense of isolation.

Our study indicates that isolation as a result of the social organization of care work in the older adult care sector is exacerbated for foreign-born care workers, particularly those who are migrant or newly arrived immigrants. That is, there are challenges that are unique to being foreign-born or immigrants that are related to their broader experiences of social isolation, lack of social network support, and the obligation to send home remittances in support of family members, which limits their own financial resources. Taken together, these factors result in precarious social and economic circumstances for immigrant care workers—a feature common across our four country case studies.

Need for Policy Reform and Investment in the Older Adult Sector

Immigrant older adult care workers have made and continue to make a substantial contribution to the older adult care sector in many high-income Western countries. Some of the challenges they face along the way are specific to the generally devalued older adult care sector in these countries, such as poor wages and a lack of full-time positions, but they also experience a unique form of social isolation specific to their recent arrival, ties to their home country, and overall foreign-born status. That is, their immigrant status intersects with the status of the work they undertake.

The one striking commonality observed across the four countries is a relative lack of prioritization of the provision of care for older people. Such a robust finding—regardless of the different immigration policies and practices—speaks to the importance of these intersecting identities. Indeed, the relative invisibility of the conditions of older adult care can be seen as being mirrored in the invisibility of the work and living conditions of their immigrant care workers. Most of the central challenges raised by the demand for migrant labor are embedded in the context of an underfunded and undervalued system of care provision, and an often-underpaid sector of employment. The increasing reliance on migrant care workers can be seen as a symptom of those challenges, and migrants or immigrants, while making important contributions, should not be the primary solution to those deficiencies.

Given the aging trends in our societies, the increasing need for a robust older adult care work force is clear. Whether these needs should be filled by migrants or immigrants is open for debate. Foreign-born workers do benefit from the relative availability of jobs in this sector, but that does little to address why these jobs are so hard to fill in the first place. Moreover, the occupancy of these positions by temporary migrants or newly arrived immigrants without recognition of the special needs of their immigration status does little to address their needs and the needs of the recipients of their care. Some of our findings suggest that policy shifts required are related to the immigration status of the care worker—such as their English or French language sufficiency and their cultural competency—but there are more general concerns with the lack of status and attention that older adult care has garnered in each national context. The major challenges lie in the reform of the older adult care system to meet the needs of an aging population adequately.

Notes

1 This section is a synthesized version of the chapter written by Margaret Denton (2009) for the report *The Role of Immigrant Care Workers in an Aging Society: The Canadian Context and Experience*.

2 For the sake of brevity, I will use the term *provinces* to refer to provinces and territories in the remainder of the chapter.

Part IV

Identities and
Meaning Making

••••••••••••••••••••••

One objective of this volume is to understand how care workers themselves define, describe, and make sense of their labor. The meanings that paid caregivers attach to their work are complex and at times contradictory. Yet, these subjective experiences of their own identities as care workers have a profound impact on worker outcomes like job satisfaction, burnout, and turnover—which in turn have important implications not only for individual workers but also for the collective provision of care to those who need it. A deep exploration of the cultural meanings of paid care work and the subjective experiences of care workers is therefore crucial to achieving an understanding of the care sector.

As these chapters show, care workers do not interpret their work in a vacuum, but often define their own identities in relation to others. Using the concept of boundary work, Fumilayo Showers describes how nurses migrating from West Africa distance themselves from the stigmatized associations of the job there by defining their work and their identities as U.S. nurses as fundamentally different from nursing in their home country. Once in the United States, some West African nurses consciously avoid jobs or institutional settings that have large concentrations of co-ethnics. These workers, like those described by LaTonya Trotter, engage in boundary work to define their own role partly by drawing contrasts between their own identities and motivations and those of other groups of workers. Trotter finds similar boundary work performed by nurse practitioners as they carve out a role distinct from both physicians and social workers.

Part of the boundary work in which paid care workers engage involves constructing a professional identity in the context of jobs that are largely devalued both economically and socially. The nurse practitioners Trotter describes claim a unique expertise that comes from social knowledge of patients obtained through clinical interactions. And in Showers's study, some of the nurses deliberately contrast their own alignment with the professionalization of nursing in the United States with the vocational orientation of nurses in their home country. Because of the racialized hierarchy in U.S. health care, the jobs held by the majority of their West African co-ethnics are also lower-status aide positions, which they also distance themselves from in order to build a professional identity.

As a group these chapters make clear that meanings of care are both individually and collectively shaped, and are linked to particular constructions of race, class, culture, nationality, age, and other attributes of workers. That is, meanings of care are social realities, born out of interaction with others. Cameron Macdonald's chapter perhaps is the most explicit example of this iterative process, demonstrating that middle-class women in search of a nanny employ "ethnic logics" to make decisions about who is best suited to care for their children. We see here that what it means to be a nanny (and whether one is hired as one) is constructed by employers in interaction with the nannies themselves, shaped by employers' perceptions of which traits are associated with particular racial profiles, age groups, and ethnic origins. Broad cultural conceptions of what constitutes good care for young children are mapped onto these personal attributes in a complex interaction among employing mothers, the expert advice literature on child care, and local cultures and networks of nannies.

Finally, these chapters illuminate the complex ways in which care workers at times integrate the emotional aspects of their work into their professional identities and at times distance themselves from these more affective dimensions. For example, the nurse practitioners described by Trotter embrace the relational aspects of their work as a way to retain their caring identity as nurses and distinguish their expertise from that of physicians. And, for nannies, the importance to employers of affective connection with children varies depending largely on the age of their child (see MacDonald).

The lifestyle workers studied by Rachel Sherman—including personal concierges, interior designers, and financial advisors—may not fit our conceptual definition of care, but her analysis offers critical insights into the relationship between power, subordination, and worker experiences of emotion work. This contrasting case allows for an analysis of workers' subjective and moral interpretations of their own emotion work outside of the scope of the ethical frame of caring for dependents, providing important clarity to questions that are often blurred in the context of nurturant care. Sherman finds that whether workers perceive emotion work as rewarding or as exploitative depends largely on the social and economic status of their occupation and the related power hierarchy with their employer. Those in higher-status jobs see the emotional, caring demands of their work as an expression of their expertise; workers in lower-status jobs or those that are in the process of professionalizing are more likely to see emotional demands as onerous and demeaning.

Sherman's analysis suggests that "increasing status and recognition [for workers] may produce affective relationships with recipients that feel more voluntary and rewarding to the provider. It thus supports the need to professionalize and upgrade care work, not only for the material rewards but because of the symbolic resources this generates in the work itself." The chapters in this section show that the symbolic resources utilized by paid care workers in interpreting their own work in relation to other workers, employers, and care recipients both shape and are shaped by the material conditions of their work.

11

The Caring Professional?

● ● ● ● ● ● ● ● ● ● ● ● ● ● ● ● ● ● ● ●

Nurse Practitioners, Social
Work, and the Performance
of Expertise

LATONYA J. TROTTER

It is not a rare sight to see the slogan "Doctors Cure, Nurses Care" emblazoned on nurses' t-shirts or announced on bumper stickers. Although perhaps overstated, this pithy catchphrase hits squarely at the core of nursing's claims to occupational legitimacy. Since its first efforts to reframe sick care done in the family circle as the province of trained nurses, nursing has sought to elevate care as both a skill and a unique area of expertise. Even though the actual work that nurses perform has become ever more specialized and technical, the profession still understands its work as unique in how it cares for patients. However as nursing stretches up the professional ladder, there are ongoing tensions between its desire to be seen as a respected profession while retaining its identity as a fundamentally and uniquely caring one.

While this tension has been evidenced throughout nursing's history, it has arisen anew in the case of the nurse practitioner. Nurse practitioners (NPs) are registered nurses, who, by obtaining a graduate degree, have acquired the skill and legal authority to enter a terrain previously held only by physicians: the ability to diagnose and treat disease states. As nurses who seem to be called both to cure and care for patients, how do they reconcile this seeming contradiction, both for themselves and for evaluating others? This chapter will address these questions through ethnographic attention to the nurse practitioner, using data from sixteen months of fieldwork among three multidisciplinary healthcare teams. I find that nurse practitioners perform a distinct form of patient care through attention to the social embeddedness of medical problems. Moreover, I find that organizational legitimacy for these practices is not primarily gained at the expense of physician legitimacy, but at the expense of another female-dominated occupation whose claims to expertise lies in attention to social context: social work. Through attention to the nurse practitioner, we can see the ways in which care can be effectively used not only as a moral justification for one's work, but as a legitimate claim of expertise. Through comparisons with social work, we can more fully understand why nurse practitioner expertise is accepted while that of other care workers is questioned.

Background and Significance

Paid care work encompasses a range of activity, from physicians to nurses' aides to high school teachers; all such work involves face-to-face interactions in the pursuit of developing client capabilities and meeting their needs (England, Budig, and Folbre 2002). Although bound together by the work's qualities, the value society accords different care work occupations is clearly unequal. For example, physicians and aides may both be care workers, but these two groups share little in the way of pay, status, or everyday working conditions. Society justifies these differences in part because we believe that what physicians do requires an expertise not required by aides. It is not simply the difficulty of discrete tasks, but our notions of expertise that elevate some work and some workers.

The sundering of many care work occupations from expertise is one explanation for their devaluation. Our difficulty in seeing expertise in the performance of care work has a distinctly gendered quality. Women's labor has been historically bound to the household; practiced at home, women's work went unremunerated by the market. Even when sold in the marketplace, such labor was seen as employing skills of the heart or of character, with workers asked to accept intangible rewards over monetary ones (England and Folbre 1999). The success of physicians, often upheld as the single care worker who has achieved professional status, cannot be understood without this gendered lens. In the United States, medicine has been a demographically male occupation. Research on comparable worth has demonstrated that "femaleness" lowers a job's wage rate because gender is implicitly a compensable characteristic for employers (Kilbourne et al. 1994; Steinberg 1990). Historically, physicians used both political and cultural strategies to change their status from slightly above household servant—beholden to domestic rhythms and worldviews—to respected expert (Foucault 1994; Starr 1984). However, scholars have noted that the political strategies male physicians had at their disposal were different from those available to female-dominated occupations (Witz 1990). Culturally, medicine's increasing reliance on scientific explanations of disease provided a new way of perceiving and treating the body that increasingly separated medical understandings from lay understandings (Foucault 1994). Medical treatment of patient bodies also increasingly moved from the domestic bedside to the hospital, removing physicians—and their practices—from the domestic and social contexts in which their patients lived (Howell 1991). Moving patients from home to hospital and learning to see generalizable disease in specific bodies were both processes that culturally masculinized medicine.

If the success of medicine is, in part, a result of masculinization, it is not an instructive model for care workers seeking greater social recognition. Most care work occupations remain not only female dominated but characterized by the gendered features of interpersonal interaction, relationship, and particular forms of emotional labor. In an analysis estimating the pay penalty to care work, Paula England and her coauthors found that in almost every case, workers involved in nurturant care work are subject to lower wages, all other characteristics of the work and the worker held constant (England, Budig, and Folbre 2002).

Nursing, although sometimes called a failed profession because of its subordinate role to medicine, might be worth a second look as a more useful model (Freidson 1970; Gordon 2006). In the same work by England, Budig, and Folbre, the singular exception to the care work pay penalty was nursing. While it may lose in a competition with medicine in terms of status and income, when viewed on its own terms, nursing is a trusted and respected occupation that affords a middle-class income for 2.7 million women and a growing number of men (Gallup 2010; U.S. Department of Labor Bureau of Labor Statistics 2013). Despite its success, the dilemma of nursing's professionalization project has always been to "attempt to professionalize altruism," without seeming to compete with the interests of more powerful physicians and hospitals (Reverby 1987). It has done this, in part, by continuing to retain care as an organizing principle and as a core part of professional identity. This balancing act has created tensions and rifts throughout nursing's history (Melosh 1982; Nelson and Gordon 2006; Reverby 1987). However, as the credentials for entry to practice continue to rise, and as nursing aides and other caregiving personnel increasingly do more interactional work, the stresses on care as an organizing principle for nursing are ongoing.

The nurse practitioner becomes an interesting case through which to understand how nursing reconciles these tensions, not just through position papers or internal politicking but through performative practices of expertise. The NP represents a segment of nursing that is at the forefront of acquiring the empirical markers of professional status. Professional nursing organizations spend most of their budget advocating not just for the rights of NPs to practice but for their right to practice autonomously without physician supervision. These organizations continue to push for increases in NP credentials: in 2004, the American Association of Colleges of Nursing released a position statement supporting the doctorate, rather than a master's degree, for NP entry to practice (American Association of Colleges of Nursing 2004). However, as NPs move into the realm of diagnostic medicine, the idea of the nurse practitioner pushes both the practical and rhetorical boundaries of what it means to be a caring profession distinct from medicine. As nurses rather than as physicians, armed with a professional logic of nursing work as care work, how do NPs actively and rhetorically perform nursing care within these arenas while maintaining their role as primary care providers? What kinds of expertise does the logic of care make possible, and which are rendered invisible? And, more importantly, in what ways is the nurse practitioner understood to care differently than other kinds of expert care workers?

The specter of other kinds of care workers must be analytically attended to. In his field-changing work, Andrew Abbott asserted that in order to understand claims to occupational legitimacy, it is less useful to study occupations as isolated cases. Rather, he charged scholars to study them in relationship to other groups within the same occupational field (Abbott 1988). The obvious comparative group for nurses is the physician. As the NP moves into the sphere of diagnostic medicine, scholarly accounts are focused on comparisons between the two (Harris 2011; Laurant et al. 2005; Lenz et al. 2004). However, in terms of the marketplace, nurse practitioners are rarely jockeying for position with physicians. The space for nurse practitioners was opened not through competition but because of physician absence in primary care specialties. Demand for physicians remains high, and their status as "the" medical expert remains structurally unchallenged by hospitals, insurers, and regulators. However, as physicians continue to move ever farther away from direct bodily and social care of patients, this vacancy has opened the door for many possible occupants to attend to these needs. While understanding how nurse practitioners gain access to medical authority is an important line of work (Fisher 1995; Trotter 2013), it is equally important to understand the ways in which other occupations are successfully kept out. This chapter will examine the ways in which nurse practitioners perform expertise as care workers, not only by accessing medical knowledge but through their creditable wielding of this knowledge in caring for the socially embedded bodies of patients.

Researching Clinical Practice

The Center

This chapter draws from ethnographic fieldwork conducted at a community-based healthcare center that provides primary health care to a geriatric population.

The center relies on a comprehensive, multidisciplinary, team approach to care, which makes it an analytically useful site for observing clinician negotiations. The team approach is part of the structural mandate of being a federally funded site under the Program of All-Inclusive Care for the Elderly (PACE). All PACE sites have a mission to provide comprehensive support to medically frail older adults (55+) to help them remain in the community. To carry out this mission, each center provides primary care services as well as access to physical therapists, occupational therapists, wound care nurses, recreational and art therapists, and social workers. In addition to providing direct services, teams coordinate and manage all patient care. This center cares for approximately four hundred patients.

The center is distinctive among PACE programs in that it defines itself as a nurse-managed healthcare center. Organizations with this identity have three things in common: an explicit recognition of nurses as the primary provider of patient care, a commitment to a nursing model of health care, and a commitment to serving those with the least access to quality health care (Hansen-Turton et al. 2009). While such organizations are far from normative, aberrant cases provide a different and often clearer view of social phenomenon through more clearly exposing our taken-for-granted understandings of the world.

The Fieldwork

I began my relationship with the center as a volunteer, spending twelve months working with the patient population. This chapter uses data collected about the staff who cared for them. From October 2010 to February 2012, I spent time following nurse practitioners, physicians, primary care nurses (registered nurses without an advanced degree), social workers, and occupational therapists. Standing in hallways, sitting in waiting rooms, and attending regular meetings, I tried to understand how these different clinicians negotiated claims to caring expertise. This chapter focuses on interactions between the NPs, the physicians, and the social workers on the three teams that worked with the center's general population.[1] In addition to fieldwork, this chapter draws from both formal and informal interviews I conducted with the primary members of these three teams: the three nurse practitioners, the two physicians, the three primary care nurses, and the three social workers.[2] In the descriptions that follow, all names are pseudonyms; some details about patients have been altered both to mask their identity and to protect private health information. Text in double quotations is a direct quote; text in single quotations was reconstructed from field notes.

Placing Nurse Practitioner Care in Context

I began my fieldwork by trying to understand the role that the nurse practitioners played in the organization. I spoke with Norah, a nurse practitioner, one afternoon about what the NPs did: "We're like the air traffic controller of the members and their needs. I hear things or identify needs and then direct it to social work or to PT [physical therapy]. Now, of course, sometimes it works the other way around, but usually, it comes through me. NPs have really taken on that kind of responsibility. It's the nature of the profession. Dr. Barnes and Dr. Sidney, they're geriatricians, so I'm sure they see the members in the same way. But still—it's different. And I'm sure they are happy to let nursing do what it does." This view of the NP role as somehow different from physician practice was shared among the NPs. Norah was convinced that this distinction was so self-evident that she assumed the physicians "were happy to let nursing do what it does."

As I spent time with the physicians, I wasn't so sure that the physicians were happy with the state of affairs. Dr. Barnes was a full-time physician at the center. I began my fieldwork just a few weeks before she began working at the center; it was instructive to watch how a physician made a space for herself within an organization where nursing held such a prominent role. About ten months into her tenure, I asked her what had been the most difficult thing to get used to. She replied, "That they're not my patients. Usually, as a physician, they're your patients. Here, they're our patients. They're transportation's patients. They're the caregiver's patients. They're the nurse's patients. They're everyone's patients." As we continued our conversation, I understood her statement as more lament than complaint. Dr. Barnes appreciated the holistic, team-based approach to care. However, there was something professionally unsettling about having multiple decision makers. But not all team members expressed this sentiment. I began to suspect that there was something particular to the physician experience. As I observed the teams' interactions, I came to have a more nuanced understanding of loss of physician control and its relation to the role of the nurse practitioner.

Team Meeting

The center had a traditional clinic, complete with a waiting room and exam rooms. But many of the decisions about patients were made outside the clinic during team meetings. Each team met weekly for and hour and a half to two hours. The primary organizational purpose of these meetings was to discuss and approve the comprehensive, PACE-mandated assessments that had to be completed for all members every six months. Either an NP or a physician could have completed the required medical assessment. Although I expected to see NP and physician conflict as they discussed these assessments, my expectations were almost never met. The medical assessments were typically delivered in a pro forma style; in many teams, the written notes from the medical exam were simply read out loud, often at a galloping pace. It was clear that little discussion was expected about decisions considered strictly medical.

Occasionally, a physician would ask a question or make a recommendation. On these occasions, there would begin a carefully choreographed dance of civility. The physician making a recommendation would usually practice restraint, phrasing it as a suggestion rather than an order: 'You may want to think about trying a different regimen for her hypertension' or 'I've heard that Paxil is good for uricemic itching. It's worth a try.' Upon hearing these suggestions, the nurse practitioners would usually perform an almost jovial deference, with responses like 'Oh, that's a good idea!' Although there was variation in how the nurse practitioners understood their practice relationship to physicians, during team meetings when a problem was structurally demarcated as distinctly medical, the nurse practitioners almost uniformly practiced deference to medical authority. Within this organization, nurse-managed though it was, physicians had (when they cared to use it) complete control over decisions that both the NP and the physician understood as wholly medical: diagnosis and medical intervention.

Interestingly, though, very little organizational decision-making or action in this particular setting was clearly marked as entirely medical. When I first began attending team meetings, I was initially surprised that the six-month assessments—the federally mandated assessments that were the primary organizational purpose of these meetings—were not more dynamic. However, after the routine of assessments, the meeting switched to the nonroutine of "member issues." It was here that perspectives differed and conflicts arose.

Different Problems, Different Solutions

On a Tuesday morning, one team met in the conference room for their weekly meeting. One of the more organized teams, they always followed the same agenda: assessments came first and then member issues. After forty-five minutes of going through the assessments, the facilitator opened the floor: 'Who has member issues?' One of the first to respond was Katie, the occupational therapist. She had received a call from the daughter of a Mr. Flack: 'When I talked to her, she really sounded like she was at her wit's end.' Mr. Flack has dementia, a condition of cognitive decline that often creates behavioral problems. Mr. Flack often lost his temper and sometimes turned violent. Katie posed a question to the team: 'Do you think emergency respite [a brief stay in a nursing home] might be a good idea?' Her question ignited a passionate discussion. A debate ensued between the two nurse practitioners present and the social worker. The social worker argued against emergency respite, retorting that the problem was more fundamental, and that the team "can't change their family dynamics with respite." While everyone on the team had the opportunity to share his or her opinion, some opinions came to matter more than others. When the social worker introduced "family dynamics," one of the nurse practitioners countered, "Yes, I've known that family for a long time" and began to describe her own history of conversations and interventions with the Flack family. This conversation, and many like it, was part of a larger narrative contest that I saw repeated again and again within team meetings: who knew the patient and the family better? Who had the appropriate knowledge to diagnose the real problem and provide the appropriate solution? In this case, the requisite knowledge was not about a medical understanding of dementia but a familiarity with Mr. Flack and his family.

The lengthy discussion was ended by a nurse practitioner, who said in a definitive tone of voice, 'I will call the daughter and recommend emergency respite from both a safety and behavioral health perspective.' This problem of Mr. Flack's family, that involved neither medication changes nor specialist referrals, was a problem that was not perceived as wholly medical. Dr. Barnes, the physician who was present, did offer an interested opinion, but it was the nurse practitioner and social worker whose ideas were in conflict. The heat behind this discussion was not typical in team meetings. However, this inter-action does make plain the grounds upon which decisions in the murky world of "not wholly medical" were often decided. Decisions about whether Ms. Jones should still cook for herself, or whether it was time to call Mr. Stein's sister about the state of his apartment, were made in free-ranging discussions that included everyone—from NPs to aides. But when there were competing plans of action, the nurse practitioner would use her knowledge of patients—their history, their family connections, and their conditions—to achieve an NP-led consensus. In the case of Mr. Flack, the nurse practitioner explicitly made the decision. However, it was more usual for a discussion to be more subtly ended by the NP making a suggestion of action to another team member, such as 'Why don't you call Mrs. Jones's daughter and see if that will work for her.' These suggestions for action had a clear hierarchy; they were often delivered from NP to social worker, rarely from social worker to NP.

The behavior of the physician regarding these team meetings was also strik-ing. Although attentive during the medical assessment presentations, their attention visibly shifted during the long conversations and debates about member issues. The physicians spent this time signing written orders, reading e-mail, or doing clinical work via smartphone. When physician time was in short supply due to vacations or competing workplace concerns, team meetings were treated as optional—they arrived late, left early, or skipped them entirely. Their behavior communicated their evaluation that little of their expertise was required during these meetings. After all, disagreement about the medical exam was so rare that even the dance of civility between themselves and the NPs was rarely required. However, in choosing to absent themselves from decisions related to member issues, the physicians left themselves out of an expanding universe of decisions, conversations, and information sharing about patients. In this population, very few member issues required diagnosis or a distinctly medical intervention. Given this finding, we can understand Dr. Barnes's feelings of discom-fort in a different light. Despite deference to medical authority, such authority was required in a shrinking proportion of clinic concerns. By comparison, the nurse practitioner's presence was deemed as essential to these meetings. If the NP was late, the meeting would wait for her appearance. In her absence, meetings were often cancelled or truncated.

Caring in Context

Although we have seen how the nurse practitioners perform expertise in team meetings, why is their performance so often convincing? The nurse practitioners did not explicitly pull rank about distinctly medical conditions but about social knowledge of patients. How did the expertise they performed differ from that of the social workers? During my fieldwork, I followed each of the nurse practitioners in turn. One of these nurse practitioners was Maura. One afternoon, I sat inside her office as she caught up on her e-mail and wrote up patient notes. At 2:35 P.M., the phone rang. Answering, she put the call on speakerphone. "Hi, it's Susie. I'm calling about my mom." Susie's mother is Ms. Bly. Susie described her mother as behaving nervously. Maura, familiar with Ms. Bly's conditions, wonders if the behavior change could be attributed to her diabetes. "What's her blood sugar?" Susie doesn't know but suggests that Maura call her sister who is currently with Ms. Bly. Maura agrees, hangs up and calls Debbie, the other sister. After some back and forth, Maura figures out that the nursing visits that normally assist Ms. Bly with her insulin injections were never restarted after she returned home from a recent hospitalization.

Ms. Bly lives alone; having assistance with her insulin is one of the key supports she needs to keep her living in the community. Throughout the call I could hear an angry Ms. Bly yelling at Debbie, and Debbie, though trying to concentrate on Maura's call, intermittently yelling back. Maura ends the call by asking Debbie to check her mother's blood sugar and then call her back. Maura follows this encounter with a quick e-mail to the department that provides home care. The e-mail is only the first of a multistep process of both troubleshooting why the nursing visits were not restarted and attending to the urgent problem at hand by arranging a nurse to make a home visit before the end of the day. As Maura navigates the organization, she will also have to navigate the family. She will make decisions about which daughter will be most likely to assist in this crisis, which daughter might be able to assist in her long-term management, and perhaps which daughter is less likely to bend under Ms. Bly's abuse.

The center's patient population was medically frail, with most having complex combinations of chronic diseases, functional impairments, and cognitive deficits. As evidenced by the case of Ms. Bly, caring for this population is less about providing cures and more about management. In the context of troubleshooting a sudden behavior change, Maura found herself inside a family argument, getting to know each daughter and learning about their different relationships to their mother. To solve the problem, she reacquainted herself with the practicalities of Ms. Bly's insulin routines. Her approach to the problem of an abnormal blood sugar was to immerse herself in Ms. Bly's social life, a life that included not only domestic routines and relationships but organizational routines and relationships. So when things went wrong, the nurse practitioner did not just provide information about particular patients or situations, she performed expertise through narrative, storied detail. In an organization with multiple layers of care providers, the successful NP became the resident patient expert.

While noting the pivotal position of NPs in this organization, I began to wonder about the role of the social worker. Much of what the nurse practitioners claimed as their unique area of expertise could also be claimed by social work: knowledge of the social situation, understanding an individual's social history and family dynamics. However, in ways both small and large, the social workers were not treated as having a unique expertise. A constant complaint by several of the social workers was about how they were treated. One complained about the way the center's receptionist would "tell her how to do her job." Another expressed frustration when a woman from the marketing department talked to a member of administration in order to circumvent her decision about a patient. This was not simply a persecution complex; in the center's daily, morning meetings, the only public discussion I ever witnessed about staff decisions was about those made by the social workers. In team meetings, I observed that social worker knowledge about patients would often be trumped by not only the NP but by aides, the nurse, or the occupational therapist. In an organization where everyone had social interaction with patients—from clerks to aides—social worker knowledge was not accorded any particular status.

In part, this was because they simply had less patient-related knowledge. Given the frailty of the center's population, all medical complaints were urgently attended to. Accordingly, much of the clinic's work was generated by patients who either walked in or called in to make their concerns clinic concerns. When I spent time with the social workers, I noted a different rhythm. Social work concerns most often came through intermediaries rather than directly from patients. Much of this work came filtered through administration. Social workers were responsible for filling out paperwork required by the state whenever a patient moved between home, rehab stays, assisted living facilities, and long-term care. Similarly, whenever a patient request for treatment, device, or service was declined, it was a social worker who sent out the denial letter. Even in team meetings, member issues were rarely brought up by social work. However, the social worker would often be left with a member-related task generated by the team. Although social workers provided patient care, in the carrying out of their work, they had much less direct patient interaction than most of the team members.

However, I also posit that it mattered that NPs knew what they knew about patients through clinic encounters rather than through social work encounters.

The medical clinic is an accepted site of expertise. These NPs transformed everyday knowledge into specialist knowledge through expanding the clinic to include social problems. Once these problems became clinic problems, their solutions lay with the NPs rather than the social workers. The social workers might have been asked to address these problems, but they were not able to perform an expertise that appeared sufficiently different from the aide, the medical assistant, or the clerical staff.

Constructing Expertise

In this site, nurse practitioners expanded their domain of action through reinscribing an everyday body into a specific kind of nursing body that then required NP skill. This specific translation of nursing care allowed for the construction of a unique area of expertise, both against the differently credentialed physicians who were not professionally called to care and the similarly credentialed social worker who could care, but whose access to greater knowledge of the patient was constrained. The NPs were better able to leverage their knowledge of the social needs of their patients, in part because the organization has created a situation in which they have more opportunity than others to garner this expertise but also because of the context in which they come to know these needs, which is from within the medical encounter rather than from within a social work encounter.

The case of the clinic provides a way of understanding the interactional processes through which nursing is able to attain a measure of success that other care work providers find elusive. "Doctors Cure, Nurses Care" is not simply a slogan that makes lower-status workers feel better about their organizational position; it is a staking out of turf. Nursing has been successful in making the case that nurses care in fundamentally different ways from unpaid family members, but also from paid aides, social workers, sonogram technicians, and a host of other care workers in the healthcare domain. Individual nurse practitioners acceded to physician authority in questions of medical diagnosis or intervention, but they were able to wield their own authority convincingly in the domain that physicians have increasingly absented: the embodied problems of everyday life.

Acknowledgments

This material is based upon work supported by the National Science Foundation Graduate Research Fellowship under Grant No. DGE-0646086. Partial support for this research was provided by a grant from the Eunice Kennedy Shriver National Institute of Child Health and Human Development under Grant No. 5R24HD047879.

Notes

1 This site had four teams. I excluded the fourth from much of my observations and from analyses in this chapter because this team cared for patients with Alzheimer's and advanced dementia. This made this team different both in terms of its practices as well as the level of protection these patients were accorded from research.

2 There were other clinicians who assisted the primary team members, such as two part-time NPs, the medical director (MD), and one part-time physician, as well as another level of nurses who dispensed medications and provided wound care. However, this chapter is focused on negotiations among those team members who were directly responsible for patient care.

12

Building a
Professional Identity

• • • • • • • • • • • • • • • • • • • •

Boundary Work and Meaning
Making among West African
Immigrant Nurses

FUMILAYO SHOWERS

I met Arthurlina, a fifty-year-old nurse from Sierra Leone, on a hot summer's day in Washington, DC. Arthurlina is a tall, imposing woman with a booming voice and an even bigger laugh. She reflected on a career that began when she trained as a nurse in her homeland after completing her high school education. After migrating to the United States, she worked as a certified nursing assistant while going to nursing school. At the time of our meeting, Arthurlina was the director of nursing at a nursing home in a DC suburb. Women like Arthurlina who migrate from West Africa to the United States create distinct professional identities in the nursing field once here, navigating within workplaces characterized by hierarchies according to race and gender.

This chapter draws on interview data obtained from a sample of forty-two women from four West African countries—Nigeria, Ghana, Liberia, and Sierra Leone—who work as skilled nurses in the Washington, DC, metropolitan area. It explores in particular the subjective meanings that they attach to their work and how they craft and manage their professional identities as nurses. Care work in the United States is a field that is increasingly characterized by the incorporation of migrant women (George 2005; Guevara 2010; Hondagneu-Sotelo 2007; Parennas 2001). Studying women healthcare workers from countries in West Africa allows for an exploration of how immigrant women understand paid caregiving work and how they navigate oppressive racial and gendered hierarchies. Using an intersectional lens, this chapter builds on previous research that documents how nurses construct professional identities in their field of work (Cowin 2001; Davis and Olesen 1963; Fagermoen 1997; Ohlen and Segesten, 1998). Focusing on a group of skilled nurses from West Africa and their experiences of work in the United States adds a transnational dimension by exploring how ideologies of care in immigrant-sending countries influence the professional identities of immigrant care workers in the United States.

In this analysis, I discuss how a group of immigrant women craft professional identities in the nursing industry by engaging in a strategy I term "professional distancing." These nurses discursively and actively separate themselves both from work settings that have large concentrations of other West Africans and from lesser-skilled occupations within the healthcare hierarchy, such as certified nursing assistants. To understand this particular strategy, I investigate the perception of the field of nursing in the sending countries in West Africa. Gaining a subjective understanding of how nursing is perceived in the home countries allows me to begin to understand the meanings respondents attach to their job in the United States. I am able to point to the ways in which the ideologies and meanings surrounding this work are transformed in the United States.

Migrant nurses experience their labor in the context of a racialized U.S. workplace. Existing scholarship on nursing has reported concentrations of women of color in less desirable and labor-intensive specialties within hospitals and other institutional settings (Hagey et al. 2001; Raghuram and Kofman 2004; Yeates 2009). While expressing these general racialized hierarchies, women in this study also hold the perception that their positioning as Black and foreign women from Africa places them at the bottom of all the hierarchies within their field of work. I argue that their subjective understandings of work must be analyzed within the general framework of racial hierarchies within the nursing field that resulted in segregation of Black women from Africa into occupational ghettoes. I also argue that the ideologies surrounding nursing in their home countries are important to understand how they carve professional identities in the United States.

Researching African Immigrant Nurses in the United States

The participants in this study (N = 42) were drawn from two counties in Maryland and in the District of Columbia. All work in hospitals and nursing homes within this area. The women ranged in age from early twenties to late sixties, which captures multiple waves of immigration and a range of experiences in the field. All of the women held legal immigration status. Some were naturalized U.S. citizens but the majority of participants were permanent residents. All of the women had received nursing training in the United States. Some (N = 8) were qualified nurses in their home countries but had to retrain and/or go through licensing and credentialing transfer procedures. Others (especially the younger women in the sample) had received their nursing training in the United States. All of the women had been in the United States for at least five years. Interviews were conducted mostly in the homes of participants but sometimes at churches and other immigrant gatherings. All interviews were conducted in English. The interviews lasted on average between sixty and ninety minutes. All the interviews were transcribed verbatim and analyzed using a grounded theory approach (Strauss and Corbin 1998).

Professional Distancing: Work Experiences and Orientations

In conceptualizing professional distancing, I draw from Michèle Lamont (2000) and her concept of "boundary work." This refers to the process by which working-class men in the United States and France draw moral boundaries that define them as distinct from groups they do not belong to, relying on racialized and gendered tropes that link work and dignity to moral traits. In this instance, professional distancing is a type of boundary work used by a group of West African women who want to project an image of professionalism and caring. Respondents distanced themselves from other West African women by avoiding specializations and institutions with large concentrations of co-ethnics. This group also distanced themselves from lower-skilled sectors within their workplaces.

Nursing "Back Home": A Stigmatized and Gendered Occupation

Interview data shed light on stigmatized views about nursing found in research participants' countries of origin. Maryam, a woman in her mid-twenties who had migrated to the United States in her early teens and subsequently trained to be a nurse, recalled the perception of nursing in Sierra Leone, drawing from family members' opinions on the subject. She explained her initial reluctance to become a nurse:

> My aunt is a nurse, my other aunt is a nurse. And the stigma in nursing is that nursing is a prostitution job. And I didn't want that. I picked up on that at an early age . . . and from people teasing my aunt, saying that "Oh . . . so you see when you live in hostels." They say "Oh, hostels is a brothel." . . . My grandmother told me to be a nurse. I never picked up on that when I came here; I was taking classes to go into pharmacy school because I did not want to be a nurse. People were still looking down on nursing; so was I.

Maryam's words show the gendered ideologies at play that add to the stigmatized view of nursing as a profession in the sending countries. Nursing granted women a certain amount of independence by offering them the opportunity to stay in female hostels free from the patriarchal control of family homes but also opened them up to accusations of prostitution or sexual promiscuity. Nursing was therefore deemed unacceptable for women from class-privileged and respectable families. A similar finding was expressed by Sheba George (2005) who noted that nurses from Kerala, India, were always vulnerable to allegations of sexual immorality and impropriety.

Another respondent, Viola, described nursing as a field that was deemed unacceptable for women from middle- and upper-middle-class families. She described the way nursing was viewed by class-privileged people in her native Nigeria and her initial view of nursing work when she entered the field upon migration to England. She states, "You know in Nigeria, the kind of mentality we have about nurses. Nursing in those days used to be for those whose parents cannot pay for university education. That was how nursing in Nigeria . . . this is the mentality that we have. So, it wasn't like something I ever thought about doing."

Another reason for the stigmatized view of nursing had to do with the type of duties associated with nurses. Nursing was viewed by this group as an unskilled occupation, with few options for demonstrating initiative and achieving professional growth. The personal care that nurses performed made the profession seem unappealing for women from class-privileged backgrounds and their families. Furthermore, nursing care, especially care provided for the elderly, was viewed in the sending countries as the natural care that children and families (specifically, women) provided for the elderly. In this context, this type of work was not seen as "real work" or skilled work.

Another research participant, Rose, migrated to the United States from Ghana for undergraduate education. After graduating with a psychology degree, she planned to attend medical school. Realizing that her grades were not stellar and that getting into medical school would prove difficult, Rose started looking into other options. She decided to go to nursing school after contemplating options like dentistry and pharmacy. She discussed her thought process in contemplating entry into the nursing profession:

So I was in the process of doing research . . . and I thought why don't I go and do nursing? And then of course everyone [her family] was opposed to it, because the whole perception of nurses back home is so different. Back home, nurses are not paid well. It's like they are looked down upon because of the kinds of stuff they do. Of course they do all the dirty work after the doctors. They take instructions.

Her description highlights the perception of nursing in her home country from the point of view of her own privileged background.

Immigrant Women and Professional Identity Formations in the United States

After migration, women like Rose, who come from class-privileged backgrounds in their home countries, craft professional identities as nurses in the United States. Rose detailed the transformative process that takes place upon migration and described how nursing as a profession is perceived differently in the United States. She listed the potential rewards of getting into such a field within the United States: "And of course from doing research I realized that nursing is not what everyone thinks. It is different here . . . you can do more. You can do nursing, you can go further, you can do your master's, even get a doctorate . . . do anything you wish to do." Rose further provides a glimpse of the ways she crafts her professional identity within the field while making clear professional distinctions between nursing in the United States and in her home country of Ghana:

> Then also by reading, I also realized that it is such a broad field. So I don't even have to do bedside nursing if I don't want to. . . . Back home you don't find nurses progressing from bedside to doing research, you know, doing public health. We have school nurses, nurse practitioners that work directly with the doctors, we even have nurses that prescribe medication. So I'm like, this is broad and maybe I don't even have to end up maybe like my fellow nurses back home.

Rose's words express clearly her professional distancing from nurses in her home country of Ghana and nursing as practiced there. She claims a professional identity and discusses nursing as a field that has had ample opportunities for professional growth and development in the United States.

Rose also distanced herself professionally from co-ethnics in the United States by discussing her educational credentials and choice of specialization within the field of nursing. In discussing her educational history, she distances herself from other West African nurses by stating that she attended one of the prestigious schools in the area with highly ranked medical and nursing schools. In Rose's view, the majority of West African nurses in that region were more apt to attend community colleges rather than prestigious teaching and research institutions. In discussing her initial entry into the field, Rose details her excitement at being accepted into and getting her training from one of the best nursing schools in the country. When probed about how much the training that she received meant to her or for that matter the academic reputation of her nursing program, she responded, "Oh yes . . . oh yes . . . It mattered a great deal. And it's like it makes me a different nurse. I bet you if I had gone to one of these different community colleges, I would not have vision. I wouldn't know what is out there at all. The first time we got into nursing school . . . we are not just training nurses. We are training leaders."

Helen, a nurse from Sierra Leone, trained in her home country and moved to the United States with the determination to gain the necessary qualifications to work as a registered nurse. She crafted her professional identity in two ways. First she engaged in professional distancing from other Africans and Sierra Leoneans within the field through the choice of specific specialties and hospitals that did not have a sizeable African staff. Helen distanced herself from concentrations of co-ethnics in nursing homes and in low-prestige units of hospitals by actively seeking out areas with few other Africans. Second, she highlighted her professional orientation to the work. In speaking about her desire to migrate to the United States, Helen mentioned her desire to further her career in nursing as well as to gain the financial rewards that were impossible to achieve as a nurse in her home country. She stated, "My decision to come to the United States was actually based on of course moving up academically and moving up financially." She recalled the advice given to her by someone in her country about the benefits of migration for her professional and financial advancement: "So the person said to me, 'If you have a way to go abroad, your career will pay off big time, as when you go abroad, if you decide to act on your goals and your dreams, you will succeed.'"

Helen's words encapsulate the dreams and desires of many migrants. However, in her narrative, Helen also exhibits a firm sense of her identity as a skilled professional who views migration to the United States as a way to further her professional goals: "My goal was to continue nursing to the highest level that I could." She expands this professional identity further by explaining that upon migration she was able to obtain a job at a nursing home, but she did not like the job. She said, "I started working in a nursing home and I did not like it. Because I knew, of course, that wasn't my goal either. I mean I wanted more, you know, out of the profession, than that."

Rachel, another nurse participant, exhibited a similar drive and ambition and also crafted her image as a professional nurse by distancing herself from low-prestige work in the nursing field. By distancing herself from lower-prestige jobs such as nurses' aides in nursing homes—the types of jobs that have typically seen a concentration of Black African women—this woman is crafting an image as a skilled professional. Rachel detailed her struggle to make a life in the United States when she first migrated. She discussed the challenges of trying to get recertified as a nurse while going through difficulties in her marriage, severe hardship, and changing her immigration status from a temporary visa to a more permanent settlement. However, in stressing her determination to make it in America, she also expressed a particular disdain for lower-prestige healthcare work. She expressed vehemently her refusal to perform lower-prestige care work because she was already a licensed nurse in her native Ghana. She stated, "So when I came, people advised me to be a nursing assistant, and I said I am going to take the exam. I would do whatever to take the exam and pass, because I am not going to work as a nursing assistant with my certificate. . . . So the difference is . . . I refused, and they [other African immigrants] told me, 'Oh you can do it.' I said 'No, I am not going to do it. I am not going to do it. I am a nurse, and I am a nurse . . . and a good one at that.'"

Helen also expressed pride in her career as a nurse, but unlike Rachel, who speaks about being a middle-class professional, Helen viewed nursing in terms of skill required and the types of duties that she needed to perform. Helen differentiated between work as a registered nurse in a nursing home versus a hospital in terms of the perceived skill requirement and professionalism of both jobs. In discussing her experience working in a nursing home, she states,

> It really, really wasn't satisfying for me; despite it was a nursing job it wasn't satisfying for me. In terms of skill level, in terms of professional development, it wasn't really, really satisfying for me. . . . So I was in this nursing home, I was still not satisfied with what I doing. I said this is not my own calling. I want more in terms of academical skills, in terms of professional, in terms of all that. So I left this nursing home, and I started speaking with people, you know, talking to different people, asking people how I could manage to get a job at the time.

Helen's interview describes how, in a bid to craft a professional identity as a skilled and professional nurse, she employs professional distancing from other African women. She embarks on a deliberate strategy to both physically and discursively separate from others like her. Discussing the hospital where she worked at the time of the interview, she was extremely proud of the fact that it was a nationally ranked teaching and research hospital. However, in addition to describing the hospital in terms of its reputation, Helen characterized the hospital and its staff in explicitly racial terms. She took pride in the fact that the racial composition of both staff and patients at the hospital was predominantly white.

> It's a hospital that I want to proudly say is . . . it's a predominantly white hospital. And so given the fact . . . that I wanted to surround myself with people who are . . . first of all, number one, I wanted to get out of an area . . . I wanted to surround myself with people who actually I could learn a lot from and I when I say learn a lot, in terms of professional development, you know. And so, my aim was to move away from hospitals that employed a lot of Sierra Leoneans, you know. I said in order for me to get where I needed to go I needed to get away from all of that.

Another Sierra Leonean nurse, Harriet, similarly elaborates on professional distancing as a discursive and material move enacted by some West African nurses to actively separate themselves from co-ethnics and gain entrée into specializations that were predominantly white. Harriet explained that that she was active and engaged in the Sierra Leonean community in the Washington metropolitan area. She even attended a church with a majority Sierra Leonean congregation, but when working she actively distanced herself from co-ethnics. She stated,

> Okay, but in terms of work, I decided to stay away from Sierra Leoneans. The ER [emergency room] where I work, there is only one other Sierra Leonean working there, and people there don't even know that we are from the same country. So in terms of work I try to stay away. Sierra Leoneans work in the hospital but in the ER . . . well, this is another thing. I always pick areas where I know that Sierra Leoneans are not in. Because as long as it's very, very challenging, they would not be there. So I always pick the areas that are very, very challenging.

Harriet's words show that professional distancing for West African women involves not only physically separating from co-ethnics but also seeking specializations that were predominantly white.

Professional Distancing and Racial Identities in the United States

So why would a group of women from Africa make the choice to distance themselves from others within the same employment field and why would they seek to work within institutions that are characterized as predominantly white? Analysis of the narratives of the women in this study shows that professional distancing occurs as direct result of nurses' perception of racial hierarchies within the field and their experiences with racism and discrimination. In their experiences with nursing, African women become aware that Black women from Africa occupy the lowest rungs of the nursing hierarchy and are concentrated in specializations viewed as mundane or less complicated, presumed to require little skill or intelligence (Barbee 1993; Hagey et al. 2001). They also experience discrimination on the basis of their race as well as their geographical origin as women from Africa. While the women in this study clearly understand and articulate racism and racist practices within the institution of nursing, they have internalized the racial hierarchies within the field as natural. To combat these negative associations of Blackness and Africanness with professional stagnation, African women employ professional distancing as one strategy to differentiate themselves from those negative connotations and advance themselves within the field, achieve professional satisfaction, and realize personal ambitions.

One participant sees clear racial hierarchies and stratification within the field. She states, "You see I've enjoyed nursing very much. But one thing, when I came over here to the United States as a registered nurse, the nurses here were all white, and the nursing assistants were all Blacks. And I had difficulty." Many other participants discussed the racial hierarchies within the field and understood that as African women immigrants, they occupied the positions and specializations that were considered less desirable. Sarah, a woman from Liberia, worked as a nurse practitioner at the time of the interview. She had occupied all the ranks of the nursing profession, starting out as a certified nursing assistant, all the way to becoming a nurse practitioner. She explained the particular systems of stratification within the nursing field and detailed where Africans were located within the system. She also detailed her experiences working as a nurse in the intensive care unit (ICU). In speaking about her job in this high-pressure and demanding field within nursing, she employs professional distancing but also gives a candid view of her assessment of race relations and racial hierarchies: "One thing I will say the ICU is very, very, very . . . it's a racist place. It's a racist place. I work there, but I will say . . . you gotta be quote unquote smart, you gotta be a Caucasian to work there." Sarah's words show that whiteness was associated with specializations that required more intellectual rigor and skill.

Previous scholarship dealing with immigrant women of color documents the presence of racialized hierarchies within nursing in which immigrant women are more likely than native nurses to be in labor-intensive specializations with high burnout rates (George 2005; Ong and Azores 1994). Assessment of Sarah's words provide us with a context for understanding professional distancing both as a discursive strategy but also as a material way that these women sought to advance their careers by proving their exceptionalism. Professional distancing was enacted as a way to maneuver within racially stratified structures. Sarah's words exemplify the racial stratification as perceived by a number of the women I encountered in my research. She states,

> If you are a Black woman working in the ICU, they say, "Wow, she's smart." And I don't think that should be the case. Everyone should be able to work there. Now, working in the nursing home, when I worked as a CNA it was majority Africans. 'Cause most people don't want to do that work. 'Cause it's quote unquote, it's a dirty job. So it's the Africans, you know. . . . Now it's the majority it's Africans who work as CAN; as a medical assistant, you have mostly Hispanic. Hispanic young ladies working as medical assistant. . . . As a nurse in the telemetry unit, I found it was mostly African nurses. When I worked at the ICU, it was a different ballgame. It was mostly Caucasian in the ICU.

Professional distancing is just one response to the concentration of Black women and African women within specializations that are deemed undesirable within the field. In addition to professional distancing and discursively setting themselves apart from the concentration of co-ethnics, African women in my sample also stressed the attainment of educational credentials and their professional orientation and hardworking personas as way to inject worth and meaning into their experiences of work. They viewed getting additional educational credentials and moving into fields and specializations that were less dominated by Africans as a way to solidify their professional identities, enhance their career opportunities, and gain self-worth. They also saw education as a means to combat racism in the field. Professional distancing is therefore one of a number of strategies used to gain self-worth and professional advancement in the face of perceived obstacles.

Future Research Directions and Implications

Professional distancing, a type of boundary work enacted by West African women to distinguish themselves from co-ethnics at work, raises questions about racial and gendered identities among Black immigrant groups in the United States. Those cases wherein women express pride in working in institutions and specialties that are predominantly white raise questions about the meanings nurses attach to race and their identity as Black women in the United States. The particular location of this group, as Black immigrant women from West Africa who faced racialized and gendered hierarchies in the nursing field, suggests that future work on immigrant care workers should take into account intersectional analyses of race, class, gender, ethnicity, and national origin in interrogating immigrant experiences within work settings in the United States. Furthermore, this chapter has shown that taking into account transnational understandings of care work and contexts of care in immigrant sending countries could add useful and nuanced understandings of care in the United States.

13

Ethnic Logics

• • • • • • • • • • • • • • • • • • • •

Race and Ethnicity in Nanny Employment

CAMERON LYNNE MACDONALD

Care for very young children is arguably one of the most emotionally fraught areas of market-based care work. Although most Americans accept the educational benefits of institutional kindergarten and even preschool education, care for children birth to age three is still considered to be the realm of mothers (Duffy 2011; Hays 1996). Given their role as maternal substitutes, childcare workers must navigate a perilous line between giving good care and threatening the mother's place as primary parent (Macdonald 2010). Further, care for the very young has yet to be fully professionalized, so outside of institutionalized day care, education and credentialing rarely plays a role in the construction of skill in early child care. Instead, workers are generally hired based on their personal characteristics, and thus race and ethnicity become salient in unusual ways in employer preferences.

My research on in-home childcare employers indicates that they use what I call "ethnic logics" as they search for the right provider. Ethnic logics are strategies designed to match a certain set of desired services with the presumed characteristics of prospective employees. These sorting mechanisms operate in hiring for nurturant care, but they vary from context to context and employer to employer, as well as within a given labor market. They are systematic only in how employers delve into a "cultural toolkit" to solve particular life problems (Swidler 1986). Ethnic logics bring together two sets of cultural assumptions: about the nature of the care to be provided and about the characteristics a worker needs to provide this care. In the case of child care, cultural norms articulate the kind of nurture a child purportedly needs at each developmental stage, providing a basis for childcare employers to match children's developmental needs with a range of stereotypes associated with particular racial and ethnic groups.

The employers I studied deployed ethnic logics strategically to help them make the best possible match between their beliefs about the personal characteristics of an ethnic or racial group (for example, West Indian women have soothing, gentle dispositions; Irish women are energetic and extroverted) and assumptions about the nature of the service to be provided (for example, calm, reassuring care helps newborns thrive; toddlers need help developing physical coordination and social skills). I observed these logics in action as employers resolved a variety of childcare problems, including recruiting and selecting their first nanny, changing nannies, and retrospectively justifying their choice of a particular nanny. In this chapter, I present an analysis of the hiring strategies used by employers in my study. I show that race, ethnicity, and gender count in care work hiring decisions, but they do so in more complex ways than the dominant theories about discrimination in nurturant care labor markets might lead us to expect.

Accounting for Discrimination in Hiring Home-Based Care Workers

Two theoretical approaches dominate the literature on how race and ethnicity shape the market for domestic workers and childcare providers. The first approach focuses on how supply and demand affect labor markets and sort workers into jobs; the second gives culture a central role, arguing that racial and/or ethnic stereotypes determine whether employers view specific groups as likely (or not) to "fit" in a given employment setting. My research suggests that while supply and demand for low-skilled workers may structure the local labor market for childcare workers, the hiring process within a given labor market is primarily culturally determined, although not in the ways that scholars have previously indicated.

Most research on the structure of labor markets for domestic workers and nannies relies on queuing theory (Reskin and Roos 1990; Thurow 1969). This model asserts that employers rank groups of prospective employees according to such factors as their education, job skills, gender, and race. Workers rank prospective jobs, ordering them in terms of wages, working conditions, and prestige. The ordering of these two queues varies according to worker supply, changes in the relative composition of a given occupation, and changes in customers' needs and expectations.

Scholars who apply queuing theory to explain the racial/ethnic mix among domestic workers in the United States use a globalized version of queuing theory that adds the worker's place in the global economy and migration status as sorting factors in hiring. This model leads to the conclusion that low-wage nurturant and non-nurturant paid care workers will be recruited from the most exploitable groups in the population, particularly recent immigrants and women of color (Colen 1995). The specific immigrant and ethnic groups scholars have identified using global queuing theory vary by region. This is not surprising, since migration flows and labor markets, though shaped by the same broad economic, social, and political forces, are also regional in nature. For instance, domestic and childcare markets in New York City are dominated by West Indian women (Brown 2011; Colen 1990; Wrigley 1995), while in Los Angeles the overwhelming majority are Latina (Hondagneu-Sotelo 2007).

Hiring patterns in the nurturant care sectors of domestic work, however, suggest a more complex process than global queuing theory indicates. Unlike non-nurturant domestic workers such as housekeepers and cleaners, childcare workers and home health aides are not drawn from a single group but rather from a wider range of ethnic and racial groups (Duffy 2011; Stacey 2011). This difference implies that for nurturant care workers, factors other than job and labor queues shape employers' decisions.

Scholars who emphasize cultural influences in employers' hiring practices focus on ethnic and racial stereotyping. They argue that employers base their hiring decisions on ethnic similarity or difference, seeking the "cultural comfort" this similarity or difference brings. For instance, in the area of child care, employers from racially disadvantaged groups have been found to prioritize "racial safety," leading them to hire care providers whose race or ethnicity is the same as or similar to their own (Hertz and Ferguson 1996; Tuominen 2003; Uttal 1996; Uttal and Tuominen 1999). Conversely, white employers may seek women of color to create race-based status hierarchies in childcare situations (Wrigley 1995).

Thus, two types of stereotypes come into play in hiring for care work: in the first, a racial-ethnic group signifies hierarchy and power in the employer-employee relationship; in the second, ethnic stereotypes signal similarity. Yet, in paid child care, hiring for subordination or hiring for similarity are insufficient strategies. Working mothers cannot directly supervise all of a childcare worker's interactions with their young children. They must rely on the caregiver's judgment and "natural" inclinations. Hiring decisions therefore involve screening for personal qualities such as nurturance, intelligence, and responsibility—characteristics that are culturally gendered and raced. Although we have rich evidence that hiring the "right type" of caregiver for a particular kind of care is an inherently racialized process (Glenn 1992; Sacks 1990), very little research has explored how employers link certain gender or racial/ethnic characteristics with particular interactive skills.

A careful examination of the choices made by Boston-area employers of in-home childcare workers shows that although ethnic logics may operate in conjunction with forms of discrimination based on similarity or difference, or on racial hierarchy, they themselves are distinct mechanisms for taking race/ethnicity into account in hiring.

Hiring In-Home Child Care in Boston: A Case Study

I conducted in-depth, semi-structured, and open-ended interviews with one hundred individuals (thirty working mothers, fifty nannies and au pairs, and twenty childcare placement agency owners) in the greater Boston area.[1] The employers worked at least thirty hours per week outside of the home and employed in-home care for at least one child under school age. The majority held managerial and professional jobs. Within these parameters, however, there was variation: employers with one to five children, with children at different developmental stages, and from various ethnic and socioeconomic backgrounds.[2]

Because I sought nannies who would be representative of all in-home childcare providers in the region, I conducted surveys in thirty-seven parks and playgrounds in affluent communities around the greater Boston area. My goals were to collect data (the mix of live-in and live-out nannies, the racial-ethnic mix of nannies and au pairs) for each area and to recruit potential interview respondents.[3] I also interviewed representatives from every greater Boston area childcare placement agency to learn how agency personnel thought race/ethnicity affected their clients' hiring decisions.

I expected to find the ethnic stratification in childcare other researchers had reported for large urban locations in the United States. However, surveying the region's parks and playgrounds turned up a much greater variety among the childcare work force than other studies have indicated. Instead of finding one low-status immigrant group that dominated the childcare labor market, like West Indians in New York City or Latinas in Los Angeles, my research assistant and I encountered immigrant childcare workers from Ireland, various parts of Latin America and the Caribbean, and from China. We also met nannies who were college-age white women from Boston and from economically depressed regions of the United States, and au pairs from all over Europe.[4]

Ethnic Logics in Action

The wide range of women we found working as full-time nannies for preschool children suggests that Boston area employers did not seek the lowest-cost childcare providers. Had they followed the logic of queuing theory, seeking the most populous and lowest-skilled workers from among the immigrant population in the Boston area, they would have employed immigrants from Haiti or the Dominican Republic, or women from Puerto Rico (the latter offering the added benefit of being American citizens). Instead, women from these sending countries were more likely to be clustered in lower-status, lower-paying housekeeping and elder-care jobs. Among nannies, no single group dominated the market. Instead, a wide array of individuals—immigrants, U.S.-born white women, and European au pairs—cared for preschool age children. It is possible that Boston is unique in its diverse nanny population, or, conversely, that researchers in other cities have focused on one ethnic group to the exclusion of others, creating an illusion of homogeneity.

This racial/ethnic variety among Boston-area childcare workers does not mean that stereotypes played little role in employers' hiring decisions. Rather than seeking workers lowest in the labor queue, or hiring merely for ethnic similarity/difference, Boston area employers used ethnic logics to hire the right nanny, or at least to justify (in retrospect) that they had done so. First, they interpreted the cultural norms regarding the proper care of young children, relying mainly on child-rearing advice literature, which emphasizes the importance of intensive mothering and concerted cultivation (Hays 1996; Lareau 2003). Based on what they learned from these manuals about children's changing developmental needs, employers then envisioned a set of personal qualities a caregiver must possess in order to meet those needs. Finally, using that image, they interpreted existing racial/ethnic stereotypes to produce an ethnic match for the developmentally ideal nanny. Importantly, while the outcome of this process differed from one mother to another, the interpretive calculation, the ethnic logics in play, remained consistent across mothers of children in each age group.

The employers I interviewed believed the birth-to-three period to be crucial to their child's emotional, social, and cognitive development and worried about experts' pronouncements that during this early period, maternal care is essential. Since these mothers could not provide full-time care, they compromised and convinced themselves that, as one employer termed it, "maternalesque" nurture, along with social and cultural capital, could be transmitted via a nanny. At the same time, these employers believed themselves alone to be ultimately responsible for how their children turned out. Lastly, they articulated a strong belief in an early childhood model of concerted cultivation (Lareau 2003). This meant an emphasis on cognitive and verbal development, closely supervised social lives, and involvement in activities structured to stimulate growing brains (Macdonald 2010). Employers justified work time outside the home as a way to finance the early development activities designed to ensure their children's upward mobility. This complex set of beliefs meant that hiring the right nanny was a high-stakes maneuver in a mother's plan to ensure her child's overall development and her success as a mother.

Care Criteria by Developmental Stages

Given the stages-of-development approach taken by most child-rearing manuals and the high level of familiarity with these books demonstrated by the employers, it is not surprising that they understood their children as having distinct, developmentally specific needs, even during the brief period from birth to age three. Employers tailored their hiring practices for the stages of infancy, toddlerhood, and preschool.

Infancy

For children from birth to approximately age one, employers had two overriding concerns: safety and nurture. Employers screened for safety by interviewing only nannies trained in infant CPR and expressing a preference for nannies with infant care experience. They satisfied the need for a nanny able to form a secure bond with their child while leaving the mother-infant bond intact by carefully observing baby-nanny interactions and by using ethnicity as a proxy.

To evaluate a care provider's interactive skills, employers watched closely during the employment interview, and often for a period after the hire. Did the nanny cuddle the baby? How did the baby respond to her? One white employer explained why she hired a forty-two-year-old woman from Jamaica this way: "And I think I knew pretty soon after she came that she was the right person for us, because she seemed so comfortable with the baby. She just picked her right up, bounced her, and the kid was asleep." A second white employer hired a fifty-three-year-old woman from the West Indies because, in her estimation, women from the Caribbean were "very religious" and "very good with children and stuff like that." A third noted that her West Indian caregiver had "always worked as a domestic . . . and she did more than just babysit. She really *took care* of people." A fourth employer praised her nanny's ability to soothe children, referring to it as "Jamaican voodoo."

Other mothers specifically sought out undocumented immigrants because they were likely to be older than legal nannies who often looked to switch out of nanny work as they got older. These employers generalized from characteristics such as older and Caribbean to "grandmotherly," and therefore able to create a stable, loving bond with an infant without encroaching on maternal territory. This kind of stereotyping extended to European au pairs and to American-born nannies. In these cases, rather than using age as a signifier for nurture and safety, employers sought what they described as "wholesomeness," equating it with whiteness. The owner of a nanny placement agency explained to me that nannies from Rust Belt states were affordable because of the relative lack of economic opportunities there. But midwestern nannies also held appeal because most of her clients were looking for "a nice fresh-faced kid," "someone from young white America" to come live with them. Her clients were "not open to" candidates of color.

A similar calculus around wholesomeness functioned in hiring European au pairs, but in these cases, wholesomeness derived from country of origin or rural upbringing. For example, a white employer felt that a Scandinavian au pair would be superior to a British au pair: "I didn't go with British au pairs.

We had just recently been to London and . . . having seen London and seen what the teenagers and the young women there were looking like, it struck me much more like it was too city, and sophisticated. . . . I sort of had an image of it being more quiet, a little bit more laid back in terms of the Scandinavian countries. . . . I've never been to a Scandinavian country in my life, but I had been in London, and it was a lot of hustle and bustle and people moving around." Employers of European au pairs voiced a general preference for Scandinavian girls based on the view that Scandinavian origin signified rural wholesomeness.

Toddlerhood

As children developed mobility and early language and interaction skills, employers grew more concerned about cognitive stimulation, socializing, and exploration of the wider world. "Grandmotherly" nannies, lauded for their patience during infancy, often came to be viewed as too sedentary to meet a toddler's needs. These needs were not defined in terms of play or activity, which could be obtained at a playground, but rather in terms of taking classes, going to library "read-alongs," visiting museums, and building social capital through playgroups with children in the care of other nannies.

For example, one mother explained that she had been happy with her sixty-year-old Chinese immigrant nanny until her daughter passed the one-year mark (at the time of our interview the child was eighteen months old). The mother confessed that she was secretly seeking to replace her nanny: "[Initially], I liked the idea of an older person, because I think that's a really good influence on the child. Now I'm sort of thinking that maybe I would like someone a little younger . . . 'cause now that she's a toddler, she's very active and . . . The babysitter I have is very nice, [but] she's very shy, so she doesn't take her many places where there [are] lots of people. So [she] isn't really socialized very well, I think, with other children." Unbeknownst to this employer, her nanny was aware of these concerns. She knew her employer wanted her to take the baby to the larger parks and playgrounds, to the Museum of Science and the library. "The farther we go, the happier [the parents are]," she explained. She resisted these outings not because of her own age, but because of the child's: "[She] is too young, I mean to excel right now, you know?" She added, "She is a baby. Just a baby. And they have expectations [spreads her arms apart] like this, you know? And how long is babyhood?"

Conflicts about what was best for a given child at a specific stage played out silently and drove nanny turnover. Nannies viewed themselves as adapting day-to-day to their grounded knowledge of the particular child, while mothers looked ahead to the next developmental stage. As one mother noted, "I read so many books because I don't know what to expect from the next developmental stage until it hits me in the face." For employers, preparing for a child's next stage often meant recruiting a new nanny. This developmentally specific turnover explains why, although most of the nannies I interviewed stayed within the occupation for many years, they averaged only about eighteen months with a given employer.

Language acquisition also became an increasingly important concern during toddlerhood. Employers who had no objections to the lilting accents of West Indian nannies during infancy began to worry as their toddlers started to mimic their childcare providers' language patterns. Others began to strategize about bilingualism. The mother quoted above thought she might replace her nanny with "an au pair from Europe who could expose [the baby] to a new language." Employers who hired Latina nannies did so in order to give their children the advantage of being bilingual. However, they too were concerned that the nanny speak the "right kind" of Spanish. A Honduran nanny described the emphasis her employers placed on her language skills this way: "The children spoke Spanish [with me] because the parents wanted the children to learn Spanish well," and they told her, "They learn Spanish with you because Puerto Rican Spanish is not good. . . . The Mexican Spanish, they sing." The employers I interviewed who hired Spanish-speaking nannies specifically sought nannies from Cuba and South and Central America for their language skills.

Finally, toddlerhood brought socializing, and with it a concern about a child's potential exclusion from the right playgroups. Neighborhood playgroups were organized around nanny and au pair networks, and along strict ethnic lines. At any large area playground, one could observe West Indian nannies and their charges in one corner, Latina nannies and the children in their care in another, Scandinavian au pairs' children in a third, and at-home moms in a fourth. These conventions had drawbacks. As one employer noted, "My kids are not socializing with our friends' kids. They are basically hanging out with the nanny's friends' kids. That bugs me." All the employers I interviewed complained that stay-at-home mothers were not open to including nannies or au pairs in informal playgroups. One admitted that this made her feel additionally guilty about working: "There are certainly lots of playgroups in which a nanny is not welcome, because the playgroups are to some degree for the kids, but they are largely for the mothers. So there is a piece that [my son] misses out on because I'm not at home."

The ethnic profile of the typical nanny varied by neighborhood and urban/suburban location, and cross-socializing was uncommon. Immigrant Irish women who populated Boston's Beacon Hill neighborhood did not socialize with West Indian nannies who dominated child care in Cambridge, for instance. Nanny networks have been described as an important job search avenue for nannies (Hondagneu-Sotelo 2007). Networks' role in building social capital for children has not received similar attention. Employers, however, were well aware of the importance of hiring from the local nanny network in order to foster social connections and ensure that their children would not be ostracized.

One employer's hiring strategy was perhaps the most striking example of this phenomenon. An African American physician with Caribbean roots, she had initially sought to employ someone "like me": "I would have liked to have someone Black. Just because of—some identification issues—and because we were in a neighborhood that is almost all white, so just to have a little bit more . . . diversity." However, in her affluent suburb, young, white migrants from the Midwest dominated the nanny network, mainly for logistical reasons. Unlike some immigrants, migrants from Iowa and Nebraska could drive. And unlike older immigrant nannies with families of their own, young women did not object to living in and earning lower wages in exchange for room and board.

After rejecting several Afro-Caribbean applicants, this employer hired a young white woman from Nebraska who had been a nanny in the area previously. One of her primary reasons for abandoning her commitment to ethnic similarity was that the white nanny was already well-connected in local nanny networks, and she viewed these connections as advantageous for her one-year-old son. "As he gets bigger and more interactive, it will give him the opportunity of having other kids to play with." A white urban-dwelling employer used a similar ethnic logic, but in the opposite direction. She described hiring her African American, live-out nanny this way: "[She] is great with [my daughter]. . . . She has all these friends in the area who are working around here, so it was actually a nice match in that way." Like many Cambridge employers, she chose a live-out Caribbean nanny whose ethnic group was populous enough in the neighborhood that she could create a social life for her child.

Preschool

As children moved closer to preschool age, employers faced two primary decisions: how to prepare their child cognitively for the fierce competition for admittance to the best schools; and how to pass on their own cultural capital via the nanny. This transition brought on concerns about the nanny's early-childhood education credentials and her ability to both cognitively stimulate the child and provide the proper class-based cultural exposure.

A Latina employer described this conundrum. As a second-generation Venezuelan immigrant, she was deeply concerned that her children be bilingual and understand some of their heritage. Her desire for cultural comfort and security in being able to trust her nanny in her children's infancy was so strong that she chose to employ the Venezuelan housekeeper who had worked for her mother and helped in her own upbringing. Her nanny, by then in her sixties, had adopted the two girls into her own extended family, which thrilled the employer during her daughters' infant and toddler years. But as her older daughter approached preschool age, she was concerned that the girl "really missed out on being with other kids." When that daughter entered preschool, she planned to replace her nanny and the extended family. She explained, "This time I'm going to do a full-interview process. . . . The ideal would be possibly someone who was doing work in child development or something. . . . I would still love someone who is Spanish speaking, because being bilingual is important to me."

In planning for preschool, employers had a new set of concerns, primarily around education, and, not incidentally, social class. They wanted a nanny who could provide the cognitive stimulation that would prepare their children for school and who could supply cultural capital resembling their own. This often meant moving away from an immigrant caregiver. As one employer remarked regarding her West Indian caregiver, "I don't know what the right answer is . . . like when [the baby] starts like going, 'Why, why, why?' I don't know how [the nanny] is going to respond, if she's going to give answers that I [pause] like. If she will be able to provide the sort of breadth and depth of experiences. Will she take her to, like, the Children's Museum?" An African American employer looked ahead to a time when her child's developmental needs might go beyond what her nanny's working-class upbringing could supply. "His needs will change over time, and that will call for reevaluation of what his child care is, and we've begun to think about that in terms of when he gets to be two and needs more structured exposure to other kids to learn things like sharing and how to play, and more developmental things."

Children's transition to preschool also marked the beginning of unease for employers of color who had hired for ethnic similarity. The Latina (or Black, West Indian, or Irish) nanny who had been nurturing during infancy, provided the language skills needed in toddlerhood, and fit into the local nanny playgroups, now lacked a key characteristic: class similarity. Another African American employer explained the problem she faced with her African American nanny: "I thought that if there was sort of racial parity among us, then there's a common ground, there's a sense of solidarity in the project of caring for these children. And that maybe it would take away some of the edge of inequality inherent in the relationship of employer/employee, to the extent that, well, they might feel more comfortable working for a Black couple as opposed to a white one. And assuming that they do feel more comfortable, and they can feel more comfortable because, after all, we are all Black." Racial and ethnic similarity added comfort (on both sides), but it did not close the gap in social class and culture. She continued, "In cultural terms, we don't have a lot in common. . . . It's mostly because of class, it turns out. So, politically we're not similar; our education and backgrounds are hugely different. . . . So the racial as proxy for cultural commonality equation doesn't work. Because we don't even like the same Black music, you know?" This employer also bemoaned her nanny's tendency to take the children to McDonald's for lunch. She stressed healthy eating with her nanny, but she avoided discussing McDonald's because the topic was freighted with class connotations. She found that racial similarity did not translate into the cultural comfort she sought. For her, class trumped race as her children developed. Her next caregiver was a Brazilian au pair from a middle-class background.

Are Ethnic Logics Unique to Care Work?

Analysis of hiring in paid in-home child care shows how employers attempt to hire for developmentally specific caregiving qualities using ethnic logics. Working mothers are understandably concerned that the full-time parental substitute for their young children provide care that mirrors what they believe they would offer if they could. As a result, the quality of the "service triangle" (the interrelationship among the childcare worker, parent-employer, and child) is crucial to maternal success, and employers manage these relationships carefully (see Leidner 1993 for discussion of the service triangle). This makes the process of defining and hiring the "right type" of worker a more conscious and explicit undertaking, which also makes it a more observable phenomenon.

This study has demonstrated how childcare employers perform interpretive work that results in hiring nannies based on stereotyped assumptions about what race or ethnicity signify regarding a worker's emotional, intellectual, or cultural capacities. For working mothers, using ethnic logics involves hiring a nanny who is tailored to meet their child's developmental needs, or at least convincing themselves that they have done so. For nannies, ethnic logics result in being hired and fired based not on expertise but on personal characteristics that may have nothing to do with their skills as childcare providers. Further, the use of ethnic logics as a hiring strategy means that nannies often enter jobs with an invisible yet predetermined expiration date. Ironically, parents assume that they can and will adapt to their children's changing needs, but they often fail to apply this adaptability to paid caregivers.

Early child care is unique among paid care work in that it is the sole area of commodified care in which Americans have not reached cultural consensus on whether child care by someone other than the mother is appropriate and, if so, what good care looks like. Employers translate intensive mothering ideologies into racial-ethnic hiring strategies precisely because of this lack of consensus regarding what constitutes quality paid care for infants and toddlers. While ethnic logics are consistently applied in child care, the outcome of this process varies from one hiring situation to another. Each employer applies ethnic logics to the problem of compensating for maternal absence in a similar way, but they achieve varying results. The employment outcome varies from one employer to another because each employer's fantasy of her full-time presence in the home varies. Yet the process of translating ethnic characteristics into caregiving potential remains the same across settings.

The question remains, are ethnic logics unique to child care? No, but they are most prominent in the nurturant care sector. Karen Brodkin Sacks (1990, 188) argues, for example, that health care is "so stratified by race and gender that the uniforms worn to distinguish the jobs and statuses of healthcare workers are largely redundant." Similarly, home health aides are hired based on how different ethnic markers signify dedication to care, subservience, or the possibility of fictive kinship with the client (Stacey 2011). Ethnic logics are salient to hiring in the nurturant care sector because, given a dearth of measureable skills, client perceptions of worker's characteristics become a stand-in for an idealized notion of what the care entails. Therefore, the process of applying ethnic logics—of equating an employee's racial-ethnic characteristics with the qualities necessary to offer a set of services—are likely to be more common in paid care work, and also likely to be more resistant to change, than other forms of racial-ethnic discrimination in employment.

Notes

1 For details about the interviews and other aspects of the research methodology, see Macdonald (2010).
2 Of the thirty employers interviewed, six were women of color (three African Americans, one Asian American, and two Latinas) and two were single parents. Thirty-two of the eighty respondents were from mother-caregiver dyads. The remaining childcare providers and employers were not interviewed as part of dyads.
3 To ensure variation, I conducted individual interviews with no more than three individuals from the same network, although I did conduct a number of group interviews with childcare workers at parks and playgrounds. The analysis here is based primarily on the individual interviews.
4 Au pairs usually are women between eighteen and twenty-two who participate in a one-year cultural exchange program. In 2009, in exchange for forty-five hours per week of childcare, they received a stipend of $195 per week, plus room and board.

14

Caring or Catering?

• • • • • • • • • • • • • • • • • • • •

Emotions, Autonomy, and
Subordination in Lifestyle Work

RACHEL SHERMAN

In interviewing providers of a wide variety of lifestyle services, from personal assistance to interior design to real estate, I was struck by how much they talked about the emotional aspects of their work. Personal concierges,[1] for example, described having to listen to clients' personal problems "like a therapist." Gabrielle, a financial advisor, recounted repeatedly driving three hours round trip to have tea with an elderly, recently widowed client not to talk about her portfolio, which was "fine," but simply because "she's lonely, and she's scared." Zoe, an art advisor, told me her job involved providing "a lot of reassurance" to collectors worried about their decisions. Although they are hired explicitly for their skills in logistics and organizing, art advising, and financial planning, these respondents—like most others I interviewed—described intimate relationships with their clients in which emotional attention and support played a significant role.

These respondents do "lifestyle work," meaning that they use their expertise to help their (mostly wealthy) clients spend and invest money. The emotional work they perform in the course of their jobs is not "care" as it is typically defined in this volume and elsewhere because these service recipients do not depend on providers for basic needs fulfillment; indeed, the non-interactive skills providers deploy and the tasks they perform are not usually those associated with caring (except among personal chefs and some concierge work). The kind of attention lifestyle workers offer may, in fact, seem unnecessary or excessive, simply enacting and reproducing the class entitlements of consumers (Sherman 2007). On the other hand, this affective labor fits into a broad definition of care as customized, person-specific work "in which concern for the well-being of the care recipient is likely to affect the quality of services provided" (Folbre and Wright 2012, 4). This nurturing attention is also similar in some ways to the intangible, often invisible emotional engagement provided by caregivers in private homes or institutions (Lopez 2006b; Stacey 2011) or by "expert" care workers (Duffy 2011) and valued by analysts as a critical part of care.

At the same time, lifestyle workers' emotional work is not "emotional labor" as it was originally defined (Hochschild 1983; Lopez 2006b) because their interactions with clients are not scripted, standardized, or otherwise prescribed by and benefiting employers. Indeed, lifestyle workers usually work for themselves and thus are not supervised closely, if at all. The emotional work they do,[2] therefore, falls more under their own control. Furthermore, they are hired for their expertise in particular areas (financial planning, home organizing, interior design, and so on), which gives them power in relation to their clients. However, they depend directly on clients for continued employment. Thus they cannot refuse implicit or explicit demands for emotional support and attention, as some other providers of skilled services (surgeons, for example) can. In addition, because client-employers typically have more money and status than lifestyle workers do, these relations take place in a context of inequality and thus may feel subordinating to service providers.

This chapter looks at lifestyle workers' responses to the affective dimension of their jobs as it relates to this tension between autonomy and subordination. Drawing on interviews with thirty service providers in a range of occupations, I address the following questions: how do lifestyle workers experience the emotional aspects of their work and their relationships with clients? Do they see clients' emotional requirements as legitimate "needs" or excessive "demands"? And are their responses to these questions patterned according to particular features of their work?

I found that respondents did not experience the emotional dimension of their work as either exclusively negative or positive; most enjoyed at least some elements of their affective relationships with clients. But, as I will demonstrate, lifestyle workers did vary systematically in how they talked about their emotional work overall. I classify them into three groups. Those in the first group took the most positive view. They saw their emotional work as essentially voluntary, felt their clients' emotional needs were legitimate, and enjoyed their relationships with clients. Those in the second group were ambivalent, enjoying relationships with some of their clients but often feeling overwhelmed by clients' emotional demands; these respondents were more likely to see these demands as unreasonable and/or to feel subordinated by them. Those in the third category (primarily personal concierges) enjoyed giving their clients relief from stress by taking care of mundane tasks for them, but drew strong boundaries against forming close relationships. Those in the first category, in essence, tended to see their affective work as caring, while those in the second and third categories were more likely to perceive it as catering. I will argue that these differences arise primarily from differences in the professional status of the service provider.

Autonomy and Subordination in Emotional Work

Scholars of caring labor and in the broader field of interactive services have looked closely at workers' responses to the emotion work required of them. Arlie Hochschild (1983) believed that performing "emotional labor"—commodified feeling management and display, prescribed by managers in order to produce certain emotions in customers—had primarily negative effects on workers, particularly their alienation from their own feelings. However, copious research in the three decades since her groundbreaking study has shown that performing emotional labor is not necessarily detrimental to workers (see Lopez 2006b, 2010, and Wharton 2009 for reviews).

In particular, workers with more autonomy from bureaucratic routines and freedom from close supervision by managers have been shown to enjoy this work more and suffer fewer negative consequences such as burnout (Wharton 1999, 2009). Emotional work may feel more voluntary or altruistic to these workers, and it may be more likely to arise from basic imperatives of social interaction and/or from occupational norms rather than prescription by employers (Bolton and Boyd 2003). However, despite the burgeoning literature on emotional labor, work outside bureaucratic settings and free of managerial directives has rarely been investigated (but see Stacey 2011).

Particularly relevant here, the minimal literature on emotional work among professional and semiprofessional interactive workers has shown that providers of these services value and often enjoy the emotional work they do (George 2008; Gimlin 1996; Smith Maguire 2008). These researchers have identified a relationship between emotional work and professional identity among these workers, although this relationship is ambiguous (Gimlin 1996). Workers such as paralegals and beauty therapists use their emotional work and emotional self-management as the basis for claiming professionalism, seeing emotional work as a skill (Lively 2001; Sharma and Black 2001). But others, such as personal trainers, claim professionalism by distancing themselves from clients' emotional demands (George 2008; Sherman 2010).

My respondents provide an especially good case with which to continue investigating emotional work among "expert service providers" (George 2008), for two reasons. One, my respondents work in multiple fields and thus can provide comparative leverage that has largely been missing from previous occupational case studies. Two, because they serve predominantly wealthy clients, my respondents face a particularly notable tension between expertise/autonomy and dependency/subordination. On the one hand, these workers have power on the job for the reasons outlined above: they typically work for themselves, outside organizational hierarchies and managerial supervision, and they have some claim to expertise in their fields (which in some cases requires a license or credential). On the other hand, however, they are dependent on their clients, who are typically significantly wealthier than they and who (explicitly or de facto) function as their employers (not unlike domestic workers such as housecleaners and nannies). They thus walk a line between being servants and being experts—a line that depends largely on how clients treat them and what kind of deference and attention clients desire. This relationship also brings up empirical and normative questions about the difference between legitimate "needs" and unreasonable "demands."

Data and Methods

This chapter is based on two related sets of data. One set comes from an occupational study of personal concierges, for which I interviewed twenty-three people (primarily small business entrepreneurs) and conducted 160 hours of ethnography at a Manhattan concierge and personal assistant company (Sherman 2010, 2011). The other evidence comes from an ongoing exploration of the production of lifestyle among New York elites. As part of this project, I have interviewed expert service providers in several lifestyle work occupations. The sixteen respondents included here consist of four interior designers, one architect, three financial and philanthropic advisors, two art advisors (consultants who advise clients on purchasing and collecting art), one wedding photographer, a parenting expert, a personal chef, a real estate broker, and two educational tutors.

In total, I draw in this paper on thirty interviews with personal service providers, including fourteen interviews with personal concierges (two of whom had also worked as full-time personal assistants).[3] I use the variety of occupations represented here to look inductively at variation in providers' responses to the relational dimensions of their jobs. Although these respondents do very different kinds of work, they all have expertise in some field, work without managerial supervision and outside organizational hierarchies, and have significant face-to-face contact with their employer-clients, quite often in long-term relationships.

Interviews lasted one to two hours. Except for the parenting expert, who is a professional therapist, none of the respondents did jobs explicitly associated with the face-to-face provision of care. Only six of my respondents were men. All but three were whites born in the United States (one was African American, one Latin American, and one southern European). Most were in their thirties and forties, and all were college educated. These interviews were conducted between 2007 and 2012, primarily in and around New York City. (Four were telephone interviews with practitioners in other parts of the country.)

Emotional Expectations

Although they are presumably hired for their non-interactive expertise, respondents clearly demonstrated that part of what their wealthy clients expect from them is a high level of personalized, nurturing attention. As the examples below show, concierges provide this attention in response to implicit or overt client desires. This emotional work depends on a high degree of intimacy with clients. Providers often have access to clients' homes, mail, and/or personal documents or financial information. Knowledge about clients, from food preferences to renovation budgets, is essential to the provision of services. Furthermore, many of these service providers, particularly those who spend time in the home, interact with clients in the "backstage" areas of their lives, witnessing "private" moments.

Respondents overwhelmingly recounted listening to clients talk about personal issues. Marco, an art advisor, told me that "the joke is that you are trauma counselor, couples therapist, champion or booster, [and] curator." Lucy, a personal concierge who had been in the business for several years, said, "I think all the time I should put 'therapist' after my name on my business card. You know, because I get the whole life story. . . . You know everything about people. You know when the husband and wife have had a fight. You know what the resolution of the fight was. You know when they've gone to the lawyer."

Lifestyle workers were also often expected to provide reassurance to clients. Cora, who offered organizing, cooking, and errand services, said of organizing that part of her job was to help clients stop punishing themselves:

> A lot of people beat themselves up about what they haven't done. . . . They want, I think, a motivator, someone they can relate to, someone that understands, someone that's not judgmental. Judgmental is what they're most afraid of, because they're judging themselves so harshly. . . . And there's a lot of anxiety there, so I try to put people at ease right away and get to work and get them involved and whatnot.

Gabrielle, a financial advisor, recounted how her clients turned to her during the financial crisis. She said, "I mean, when the market was crashing . . . [my clients] would call me hysterical. 'Oh my God. Aaahh!' You know, full-bore crazy, out of their mind. 'What do I do? I'm gonna sell everything.' And it was everything I could do to calm them down." These examples show that responses to clients can involve both a kind of generic comfort ("You can do it") and, sometimes, a reassurance rooted specifically in the expertise of the service provider ("Don't sell everything").

Because lifestyle workers facilitate clients' consumption, they also have to assuage clients' insecurities about class and money. Zoe, an art advisor, talked about the buyer's remorse that sometimes set in after collectors purchased a piece of art, when they would panic and think they had made the wrong decision. She told me, "And then I have to remind them, they have a good eye. They're really knowledgeable. You know, [to remember] the core focus of their collection, et cetera." Here Zoe is indicating to the collectors—on the basis of her own expertise—that they do have an appropriate and reasonable taste in art, which is a form of class reassurance. Many providers described explicitly dealing with clients' issues about money. Judy, a financial advisor, called herself a "money therapist," because she directly confronts emotional and family conflicts around having and spending money. The prevalence of the "therapist" analogy in these interviews indicates the level of intimacy, as well as the client's expectation of listening and reassurance; implicit as well, perhaps, is a lack of reciprocity.

Responses to Emotional Work

I identified three types of response to this work among my interviewees, which varied according to their professional status. Respondents in more recognized professions, or with more established standing in semiprofessional occupations, spoke positively of their emotional work and relations with clients, and they framed clients' emotional demands of them as legitimate. Respondents in the second category, typically semiprofessionals working independently, expressed ambivalence, describing clients' emotional demands as excessive, overwhelming, and sometimes subordinating. The third type of response, common among personal concierges, who struggle for occupational legitimacy, emphasized the desire to help clients by taking care of tasks while retaining emotional distance from them.

Voluntary Intimacy and Legitimate Needs: High-Status Lifestyle Workers

Lifestyle workers who could claim higher status tended to see their emotional work in a positive light. These were service providers in recognized professions such as financial planning and therapy, as well as more successful or established entrepreneurs in occupations such as concierge service and interior design. First, they talked about relationships with clients as a favorite aspect of their work. Asked what she liked the most about her job, Judy, a financial advisor, said, "I think the part that I appreciate the most is clients' willingness to share such intimate parts of their life with me. You know, I think that's what makes this so much more than just a financial, numbers-crunching job."

Providers who responded positively to clients' emotional requirements tended to frame these as "needs" that it was reasonable to expect them to fulfill. They took a magnanimous view, often portraying the "need" as legitimate by virtue of being universal ("We all have our quirky stuff," Hannah, the owner of a concierge business with several employees, told me). These respondents did not typically describe setting boundaries with clients. For example, Gabrielle told me of her clients, "Everybody has my cell phone number, which I don't mind. I'm happy to take the call." She even spoke sympathetically of a client who had aggressively demanded her attention when Gabrielle was in the hospital. These respondents tended to describe the provision of attention as voluntary and the attention itself as genuine.

Indeed, some of these respondents described becoming close friends with clients over time, and their narratives tended to focus on these clients or on clients they liked. Hannah said, "My friends are my clients and my clients are my friends." Brooke, a longtime interior designer, told me how much she loved her clients, saying, "I feel it's very important to have a closeness." This emphasis highlights equality and reciprocity between service providers and clients. Notably, Hannah and Brooke are semiprofessionals, but Hannah is a very successful entrepreneur with several employees and very wealthy clients, and Brooke is a well-established designer with high-status and celebrity clients.

Respondents using this approach also typically took a sympathetic view of clients even when clients treated them badly. They reframed rudeness or making many demands as symptoms of legitimate emotional distress. Sarah, a parenting expert, told me she becomes irritated when her wealthy clients are "abrasive" and expect her to "fix" their children's problems immediately. But, she said, when she gets a sense of their issues, she becomes less annoyed. For example, when they talk about their childhood, she said, "you instantly have the insight into what it is they're trying to escape, and what it is they're trying to repair, and what is they're afraid of. And then of course you have total empathy for them." Gabrielle made a similar interpretive move. Asked how her clients treated her, she said, "I work with a lot of really nice people. I mean, if anything, you know, I would say, you know, do my clients express fear emphatically, when something has gone really wrong? Yeah." This is a generous interpretation of their behavior, which highlights their vulnerability even as they make extreme demands on her (such as yelling "I need you!" over the phone when she is in a hospital bed).

Weak Boundaries and Excessive Demands: Independent Semiprofessionals

In contrast to respondents in higher-status occupations, independent semiprofessionals expressed ambivalence about the emotional dimensions of their work. These lifestyle workers interpreted some client desires as unreasonable demands rather than legitimate needs. Zoe, the art advisor, spoke derisively about "massaging" the "tender egos" of the collectors she worked with, whom she described as "shockingly insecure." Alice, a former personal assistant, described the woman for whom she had worked as unbearably needy, saying, "I think she really needed the idea that there was, like, this closeness . . . it was this need to have, like, this rapport that wasn't really there." Contrast Alice's response to Brooke's desire, quoted above, for closeness with her clients.

Demands for attention that seemed excessive often connoted subordination. Talia, a personal chef, distinguished between clients on the basis of "what they expect from me: if I'm serving them, or I'm, like, helping them." She loved her relationships with clients who were "normal, appreciative, down to earth, [who] understand that they're human and I'm human." She contrasted these relationships of mutual recognition to relations with clients who are "used to just being served, giving orders, not being personal, and expecting everything to function around them and to their satisfaction." Talia characterized these clients as demanding an unreasonable amount of her caring attention. "Some of these people are spoiled in a way that they need constantly to feel like they're catered to and taken care of and nourished. . . . In a way, I do have to be like caring and loving like their mother and show that I'm taking care of them." These clients want to feel taken care of. But Talia believes they also want to feel "catered to," which she thinks is not legitimate.

While these lifestyle workers talked about enjoying their relationships with some clients, they also described being depleted emotionally by the affective elements of their work (not unlike home care aides [Stacey 2011]). David, an interior designer, told me he found working with residential clients "physically and emotionally draining" because of his proximity to personal information, conflict, and personal drama, such as infidelity, familial resentment, and divorce. He associated this drain with "living in servitude" to these clients, thereby connecting subordination to emotional work. Talia said, "You constantly have to give your guts [emotionally]. . . . It can wear you out."

Indeed, several of these respondents described feeling that their own lives were overwhelmed by clients' needs, and they struggled to set limits. Zoe, the art advisor, told me that clients would cry on her shoulder about their personal problems to the point that she had to address these boundary issues in therapy. She said, "I'm much better at the boundaries [now]. . . . A shrink helped me on that one. Because I'd be like, 'And [my client's] getting a divorce, and this is happening, and that's happening [to her].' And my shrink would be like, 'And in *your* life?' I'd be like, 'I don't even know! It's horrible for [the client].'" A high-end real estate broker told me that he had to go to therapy to work through similar concerns related to his wealthy clients' conflicts about money. He said, "Since I'm bombarded with so many people's different issues about money, and all of these things, I need to keep myself grounded. Because I can't get all wrapped up in your issue."

These service providers often felt genuine concern for their clients, as Zoe's quote indicates; indeed, it is the attachment itself that can become problematic. Nancy told me how her life had been subsumed by her employer's when she was a personal assistant: "The more his life got complicated, I kept simplifying my life. I really wasn't living." She described feeling "incredible" and "liberated" when she left this job. Yet when I asked her why she had stayed with the employer for several years, she said, "I liked being needed." In general, these respondents liked having meaningful relationships with some of their clients, but felt it could easily go too far. Their desire for boundaries was not related to professional identity but rather to their need for a barrier against being over-taken by their clients' needs.

Executing Tasks and Maintaining Distance: Concierges

The third category was composed of people (primarily concierges) who liked helping clients but drew strong boundaries against close relationships. On the one hand, they enjoyed "helping" and often spoke positively about how their work had positive emotional effects on their clients, and sometimes on them as well. Louise, a concierge, described a client from out of state who asked her to deliver a birthday cake to a local friend. She said, "Her friend was just like, 'Wow,' starts crying. It was amazing. . . . It was very reward-ing, you know, and she said, like, 'Wow, thank you so much.'" Laura, another concierge, illuminated the link between completing practical tasks and alle-viating the client's anxiety. She described a client who "was just so stressed out with a medical proxy for her parents, and she just needed somebody to talk to and needed to reaffirm that everything is going to be okay. You know, 'I'm gonna get your iced tea. It was specially ordered and it'll be there today.' 'Oh, great!' . . . Sometimes it's a grounding mechanism to just reaffirm and, a friendly voice is going to take care of it." In this sense, concierges and others who do this kind of task show that "taking care of" tasks is implicitly "taking care of" people.[4]

Yet these respondents, for the most part, drew strong boundaries against inti-mate relationships with clients, trying to avoid being the "therapist" many of them thought their clients wanted. They preserved distance not because they found these relations draining but because they considered them unprofes-sional. As Claudia said, "You have to be friendly, you have to have some kind of relationship, because you are in their life doing these intimate types of tasks. However, you have to keep yourself separate because you have to be objective in what you're doing. . . . So I try and draw that line so that they know I like them, I know what their needs are, I take care of it, but at the same time it's a business relationship." As I have argued elsewhere (Sherman 2010), concierges struggle to professionalize their work, which has strong associations with uncommodi-fied family labor; maintaining this distance is part of that effort (see also George 2008, 2013).

Concierges were also the only respondents who mentioned cultivating emo-tional relationships with clients instrumentally, in order to get more business. Rebecca, a concierge, told me, "We push the relationship," meaning that the quality of the interaction will keep the client coming back. Laura, speaking of the same client mentioned above, said, "I try to keep the door open, because if there's a lot going on, I might be able to, like when I drop off the iced tea, [ask] 'Is there more that I can do for you today? How about the rest of the week?' . . . So it works for me too." Although this admission was not common, it exemplifies the kind of distancing view that most concierges took.

Implications for Emotional Work and Care

Individual characteristics doubtless play a role in the kind of attention clients desire and in how lifestyle workers experience those desires. But I have argued that lifestyle workers' responses to their own emotional work are also patterned according to their occupational status. The lifestyle workers in more professionalized occupations, or in privileged spaces within semiprofessional occupations, were more positive about their emotional work. Those in less established occupations wanted more emotional distance with clients and were more likely to see clients' emotional demands as excessive or inappropriate. This was true both of semiprofessionals such as art advisors and personal chefs and of personal concierges, although concierges tended to be more adamant from the beginning about maintaining distance, more concerned with professional status, and less drained by clients' needs.

The question then arises of what factors underlie this pattern. It is possible that clients ask less emotionally of higher-status lifestyle workers. But I also suspect that these workers interpret clients' emotional requirements more generously because they have a greater capacity to protect themselves emotionally and symbolically from subordination (see Hodson 2000; Sherman 2007). Professional recognition serves as a "status shield" against emotional demands that might otherwise feel subordinating (Hochschild 1983). And professionals in some categories (especially financial planning) may perceive less social distance between themselves and their clients since they are also quite affluent, which may also protect against feeling subordinated by demands for attention. Furthermore, professionals and successful entrepreneurs (such as Hannah) are essentially employed by clients, but they also typically have colleagues and employees, which may mitigate the intensity of the one-on-one relationship described by those who work alone with clients. More sustained comparative analysis would be needed to trace any of these patterns conclusively.

This analysis has several implications for emotional work in general, and for care work more narrowly defined. First, my findings support previous research suggesting that emotional work is neither inherently good nor bad, at least in the eyes of those providing it, and that the conditions under which it is done are critical in influencing workers' experience of this labor (Lopez 2006b; Wharton 2009). This conclusion is important for dependent care work in other contexts (such as those described elsewhere in this volume) because it suggests that increasing status and recognition may produce affective relationships with recipients that feel more voluntary and rewarding to the provider. It thus supports the need to professionalize and upgrade care work, not only for the material rewards but because of the symbolic resources this generates in the work itself.

My analysis also suggests that a critical dimension of workers' feelings about this work is the extent to which they perceive it as subordinating. The concept of commodification has dominated much of the discussion of emotional work. Hochschild and others have argued or implied that the commodification of emotions affects workers negatively; more recent researchers have questioned this claim, arguing that the "love or money" dichotomy is often neither empirically accurate nor normatively useful (Bolton and Boyd 2003; England 2005; Folbre 2012; Folbre and Nelson 2000). I would suggest that perhaps more important than commodification, from workers' perspectives, is being able to avoid feelings of subordination (Sherman 2007). This capacity may emerge when they have autonomy from managers, but it is also fostered by positive relationships with clients and by professional recognition more broadly.

As I noted at the beginning of this chapter, the work done by lifestyle service providers is not care as it is defined in this volume. But there are similarities. Emotional work in both contexts involves listening and reassurance, often in the context of an ongoing relationship. This work is not managerially prescribed or routinized. And all of my respondents do feel a genuine concern for the well-being of (at least some of) their clients (Folbre and Wright 2012); indeed, this concern sometimes becomes overwhelming, a pattern Stacey (2011) has identified in the case of home health aides. Thus a final implication is that scholars should try to integrate analyses of emotions at work across different settings, comparing workers' experiences of emotion work in situations that differ in terms of autonomy, professionalism, class distance, or other features.

Of course, such a proposal raises questions about the normative aspects of emotional work in lifestyle and other service work occupations. The affective labor I have described does not immediately appear to be socially necessary; in fact, it may seem quite the opposite—wealthy people trying to get excessive amounts of attention and labor from others. This attention is unequally distributed according to class (Hochschild 1983) and likely to reproduce class entitlements (Sherman 2007). It does not fit into definitions of care predicated on social parity rather than asymmetry (for example, Waerness 1996). And this kind of attention is clearly not as socially important as basic care provided to elderly people or children.

At the same time, however, normative assumptions and claims about the difference between "attention" and "care" or between "excessive" and "reasonable" demands should be examined. In particular, scholars' notions should be held up against what producers of emotional work themselves think about "real" dependency or "legitimate" personal needs. I believe scholars do, and should, make normative commitments and distinctions that their respondents might not share. But we need to be explicit about thinking through the relationship between attention and subordination and where we draw the line between caring and catering.

Notes

1 Personal concierges typically offer a wide range of services to their clients, including errand running of all types, gift buying, personal organizing, and supervising minor renovations or home moves. They almost always refuse to do household work such as cleaning, child care, or food preparation (Sherman 2010).

2 The term "emotional labor" is now widely used to describe all kinds of commodified emotional work, although this was not its original meaning, as Lopez (2006b) has pointed out. I use "emotional work" (rather than "emotion work," which Hochschild [1983] used to mean uncommodified work) to describe work with an emotional dimension that has not been prescribed by managers.

3 I include only fourteen of my twenty-three concierge/personal assistant respondents because nine of them did not have sufficient experience with clients to speak to these issues in depth.

4 Concierge tasks constitute "support care" (Folbre and Wright 2012) or non-nurturant care (Duffy 2011) because they enable clients to care for others, especially children. But providers also saw emotional benefits, especially stress relief, arising directly from this kind of work for clients themselves.

Part V

Work and Family

• •

It would be impossible to offer a comprehensive view of paid care without also considering the question of family. Work and family intersect for paid caregivers in many noteworthy ways: paid care workers often must juggle their job obligations with unpaid care responsibilities at home, many families rely on paid care workers to meet their essential care needs, and cultural ideologies of family and work permeate the experiences of paid care workers. These chapters show that paying people to do care work is not, as it is often posed, the *opposite* of family care. In fact, family care is both practically and ideologically intertwined with paid care.

The idea of family in the United States is inextricably linked with norms of reciprocity, obligation, and reward. For paid care workers, the definition of family and the role of these "family" norms become often blurred and sometimes transformed. Lisa Dodson and Rebekah Zincavage describe how the language of family is used in nursing homes by both workers and managers to describe ideal relationships between aides and residents. And yet the resulting norms of family obligation are used to exploit low-wage workers who work extra unpaid hours to care for their fictive grandparents—and then are not allowed to take time to grieve when those residents die. As previous chapters show, long, unpredictable hours, sometimes around the clock, inhibit care workers' ability to balance work with their own family needs. Naomi Gerstel and Dan Clawson argue that nursing assistants respond to these structural conditions by using an expansive definition of family to include a wide range of relatives in their network of reciprocal exchange.

Ideologies of family obligation and reward not only play a role in the experiences of workers and the organization of workplaces but are implicated in the creation and implementation of policy. Both the California home care program (see Clare Stacey and Lindsay Ayers) and the Swedish parental leave program (see Mary Zimmerman) offer some form of government-subsidized payment to family caregivers. However, in the California case, family caregivers describe feeling like "employees in their own homes," while the Swedish policy is clearly framed as paid leave to attend to unpaid family responsibilities. The conflicts between the norms of worker and the norms of family member that Stacey and Ayers highlight among California family home care providers seem to be largely absent in the Swedish case where the participants are seen not as working but as parenting.

Because of the blurring of boundaries between work norms and family norms in paid care, workers often engage in boundary work to define their roles. Depending on the context of care, ideas about work and family (and what it means to be a caregiver in either context) powerfully shape the daily work of caregivers and their capacity to advocate for themselves on the job. For example, managers encouraged the nursing aides described by Dodson and Zincavage to adopt the norms of kinship. After all, when you are told and believe that you are caring for your fictive "grandma," it becomes difficult to question managers when asked to work during your break or when you are subjected to racial epithets by residents. By contrast, the family home care providers described by Stacey and Ayers struggle to move away from the rhetoric of kinship and obligation to family. Rather than embrace the language of kinship, these home care aides create accounts of their work as a public service that is skilled, in large part to justify receiving pay for something considered by many to be an obligation of love.

The way that family ideology is deployed depends not only on the context of a particular caregiving situation but on the social location of the caregivers and care recipients. The California home care program is a means-tested program targeting low-income families, and thus is vulnerable to stigma as an undeserved welfare benefit. Caregivers' distancing themselves from family ideology and identifying their role as public service and skilled labor are in part responses to this stigmatized status. By contrast, the Swedish parental leave policy is universal, and it is widely perceived as essential family policy rather than as a marginal program. Gerstel and Clawson emphasize that the ideology of extended family embraced by nursing aides is a result of their class position, which is deeply intertwined with racial hierarchies as well. And nursing home managers incorporate into their hiring practices the perception that there is a cultural proclivity among women of color to build the type of fictive relationships with residents that make them "good" care workers (see Dodson and Zincavage).

Taken together, these chapters explore the intersections of work and family in the realm of care. The scholarship of care, as well as care policy, must take seriously the way in which the very existence of paid care challenges the notion of the separation of work and family. Ideologies of family are ubiquitous and used to specific purposes within the realm of paid care. This view challenges us to move beyond a model of work-family tensions or work-family balance to explore the complex and interrelated ways that family and work intersect.

15

Low-Wage Care Workers

• •

Extended Family as a
Strategy for Survival

NAOMI GERSTEL AND

DAN CLAWSON

One might not expect a union bargaining session to be the best place to uncover conflicts over views of the family, but sometimes it is. Take this example. We observed a bargaining session between nursing assistants and the nursing home where they worked. Six "bosses" (as the workers called them), including the white lawyers and the management of the nursing home, sat at the front across from the fifteen people who made up the union negotiating committee (union staff and worker representatives, almost all women and mostly people of color). There were fifteen or so workers in the audience in this large hotel room where the negotiations took place. There were, of course, various points of contention. But the lawyer and managers seemed genuinely surprised when the talk turned to family. The topic was bereavement leave, and it became clear that professionals/ managers thought the distinction between the nuclear family and the extended family was simple: nuclear families counted more.

The nursing assistants they were bargaining with suggested something different. The contract they were negotiating contained two clauses on bereavement leave: "(1) Up to 3 days will be allowed for death of an Employee's: (a) Spouse/ Partner (b) Parent or (c) Child. (2) Up to 2 days will be allowed for the death of an Employee's (a) Brother; (b) Sister; (c) Grandparent (d) Grandchild, (e) Stepchild, or (f) Parent-in-law." The workers launched an attack. A worker at the table said, "They're telling me I can only take two days for my grandmother. Only two days for my grandmother. No way. And then you gonna tell me I can take three for my partner. Don't tell me that they didn't love their grandmother and don't need three days for her. At least three days, oh no." Heated remarks came from the workers in the audience, who before this exchange had been sitting rather quietly. One worker member yelled, "I need a week for my grandmother." There was some indignant muttering in the crowd about how their grandmothers took care of them. Another spoke up: "And only two days for my sister?" The worker at the table jumped back into the discussion, criticizing the distinction these clauses made between partners and other relatives.

As this negotiation makes clear, what family means to these nursing assistants is the extended family. The low-wage nursing assistants we studied—overwhelmingly women, often women of color—not only had a different view of family than their managers, but their views and strategies were not the same as those of nurses or doctors, also caregivers but caregivers with higher status and incomes. The nursing assistants' distinctive understanding of family, we will suggest, is shaped by the kinds of jobs they hold.

Race, Class, and Extended Families

This incident, and our research more generally, is in accord with a fair amount of previous research that suggests racial differences in reliance on extended families. Those who identify as people of color—in particular, Blacks and Latino/as—rely on extended kin more than do whites (Folbre 2012; Gerstel 2011; Sarkisian and Gerstel 2012; Swarz 2009; but see also Roschelle 1997). Compared to white non-Latino/a families, Blacks and Latino/as are more likely to live with relatives, to live near and see each other more often, as well as to exchange more practical assistance with family members.

These comparisons suggest that an emphasis on the nuclear family is inadequate to describe the realities of family life. But why do these differences exist? Analysis of large national surveys suggests that to a significant extent, they are a function of economic differences. Individuals' lack of economic resources increases their need for help from kin and boosts their willingness to give help in return. White, Black, and Latino/a individuals with the same amount of income and education have similar patterns of involvement with their extended families. Whether white, Latino/a, or Black, those who are poorer more often engage in mutual exchange of practical help with extended kin than do their wealthier counterparts. In contrast, just like educated affluent whites, more educated and wealthier Blacks and Latino/as are less likely to provide practical assistance to relatives outside the nuclear family. It is the relative economic deprivation of racial/ethnic minorities that leads to higher levels of extended family involvement (Gerstel and Sarkisian 2008; Sarkisian and Gerstel 2012).

Prior research on work and family, and on extended kin in particular, has not looked beyond money and education to features of jobs. By focusing on low-wage care workers, we will show here that while money matters, so, too, do the conditions of the workday. Paid work and family are deeply intertwined in ways that prior research has not made visible.

Data and Methods

The data we present here comes from research we conducted on the jobs and families of paid caregivers in the Northeast. In the larger study on which this chapter is based, we examined four occupations to create a two-by-two, gender-by-class table: nursing assistants and nurses, emergency medical technicians and physicians. In this chapter we focus on nursing assistants (also referred to as certified nursing assistants or CNAs), with occasional comparisons to doctors and nurses who, while also caregivers, are professionals with more education, income, authority, and societal recognition; doctors are also more likely to be men.

We collected multilevel data, including a mail survey, 220 in-person intensive interviews, fieldwork observations at eight work sites, official schedules showing both who was projected in advance to work and who actually worked, and observations of union negotiations. (For a more detailed discussion of our research methodology, see Clawson and Gerstel 2014.)

Mirroring national data, the large majority of nursing assistants in our data (89 percent) are women, most of whom earn wages (often as single mothers) close to the poverty line. Nursing assistants have less education and lower pay (a median of $10.05 an hour in our study) than any of the other occupations we studied. With limited education (typically a high school degree), nursing assistants can be certified with as little as three weeks' additional instruction. Close to half (44 percent) of nursing assistants in our study are nonwhite (mostly African American and Hispanic), while the large majority of doctors and nurses were white (over 80 percent).

"Family" Is Extended Kin

Whether Black, white, or Latina, many CNAs agree that their concept of "family" includes extended family members: they talked often about their mothers, brothers and sisters, aunts, uncles, grandparents, and cousins. They talked more about extended kin than any other occupational groups, whether that was about living together, exchanging child care and transportation, or helping with medical care. In the interviews, one-third of the nursing assistants' discussion of family focused on extended kin (among doctors it was only

11 percent and nurses only 1 percent). In addition, note that most of the CNAs' discussion about extended kin was about giving or receiving care; in contrast, much of the doctors' discussion was about contact and visiting with extended kin rather than caregiving. Many nursing assistants made comments like, "I don't know what I would do without my sister" or "She [my mother] is my rock. She is my life." Another nursing assistant's comment made clear just how pervasive kin were: "Well, I'm a single parent. That's my aunt [pointing to another person who worked in the same nursing home], so I stay with her. . . . Usually if both of us have to work that same day, that guy that you just saw in here, that's my cousin, and that's his girlfriend. So if we all have to work, I'll stay here till 8:00 and bring the kids to their house, which is the next block over. Right, we all kind of work together to make it happen."

Even when they could not routinely rely on daily exchanges with kin, it was clear that the extended family is family for those low-wage nursing assistants. A twenty-year-old who lives with a male partner and a six-year-old son remarked, "I don't actually have family out here. My family's in Philly." For her, family is not her partner and son; family is her mother, cousins, and grandparents.

Why these differences in the meaning and practice of family? Two broad theories are typically used to explain them: a difference in cultural schemas, morality, or values attached to family, or a set of structural conditions that produces what we have come to call a strategy for survival. While we do not think that structure and culture should be juxtaposed as opposites, and do not want to deny the importance of culture, we do want to make the argument that structure matters. More specifically, we found that job conditions are key. It is the money they make (or do not make) and their hours and schedules that are central to worker reliance on family.

First the money: as we noted, nursing assistants are low-wage workers who earn on average only about $20,000 a year. To put it bluntly, one doctor earns on average what eight nursing assistants earn. Not only do the nursing assistants earn a wage close to the poverty line, many are the breadwinners for their families. In our survey, only 48 percent report they are married; another 20 percent live with a partner. Even for those who were partnered, the nursing assistants tended to earn more than their (often unemployed) partners. As one notes, "I'm more of the breadwinner in the family, so I have to pick up extra [shifts]." They have to stretch their income to support their children. Some stories bring this home. A scheduler in a nursing home asked us to explain our research to a nursing assistant who had just taken on an extra shift and joked about it. Saying something like we are studying "why you work so much," the worker responded, "Number one, I'm single. Number two, I got two kids. Number three, the rent is $750. So I have no choice; you can see it, right?" This was emphasized in another interaction: we observed the nursing assistants' family pictures around the office desk of a sympathetic scheduler in a nursing home. Asking about the dozens of pictures on the bulletin board next to her desk, the scheduler said she put them there because nursing assistants aren't allowed to post pictures anywhere near where they work. "So," she continued, "this way they can put up pictures of their family someplace." A nursing assistant listening to the conversation piped up: "She has them up so when you come in and say 'I quit,' she can point to the pictures and say, 'You remember why you are working?'" This exchange makes clear the necessity these CNAs feel to serve as their family's primary breadwinner.

Moreover, these low-wage care workers are often called on to provide financial or practical support for their mothers, sisters-in-law, or cousins—whether lending money or providing rides, which, they reminded us, meant that they not only had to pay for a car and its upkeep but they also had to pay for expensive gas. In this sense, we can see that kin also can constrain the lives of low-wage workers—making their jobs, and the wages (even if low) they provide all the more necessary to support the much needed reciprocal relations with kin.

Job Hours and Schedules

To meet all these family responsibilities, wages matter, but so do job hours and schedules. Nursing assistants' reliance on extended kin is in part due to the fact that many work so-called alternative shifts. Because nursing homes, where most CNAs work, operate 24/7, the shifts for nursing assistants include the day shift from 7:00 A.M. to 3:00 P.M., the evening shift from 3:00 P.M. to 11:00 P.M., and the night shift from 11:00 P.M. to 7:00 A.M. In our study, four out of five (82 percent) of the CNAs are also required to work weekends. Nursing assistants and their managers told us that availability for such "unsocial hours" was a criterion of hiring. The workers themselves are drawn to the evening and night schedules because they received an extra $1.00 per hour and because, for some, these shifts enable them to better care for their children during the day when their children are awake and their parenting work is visible (Garey 1995, 1999). National surveys show that minority women, especially those in the lower levels of the service sector, are more likely to work such alternative or unsocial hours than other groups (Presser 2003).

The paid hours of these low-wage care workers were, moreover, unpredictable. We found that the schedules people actually work often do not match those that are officially scheduled in advance (about one-third of shifts were not according to schedule). Instead, there is a great deal of what we have come to call "churning" among the care workers in nursing homes. Nursing assistants changed hours and shifts by both adding and taking time off.

When we asked the nursing assistants why they pick up extra hours, we heard again and again that they needed to add hours to manage economically. Like other low-wage workers, nursing assistants are often hired for fewer than forty hours a week—typically twenty-four to thirty-two hours a week. Employers, quite purposively, hire nursing assistants for less than forty hours and simultaneously leave the organizations understaffed. The employers then expect the workers to stay extra shifts but do not need to pay them overtime. Floor supervisors and schedulers regularly ask nursing assistants to sign up for extra shifts and often do so without much warning on a day, evening, or night when the nursing assistants are already working a shift. Managers told us, "They [the workers] have to be flexible." Workers said to us, "If I was to only make my thirty-two hours, I'll be short of money." Or as another CNA commented,

Q: So, you do three twelve-hour shifts in a row?
R: Mmmhmm.
Q: Wow. So why do you have to do that?
R: Because, I wanna work, I gotta make the money, I need the money. Yeah, and since I'm a single parent I really have to work harder, 'cause I gotta bring the money home.

Nursing assistants do have a choice about whether to pick up additional shifts, or to work a second job as one-quarter of them do, but that choice is constrained by economic necessity; many feel compelled to pick up shifts if possible, since a thirty-two-hour-a-week schedule, at $10 an hour, leaves them below the poverty line.

Another reason we see a lot of churning is because nursing assistants need not only to add time but also to take time off. Their schedules outside of work are unpredictable. Unexpected events recur that require they take time off from work. More than any of the other care work occupations we studied, however, nursing assistants are also likely to encounter policies making it difficult to get time off; even their ability to take a sick day is restricted. At one nursing home we observed, workers receive six paid sick days per year but are penalized any time they use one. Other research on nursing homes suggests this was not an exceptional situation (Lopez 2006a). Many of the nursing assistants told us they are afraid to take a sick day, even though officially they are granted it: "Even if I'm sick I will still go to work [laughs]. . . . Somehow I am going to make it." Another nursing assistant talked about how management told them that they "were not going to tolerate sickness" and said, "If you've got diarrhea or vomiting, they still want you to come in. At our meetings, they say a sore throat is not really a sore throat. Lots of times they'll say to come in and do what you can and if you can't stay, we'll let you go home. But lots of times they won't let you go home. The whole idea is to intimidate you so you won't call out." Those who objected to the policy, she reported, lost their jobs.

A number of nursing assistants described situations that should be covered by the Family and Medical Leave Act (FMLA) but were not (Gerstel and Armenia 2009). One nursing assistant described the policy of no excused absences:

I think that the administration needs to be more understanding of the fact that we have families; some of us don't have the healthiest families. I mean, my daughter has a seizure disorder. My other two boys [one of whom is a nephew living with her], they're all right. The baby has real bad asthma. So there's times where I have to stay home or whatever because he can't breathe, she's having seizures, whatever the case. I think that if we come in with a doctor's note it should be considered an excused absence—it's not. There's no excused absences. So it's not fair to us as parents. Basically they want us to put our jobs ahead of our families. But they want to pay us chump change.

The wide range of relatives that the nursing assistants cared for exacerbated this problem. In one hospital staff meeting about schedules that included both CNAs and nurses, there were arguments between those who had children and those who did not. One CNA remarked, "Single people often have someone else to care for, like I have my parents at home to care for. That should matter as much as children." They are expected (and themselves expect) to care for a range of kin, which, in turn, affects their work lives. In other words, constraints, like unpredictable events that require a response, operate both in their work and their family lives.

Administrators legitimate their sick leave policy by claiming, for example, "There are times when people can't survive with this business." These managers are certain they can replace the nursing assistants who leave: the unemployment rate for nursing assistants was about 9 percent over the last ten years (U.S. Department of Labor Bureau of Labor Statistics 2010b). The nursing assistants do not have the market power to force their workplaces to provide time off.

This management control strategy for these care workers—which entails the moral frame that they cannot be trusted and penalties must be invoked for any absence—has negative health consequences not only for workers but also for clients. As one nursing assistant pointed out, "You know, you work in a healthcare facility and somebody has a real bad cold. But they still have to come anyway."

Contrast this to the doctors and nurses we studied. To put it simply, these two professional care worker groups not only make far more money than nursing assistants, but they have far more control over their work hours. In stark contrast with the nursing assistants' sense of a fate that could not be controlled was physicians' and nurses' taken-for-granted view that if there was a problem it would be addressed. One doctor (a surgeon in a private practice) was explaining his hectic schedule to us, contrasting his situation with that of other (subordinate) occupations within the office. Deciding not to come in one week, he said, "I just cancelled five days of appointments and went on vacation. They can't do that. They can't just decide not to come in. I can."

With relative ease, nurses also often can and do get time off for sickness, sometimes for themselves and sometimes for family members. Nurses reported to us that they do not come in if they are sick; they call and the full-time (and overburdened) scheduler finds someone else to work in their place. In contrast to what the nursing assistants experienced with the same symptom, one nurse explains that even if she isn't physically ill and just wants a day off, "A good one is I have diarrhea, because they go, 'Ohhh! Don't you dare come to this place with diarrhea.'" These professionals enjoy the privilege of flexibility in work hours and schedules that the nursing assistants do not imagine.

Consequences for Family Form

Other researchers have highlighted the limited economic wherewithal and unsocial hours of such paid care workers. Missing from these analyses is an understanding of how income and hours of employment affect worker reliance on family. Because they cannot get the time off, nursing assistants often have to turn to a range of extended kin for the recurring needs, even crises, that come up when one of their children gets sick or they have an appointment at school that requires the attendance of parents. Given their intense relations with other kin, they often must take time off for them—when a sister needs a ride to the doctor or a brother needs help with child care. Thus, the inflexible job of the CNA makes it all the more likely that these care workers will give and get a great deal of unpaid care outside the workplace.

We have come full circle: Because of their low pay and unpredictable, unsocial hours and additional jobs, these paid caregivers turn to kin for help, especially (but not only) with child care. The problem is not just that their hours are long and unpredictable; it is that their hours are out of synch with the hours formal child care is available because they work weekends, evenings, nights, unexpected extra shifts, and second jobs. The large majority (over three-quarters) of the CNAs told us they relied on their relatives for assistance with child care. They turn to their mothers and siblings but also cousins, aunts, and occasionally uncles for help. One nursing assistant told us that if somebody calls out on the night shift, she says, "Oh, I'll stay till six." How does she do that? This nursing assistant calls her disabled mother, who is available because her bad back made it difficult for her to work outside the home. Asking her mom if she can watch her son overnight is not so easy: "You know, of course, here she is watchin' him 3 to 11. And now she's gonna stay with him overnight and then have to get up with him in the morning and then watch him all day. As much as she probably doesn't want to sometimes, she does. 'Cause she knows I need the money."

It is not only their mothers. One nursing assistant offered a typical example: "On a weekend I'll ask one of my brothers if they could take care of our aunt who needs a lot of help. In the nursing field you *have* to—it's a *must*—you have to work every other weekend. . . . Right now I'm watching my nephew for my brother. His girl, she works where I work." Even a thirty-seven-year-old married mother nursing assistant who sometimes alternated shifts with her husband also needed to rely on her sister and mother. "Sometimes it's hard to find a babysitter from 3 to 11, 'cause people got lives, like my sister, she got two other kids, and it's hard, so. . . . She just goes, pick him up in school, then she drops him off at my mom's house. That's what she does. He sleeps with my mom." Reliance on extended family is pervasive among the low-wage care workers we studied.

Conclusion

While many researchers and commentators focus on the nuclear family, we have shown here that family means something different to low-wage workers, specifically nursing assistants. Our argument is about the intersection of low-wage work and care work, and of course these are often related. The CNAs—whether white, African American, or Latina—talked about and depended on extended kin; we found little racial variation because, as we have shown, that reliance is a result of structural conditions of the jobs. These are conditions CNAs of all races share.

Our structural argument is not just about workplace conditions. There are probably a number of other factors shaping the character and meaning of "family"—for example, propinquity (or whether relatives live near one another) and marital status. Low-wage workers are more likely to live with or near kin than are those higher up the class structure. This makes it easier to give and get care. But in analyses of national surveys, Sarkisian and Gerstel (2005, 2012) find significant class distinctions in kin reliance even controlling for propinquity. In addition, the greater exchanges with kin among these low-wage workers may be tied to marital structure. Marriage cuts off both women and men from other social connections; it does so for the wealthy and the poor, the middle class and the working class. Even controlling for education and income, married people are less involved with their extended kin than those who are never married or previously married (Gerstel 2011; Gerstel and Sarkisian 2006). Low-wage workers, like CNAs, are less likely to be married than those higher up the class structure. As the much cited 2010 publication from the Pew Research Center reports, "Marriage, while declining among all groups, remains the norm for adults with a college education and good income but is now markedly less prevalent among those on the lower rungs of the socio-economic ladder" (Pew 2010). Because the reliance on kin we have outlined here is not primarily a result of particular values but rather of social conditions, we heard these stories of reliance on kin from Blacks, Latino/as, and whites. Class here seems to trump race. But class is deeply intertwined with race. Many of these workers are women of color and to separate race from their class position is in some sense to do injustice to our understanding of both.

Some of what we analyze would apply to any low-wage worker, but care work adds an extra dimension. Care work is much more likely than other work to operate 24/7, which means that care workers are likely to need to find child care on weekends, evenings, and nights; that in turn typically means reliance on relatives. Much care work must be continuous: a nursing home or hospital patient cannot be left unattended for an eight-hour shift (see chapter 16 this volume;

Zerubavel 1979). Employers thus impose harsh penalties on workers (especially low-wage care workers) who don't report for duty. The extra penalties for absences further reinforce the need for emergency backup for, say, a sick child; for low-wage workers that usually means extended kin. It is the intersection of care work and low wages that is critical here: physicians also provide care and also must be available nights and weekends, often on an emergency basis. But 39 percent of the male physicians who need to respond to emergencies can rely on a stay-at-home wife, and two-earner physician families often have a nanny, in some sense a market substitute for extended family.

The perspective we have presented here has two faces. It is, on the one hand, a critique of those who argue that poor and working-class families are disorganized—a position that is reappearing with the reinvigoration of the Moynihan Report. The low-wage nursing assistants we studied were not workers devaluing families as some recent commentators would lead one to expect (Murray 2012). We can argue that low-wage families are disorganized insofar as we think of the nuclear family as the only functional family. It isn't.

At the same time, while we can insist these families are not disorganized, we should not romanticize them or argue that what relatives provide easily replaces what state policy could and should provide. The nursing assistants occasionally complain or express ambivalence about their relatives. Taking care of kin is often hard. It wears people down. It even costs money. It certainly can be stressful. As Carol Stack (1974) showed a number of years ago, caring for kin can make it difficult to be upwardly mobile. With the system of reciprocity so many used, the same kin who offered support expected help in return. Sometimes these care workers talked about how their hours and schedules made it difficult to provide care for relatives who needed it, adding another layer of stress to their already complicated lives. One married nursing assistant, whose mother-in-law had moved in with them about four months earlier, remarked, with almost saintly aspirations, that she hoped this would make her an even better [nursing assistant] "because I realize how much responsibility this is." But then she trailed off: "My mother-in-law lost her husband. Today she is home alone by herself. And I am worried about whether she will maintain her food restrictions. I cry in the car every day about her." This strategy for survival, then, has its own tensions and costs.

Acknowledgments

We gratefully acknowledge research support provided by NSF (SES-0549817; SES-0959712), the Alfred Sloan Foundation, the Russell Sage Foundation, NAEMT and PERI and the assistance of Jill Crocker and Jackie Stein.

16

"It's Like a Family"

• • • • • • • • • • • • • • • • • • • •

Caring Labor, Exploitation, and Race in Nursing Homes

LISA DODSON AND

REBEKAH M. ZINCAVAGE

> "The same way I think about my mother, this is the same way I'm thinking about these residents. I consider them like they are my own. But it's a very hard job, we don't get paid enough for the job, and sometimes you feel like every day you do more and more and more, and the money is less."
> —Certified nursing assistant

Over the last two decades, a "crisis in care" has provoked difficult questions about the meaning and value of purchased care in contemporary society. Historically, family relationships and the market have been considered separate worlds, yet care work, traditionally a taken-for-granted female activity, has increasingly demanded market valuation as millions of women left homemaking for paid employment, expanding the need for hired care providers. The United States' ever-growing population of elderly and chronically ill people has made long-term care an urgent and complex demand. As in the past, those who enter the low-paid care labor market tend to be poor women, native-born women of color, and immigrants (Dawson and Surpin 2001; Duffy 2007; Glenn 1992; Romero 1992).

This chapter draws from interviews, focus groups, observational data, and a survey from research in eighteen long-term care residential facilities in Massachusetts. From these multiple sources, we explicate an ideology of family that consistently emerged as integral to the design and understanding of care for residents. Further, we examine how family ideology drives expectations of the kind of care provided by certified nursing assistants (CNAs) who, as one facility director put it, are "the backbone of the nursing home industry." As theorized in scholarship on caring labor across disciplines (DeVault 1991; Folbre 2002; Kittay 1999; Stone 2005; Uttal and Tuominen 1999), our research uncovers the tension experienced by care workers, disproportionately women of color, as they manage their work as both a job and as a commitment to care for fictive family members.

At the Intersection of Family and the Long-Term Care Market

Critical social theorists have focused on how family ideology structures care work within the domestic sphere in ways that disadvantage low-income women who sell their care labor (Dill 1994; Hondagneu-Sotelo 2007; Rollins 1985; Romero 2001). Beyond gender and class, Mignon Duffy (2007) points out that racial-ethnic hierarchies remain entrenched, even as care work is increasingly part of the paid labor market.

Care scholars have suggested that the family model is considered the standard of care. Mary Tuominen has described the "golden rule" of paid care work as the obligation to care for others as you would care for your kin. Yet this model may prove tyrannical as appeals to kinship invoke a set of expectations that can remain unstated yet spin a complicated web of obligations (Anderson 2000; DeVault 1991; Hondagneu-Sotelo 2007; Romero 1992). Childcare research has uncovered how paid care workers must walk a confusing line between the overlapping role of paid employee and substitute mother who is sincerely attached to children in her care (Macdonald 2010; Nelson 1994; Tuominen 2003). The complexity of balancing kinlike relationships and workplace roles converges in the lives of low-paid care workers who are disproportionately women of color (Hondagneu-Sotelo 2007; Paraprofessional Healthcare Institute 2012; Romero 1992; Uttal and Tuominen 1999).

Recent scholarship has engaged in the debate about the commodification of intimacy, directly challenging the "hostile worlds" notion that care work and compensation are incompatible (Folbre and Nelson 2000; Himmelweit 1999; Stone 2005; Zelizer 2005). Viviana Zelizer (2005), in particular, suggests that caregiving may be bought without the loss of authentic feeling, arguing that intimacy and economic transaction overlap along the spectrum of care activities.

However, she also points out that purchased intimacy is a carefully circumscribed exchange, marked by a clear boundary and distinct sets of understandings and practices (Zelizer 2005). While a market exchange does not preclude a meaningful relationship, neither does it ensure that the terms of purchase will be negotiated among equals.

Currently more than 1.9 million individuals receive nursing home care (American Association of Homes and Services for the Aging [AAHSA] 2007). Within these nursing homes, CNAs are on the front lines and work under the supervision of nurses. Comprising 65 percent of the total nursing staff, CNAs provide between 80 and 90 percent of direct care to residents (Dawson and Surpin 2001; Page 2004). Contrary to a widespread representation of this work as unskilled labor, CNAs actually carry out a variety of complex tasks crucial to the well-being of residents. In this research, we examined the role of CNAs, who have been described as the critical front line of long-term care (Glenn 1992; Himmelweit 1999; Tuominen 2003). We explored the effects of an institutionalized family model of care in nursing homes, analyzing the benefits and burdens of an ethic of kinship reciprocity (DeVault 1991; Kittay 1999; Stone 2000; Uttal and Tuominen 1999). We also drew out the kinlike relationship between paid caregiver and receiver, highlighting CNAs' personal concern for vulnerable residents (Stone 2005; Zelizer 2005).

Our examination of family ideology in long-term care comes from a study of work practices and relationships in nursing homes completed over the course of two years (2004–2005). The research included focus groups with CNAs (N = 105), interviews with administrators (N = 18), assistant administrators (N = 2), directors of nursing (N = 16), nurses, both LPNs and RNs (N = 77), as well as various other management staff (that is, activities directors, assistant directors of nursing, directors of human resources, directors of quality assurance, chief financial officers, social workers, staff development, and union stewards; N = 32).

Fictive Kinship Goes to Market

> "I tell them, think of this as your mother, how would you want her treated?"
> —Manager

> "Sometimes, we're the family, but that's part of being a CNA."
> —CNA

Across the eighteen nursing homes in our study, whether nonprofit or for-profit, union or nonunion, "compassionate" and high-quality care was commonly expressed in the language of a family model of caring. In the many discussions about care quality and institutional approach, both management and frontline workers described creating a family as the best model of care for elderly and dependent residents.

In the facilities adopting the increasingly popular "person-centered care" approach to long-term care, allowing the residents to reclaim feelings of autonomy and living at home are care priorities. In describing this approach, managers would regularly talk about how a family would treat a fragile member, based on personal preferences and needs. As one manager asked, "Why should you have to get up when the facility wants; why can't you get up when you want to, the way you do at home?" critiquing the traditional institutional custom of waking all residents up in the morning at one prescribed time. Across the nursing homes, administrators, nurses, and CNAs spoke of residents as having been abandoned by their biological families. In response, some managers described encouraging CNAs to, as several put it, "adopt" residents, to regard them as actual family members. Managers saw this as a strategy to promote empathy and patience among CNAs, particularly with residents who were sometimes uncooperative. One assistant director said, "I encourage [CNAs] to think of [residents] as their own mothers." Another manager advised CNAs to provide care for the residents "the way you would care for your own parents." One administrator put it poignantly, indicating she teaches CNAs that "[CNAs] are [residents'] family now. The last face they see will be [the face of the CNA]." Certainly this is a compelling image of the job.

This theme was reflected in conversations with CNAs as well; many regarded themselves as fill-ins for absent family members. Many took on these roles in the belief that elderly people deserved kin care and because a personal relationship was an attribute of the job that was gratifying. We heard variations of these kin obligations, "You have to be their family. You have to be there for them." One CNA told us, "You get attached to them. . . . It's like having forty grandparents in one room. Being there when the residents need things. When they don't see a family member that don't come in, we're there."

During focus groups and open-ended discussions with CNAs, many described kinlike attachment as part of how they conducted intimate and demanding care. "I think of my grandmother" was a common refrain. In some cases, CNAs, particularly those who were immigrants, were separated from their own kin. They described providing care to elderly residents as a substitution; doing paid care work in this setting allowed them to offer love and understanding that, under other circumstances, would have been given to their own family. One CNA said, "I can tell you that I miss my family probably in a lot of stuff that I have to do here. . . . The thing is I focus on my mother here. And that made me do the best because I think if it was my mother, I want to give her—I think I take this job personal." Another CNA echoed this connection: "I love them. . . . I feel when I'm here, I [think about] my mother and my brother, that's the way I feel. I love them."

The combination of managers encouraging CNAs to adopt the residents and the willingness by CNAs to establish family-like bonds emerged as the pervasive culture in all these facilities. We note, however, that not all CNAs expressed attachment to all residents and a few claimed they attempted to limit their attachments because they were too emotionally demanding. We also heard from some managers and CNAs that they had known staff people (CNAs as well as nurses and managers) who, given their cold and even abusive tendencies, "had no business working with [the] elderly." Yet overall, family connection was the most common understanding of how care work should be done.

When asked what CNAs "liked best about their jobs," overwhelmingly and across all types of nursing homes, they identified the residents or "doing something to help these people." Nearly 90 percent of the CNAs surveyed regarded themselves as the person closest to the residents in their care. While many CNAs were critical of various aspects of how specific nursing homes were managed, CNAs most frequently identified attachment to residents as the most gratifying part of their jobs. "The residents are what make the job good" as one CNA put it. Another explained, "A lot of [CNAs] treat [residents] like they're family. You are their family. This is the only place they know."

The Burdens and Benefits of "Making Family" in Nursing Homes

From the viewpoint of the managers, the bonds of kinlike relationship between CNAs and residents were very helpful. The general consensus was that CNAs possessed a critical understanding of residents' preferences, recognized day-to-day changes in resident status, and were the most capable of providing care centered on the individual. Managers referred to CNAs as being the "eyes and ears" of the facility or the "hearts and hands" of care. Numerous managers spoke in heartfelt terms of their responsibility to promote quality of care within their institutions. "These people have lived their lives and made contributions and this is their end of life. We are the ones who are responsible for what that's like," said one nursing home director.

But managers also discussed care strategies in more pragmatic terms. Competition for residents and demanding regulatory standards were major considerations in care styles and quality. Managers claimed that family members wanted to see their elderly kin clean and fed and, equally as important, receiving compassionate and affectionate care. Nursing homes are highly regulated by state and federal mandates and state officials periodically conducted visits to evaluate quality of care; infractions resulted in loss of revenue. Encouraging caregivers to form deep bonds with residents and go out of their way to take good care of them was discussed as humane as well as a boon to the institutional bottom line. Without a doubt, the family model was good for business.

When queried about characteristics desirable in CNAs, one director of nursing said, "They [CNAs] have to be really caring," while another expressed a similar sentiment: "I want to see a lot of hugging, touching, very loving and caring." Managers also sometimes encouraged family-like "extras." As one put it, "[CNAs] should bring in birthday cakes for the residents, or, go shopping on their own time for residents, make a big deal out of their birthdays." Preferences for people who were more likely to adopt or bond with residents had, in some facilities, become institutionalized. In this vein, we heard that managers were "looking for someone who is flexible, who is willing to go more than the eight hours." The standard behavior for a CNA had evolved into a willingness to go above and beyond simple task completion and develop a kinlike relationship with residents as part of the job.

Certified nursing assistants, as the people who were performing the majority of duties that constructed family, expressed a more ambivalent attitude. Most CNAs valued the affection that some residents were able to offer in response to their care. Yet as the primary direct care providers, CNAs also pointed to the stress and physical exhaustion involved in caring for seven to fourteen dependent people (as many as twenty-two in the evening and during the "graveyard shift"). In the survey, 93 percent reported that they work short-staffed occasionally, often, or always (44, 36, and 13 percent, respectively). One summed it up this way: "It's really just a big rush, the whole day. . . . like an assembly line, you know?" Moreover, the emotional challenge of fulfilling the expectations of a dozen "grandparents" was sometimes overwhelming. Many CNAs expressed sentiments similar to one who said, "It's not so much the [activities of daily living], helping them get washed up, helping them get dressed; it's to be able to spend that quality time with them, other than doing the patient care. There's more to being a CNA than just doing patient care. And these people don't, some of them don't have families that come in, so they kind of appreciate when you take that little bit of time and spend it with them."

Certified nursing assistants spoke of worrying about the residents over the weekends or in the evening. In fact, almost half indicated that they visit residents, unpaid, on their days off. CNAs suggested that in order to do their job they had to do more, feel more, and stretch themselves for the residents "because we are their family." Three out of five CNAs reported that they came in early or stayed late to provide care to residents without being paid to do so, and 80 percent of the CNAs indicated they worked through their breaks in order to provide adequate care.

Despite authentic concern for residents, CNAs expressed criticism about how they were valued in the nursing homes. It was common to hear CNAs remark that the pay was low and the benefits limited or nonexistent; some pointed out that their wages were not enough to cover their monthly bills. Most earned between $9 and $14 hourly and did not receive medical or other employment benefits. Overtime work was common, with three-fifths of the CNAs reporting that they worked overtime at least once a month and a few admitting that they worked double shifts frequently. Moreover, at least one-third indicated that due to low wages they held more than one full-time CNA job.

While at all staffing levels individuals pointed out that "no one gets rich who works with the elderly," many of the managers and directors agreed that the CNA staff were notoriously underpaid and that there was little or no room for advancement without further schooling. Many managers expressed the belief that CNAs deserved more for the work that they did, and few denied the importance of their work. Yet given the "dead-end" trajectory of the job, the hard work of caring for dependent, even immobile, people, and "bad wages," some administrators suggested that the work had to be "a calling." Several others echoed this sentiment, claiming that CNAs "can't be in it for the money." This framing of the work in terms of nonmarket motivations was echoed in numerous ways. It was common to hear managers and CNAs explicitly describe putting affection and family duty before money as the motivation for this job. One CNA described the job as being about love: "Got to love them to do this type of work. You have to be caring; have to be honest with them, patient, loving. All that counts to be a good CNA. If it was for the money, I wouldn't be here. I'm here because of the residents, I love them." Another explained, "It's not the money. It's like you're doing it for them to do it really is your heart. It's your heart, you do it with all your heart."

Race and Fictive Kinship Labor

In our sample, 75 percent of the CNAs were people of color, mirroring national trends of disproportionate representation. Issues of ethnicity and race emerged in the descriptive discussions among supervisors in describing the work of CNAs. Specifically, some supervisors considered racial identity to be a factor in the provision of authentic affection to residents and described a cultural—or racialized—proclivity among women of color to do care work. Several managers spoke of the warmth of Caribbean people's cultures and one manager suggested that Haitians are "naturally" suited to providing care for elderly people: "They [Haitian CNAs] have a culture of respecting the elderly . . . they are warm and patient . . . they have that approach." Other supervisors alluded to how Latino, African American, and Caribbean people are more "family oriented" and they brought that quality to the workplace. While language limitations among immigrant workers were discussed as detraction from their performance, this seemed to be offset by an assumed capacity that "foreign" CNAs would adopt fictive kin with ease, more naturally. In most cases when these racialized references were made overtly, they took the guise of a "compliment" as a nurse supervisor put it.

In the nursing home corridors, this characterization of CNAs of color as possessing an essentialized capacity for kindness suggested a particularly deep level of selflessness. In some nursing homes, "racial slurs" expressed by the people receiving care were reported as commonplace. In this vein, Celia Berdes and

John Eckert (2007) examined how the family care model interacts with racial abuse in nursing homes. They suggest that the family model is useful to offset the potential for lowered care quality that might be expected when workers are racially abused. As the authors put it, "When neither good wages, benefits, nor job prestige are present to serve as motivators, when hope of advancement is slim, when the work itself is onerous," one of the only pillars of maintaining good care is the "emotional 'currency'" that may sustain quality, "even [to] those residents that actively abuse them" (Berdes and Eckert 2007, 347). Critical race theorists have long pointed to an archetypal figure, the caregiver of color, as engrained in the American social imagination (Collins 2005; Glenn 1992; Harris 1982; Jones 1985; Omolade 1994).

Supervisors and nurses expressed distaste at the racist comments from some residents. As one nurse put it, this unfortunate aspect of their work was "really unfair" to the CNAs. Yet she spoke with an air of inevitability. Embedded in this was the assumption that such comments would not fracture the kind of care residents received and that CNAs of color would overlook such comments as part of the altruism that characterized their approach to this work.

With some variation in the different worksites, white CNAs and CNAs of color were encouraged to adopt a culture of fictive kinship as an approach to provide better care, despite the burden of intensified emotion labor that this model entails. While authentic attachment to residents is common among direct care workers, the strain of providing kin care is hard to measure and thus easy to overlook as a considerable work demand among direct care workers. Furthermore, for CNAs of color, the kinship model represents a disproportionate burden in a work setting that tolerates, if reluctantly, worker experiences of racism as part of the job.

Boundaries within the Family

For nursing home managers, the family model was a way to improve quality of resident care and to deepen a worker's sense of relationship and responsibility, despite low wages and strenuous job conditions. For the institutions, the promotion of a family ideology offered considerable benefits and few burdens. But for the people who were performing the majority of direct care, the family model was much more costly. Set in the context of compensation that was by all accounts very low, the burden of "making family" was materially undervalued and largely borne by the CNAs.

Beyond the imbalance in costs and benefits, this formulation of fictive kinship had distinct boundaries. While kin claims made on CNAs were part of nursing home culture, kin claims made by CNAs were received quite differently, often exposing the nonreciprocal nature of the family model. In particular, we found examples of a carefully delineated version of family in policies regarding the death of residents, the response to CNA family concerns, and a consistent lack of recognition of the knowledge that CNAs develop regarding the care of residents.

As expected, we found that the death of residents was inevitably part of the experience of work in nursing homes. But CNAs' accounts of losing one of "their" residents raised a challenge to the nursing home mystique about being "part of a family." Several CNAs said that while they had been encouraged to care for a resident as a grandmother, they were discouraged from mourning her in that way. For nursing home managers, grief meant a potential disruption to an orderly workflow. Only a few nursing homes integrated the practice of allowing CNAs to attend residents' funerals. While some CNAs reported that they appreciated the chance to participate in grieving, many could not give up a day of income to attend a funeral. In a more general sense, others found that the profound grief they felt did not dry up immediately after the funeral. As one woman explained, "It's like your own family, is the way I see it. It's not like for me it's a stranger anymore. You know that person deeply, and then that person, one day, is just gone."

Another element of the CNA role that indicated a distorted version of kinship was the way CNAs' own families were treated. These families were excluded from the family model incorporated into the work, treated not as an extended part of a family circle but largely as work obstacles. "Family issues are big [problems]," one manager acknowledged. Understaffing is a major impediment to good care and countless managers described families as a primary obstacle in supervising CNAs, specifically pointing to childcare issues, school vacations and holidays, and family health problems. A few supervisors were flexible, acutely aware of the problems facing working mothers, but others said they could "only go so far." As one manager put it, "They have a real obligation here; these people [the residents] count on them and we count on them." Another remarked, "This is a business; we have staffing levels we have to meet." One manager framed this as the need for CNAs to behave appropriately at work by keeping private family matters outside: "'Leave them at the door,' I say. We don't want the residents to get upset."

Some CNAs recognized the paradox of their role. One said reflectively "I mean, I give [the residents] 100 percent of what I got. Maybe too much. More to them than I give my family." Another young CNA said, "I spend much more time with [residents] than I do with my son." Pointing to the institutional culture that puts the real and fictive families in competition, one CNA said, "[Supervisors] give you the feeling, they kind of make you feel like 'We're first and your family's second.' They try to put you on that track."

Another contradiction in the model of family was failure to include CNAs in discussions of the care for "their" residents. Seventeen out of eighteen facilities did not include CNAs in routine meetings regarding care concerns for each resident. This omission sometimes baffled supervising staff, as one nurse manager expressed: "Some of the aides know far more about the people [her residents] than I do." Supervisors reflected that, generally, CNAs were supposed to "report" their observations to supervisors but not be included in the collaborative process of planning. One CNA said, "They [management] don't really ask us too much what we think." In fact, despite their proximate role in caring for residents, less than a quarter of CNAs surveyed indicated that their supervisors even consistently asked for input in care plans.

This gap between being credited as critical kin who are closest to the care receiver yet extraneous to the "thinking" part of care was critiqued by some CNAs. One remarked, "Sometime you come to work. . . . you don't feel like . . . we are family too. . . . Like [management] don't think you are nothing. You're here only to clean people but you're not really a person, you know? . . . They don't treat you as a person." Another added, "Yeah, they think we are nothing but butt wipers . . . that's all."

Care and Reciprocity

In the course of this research, an ideology of family emerged as integral to the way that care was conceptualized by managers and direct care workers. We have examined the contours of this family model as one that can offer considerable benefit to frail and dependent people and also to the institutions responsible for providing them with decent care. As we so often heard, the devoted "hearts and hands" of CNAs are good for residents and good for business. Encouraging CNAs to consider residents as their own mothers and fathers builds a morally obligated and emotionally devoted worker, likely to stretch herself to give good care to her kin.

We do not mean to diminish the degree to which CNAs valued their relationships with many of the residents in their care; overwhelmingly they identified these relationships as the best aspect of their job. Many CNAs used fictive kinship to establish connections with elderly and infirm strangers for whom they were going to provide the most intimate care duties: changing soiled undergarments, washing, feeding, soothing, and, in most cases, witnessing their deterioration. And many nursing home managers spoke admiringly of their work.

Yet the family construct appeared to institutionalize an expectation of self-sacrifice or of putting "adopted" kin above all else. The gendered role of family caregiver is without boundaries, orbits around the needs of others, and is "a calling" too sacred for such base calculation as market valuation; in words from this research, "It is not about the money" (Crittenden 2001; DeVault 1991; Folbre 2002; Nelson 1994). While relationships emerged as foundational to high-quality care for people who certainly need it, emotional work comes at a high cost. The institutional use of a family ideology creates a workplace culture ripe for the exploitation of the lowest-paid direct care workers.

Our findings reflect those of others who have uncovered how determinedly paid care givers resist a commodification of their labor that negates their feelings, even to the point of bending or breaking rules (Stone 2000). We also agree that authentic caring can be purchased. The fact that CNAs received wages did not turn their care into market exchanges devoid of affection. Quite the contrary; above all, they valued relationships with residents. Yet we also found these monetized care exchanges do have distinct boundaries and, importantly, "differentiated social ties" (Zelizer 2005), with lines that are drawn markedly in favor of resident need and nursing home interests. Similar to the sharp imbalance of power between employer and domestic worker, nursing home managers have the freedom to vacillate between the CNA as trusted kin or contracted worker, whichever offers the greatest advantage at any particular moment (Dill 1994; Glenn 1992; Hondagneu-Sotelo 2007).

Despite the ways that this model of family served to exploit CNAs, we believe that a version of familial relationship is at the heart of good care and of gratifying care work. CNAs taught us that their job demands not only physical strength but also artistry, intuition, skill, patience, and finally (though certainly not in all cases) affection or, as so many said, love. When this critical work is rooted in an ethic of reciprocity, the kinship model is not inherently exploitive. But so long as CNAs are relegated to that particular "part of the family" where women of color and immigrants have been assigned for centuries, the use of family ideology can easily become tyranny at work (Childress 1986). From another angle, collective bargaining and strong union representation may be the most viable means of ensuring that this growing work force is paid a sustainable income and receives job benefits. Unions may also be the channel through which CNAs enjoy a change in their institutional status and gain the respect that their critical work merits.

From all quarters of this study, administrators and frontline workers regarded a caring relationship between CNAs and residents as essential to the well-being of elderly, chronically ill, and dependent people. Managers and frontline care workers alike spoke of family relationship as an essential ingredient for long-term care. Reflecting the thinking of those who do the work, we argue that, when fully valued, kinship in care work is not inherently exploitive. Yet a critical concern for dignified and family-like care of one segment of our people does not justify sacrificing the humanity of another, in this case, those who do the job of caring.

Acknowledgments

This chapter is a revision of "'It's Like a Family': Caring Labor, Exploitation, and Race in Nursing Homes" first published in 2007 in Gender and Society 21: 905–28. Data reported on here were gathered as part of the project entitled "Improving Institutional Long-Term Care for Residents and Workers: The Effect of Leadership, Relationships, and Work Design Project." Research was funded by the Better Jobs Better Care collaboration of the Robert Wood

Johnson Foundation and Atlantic Philanthropies administered by the Institute for the Future of Aging Services. The project was approved by the Institutional Review Boards at Brandeis University, Boston College, in addition to facility-specific IRBs for NFs that had their own IRBs. For a more detailed discussion of study design and methods, please see the final project report at http://www.bjbc.org/.

17

Caught between
Love and Money

• •

The Experiences of
Paid Family Caregivers

CLARE L. STACEY AND
LINDSEY L. AYERS

In her afterword to the twentieth anniversary edition of *The Managed Heart*,
Arlie Hochschild argues that new scholarship on work and emotional labor
must consider what she calls the "third sector" of social life, where forces of family and market collide (Hochschild 2003b). Instead of considering labor solely
in the context of public life, she asks us to investigate what happens to social
norms and work expectations when private space (that is, the home) becomes
a site of work. Put succinctly, Hochschild seeks to understand what happens
when private life becomes "marketized."

Here we take up Hochschild's call by examining the work experiences of
family home care providers, who are paid a wage by California's In Home Supportive Services (IHSS) to care for sick, elderly, or disabled family members.
These caregivers, most of whom are poor and qualify for state support, essentially become employees within their own homes, in charge of family "clients."
Following Hochschild, our research is guided by the following question: How do

family providers experience and manage the marketization of their private lives and space?

Drawing on in-depth interviews with sixteen family providers and six months of ethnographic observation of home-based care, we find that caregivers struggle to make sense of their care work, torn between wanting to provide free care to family and circumstances of poverty that prevent them from easily doing so. Employment through the means-tested IHSS program helps alleviate some of the pressures associated with care, but social costs associated with paid family care work remain. Caregivers perceive waged care as a violation of social norms surrounding family care, namely that care should not be exchanged for pay. Family caregivers manage the norm violation associated with their care work by offering "accounts" (Scott and Lyman 1968) that justify their work as socially valuable and altruistically motivated. Specifically, providers construct accounts that (1) emphasize the tasks and skill associated with caregiving and (2) frame paid family care as a public good or service. These accounts allow family providers to claim their work as legitimate and to reconstruct their actions in a positive light.

The Obligation to Care

Americans generally view the care of family as a private affair, something that family members are expected to do out of love or obligation (Folbre 2002). U.S. institutions (workplaces, governments, medical systems) and policies that fail to acknowledge or support family caregivers reinforce this norm (Bashevkin 2002; Harrington Meyer 2000). Without caregiver pensions or a substantive long-term care benefit, families in the United States often struggle with the emotional and financial costs of caregiving (Chorn-Dunham and Dietz 2003; Gallagher et al. 1989; George and Gwyther 1986).

The implicit notion that care should be provided quietly, altruistically, and without remuneration runs deep in our culture, stemming from what Viviana Zelizer (2005) calls the hostile worlds of love and money. Zelizer argues that when economic transactions mingle with intimate life, concerns abound that "contact between the personal and economic spheres corrupts both of them" (2005, 207). She raises the case of paid family caregivers specifically, whose paid work stirs "acute political and moral debates, often with hostile worlds warnings about the contamination and undermining of moral obligation" (2005, 171). In other words, payment for care sullies the gendered, idealized notions of caregiving that dominate our cultural imagination.

Family caregivers necessarily violate the hostile worlds tenet that money and love should be separate since they provide care in a "third sector" of social life where home and work converge (Hochschild 2003a, b). Paid an hourly wage, these providers experience a "marketization" of private life that complicates social norms associated with caregiving. When private spaces such as the home become sites of waged labor, social actors are unclear whether norms of workplace or of kinship/family apply (Hochschild 2003b, 204). This confusion has been observed in a wide range of empirical contexts, including telecommuting (Mirchandani 2000), domestic work (Hondagneu-Sotelo 2007), nursing and personal care (Stacey 2011), home-based child care (Tuominen 2003), and in homes where personal concierges are employed (Sherman 2010). In each of these cases, individuals internalize to some extent the idea that love/money and home/work are hostile worlds, and they must therefore strive to justify what is seen as nonnormative by others. The hostile worlds problem is particularly acute for paid family caregivers precisely because they are family, rather than fictive kin or pseudo-family (as is the case with non-family aides, childcare workers, personal concierges, and so forth). It is not surprising, then, that family providers construct accounts, "stories" that allow them to "make their behavior accountable in a moral world" (Shotter 1984).

Accounting for Care Work

Marvin Scott and Stanford Lyman suggest that accounts are "linguistic devices employed whenever an action is subjected to valuative inquiry" (1968, 46). Social actors use accounts to distance themselves from or justify behavior that society views as deviant or non-normative (Scott and Lyman 1968). Constructed accounts act as a way of avoiding detrimental consequences to the self in light of a violation of social norms (Orbuch 1997). Accounts can therefore be viewed as a type of "aligning action" that demonstrates how individuals interpret and narrate behavior in synch with broader cultural beliefs or understandings (Orbuch 1997, 463). Accounts do not simply align people's behaviors with social norms; they also help people cope with life events. Scholars have found that accounts give people a greater sense of control over their environments, allow them to deal with stressful life events, and help "establish order in daily relational experiences" (Harvey et al. 1990; Orbuch 1997, 459). Caregivers offer their accounts in two broad ways: by emphasizing caregiving as a "real" set of tasks worthy of remuneration and by framing their labor as a public good that benefits the broader community. In both cases, the accounts serve to remind caregivers—as well as "generalized others"—that their labor is worthy of respect.

Sample and Methods

Data are drawn from a two-year qualitative study of home care providers in Central City, California, a medium-sized city with approximately 500,000 residents. We focus on in-depth interviews and ethnographic observations of sixteen paid family caregivers who are part of a broader sample of home care aides studied (N = 43). Family providers are paid an hourly wage ($9–11 per hour) by a state program, In Home Supportive Services, to provide care for a relative.

The clients served by IHSS are generally elderly, disabled, and low-income and qualify for some form of subsidized in-home care via Medicaid waiver programs. Disabled children are also eligible for IHSS support, and parents often become paid caregivers to their dependents. In our sample, three of the caregivers are paid to care for their children. Family caregivers interviewed for this study, as well as the "clients" for whom they care, openly identified themselves as struggling financially; the average monthly income of IHSS providers in California is $430 (Berg and Farrar 2000). IHSS family providers in the sample generally have a long history of caring informally for family (child care, elder care) but as a rule have little formal experience and job training in home care. Just three of the sixteen family providers in the sample are licensed certified nursing assistants, or CNAs.

The family providers range in age from twenty-one to seventy years. The median age of the family providers is fifty-two. Eight providers are white, six are Black, and two are Latino. Three caregivers are male. Six providers also work outside the home as nursing aides for nonrelatives. The sample roughly mirrors the general population of home care workers in California and the United States, with a high percentage of women and an overrepresentation of racial and ethnic minorities (Smith and Baughman 2007).

Because family providers perform their waged labor in the home, formal interviews with respondents often led to observations of the daily routines and tasks associated with home-based care work. While interviews generally lasted one to two hours, the first author routinely spent three to four hours on site with caregivers and their families, sometimes returning for a second visit. In addition to the ethnographic data collected in caregivers' homes, the first author also accompanied IHSS public health nurses and social workers on visits to the homes of family providers. The ethnographic data collected in caregiver homes helped contextualize some of the claims made by respondents during formal interviews, thereby providing a richer account of what it means to be paid for familial care. Pseudonyms are used to protect the confidentiality of research subjects (Central City, the location of the study, is also a pseudonym). Although the interviews yield a wide variety of caregivers, the fact that we sampled caregivers from voluntary trainings and orientation meetings suggests that a certain selection of workers may be overrepresented in the sample (such as conscientious workers, aides with more time to attend meetings, and aides who are better connected to IHSS resources and programs). That said, training workshops attract caregivers through incentives of free dinner, gifts, or money, which suggests our sample might in fact reflect a range of caregivers and caregiving orientations.

Note also that while this chapter focuses almost exclusively on paid family providers, the first author has conducted extensive interviews with home care workers who are not related to their clients (Stacey 2005). We reference this group of aides in the current analysis where we feel it relevant to the discussion at hand.

When Love and Money Converge

On the surface, the story of the paid family provider mirrors that of family caregivers everywhere: a family member falls ill or becomes disabled, tough decisions are made about who will provide care and where, and someone (usually a mother, daughter, or sister) assumes primary responsibility for care. There is, of course, nothing particularly unusual about such a scenario. Family care is generally held in high moral regard—at least in a superficial sense—by a public that tends to view caregiving as an act of altruism.

For providers in this study, however, receiving wages from a means-tested program (IHSS) sullies the altruistic dimensions of care by bringing love and money together in the space of the home. Specifically, family providers are in violation of an implicit axiom of the familial obligation to care: tending to one's family, while honorable, is not something women (or men) should do in exchange for pay.

Most providers are aware that their paid work is non-normative. This perception is further reinforced in interaction with others, who overtly judge or condemn the decision to apply for IHSS support. Melanie, a white provider taking care of her brain-impaired father, lives paycheck to paycheck and often feels belittled by people who do not understand her commitment to her father. While on IHSS, she has had numerous encounters with a family lawyer who fails to recognize her paid caregiving as work and chastises her for not having a "real job" outside of the home.

Callie, a white caregiver in her late forties who cares for her disabled cousin, routinely encounters friends, acquaintances, and neighbors who question why she is being paid for the care of family: "They think, 'I don't know why you get paid for taking care of a family member when you could do it for free.' Well, you know, if PG&E [a utilities company] would recognize and say 'Oh, yeah, you don't need to pay for your bill because you're taking care of your brother or your sister or your daughter; we won't charge you anything.' If you didn't have those living expenses, I'm sure you could do that. But unfortunately, we all have bills to pay, you know? Even the grocery store won't give us a 'buy groceries free' card."

Charlene, a white woman with a disabled child, learned about IHSS from a friend and was relieved that she could provide direct care to her daughter without sinking into poverty. Even though receiving a wage for the care of her daughter enabled Charlene to meet her obligations as a mother, she was initially very reluctant to talk to others about her employment situation for fear they would react negatively: "I had a real problem at first when I went on the program, probably the first two years. I would almost cry when I had to tell people what I did because I felt like a welfare recipient. I had to readjust my thinking, and really recognize what I was doing. I mean . . . my first two reviews with [the social worker] I almost cried through the whole thing. I don't like to tell people that I stay home and I'm paid to stay home and take care of my kid, because people really did treat me like I was, you know, on the dole."

Most family providers encounter people who overtly or subtly communicate that it is not "right" to receive pay for the care of family. Whether encounters involve egregious behavior or subtle commentary on the part of unsympathetic others, caregivers seem to internalize the idea that their paid labor is deviant and against the social mores of family care. Family providers sometimes struggle to understand their care as work and are unsure whether they are entitled to the wages that IHSS provides.

Joyce, an African American woman caring for a brother with cancer, finds it nearly impossible to ask her case worker to increase her paid hours, even though tending to her brother is an around-the-clock affair that precludes her from taking another job. Joyce's sister implores her to ask for more hours, but Joyce feels unsure about asking for more money for the care of a relative: "My sister was complaining, she wanted to know why I didn't go to them [IHSS] and complain, make them give me more hours. I said, 'He's my brother,' so I feel that they kind of figured the same thing . . . that he was my brother and they shouldn't be paying me at all. But under the circumstances, you know, [I am] up in the morning . . . it is, it is a full-time job. Really, really it is."

Lucia, a Latina caring for her developmentally disabled daughter, reluctantly accepted the support of IHSS after realizing that she could no longer balance work outside the home with care for her daughter and commitments to her husband and other children. Refusing IHSS services for nearly ten years, Lucia initially found it difficult to accept that she could be paid for the care of family, "So the first time that they let me know [I could apply for IHSS], my daughter was very little. I say, 'You know, forget it!' I was too proud, you know? I had too much pride, so I just [cared myself] until she was nineteen years old. I was thinking, this is ridiculous, you know? I've been doing this for such a long time, you know? This is my child, this is my job, it's my responsibility."

Other caregivers are initially confused about how they should identify themselves to others, further evidence that they are uncomfortable with the way that love and money coalesce in their homes. Sally, a fifty-two-year-old African American woman caring for her brother, has worked as a nursing aide on and off for most of her adult life. When asked whether she is forthcoming to friends and acquaintances about being paid to care for her brother, she responds, "Oh no, I don't tell people I am a caregiver, even though I receive a check for caregiving. I did it for many years, but to give myself a title? No, females are caregivers."

Similarly, Lete—who cares for her son—routinely tells people that she is a "cook," referring to her five-hour-a-week job preparing meals for her church, even though she spends a majority of her working hours providing paid care at home. Both women generate most of their monthly income through the care of family, but neither discloses the fact to outsiders.

Not all caregivers withhold information about their care work. Paul, an African American man caring for his mother, believes his work is misunderstood, but, unlike Sally and Lete, he is forthcoming about his work as a paid family caregiver. He explains "I'm a care provider, yeah, I'm proud of what I do. . . . I consider my employer to be the county IHSS. They're the ones who send me my check!" Paul is comfortable talking to his male friends—most of whom are police officers—about his care work, and he believes they "understand and respect" what he is doing, even though they occasionally joke that they "hope they never have to do that."

Another male caregiver in the sample, Jose, is similarly open about his job as a paid caregiver for his wife. Given the sample size, it is difficult to say whether gender is a factor in Paul and Jose's willingness to disclose the nature of their paid employment, but it is certainly reasonable to assume that for the men in the group, receiving pay is less a violation of caregiving norms than it is for women. Indeed, Paul and Jose may well feel entitled to pay because they are less likely to experience gender norms that render love and money incompatible in the context of care (Folbre 2002).

Justify My Love: Constructing Accounts of Paid Family Caregiving

Feelings of shame, discomfort, and embarrassment that come from receiving a wage for the care of family persists for many caregivers, even after years of employment with IHSS. Joyce, for example, continues to care for her brother without asking for increased hours or pay from her social worker, all the while remaining discreet about her status as a paid family provider when she encounters friends or acquaintances. Other caregivers, by contrast, learn to reframe their caring labor in a way that emphasizes the broader social value of their work and provides justification for the compensation they receive. To account for their work, caregivers tend to play up the skill of caring and/or emphasize that their care is a benefit to all—a kind of public good.

Martha, a white family provider in her early sixties, is a paid caregiver for her ex-husband, Bill, who recently suffered a stroke. Although previously estranged from one another, Bill's stroke and shared custody of a mentally ill son brought the couple together again (although they remain divorced). Martha initially felt uncomfortable with the idea of receiving money for Bill's care, but her activism in the union empowered Martha to work for "a profession that's worth being a profession." She further explained that most people fail to understand the work associated with caregiving and, as a result, the work is socially devalued and unfairly compensated. As a union steward, Martha spends her non-work hours engaged in constructing accounts about her work, talking to other family providers, community organizers, and political leaders about the nature and value of care work.

In an interaction with a social worker who questioned whether Martha had a genuine need to be compensated for caregiving, Martha reminded the woman that even the most simple task—like brushing someone's teeth—requires time and skill: "The social worker will tell you that they can pay only for the time that you are doing it. Ok, but am I doing it if I have to stand there and wait? And when you're done, can you clean it all up? Can you put it back? Those are things that they don't understand. Do you need help with toilet items? 'Course you do. And if you can't go in there and take out what you need and clean it up afterward, you need help. Brushing your teeth does not just involve pushing the brush."

Paul likewise feels strongly that the work associated with his care is unrecognized and unfairly compensated. As mentioned earlier, Paul's friends and his wife are largely supportive of his caregiving, but he feels that generally "people don't understand what we do. Period." In particular, Paul feels that social workers assigned to his mother's case fail to recognize the hours involved in her care. He finds himself explaining to anyone who will listen about the extent of his caring commitments:

> They [IHSS] only pay you for what you say you are supposed to do. But what happens when she slips and falls at night and you got to take her to the emergency room and you got to sit there for five hours waiting? They don't pay you for that stuff. What happens if things like that come up? They'll only give you 3.5 hours a month for that. But then you have more doctors' appointments to go to, and then now there's eye surgery, you know, the cataracts. They only pay me like four hours, or allow me 4.5 hours a month for doctors' appointments. That's one morning! You got to be there at 6:30 in the morning, wake up at 5:30, and then you got to wait for the surgery, get done, you're out of there probably by 2:30, 3 o'clock in the afternoon. . . . So you're not being paid for everything that you're doing and that's what really aggravates me.

Other caregivers emphasize the emotional skills associated with caregiving, drawing particular attention to the way that the care of a family member improves the quality of life for loved ones. Callie, a white caregiver, cares for her disabled cousin and has also cared for an aunt with terminal cancer (in both instances she received pay from IHSS). She is very active in the union and feels compelled to explain—in union meetings, public rallies, and meetings with political representatives—exactly how her skills as a caregiver benefit her family:

> You work hard on them [family] for six months, exercising them, getting them ready, and then one day is the first day that they can walk and you see them take their first step after a stroke. After all that praying and exercising and working on them. . . . And people don't understand, they never will. When you've helped them get everything all situated and when you've helped them pray. . . . You

know when they pray and you pray with them through their last breath and when they pass on you know that you've done everything that you could for them and you know that they met a peaceful end.

Martha, Callie, and Paul, in different ways, use their accounts to emphasize caregiving as a set of discrete emotional and physical tasks that are necessary to maintain the health and well-being of family. They each hold strong convictions about the importance of paid family caregiving and deflect negative attention by rendering visible the effort and skill associated with their work.

From the perspective of some caseworkers and public health nurses who work directly with clients and their caregivers, accounts that focus on the "real" work of family caregiving are less than convincing. Of the four case workers and eight public health nurses shadowed and interviewed for this study, only two had positive things to say about family providers. Most openly questioned the intentions and motivations of caregivers who receive money for the care of family and nearly all criticized the idea of a union for caregivers. Providers who agitate for more hours or pay were generally seen as trying to "game" the system, that is, claiming more paid hours than actually needed for care. As one social worker commented, "The fraud [of caregivers] makes you jaded."

While fraud is part of the IHSS program, even those providers who do their work with integrity and honesty—and who have legitimate claims for greater recognition and pay—suffer a courtesy stigma (Goffman 1963; Herek 1999) due to their association with a minority of fraudulent workers. Family caregivers are fully aware that they are maligned by a subset of county workers. As one caregiver explained, "They [social workers] have always disdained us and still do. A lot of these social workers just have no idea what it's like in the real world when you are dealing with [family] patients."

Given this reality, and the widespread assumption that IHSS suffers from rampant fraud, it is not surprising that family providers also construct accounts that emphasize their care work as a public good that benefits the broader community. Charlene, the white caregiver mentioned earlier, has consciously changed the way she narrates her work in a way that emphasizes the benefits to taxpayers and the state coffers:

But I think a lot of that is how I presented the program. Now . . . I think I present it differently, because I'm totally supportive of the whole idea now. I mean I'm saving the state a tremendous amount of money, you know? I'm saving every taxpayer out there a tremendous amount of money by doing the job myself, and not only by doing the job myself, but I do a much better job. I also, I'm her educator, I'm her full-time medical person, and I'm the caregiver twenty-four hours a day. They don't have to pay the teacher, they don't have to pay a nurse, and they don't have to pay a caregiver. . . . I'm giving her better quality care then she would receive by anybody else in the home, or, in an institution, you know?

Like Charlene, Lucia believes that her work saves her fellow taxpayers money. She remembers the moment when she realized that her work was a benefit rather than burden to the state: "Some say, 'You can decide to put your daughter in an institution or another place, if you don't want her here in the house.' She [the social worker] said, 'Do you realize how much the state and the county will be paying for one person [in an institution]?' So she let me know, she wrote down the amount and everything. I said, 'Oh my goodness.' She said, 'By you keeping her home, you're doing them a favor.' I thought, 'Oh my gracious.'"

Paul, in his account, focuses less on benefits to the taxpayer and more on the broader altruism of his work. In his narrative, he emphasizes the difference between selling something and caring for something, thereby shifting attention away from the pecuniary impetus for his work and reasserting the purity of his own intentions: "You're doing things for your community, you know, instead of selling them something or doing them something. You're caring for somebody and helping them live a better quality of life. That's the kind of person I am. . . . I like to know I'm doing something helpful, you know. I mean, I've been there and did that, made money you know, done that. I was very successful at it . . . so I got a new challenge here."

Here Paul contrasts the "new challenge" of caregiving with earlier pursuits such as "making money." Although Paul is likely referring to the challenges of caring for an elderly parent, we suggest that Paul and other family caregivers also face a broader, longer term challenge of defending the legitimacy of their paid care work. As the above anecdotes illustrate, some caregivers manage this challenge quietly, while others learn to recast their work through strategic, purposeful accounts. While we cannot say with certainty that constructing accounts eliminates negative feelings and experiences associated with paid care, it is undoubtedly the case that a subset of family providers manage the norm violation of paid caregiving by reframing their labor as "real," socially valuable work.

Considering Paid Family Caregiving

Family providers employed by IHSS constitute a significant, yet relatively invisible, part of California's population of home care workers. Although considerable attention has been given to non-family home care aides in California (Boris and Klein 2006; Delp and Quan 2002; Howes 2004, 2008; Stacey 2005, 2011), very little scholarly work mentions the subset of family caregivers who comprise roughly 40 percent of the total IHSS work force (Berg and Farrar 2000). Beyond the uniqueness of the population, we suggest that an examination of family providers also contributes to ongoing discussions in sociology about the hostile worlds of love and money, and the way that caregivers interpret and account for their labor, especially when that labor is carried out in non-normative ways.

The IHSS program gives those who are eligible the ability to meet their familial obligations without sacrificing employment income. Although the program helps offset the financial costs associated with the familial obligation to care, there are social costs tied to participation in the program. Receiving roughly $9 an hour to care for "their own," family providers live and work in Hochschild's (2003b) "third sector" of social life, where the norms of private life (that is, that family should provide care to relatives out of obligation, duty, and love) sit in opposition to the market logic of paid employment. As a result, family providers struggle to make sense of whether they are employees in the conventional sense and are unsure about whether they are entitled to ask for better hours or increased pay as other workers do. These findings support Hochschild's hypothesis (2003b) that the "marketization" of private life complicates social and cultural understandings of care and work. In a similar sense, the experiences of family providers lend further empirical support to Zelizer's claims that money and love are often seen as incompatible with the private space of the home, especially when intimate relationships are changed or challenged as a result (Zelizer 2005).

The fact that love and money remain hostile worlds for family providers is of potential interest to sociologists of gender and care work, who implore policy makers and public officials to think creatively about ways we can recognize and compensate caregiving. It seems that any steps toward such a goal—especially those that involve promoting monetary compensation of women's caregiving in the home—will rely on anticipating and reframing public debate surrounding the value of care more generally.

There is no shortage of public debates over whether women should be paid for caring "for their own," whether that care is of children or elderly/disabled adults. From the era of the "welfare queen" to more recent public debates over family home care providers in California, it is clear that Americans are at best ambivalent and at worst hostile to the idea of compensating women for the care of dependents (Quadagno 1996). Even when non-family members care for the elderly or disabled in the context of the home, there is confusion at the level of public opinion and public policy about whether such caregiving constitutes work. For some time, home care aides—those unrelated to their clients—sought protection under the Fair Labor Standards Act, legislation that affords American workers, among other things, the right to a minimum wage and overtime pay. Until recently, federal labor law exempted home care aides from the FLSA because they were seen as providing "companionship" rather than "labor" to care recipients, further evidence of Zelizer's hostile worlds thesis. Scholars of care work must continue to interrogate contexts where love and money collide, especially in the space of the home, to reframe the debate around public compensation for so-called "private" acts of care.

Scholars of care work have long called for sustained funding for community-based long-term care, akin to the family pensions and stipends offered caregivers in many European democracies (Bashevkin 2002; Harrington Meyer 2000). It appears from our data, however, that family providers—like most Americans—struggle to make sense of a program that pays them for care and brings together the hostile worlds of love and money (Zelizer 2005). Extending social programs like the one detailed here will therefore rely on reframing public accounts—at a national, state, and local level—about the value and importance of care work. We suggest that the best place to start such an effort is with paid caregivers themselves, who are critical barometers of how a broader society values, or does not value, caring labor.

Acknowledgments

This chapter is a revision of "For Love and Money: The Experiences of Paid Family Caregivers" first published 2012 in *Qualitative Sociology* 35 (1): 47–64.

18

Paying Family Caregivers

• •

Parental Leave and Gender
Equality in Sweden

MARY K. ZIMMERMAN

In the spring of 2013, prominent media in the United States exploded with the report that women were the primary breadwinners in some 40 percent of American families, including single parent families but also dual earner families where wives earn more than husbands (Wang, Parker, and Taylor 2013). This trend causes us to rethink our assumptions about families. It also leads us to a long-standing care-work dilemma in American family life: how to reconcile women's work as breadwinners with the expectation that they serve as primary caregivers for young, old, and disabled family members. Family care work, still largely performed by women, is vital to individuals' health and well-being; yet at the same time, it imposes multiple penalties, interfering with women's paid employment, job performance, professional advancement, and the ability to earn an adequate income and support the family. When women who are wives, mothers, and daughters find themselves caring for husbands, children, and aging parents as well as holding down a full-time job, they endanger their own health as well as the well-being of those in their care.

This chapter argues that work-family tensions and conflicts are not simply personal problems resulting from jobs in the labor market clashing with family life. Rather, they are shaped in large part by social policies that governments either enact or neglect and resist (Zimmerman 2013). To date, the United States has adopted relatively few universally available policies that help reconcile the competing demands of employment and family, in stark contrast to many of its peer nations (Gornick and Meyers 2003). This chapter turns to one of these countries, Sweden, to examine its program of compensating parents when they leave employment to care for a newborn or young child. While parental leave policies address just one facet of family care work, learning how one established program of compensated family care (forty years old in the case of Swedish parental leave) has worked, been adjusted, and developed over time adds an important dimension to the study of paid care work.

Compensation for family caregivers challenges and blurs the distinction between paid and unpaid care work, yet such arrangements are becoming more common. Strong demographic and economic pressures point toward compensated family care as an increasingly significant part of how care work is organized in high-income countries. In the United States at the state level, there have been several instances of policies to pay family caregivers (for example, California's paid parental leave program to pay family home care providers). Nationally, the U.S. Congress, which resisted for decades adding compensation to the job protections already afforded to qualified family caregivers under the Family and Medical Leave Act of 1993 (Public Law 103-3), recently enacted a program that pays family caregivers of wounded veterans under the Caregivers and Veterans Omnibus Health Services Act of 2012 (Public Law 111-63). Nonetheless, the overall inadequacy of policies to address work-family conflict has led Joan Williams (2010) to charge the United States with having the most "family-hostile" policies in the developed world. She and others contend that it is nearly impossible for American middle-class and working-class families to hold jobs and also care for young children and other family members (Gornick and Meyers 2009; Lewis 2009). Moreover, purchasing care in the market as a backup resource is typically out of the question for many families. These scholars suggest that the best solution is to adopt improved versions of the supportive public policies found in many European countries.

Swedish parental leave is the most generously compensated among the twenty-one countries of the Office of Economic Cooperation and Development (OECD), all of which offer paid parental leave except the United States (Ray, Gornick, and Schmitt 2010). A key point suggested by the Swedish experience is that compensating family caregivers has the potential to alter the family division of labor. Thus, how public compensation policies are constructed can have important consequences for gender roles and family relationships. Policies have the potential to incentivize who performs care work, which can either promote or impede gender equality. For example, one of the key changes made in Sweden was to set aside thirty days of paid leave for each parent, days that could not be transferred. Fathers' days, therefore, would be lost if not taken. This so-called "daddy month," subsequently extended to two nontransferrable months for fathers, resulted in more equitable sharing of leave days between mothers and fathers.

This chapter presents a chronology of the challenges and solutions in the development of Swedish parental leave. In addition, it addresses the relationship between these care-work policies and gender, showing how compensated parental leave supports Sweden's gender equality goals as well as how these goals have been interpreted and framed through policy adjustments and changes over the years. The chapter presents data on changes in fathers' uptake of leave days and discusses related policy impacts such as changing cultural expectations for fathers and the overall nature of father-child relations. Finally, it considers what these developments tell us about prospects for high-income countries when they compensate parents for care work.

Sweden: Dual Earner/Dual Carer Society

In Sweden, social policies are guided by an equality principle.[1] In terms of family care work, policies have been directed toward minimizing the effects of socio-economic differences and circumstances that might unduly burden one family versus another, including illness and disability, the birth of a child, and job loss. Under the equality principle, it is intended that families with children should experience no more socioeconomic penalty for their choice to have children than families without children. The Swedish Social Insurance Agency states the main objective of Swedish family policy as "Differences in the economic conditions between families with or without children shall be reduced" (Wolf and Löfgren 2007). The equality principle also extends to equality in gender roles (the gender division of labor), embodied in the ideal of a dual earner/dual carer society where both parents earn and equally share family work.

Social philosopher Nancy Fraser explains the dual earner/dual carer model in the context of various ways to divide family labor (Fraser 2000). She argues that two-parent families where one is the breadwinner and the other takes charge of the household and care work are no longer sustainable, and then goes on to examine the various possibilities for contemporary family divisions of labor in terms of seven equity criteria for women. She finds the dual earner/dual carer form to be the most gender equitable and therefore the most preferable. Janet Gornick and Marcia Meyers embrace this model in their empirical work and offer it as their institutional proposal in their Real Utopias Project volume (Gornick and Meyers 2003, 2009). Notably, they along with Fraser name Sweden as the best existing example of the dual earner/dual carer society.

While scholars concur that Sweden merits distinction for policies that reconcile work and family, Swedish outcomes still are far from perfect. Despite the equality principle, the Swedish labor force is highly sex segregated with women and men working in different sectors and types of jobs. Moreover, Swedish women work significantly fewer hours per week than men. Many work part-time and mothers are more likely than fathers to take advantage of a family policy allowing full-time workers with young children to work six- rather than eight-hour days. In 2011, women with children worked approximately seven fewer hours per week than men with children (Statistics Sweden 2012). On the other hand, consistent with the goal of achieving gender equality in the gender division of labor, current data also show that Swedish women with children are working more hours than previously while men with children are working fewer hours (Statistics Sweden 2012).

To be both earners and carers, parents need job protection as well as income protection when children are born and during the first years of life. This enables them to maintain their place in the labor force and be able to assume a portion of family care work at the same time. The Swedish parental leave benefit offers this protection, complemented by a system of affordable preschool child care. These two types of policy—paid parental leave and publicly subsidized child care—comprise key pillars supporting Sweden's dual earner/dual carer family model (Ferrarini and Duvander 2009).

Following the Swedish way of thinking, the compensated parental leave portion of family policy is officially called parental insurance. The concept of insuring couples for parenthood conveys the idea that families with children should be sheltered from disruptive child-related economic and social costs. Reflecting on the equality principle, it is thought that the additional burdens related to having children for these families should be minimized. The insurance concept provides a culturally appropriate frame for the relatively generous Swedish program of parental leave, linking it to other forms of social insurance such as sickness leave and old-age pensions. In the social policy literature, this framing aspect of a social policy is sometimes referred to as its "policy logic" (Lewis 2009). I will return to the policy logic and framing of Swedish parental leave in a subsequent section after first reviewing the specific benefits and benefit changes over the life of the program to date.

Parental Leave Policy Changes, 1974–2012

Welfare state and care work scholars since at least the 1970s have debated, theorized, and comparatively examined the issues of family care work, citizenship, and the ideal of a woman-friendly state (Hernes 1987; Waerness 1978). Despite their complexities and the variability of benefits over time and from country to country, parental leave policies are central to this scholarship. The parental leave system in Sweden consists of three elements of paid support: a pregnancy cash benefit, paid leave in connection with childbirth or adoption, and a temporary leave benefit in the case of sick children. Together with the child allowance and other various forms of cash assistance, these policies help facilitate the dual worker/dual carer family and reduce the differences in living circumstances between families with and without children. This chapter will focus on compensated leave associated with childbirth or adoption.

Parental leave days in Sweden can be used any time before the child turns eight, although workers typically use it in the early years of a child's life. To qualify for the full benefit, a parent must have been employed for the previous 240 days. Unemployed parents are also paid for parental care, but at a lower level of compensation. When the program started, parents were entitled to 180 days with earnings-related compensation set at 90 percent of income up to a ceiling. Compensation remains at the ceiling level for those who earn more. Although the government suggested that both parents share leave days equally, the expectation was that mothers would take most days. For this reason, the extent of leave was limited to six months so that mothers' absence from work would not jeopardize their jobs or advancement (Duvander and Johansson 2012). Table 18.1 gives a historical view of how the length, compensation, and terms

Table 18.1
Swedish parental leave policy adjustments, 1974–2012

1974	Introduction of 180 days of parental insurance; open transfer; 90% earned income compensation; explicit policy focus: facilitating mothers' employment and the dual earner family
1976	Increase to 210 days of insurance
1978	Increase to 270 days
1986	Increase to 360 days
1989	Increase to 450 days; last 90 days with flat rate compensation
1993	Compensation lowered to 75%, subsequently raised to 80% (in addition, some public and private sector employers offer an extra 10% as a job benefit)
1995	Introduction of one nontransferable month for each parent
2000	Explicit policy focus: increasing fathers' use of leave days and the dual earner/dual carer family
2002	Increase to 480 days of insurance; second nontransferable month added for each parent
2005	Explicit policy focus: equality in use of leave days between mothers and fathers
2007	Fixed amount or "ceiling" for calculating the 80% of earned income parental leave compensation is increased by 35%
2008	Introduction of a gender equality bonus given as a tax reduction when parents share days more equally
2012	Gender equality bonus changed to a cash payment; introduction of 30 double days during child's first year; both parents can take leave on the same day, using two leave days at the same time.

SOURCE: Swedish Social Insurance Agency

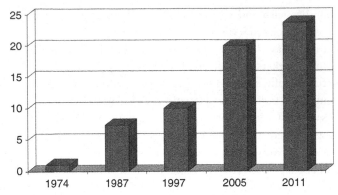

FIG. 18.1 Percentage of parental leave days used by Swedish fathers. (Source: Swedish Social Insurance Agency)

of leave period have changed. Adjustments in the early years of the program steadily increased the number of days of compensated leave available to parents.

At the end of the 1980s, despite encouragement from the Social Insurance Agency, fathers were only taking about 7 percent of the available days. Thus the agency, backed by the government's policy goals, decided to pursue the explicit policy goal of increasing fathers' share of leave days. This signaled a new phase in how parental leave was structured. Beginning in 1995, one month of leave was reserved for each parent and if not taken by that parent could not be transferred and was lost. Commonly referred to as the daddy month and mommy month, this was the first use of a quota approach for the allocation of parental leave days. By the end of the 1990s the uptake of parental leave days by fathers had begun to increase, reaching 10 percent of days in 1997 (see figure 18.1). In 2002, the daddy and mommy months were extended to 60 days of nontransferable leave for each parent. By 2005, fathers were taking 20 percent of leave days. While there was discussion among politicians of putting in place a 50-50 quota of days for parents, momentum for this idea slowed when the Swedish election of 2006 brought in a more conservative government promising greater choices for families in education and state welfare services.

Embedded in the new policies after 2006 were seemingly contradictory initiatives. These underscore a basic tension in the logic of Swedish family policy between the goals of gender equality and freedom of choice for individual families. On the one hand, the introduction of a Gender Equality Bonus offered further incentive for parents to divide leave days more equally. On the other hand, a provision that allowed municipalities to offer a child raising or home care allowance for parents of children ages one to three who stayed home and did not use publicly subsidized child care services appeared to undermine the dual earner/dual carer family model and possibly progress toward gender equality (Westlund 2007). By 2011, however, only one-third of Swedish municipalities were offering the home care allowance and parents of only about 2 percent of all children of eligible age in these municipalities had applied for it (Duvander and Haas 2013).

Despite the center-right government's emphasis on flexibility and choice, they continued to pursue policies to increase fathers' participation in family care through the structure of the parental leave program. The low level of the salary ceiling was thought to be another possible reason that fathers did not take more leave days. Parental leave compensation is set at 80 percent of each parent's salary up to a ceiling amount (an extra 10 percent is offered as an employment benefit by some employers to bring compensation to 90 percent). For parents earning above the ceiling, this means their compensation remains fixed at 80 percent of the ceiling salary regardless of how much more than that they earn. Therefore, high-earning parents' actual compensation can actually be much lower than 80 percent of what they earn. Men earn more than women in Sweden (European Commission 2013), so it was thought that fathers might be less likely to take parental leave because it would lower family income more than if mothers took the leave. Thus, in 2007, after years of only small increases, the ceiling was increased significantly, reaching approximately 440,000 crowns ($68,508) in 2012. Over this same period, the proportion of leave days taken by fathers increased to 23.7 percent (C. Wolf, personal communication, November 2012). Despite belief in the importance of fathers' higher earnings, subsequent research has shown that earnings considerations do not significantly impact their tendency to take leave (Ekberg, Eriksson, and Friebel 2013).

The overall picture in the development of the compensated parental leave program is one of slow but consistent movement toward care work equity within the family. There is also growing evidence that the daddy month reform is what has worked best to date to increase fathers' use of leave days (Duvander and Johansson 2012; Ekberg, Eriksson, and Friebel 2013). The latest reform effort is the Gender Equality Bonus, which gives parents an additional compensation (about $7.75) for each day they use the leave equally after the two "daddy months" have been taken. Since parents have up to eight years to use their leave days, more time is needed to fully evaluate this reform.

Development of the parental leave program also suggests movement toward care work equity within the family. The initial policy decision to let families voluntarily decide which parent would take parental leave resulted in fathers taking less than 1 percent of allotted leave days (figure 18.1). At that point, open choice and flexibility appeared to simply perpetuate gender-specific caregiver roles. To counter this trend, Sweden turned to a quota strategy of nontransferable daddy and mommy months. The first decade of the twenty-first century represented an active period in terms of pursuing equality in parental leave, extending nontransferable days to two months for each parent and significantly increasing compensation for higher-earning parents. By the fortieth anniversary of Swedish parental leave, the division of days by fathers and mothers is nearly halfway to full equality. There is growing evidence that what has worked best to increase fathers' use of leave days is the nontransferable sixty days; however, more recent reforms require more years of follow-up to fully evaluate their impact.

Framing Parental Leave Policies

In Sweden as in the United States, giving families flexibility and choice is a culturally appealing idea. Yet the initial parental leave policy offering flexibility and choice was heavily debated during the early years in Sweden, particularly with regard to its potential implications for gender inequality. Social Insurance Agency documents state the case against flexibility this way:

> Parents may exploit the flexibility of parental insurance in ways that adversely affect equal opportunities in working life. The lower salaries of women may partly be traced to their claiming the lion's share of parental leave and thus being branded as a more "risk-prone" supply of labor than men. . . . A less flexible parental insurance, preventing fathers from transferring days to mothers, should help promote gender equality . . . [and] a flexible social insurance can reinforce current gender structures. (Swedish Social Insurance Agency 2003, 26)

From the American perspective, flexibility is seen as a benefit rather than a risk, making the above argument against it somewhat surprising. Table 18.2 presents the language used in yearly policy directives (Regleringsbrev, literally translated as "letter of regulation") from Swedish government officials to the Social Insurance Agency, which has autonomous authority to implement them. The language and framing used in these directives is important because it guides those who plan and administer the parental leave program. As discussed previously, changing the gender division of labor was an implicit policy objective, first focusing on supporting and increasing women's employment and later on increasing men's care work. Between 2000 and 2009, the framing of parental leave goals shifted from increasing fathers' share to an explicit mention of equality between parents (see table 18.2). By 2012, the interests and standpoint of children, especially their having equal time with both parents, had become more of a focus: "the child needs and has a right to both parents" (Swedish Social Insurance Agency 2003). Also consistent with this shift, in 2012 the agency adopted a new equality measure to assess the success of the parental leave program: the percentage of children whose parental leave days with each parent have been divided somewhere between 40 and 60 percent. The previous measure, the percentage of leave days taken by fathers, shows that in 2012 complete equality was close to halfway accomplished with fathers using very close to 25 percent of the days compared to the target of 50 percent. Using the new measure, constructed from the perspective of the child, success appears somewhat further away. It shows that just 10 percent of Swedish children spend between

Table 18.2

Swedish government's annual directives (regleringsbrev) for paid parental leave, 2000–2009

2000	"The social insurance administration should work so that a *larger share of men will use more parental leave days*."
2001	"The national government requests to know the number of men using benefit days and the number of total days used by men."
2002	The one month nontransferable period for each parent was extended to two months (60 days).
2003	"The overall share of men taking parental leave the number of days used by men should increase."
2004	"*Decrease the differences between the child's parents* in terms of which parent takes leave."
2005	"The overall goal for parental insurance should be equality—that is, *the total number of benefit days should be equal between mothers and fathers*."
2006	Same as 2005.
2007	"Half each" should be the goal for parental insurance use.
2008	"The conditions for equal use of parental benefits between men and women should be improved."
2009	Through information, *parents should have better conditions for choosing* how they will share parental leave days.

SOURCE: Swedish Social Insurance Agency.
NOTE: Frame shifts noted in *italics*.

40 and 60 percent of parental leave days with each parent (C. Wolf, personal communication, November 2012) with a somewhat higher percent for children born in 2008 (Duvander and Haas 2013).

Evidence from this brief history of the parental leave program in Sweden shows the potential economic, gender equity, and child-friendly benefits of compensation for family care work. At the same time, however, the Swedish experience shows that how programs are designed and incentivized are critical elements. There are important trade-offs between flexibility and individual choices on the one hand, and more structured approaches such as quotas of leave days for mothers and fathers on the other. While flexibility and choice sound attractive, they have not been shown in Sweden to promote gender equality and the dual earner/dual carer family.

Conclusions

The daily demands of contemporary lives, whether in high-income or more moderate-income countries, require a new view of family care work and the gender division of labor. Who enters the labor force, who serves as the primary breadwinner, who takes care of the home and family needs—these are old questions that require new thinking, not just on the part of mothers and fathers but on the part of governments and policy makers. How should this work be divided? Can the competing demands of home and job be reconciled without putting parents and children at risk, either economically or socially? Social policies enacted by governments are central in shaping both divisions and solutions, influencing families to go down one path or the other. This examination of parental leave policies in Sweden not only shows that public institutions are significant forces in creating structures and rules, but suggests they influence the culture within which families construct their private lives. What are experienced every day as personal tensions, stresses, hassles, and crises can also be understood as the consequences of social policies (or their absence)—the dual earner/dual carer family model promoted by Sweden, the male breadwinner/female carer family of the past, or the dual earner/female carer model with which American families, especially those 40 percent headed by women, are struggling today.

Paid parental leave policies over the last decades have helped bring Sweden closer to fulfilling its interrelated social objectives of achieving the dual earner/ dual carer society, promoting gender equality, reconciling employment and family, minimizing the differences between families with and without children, and enabling a greater portion of Swedish children to have equal access (care time) with each parent. Much of this progress can be attributed to a relatively forceful policy approach using quotas of paid parental leave days as the incentive. Regarding the future, there is some thought that the quotas, by employing strong incentives and putting fathers into greater contact with their children, may have long-lasting effects in changing social expectations as well as male culture to accept and even encourage increased caregiving among fathers. It remains to be seen, however, if these hopes will come to fruition. It also remains to be seen how far the dual earner/dual carer family might reverse if Sweden's policies return to the flexibility and open choice that characterized the early years of parental leave when it was used primarily by mothers. So far, there is no evidence that such a reversal is occurring.

In high-income countries, public policies to pay family members for care-work are likely to become increasingly common, driven primarily by strong economic forces that require all able adults to be earners combined with increasing family care needs. Sweden's experience has shown that paying parents so they can leave work to care for their children immediately raises issues of gender equality. Of particular concern are the terms of compensation and whether they will enhance or reduce women's job advancement and overall equality. Sweden's early parental leave policies reinforced an already gendered family division of labor; however, subsequent adjustments promoted father's equal participation in order to achieve a more equitable division of family care. As shown here, the results to date show partial success: halfway to achieving full equality in the parental leave of mothers and fathers, with full equality yet to come.

Overall, the experience of Sweden in paying parents to care presents a strategy to promote both earning and caring in an equitable way. In the United States, feminists and others have criticized the federal government for having harsh family policies that fail to support employed mothers and for its general disregard for gender equity. The Swedish case shows a more proactive stance. Much depends, however, on the policy orientation and leadership of elected officials and the pressure placed upon them by the public. If, indeed, paying parents for carework becomes a more prominent part of public policy in the United States and elsewhere, the experience of Sweden instructs that the way compensation mechanisms work can have profound consequences for family relationships. Thus, it is critical that the details of compensation programs be carefully designed, implemented, and evaluated.

Note

1   Unless otherwise noted, information about Sweden's social policies and parental leave in particular has been provided by the Swedish Social Insurance Agency (Försäkringskassan) and through personal communication with agency staff in 2007, 2009, and 2012.

Part VI

Paths to Change

• •

Given the inadequacy of resources in the care work sector, it is not surprising that many of the jobs explored in this volume are what Arne Kalleberg (2011) characterizes as "bad jobs," with low pay and lack of benefits. In this section, scholars engage with efforts to improve working conditions in the care sector, exploring policy and practice innovations as well as worker perceptions of movements for change.

Some of these chapters describe efforts that focus on improving the pay and conditions of the "worst" care jobs through grassroots advocacy, unionization, or professionalization. For example, Deborah Little highlights the work of the Direct Care Alliance to mobilize groups of direct care workers to advocate for better pay and conditions for themselves and to pressure the state to change policies that disadvantage these workers. Unions have also been active in care worker movements, especially in health care and child care. Clare Hammonds examines an ongoing union movement among center-based childcare workers and explores motivations among different groups of workers to join the union. And Amy Armenia finds that some home-based childcare workers support a burgeoning professionalization movement and subscribe to professional aspirations as a way to improve their jobs.

While efforts like these strive to raise the floor under care workers as a group, other initiatives aim to provide opportunities for individual care workers to move into jobs with higher pay and more access to benefits. These strategies include employer-supported career lattices—programs that link employee training to salary increases and facilitate lateral and upward movement within a single industry. According to Jennifer Craft Morgan and Brandy Farrar, policies that support employee occupational mobility through career lattices hold great potential for low-wage workers in the healthcare sector, especially in light of recent changes to U.S. policy. Because health care is so rigidly credentialed, obtaining further education and training is critical for worker mobility but difficult to manage for lower-level workers. The partnerships described by Michelle Haynes and colleagues provide examples of collaborations between healthcare and higher education institutions that address some of the financial, logistical, and practical barriers facing entry-level healthcare workers seeking education and training. Across the care sector, efforts to improve opportunities for workers have the potential to create positive outcomes beyond the individual. Given the stratification of the care labor force by race, national origin, and other dimensions of inequality, policies that encourage mobility from lower-wage jobs to higher-wage jobs within the sector also have the potential to combat occupational segregation and increase diversity at all levels of the sector.

Some of the barriers to change in the paid care sector that are outlined in these chapters reflect the structure of the care labor force and echo concerns that have emerged in earlier sections. For example, a central issue is that overall wage levels are so low across many care occupations that worker investments in education and training may result in relatively low returns. And efforts that focus on raising the floor for the jobs at the bottom of the occupational hierarchy are facing a steep uphill climb. The chronic public underinvestment in the sector that has been implicated in these difficult conditions also makes it challenging for employers and community partners to create and sustain innovative programs (see Haynes et al. and Morgan and Farrar). More specific structural barriers include the work schedules of care workers—which often interfere with the ability to predictably attend classes as well as to participate in broader organizing efforts.

These chapters also highlight cultural barriers to change in the paid care sector, chief among them workers' orientation to an ethic of care that can undermine their ability to advocate for themselves, especially if they see their needs and the needs of those for whom they care as in conflict (see Little). Haynes and colleagues also outline cultural differences among institutions that hinder collaborative solutions. Several of the chapters in this section highlight that any movement toward change must include a discussion of how workers themselves situate their work (see Little, Armenia, Hammonds). Individual worker perceptions of their work are critical to understand in framing any social movement for change.

Despite the many barriers, these chapters offer what is ultimately a hopeful view of the possibilities for a future in which care work and care workers are more valued. Haynes and colleagues and Morgan and Farrar offer practical and inspirational models of programs and partnerships that are working to provide economic opportunities to care workers. And there is reason to believe that recent policy changes in health care in the United States will make programs like this more common (see Morgan and Farrar). The efforts of the Direct Care Alliance demonstrate a deep understanding of the motivations of care workers and explicit strategies to expand the ethic of care to link quality jobs with quality care (see Little). The advocacy of the DCA and other worker organizations was critical in the recent success in obtaining legal recognition and protection for home health workers under the Fair Labor Standards Act (FLSA). The narratives of child care workers presented by Hammonds show a range of motivations for involvement in unionization efforts that allow organizers to meet workers where their passions are. And Armenia outlines the ways in which child care workers identify—and do not identify—with efforts to professionalize their occupation, providing critical insight into the potential and pitfalls of these strategies.

19

For Children and Self

• •

Understanding Collective
Action among Early Childhood
Educators

CLARE HAMMONDS

At just twenty-five years old, Camilla already has more than a decade of
experience working in early education. Today she is the director of Happy Feet,
an early education center located in a midsized suburban community in central
Massachusetts. There Camilla manages a budget of more than a half million
dollars and a staff of over twenty teachers and assistants. The first time I met
Camilla, she was leading a professional development workshop for twenty
teachers in her region. The workshop was in a large basement classroom at her
center. Despite the absence of windows, cheery yellow paint, student art, and a
large tree mural give the space a welcoming feel. During the workshop, teachers
crouched on small chairs around two low tables taking notes as Camilla talked.

The workshop was coordinated by the Massachusetts Early Childhood
Educators Union (MECEU). The session was an outreach tool used in the
effort to form a nontraditional union of center-based early educators in
Massachusetts. When the workshop ended, Camilla encouraged the teachers
in attendance to stay for a few minutes because she wanted to share with them
information about an important ongoing effort to improve wages and working
conditions for teachers and directors.

Camilla explained that over the last year teachers and directors across the state have been coming together to form a nontraditional union. The union is nontraditional because it seeks to include both teachers and directors in a single unit that will then negotiate with the state over issues related to professional development and the recruitment and retention of the work force. Unlike a traditional union that seeks to increase wages by asking more from the employer or, in this case, the parents, the union is instead asking the state to increase their investment in the youth of Massachusetts.

Camilla then launched into a more personal story. In most ways, Camilla's career trajectory followed a pattern similar to other early educators I met while observing the MECEU campaign between 2010 and 2012. She began in high school working as an assistant at a center where her sister had been employed. After graduation, she wanted to continue working with young children, so she attended the local college where she got her bachelor's and subsequently her master's degree. Today she serves as the director at a nonprofit program located in one of the poorest counties in the state where nearly 85 percent of the center students are funded through state-subsidized childcare vouchers.

Camilla explained to the teachers why she is a part of the MECEU Organizing Committee. Her students are some of the poorest and most vulnerable in the state, and that she believes it is the teachers who can close the achievement gap between students. After spending six years in school, she is trained to notice things that parents simply do not. For example, she notices the early warning signs for autism and learning disabilities. She described her commitment to providing her students with the future that they deserve and that she believes a union for early educators will help to support that goal by giving the teachers the resources they need to provide the best education possible.

Camilla's emphasis on providing education for the most at-risk children was just one of four types of motivational narratives I found in interviews with teacher and director activists on the union campaign. While Camilla framed her motivation for participation as a desire to close the achievement gap, other teachers expressed that they were driven by a desire to support other teachers, financial considerations, or a "passion" for children. These accounts present a shared understanding of why teachers need a voice in the field and how it should be achieved. In this chapter, I summarize these four narratives and argue that the variations can be best explained with reference to both the characteristics of the individual teacher and the organizational characteristics of the teacher's center, particularly the extent to which the center is embedded in, and reliant on, the state. While focusing on four types of narratives does in some ways conceal important variations among the teachers, the use of this typology provides useful insights about how individual and organizational characteristics interact in creating motivations for workplace-based mobilization.

The unique characteristics of care work, in particular the relational aspects of this labor, have important implications for union organizing among childcare workers (Tuominen 2002). Previous scholarship has highlighted how the physical site in which the care work is carried out has important implications for the definitions of care (Fitz Gibbon 2002; Folbre and Wright 2012). Similarly, definitions of care may shift depending on who is doing the work. We know little about how these different understandings may in turn inform collective mobilization on the part of care workers themselves. How do different definitions of care, embedded in organizational contexts and individual histories, shape the possibilities for mobilization? In answering this question, the chapter examines Dorothy Sue Cobble's (2010) call for a consideration of how understandings of workplace-based collective action may change if we move beyond the traditional factory paradigm to put the experiences of personal service workers at the center of the discussion.

My analysis in this chapter is based on interviews with twenty-five teachers and directors at early education centers who were activists with the MECEU. In order to protect the confidentiality of my respondents, I have employed pseudonyms, changed the names of the centers, and altered inessential details about the individuals and their worksites. Data came in response to a specific question about what motivated them to participate in the union campaign. All of the women interviewed were formal members of the MECEU Statewide Organizing Committee. While their levels of participation varied, all committed to attending monthly meetings, making phone calls to other teachers, visiting centers with union staff organizers, and contacting legislators to win political support for their effort. These women represent the twenty-five most active educator activists on the campaign.

In addition to the use of interview data, my analysis here is informed by participant observation conducted on the campaign between 2010 and 2012, when I worked as a researcher for MECEU. In this capacity I attended organizing meetings, trainings, and leadership development workshops; visited centers with organizers; attended strategy meetings; and talked with legislators, advocates, teachers, and parents. This provided me with key insights about the overall organization and strategy of the effort.

In the discussion that follows, I first provide a brief overview of the unionization of care workers in the United States, specifically focusing on how the MECEU builds on many of these earlier efforts. I then present four different types of motivational narratives that were present among activists, demonstrating how each results from an interplay of organizational factors and individual characteristics. In particular, I focus on the how a center's relationship with the state combines with individual teachers' level of exposure to formalized professional education to shape their motivations for collective action.

Union Organizing in Early Education

Despite dramatically declining levels of union density and power in the United States over the last fifty years, low-wage direct care workers have emerged as an important site of new organizing and strength for the labor movement.

In particular this growth has occurred among a variety of "atypical" care workers who, because of their self-employed status, fall outside the structure of traditional labor law. These unionization efforts have relied on state-level legal innovations to leverage the presence of regulations and subsidies in care industries in order to establish statewide unions where care workers form a quasi-employment relationship with the state. These innovations have been made possible by a loophole that leaves states free to regulate the labor relations of workers who are specifically exempted from coverage under the National Labor Relations Act (NLRA).

Beginning with the successful unionization of home health aides in California in 1999, this national movement has spread such that today, approximately 440,000 home health aides and personal care attendants are unionized around the country. Additionally, since 2005, unions have organized about 200,000 home-based family childcare providers in fourteen states (Rhee and Zabin 2009).

Similar to these ongoing attempts to organize home care workers, the Massachusetts campaign to unionize center-based teachers and directors involves both a legislative effort to create new bargaining rights as well as grassroots effort to organize workers. In contrast to home care workers however, center-based early educators are already covered by the NLRA and have the right to bargain within their centers. As a result, center-based teachers and directors face a different set of legal barriers to organizing than home-based counterparts. Their challenges do not arise from their status as exempt workers but because they are already covered by national labor law. Consequently, the union cannot seek a collective bargaining agreement in a traditional sense but instead has chosen to develop alternative mechanisms for teachers and directors to cooperate and participate in the development of state early education policy.

The legislation that would allow an organization of center-based teachers and directors to negotiate with the state was first introduced in the Massachusetts House of Representatives in January 2011. That bill ultimately failed to make it out of committee and in January 2013, after substantial revisions, legislation was reintroduced in both the House and Senate. At the time of this writing, teachers and directors continue to engage in the grassroots work of building the union around the state while they await the decision of the Joint Committee on Public Service.

Existing studies of similar efforts have tended to focus primarily on the structure of these campaigns. In particular, scholars have been interested in how unions address the unique challenges associated with organizing low-wage, highly gendered, intimate service work that is performed in diverse settings (Delp and Quan 2002; Smith 2006). These studies have emphasized the importance of coalition building with consumers and advocates (Boris and Klein 2006; Delp and Quan 2002) and the need for strong union political influence (Reese 2011). While there is some scholarship that explores how care workers feel about these unionization efforts (Stacey 2011), there has not been a more comprehensive look at how movement activists understand and explain their motivations for participation.

Drawing on interviews with care worker activists themselves, this chapter provides an important contribution to our understanding of some of the tensions and complexities involved in organizing paid care work. These activists' narratives reveal the complex interplay between organizational structure and individual characteristics in determining the women's own understandings of their work and their explanations for engaging in collective action.

Motivational Narratives in Care Worker Organizing

The early educator activists I interviewed worked in a variety of centers that ranged in size from ten students to over two hundred. Among the activists there were teachers in nonprofit organizations, for-profit centers, religious centers, and Montessori schools. While there was a fair amount of variation among the activists' backgrounds, my interviews revealed two dimensions that were most salient to understanding which motivational narrative an activist employed.

The first dimension is the proportion of students at the center who are receiving state-subsidized care. This captures important features of the center itself. Currently there are about 53,000 children in Massachusetts who are served by the childcare subsidy program (Department of Early Education and Care 2013). The proportion of subsidized students accepted by a center serves as a proxy for a host of other organizational characteristics. Most directly, a high level of subsidies is an indicator that the center serves a high number of children in poverty. Because centers who accept subsidies are required by the state to meet additional standards related to quality, oversight, and reporting, high subsidy rates are associated with increased state regulation and control. The low reimbursement rates associated with childcare subsidies also mean that centers accepting a higher number of subsidized children also have lower overall operating budgets. As a result, these centers generally have higher student-teacher ratios and experience higher levels of turnover because of the low wages and increased levels of job stress associated with lower staffing levels (Richardi, Schuster, and Wagman 2011).

The second salient factor is the exposure an activist had to higher education. Over the last twenty years, the field of early education and care has experienced a profound move toward bureaucratization and professionalization. As a field, it has become increasingly legitimated as the site for the professional care of children. This shift has been driven by an increasing belief that early education can close the achievement gap as well as by economic research that highlights the long-term cost savings associated with early interventions (Douglas and Gittell 2012). A major consequence of this shift has been a move to increase levels of educational attainment among teachers.

Table 19.1

Motivational narratives for collective mobilization by early childhood educators on the MECEU campaign (2010–2012)

		Individual dimension	
		>Bachelors' degree	<Bachelors' degree
Organizational dimension	Subsidized students > 50%	Closing the achievement gap (n = 10)	Financial motivations (n = 6)
	Subsidized students < 50%	Supporting other teachers (n = 5)	"Passion" for children (n = 4)

In 2010, the Massachusetts Department of Early Education and Care, as a core component of its Quality Rating and Improvement System (QRIS), initiated new policies that will require lead teachers have a bachelor's degree or to be enrolled in a program and working toward that goal. Just over half of the teachers I interviewed had already completed at least this level of education. For teachers who had not, the regulation represented a significant hurdle. These teachers were generally older and had gained most of their knowledge about early education through experience in the field. The level of education, as measured by whether or not the teacher had yet completed her bachelor's degree, became the second salient factor in how activists understood their work and their collective action.

The interplay among organizational and individual factors and their related narrative outcomes is captured in table 19.1. In the discussion that follows, I describe the specifics of each of these narratives, illustrating how they can be understood in terms of the percent of subsidized students in a center and extent of professional education received by the teacher.

Closing the Achievement Gap

Among the activists I interviewed, those like Camilla who had a high level of education and worked in centers with a high number of state-subsidized students expressed motivations for unionization in terms of increasing support to close the achievement gap for at-risk children. Patricia, who works at a Montessori school in south Boston, was another such teacher. Originally from Haiti, she takes her work very seriously, adopting a no-nonsense tone when she speaks about her teaching. With a master's degree in early education, Patricia is the only activist I met who wears dress slacks and a button-down shirt in the classroom every day. When I asked Patricia about her motivations for participating in the union, she connected the way she had been supported by educators in her own life to the way she hoped to help children in need. She tells a story about her third grade teacher, explaining, "I feel like I owe her for what she has done." She goes on to say, "A union for teachers can help us to get what we need to do this work." For Patricia, the union is about providing education for the children who need it most. She says, "The children I work with need me. Most of them don't have much at home and sometimes their parents just don't know. They don't know what to look for and they need us to make sure they are prepared for school. You might be the next person to help them keep moving forward in life."

The connection between unionization and supporting at-risk students present in the narratives of both Camilla and Patricia is not surprising given that they both work at centers where more than three-quarters of the students receive childcare subsidies. The resulting high level of interaction with the state means that these teachers are more likely to be bound by the existing logic of state early education and care policy. In United States, policy in this area has historically been limited, owing primarily to an ingrained preference for maternal care that underlies historical opposition to state-funded child care (Michel 1999). The limited subsidies that have been available have been intended to provide targeted assistance in order to allow poor single women to enter the labor market and to protect the interests of their children who are not able to receive "proper" child care at home (Wexler 1997).

Activists I interviewed who worked in the centers most heavily reliant on state funding streams tended to describe their motivation for unionization in ways that paralleled these state rationales for early education support. They closely connected their activism to an understanding that this care is something specifically needed by poor children. For these teachers, their activism is less about themselves, or even about supporting students in general. Instead it takes on the specific logic of supporting students who are poor and at risk.

"Not for Me: I Do It for the Others"

While teachers with high levels of education working in centers where the majority of children were on vouchers exhibited a commitment to using their unique skills to support the most at-risk students, teachers with similar levels of education who worked in centers accepting fewer subsidies presented an alternative set of motivations for participation. These teachers were most likely to frame their participation in terms of their desire to help the other teachers who really need it.

That these teachers worked in centers that were less reliant on childcare vouchers meant that they were in locations with higher operating budgets. This allowed the center to pay higher wages and also to provide more services and resources to the students. In most cases, these centers accepted only a handful of voucher students and did so because of a moral commitment on the part of the owners to serving some low-income students. Abigail, a director at one of these centers, expressed the sentiment when she noted, "We have an obligation here to give back."

Among the activists I interviewed, more than a quarter were highly educated and worked in a center where fewer than 20 percent of the students were receiving state subsidies. These teachers overwhelmingly explained their activism as a way to lift the field but not as something that they saw as directly benefiting themselves or their work. Suzanne is a teacher who captured this perspective. Working at a small school in Boston, she was expecting her first son when I meet her. In her early thirties, Suzanne grew up in the Midwest and moved to Massachusetts only after her husband had to relocate for work. Her background is in math, and before taking this job at the Early Birds Learning Academy her teaching experience was limited to an art class she ran out of her home. The center she works at offers generous maternity leave, and she was planning to take six months off when she gave birth.

As an activist on the union campaign, Suzanne has taken a leadership role from the beginning, bringing other teachers in her center to meetings and visiting nearby centers with an organizer. When I asked Suzanne about what motivated her to participate in the union, she explained, "I feel like I am in it for other teachers that are struggling. I wish that I could understand more about the whole bill and how it gets passed and things like that. But I understand that it is for a great cause. Early childhood education. I just want to be a part of it. I want to do as much as I can. I hope that by being a part of it and contributing as much as I can it will inspire others to do the same. I have always been a person who is like, if I start something then I want to finish it. I want to see this all the way through and if I can." In this way, Suzanne is like other highly educated activists working in centers that are less financially reliant on the state. For these teachers, it is about bringing respect to the profession and supporting the other teachers who need it.

Jasmine is another activist on the campaign who employs a similar narrative to explain her participation. She has two master's degrees, one in biology and the other in early education. Employed at a wealthy center south of Boston, she explains that she is part of MECEU because "I just want to be a part of the move. I know, growing up, history was like the civil rights movement. And you know, I just want to be a part of history. I think that this field has been ignored for too long. It hasn't matured. And if I want to fight for something then it might as well be the field that I love and the children that I love. And I feel like someone fought for me. And I feel like this field is no different than all the things that this country has accomplished."

While Jasmine feels happy with her own position, she expresses a desire to both support other teachers and be a part of the movement. Another teacher who works alongside Jasmine at the same center expresses a similar sentiment: "Well, we get treated really good here, but this place is different. There are teachers who don't even get a sick day! What about them?"

"I Don't Have Time for a Second Job!"

Although discussions about the low levels of compensation certainly dominate political conversations on early education, only about 20 percent of the teachers I interviewed explicitly cited wages as their primary motivation for engagement with MECEU. All of these teachers worked in centers that were very reliant on the state subsidies. In addition, while they were at least enrolled in college, none had yet completed a bachelor's degree. Correspondingly it was these teachers who were most economically vulnerable by virtue of the fact that they were in lower-earning families. Of the six respondents who fell into this category, four were single parents.

For these teachers who work in some of the most underresourced centers in the state, this work provides an opportunity for a stable, albeit small, income. As the field has professionalized and regulations increased, however, it is those in this category who struggle the most to keep up with evolving standards coupled with stagnant wages. Because they work in centers that have limited resources as a result of minimal state investment, the teachers in this group are the most economically vulnerable activists on the campaign.

Sarah has been an activist with MECEU from the beginning in 2009. She is a petite Hispanic woman in her sixties, with a resonating voice that works well for quieting the children in the classroom. When I meet her for our interview, she is finishing up cleaning for the day. While she stops and listens intently when I ask my questions, she continues to scrub and organize while she talks. When I ask her about why she is involved in MECEU, she explains, "I don't want to keep saying this pay thing but it is that. I don't know how other people feel but I don't feel like we are getting acknowledged for what we do. They want us to do a lot. We just got accredited. And that was like . . . we were busting our ass to do that. And then they were telling us about this thing where we have to get our bachelor's. I just feel like we are pressured to do a lot."

Here Sarah articulates the heavy burden imposed by state regulations. Centers that accept subsidies are subject to increasingly strict standards intended to bureaucratize and professionalize the field. This involves a host of regulations that not only dictate what material must be taught, but also who is qualified to be a teacher. For those like Sarah who have been in the field for a decade, these regulations, particularly the requirements around returning to school, pose a real hardship and thus constitute a major factor in her decision to be active in MECEU.

Erica, a teacher in a center where about 75 percent of the students receive state subsidies, provides a similar narrative. "Why?" she asks me in response to my question about why she participates in MECEU. "What else can I do? I have to do something. I am trying to get by week to week. Like two months ago I had to choose between putting food on the table, him [her son] having clothing, paying the van, and you know. . . . I was like, wow. Every day I get out of here and I think about getting a second job. And now they like want me to do more?" It had been six years since Erica received a raise at her center. The voucher reimbursement rates in Massachusetts have been relatively constant over that same period, making it difficult for centers to raise wages.

"Because Children Are My Passion"

The fourth motivational narrative I identified in my interviews was among activists who did not hold a bachelor's degree and worked in centers that accepted only a small number of state-subsidized students. These teachers were the group that specifically connected their activism to the caring and nurturing aspects of their work. Many in this group discussed early education in terms of a "calling," using a language of emotion with terms like "love" and "passion" to express their commitment to the students and their commitment to improving the field. In contrast to the teachers in highly subsidized centers, the pressures and burdens of state interference were a less daily presence for these teachers. Furthermore, the presence of more private-pay students allowed teachers in these centers to receive better compensation overall. Without having completed a bachelor's degree, these teachers also had less exposure to the professionalizing process of higher education. The result was that they had the greatest flexibility to adopt their own meanings for their work and their activism.

Terry exemplifies the narrative found among these teachers when she explains, "The union is about kids. They are the reason I am here. I love working with kids . . . when you get that 'Aha' moment. They are so proud of themselves that they got it. Or when you are working with them to do a puzzle that they couldn't do. When they accomplish something they couldn't do. In that moment, they are learning and exploring and taking everything in for what it is."

While Terry did not articulate exactly how she thought a nontraditional union of early educators would support the kids, the two things were clearly linked in her mind. Jessica, another teacher, also explained, "I do this because children are my passion. They are my love. I love when we have them from the time they are infants and we see them get big. They become like . . . part of our family." Here Jessica connects her activism less to the specific skills that she brings to educating these children and more to her nurturing role.

Both Terry and Jessica had been in the field for over twenty years. They work at small nonprofit centers in neighborhoods that are wealthy enough to draw a base of private-pay students. Consistent with other findings on the role of higher education in forming a professional identity, these teachers' limited exposure to coursework and training means that when they spoke about the value of their work, they did not connect it to specific skills learned through formal education as did teachers like Camilla and Patricia. They spoke instead about their love of working with children and their bonds with them.

As a field, early education and care has undergone a profound shift in recent decades towards professionalization and bureaucratization. This shift is frequently referred to as the "educationalization" of child care (Noordegraaf

2007). The move has been welcomed by many teachers who seek to distance themselves from the "caring" aspects that may serve to devalue their labor, instead placing increased emphasis on scientific knowledge and standardized practices (Goldstein 1998). While evidence of this shift was found among many of the teachers I interviewed, it was the teachers in this group who most explicitly drew on the language of care and concern in explaining their motivations for participating the union campaign. These teachers were less constrained by the logic of early education and care policy–as well as by economic need–and the professionalization processes of higher education, thus allowing them to place greater emphasis on the emotionality of their work.

Using Motivation to Shape Activism

When talking with early educator activists on the union campaign, it became clear that their motivations for their participation were diverse and complex, shaped by both individual and organizational characteristics. These characteristics led the teachers to have different understandings of their work, the care they provided to children, and subsequently of their activism. Not surprisingly, teachers who worked in centers that had the greatest degree of interaction with the state often employed a logic that paralleled that of state early education policy in explaining the value of their care work. Activists in centers that were less reliant on state resources benefited from a wage buffer provided by higher overall operating budgets and correspondingly emphasized the collective value of their caring labor and more emotional aspects of the love and care they provided. These varied understandings of care work in turn were linked to different motivations for participating in collective action. Listening to these workers offers an important contribution to our understanding of care work more generally by providing insights about the relationship between understandings of care and collective action. It highlights the way in which organizational dimensions of care, most notably the role of the state in the provision of services, combine with personal characteristics of the caregiver in shaping activism.

Finally, these findings highlight the ways in which workers may draw upon unique resources associated with their labor to support organizing. For unions who continue to organize these workers, understanding this interplay may be essential for devising more effective organizing strategies.

20

Creating Expertise
and Autonomy

• • • • • • • • • • • • • • • • • • • •

Family Day Care Providers'
Attitudes toward
Professionalization

AMY ARMENIA

While most agree that something needs to be done to raise compensation levels and improve working conditions for care workers, no consensus exists regarding what that something should be. Many suggestions—including those in this volume—rely on some kind of collective action, bringing together groups of workers to advocate for change. These efforts tend to head in one of two directions: either unionization efforts that involve mobilizing as many workers as possible to agitate for change, or professionalization strategies, which attempt to draw boundaries around some workers to justify the raising of status and compensation for that group. For the purposes of this chapter, I will consider the strategies specifically related to professionalization for one group of workers: family day care providers.

By "family day care providers" or "home day care providers" (terms I use interchangeably), I mean those who provide child care for pay on a regular basis in their own homes. They are self-employed, may be relatives or nonrelatives of the children they care for, and these settings may be regulated or unregulated by government agencies.

Simultaneously located in the market and the home, family day care remains a site of devalued reproductive labor. As Margaret Nelson writes,

> If women are doing the work of child care, and if they do it cheaply at home, capital does not have to pay the full costs of the reproduction of its labor force. And as a society we can overlook altogether the fundamental challenge current trends pose to the notion of the separation between private and public spheres even as the responsibility for the care of children is moved outside the nuclear family. . . . We can also overlook the challenge these trends pose to traditional ideas about women's role when child care is defined as a "woman's problem" and is shifted from one woman to another. (1990, 8)

Concerns about the working conditions and pay of these workers are further obscured by stereotypes that suggest that most providers are stay-at-home mothers who are earning "extra money" for their families. However, recent research suggests that many do not fit this stereotype, with many workers who are primary earners for their families or who view their work with children as a long-term career (Armenia 2009). These providers also seek to gain respect by challenging stereotypes of themselves as "babysitters" (Tuominen 2003).

Like others in the growing sector of contingent and self-employed workers, these providers experience both advantages and disadvantages vis-à-vis childcare workers employed in organizations. On average, these workers earn $7.14 per hour, less than the minimum wage and less than center-based providers, who earn $9.60 per hour (Howes, Leana, and Smith 2012). Because they are self-employed, they typically do not receive health insurance, sick leave, or other benefits. Turnover rates among these workers are higher than among center-based workers, estimated between 35 and 59 percent annually (Kontos et al. 1995).

However, this tenuous position is countered by a potential for more control over their workplaces; family day care workers set their own hours, pay, and priorities for care within the limits of market demand. It is this autonomy that has allowed some space for professional movements in recent years. In this chapter, I will provide a brief examination of the goals and strategies of professionalization, and will use data from a large-scale survey of family day care workers to explore worker attitudes toward these efforts.

The Professional Project

When we think about a "profession" (as opposed to a "job"), we imagine an occupational position that is difficult to attain, requires higher standards for entry and practice, and is awarded higher levels of status, respect, and compensation accordingly. The practice of law or medicine, for example, is perceived as qualitatively different from other work—with years of training followed by a commitment to uphold the ideals of these elite careers. Early scholarly literature on professionalization accepted this uncritical view of professions, seeking to identify the characteristics of a profession and the role that professions served in society (MacDonald 1995). In the 1970s, scholars (most notably Friedson 1970 and Larson 1977) shifted their focus from structure to action. As Keith MacDonald (1995) notes, "The sociological question changed from 'What part do the professions play in the established order of society?' to 'How do such occupations manage to persuade society to grant them a privileged position?'" (6).

Magali Sarfatti Larson (1977) introduced the concept of the professional project, the idea that professionalization is a collective mobility project by a group of workers to create a "monopoly of competence" and a community of professionals who benefit from this monopoly. These movements involve the construction of boundaries around an occupational group, with the claim that this group is more dedicated, more qualified, and therefore more deserving of better work conditions. In addition, these boundaries aim to limit entry into the profession, creating higher demand for these workers and in theory, higher wages (Weeden 2002).

While this literature on professions has focused on predominantly male occupations, some scholars have addressed the particular position of women's professional projects. Anne Witz (1990) notes that historically, the professionalization process itself, based on dual systems of patriarchy and capitalism, has worked to raise status by excluding women. For example, the professionalization of medicine was at least partly an effort to push midwives and other female healers out of the field. She also notes that some groups of women workers responded to this gender inequality by professionalizing women's occupations, like nursing and teaching. However, the drawing of professional boundaries necessarily leaves some on the outside, creating inequalities between groups of workers. As a result, these movements have historically reinforced race and class stratification among women in care work occupations, as those who had access to professional training and networks benefitted at the expense of those who did not (Duffy 2011).

Professionalizing groups use various mechanisms to accomplish and present their unique qualities (MacDonald 1995). Specialized educational programs and credentials are central ways for a profession to socialize its members, create commitment and cohesion to professional ideals, and to justify occupational privilege to outsiders. Government regulation is often used to enforce entry qualifications and standards of practice. In addition, professional associations are established that can serve as forums for connections between workers, and advocacy for the group as a whole.

Family childcare workers have made use of all of these mechanisms to attempt to elevate their occupation to the level of profession: education and training, credentials, regulation, and professional associations. Licensed providers are required to fulfill education and training requirements by the state, and some providers pursue additional training to distinguish themselves from other providers. Accreditation by the National Association for Family Child Care, for example, certifies that certain standards are met by the provider in terms of physical environment, provider knowledge, and adult-child interactions. Other trained providers serve as gatekeepers to the profession; certification requires a somewhat costly and lengthy application, including observation by another accredited provider (Kontos 1992). Numerous associations for providers exist locally, statewide, and on the national level. Proponents of these efforts point to professionalization as a means to higher quality care and increased self-esteem for providers (Cohen n.d.). Some argue that training and professionalism are essential if day care is to become a highly regarded and well-paid occupation.

We know next to nothing, however, about worker responses to these professionalization efforts. Do providers themselves buy into these ideas (and mechanisms) for raising their status? To what extent do they see these efforts as part of a coherent professional project? How collective is this collective mobility project? Using quantitative and qualitative data from a survey of over five hundred family day care providers, I assess worker involvement in and attitudes toward training, credentialing, regulation, and provider associations.

Hearing the Voices of Family Day Care Providers

Data for this chapter come from a survey of licensed family day care providers in Illinois. A sample of 1,300 providers was randomly selected from the list of 10,000 individuals licensed by the Illinois Department of Child and Family Services (DCFS) in the summer of 2003. Each provider was mailed a questionnaire consisting primarily of closed-ended questions with some opportunities for open-ended response.

A second and third round of surveys were sent out to nonrespondents in the fall of 2003 and the winter of 2004 to increase the response rate. A total of 575 surveys were returned from the 1,280 valid addresses, for a total response rate of 45 percent. This chapter uses data for the 550 respondents who reported that they are currently working as family day care providers.

It is important to note that the inclusion of only licensed providers limits the generalizability of my findings. Family day care providers only need to be licensed by the state if they care for a certain number of children; in Illinois, a provider may care for up to three children (including any children of their own) without a license. Unlicensed providers (who far outnumber licensed providers) are likely to include more members of recent immigrant groups, Latinas, and undocumented workers, and are likely to be earning less than licensed providers. In addition, the presence of a large group of people who may legally operate outside of state regulation presents a challenge to those who wish to professionalize.

Using the provider survey data, I assess the extent to which providers evaluate and participate in different aspects of the professionalization project available to them. Specifically, I address how likely providers are to seek additional training and for what reasons. I also examine how likely providers are to invest the time and money in earning professional credentials, like their Child Development Associate credential or accreditation from the National Association of Family Child Care, two avenues by which they might distinguish themselves from other providers. Next, I explore providers' perceptions of state regulations that govern the standards and practice of family day care. Finally, I look at the extent of provider involvement with professional associations and their perception of these organizations as ways to connect with other providers and improve their status and working conditions.

Education, Training, and Credentials

The primary mechanism for professionalization is the establishment of education and training requirements, and the creation of specialized credentials that can distinguish workers in a field. Family child care providers encounter both state requirements for continuing education and optional opportunities for training and credentials, and express mixed sentiments about them.

Almost 90 percent of the sample report having attended some training or education for childcare providers in the last year. Attendance at some training is near universal for providers because of the state requirements for licensure. Home day care providers must attend fifteen clock hours of in-service training each year to keep their license.

The highest proportions of providers report that meeting the licensing requirements and learning about child development or education were big reasons for them to attend training (77.2 percent and 77.0 percent, respectively). Fewer providers report that learning about business skills and learning about government and childcare policies were big reasons for them to attend training (44.3 percent and 37.6 percent of providers, respectively). This difference in reasons for attending may reflect the range of training available to them, however, since these providers also appear to be eager for more training and education, including in the areas of business skills and policies. Approximately 88 percent of the sample reports that training in child development would be very or somewhat useful, and 88 percent report the same about training on early childhood education or curriculum. Three-fourths of providers report that training on business skills would be useful, and 63 percent report that training on lobbying government would be useful.

In their open-ended comments, providers also express desire for more training and education on child care and see the usefulness of these opportunities. As one provider comments, "As a childcare provider I have found that we must wear many hats. Also we must become very knowledgeable in many areas inside and outside of our field. As a result the learning aspect has been very rewarding."

Providers also express some dissatisfaction with the training opportunities available to them, either because of distance, cost, or quality of training. One respondent notes that training sessions are hard to get to for rural providers: "Having further education be a little bit more accessible would be nice. I dislike having to travel far distances to attend trainings." The costs associated with training can be prohibitive for those working with an already meager income, as noted by this provider: "Also, you have to take all these classes that we have to pay for. And you already don't make enough money to get by then have to worry about paying for classes, too."

Finally, one provider invokes an image of professional expertise and autonomy by suggesting that providers can adequately meet their own training needs, without requirements and workshops from the state. She writes, "If I could change anything it would be the fifteen training hours [the state] now requires you to have a year. I don't think those required hours are necessary for us to provide child care. A lot of us providers read about child development and are knowledgeable on our own without these hours."

As outlined above, professionalization efforts have stressed not just substantive training but credentialing for providers. Proponents have emphasized the importance of both general educational credentials (like high school diplomas and college degrees) as well as specific credentials for childcare work. These credentials involve a greater commitment of time and resources from providers than the training noted above. Providers in this sample have a range of educational levels. Nearly all (94 percent) have at least a high school diploma, and most have some additional education (55 percent with some college or associate's degree and another 12 percent with a bachelor's degree or higher).

Beyond general education, providers also have the opportunity to invest in additional credentials specific to childcare work. The most common of these is the Child Development Associate (CDA), funded by the U.S. Department of Health and Human Services Administration on Children, Youth, and Families. To earn a CDA, providers must complete a multistage assessment to demonstrate competence and knowledge in thirteen functional areas including basic standards related to safety as well as expertise in educational and emotional development and professionalism. The areas are assessed via documentation of training, parent recommendations, and formal observation.

A second credential specific to family day care providers is offered by the National Association for Family Child Care (NAFCC). Accreditation from NAFCC involves meeting standards in five areas of quality: relationships, environment, developmental learning activities, safety and health, and professional and business practices. To be accredited by the NAFCC, providers must have their CDA or ninety hours of relevant training, complete a lengthy application and self-evaluation, and be observed for two days by an NAFCC-approved observer.

While the CDA has been incorporated into licensing requirements for childcare center directors and teachers, both the CDA and NAFCC accreditations are elective for family day care providers. As such, these credentials represent a significant investment in one's career. Along with the time and effort spent in relevant training, these credentials involve lengthy and costly application processes; as of 2013, the CDA application costs $355 and the NAFCC application costs between $900 and $1,275, depending on membership status. Given the challenges that providers mention to meet a fifteen-hour continuing education requirement, we can imagine that the requirements for a CDA or NAFCC credential are insurmountable for many providers, especially given their uncertain value in the market. Not surprisingly, only a small percentage of providers in this sample have one or both of these credentials. Approximately 10 percent have a CDA, and another 10 percent plan on earning one in the future. Fourteen percent of providers are accredited by NAFCC and another 13 percent plan on earning accreditation.

State Regulation and Professional Autonomy

Just as the state requires continuing education for providers, they also enforce a number of other regulations on licensed day care homes regarding child/teacher ratios, health and safety requirements, physical environment, and many other areas. Provider attitudes toward these requirements reflect conflicting opinions about standards, self-regulation, and professionalization. While state regulation is a central mechanism for controlling professional boundaries and standardizing practice, it may also be seen as undermining the authority and autonomy of providers when those standards come from outside the group of workers.

All in all, a sizeable group of providers (40 percent) report that the Department of Child and Family Services (DCFS) has too many requirements for home day care providers. A little more than half of providers (56 percent) respond that there are just the right amount of requirements and a small group (4 percent) say that there are not enough requirements. Open-ended comments also reflect this ambiguity toward state regulation.

Some providers see state regulation as part of a necessary professionalization and hope that stricter rules would improve their own pay and status. For these providers, regulations (and the elimination of providers who do not follow them) are one route to more respect from others. One respondent notes, "I dislike not always being seen as the professional I am or appreciated as someone more than a babysitter. I would want to change the image and caliber of home day care providers, eliminating those who do not meet proper standards."

Another provider speaks more strategically, accusing unlicensed providers of driving down the market rates: "Unlicensed day care providers are constantly charging less than us and taking business away from us. Need tougher laws on unlicensed babysitters and more investigating." Other providers see state regulation as a necessary inconvenience aimed at controlling the damage inflicted by others. As one provider comments, "I dislike the pay and strictness that DCFS demands but I do understand it. Other people have messed it up for the good people." In all of these comments, providers clearly conceptualize these regulations as a way of constructing boundaries around more qualified, or more "professional" providers.

There is, however, another group of providers who challenge DCFS regulations on the grounds that they are cumbersome, arbitrary, and intrusive. Some providers see the rules and paperwork as keeping them from their real work of caregiving, as suggested by this provider, who writes, "I dislike all the red tape the government puts on the providers. I believe we could serve better if we were not so bogged down with paperwork!"

Others tell stories of requirements imposed by the state that they see as arbitrary and question the usefulness of one set of rules to govern diverse environments. One notes, "I would change the ratio of children to provider. Some providers are very good at their job and could handle a larger daycare group. . . . Every home daycare is different. Each rep should look at the daycare provider and ask parents in the daycare their opinion on the provider or handling more children." Another provider questions the "bed" rule, which is a state requirement that all children have access to their own crib, bed, or cot for naptime, invoking her own knowledge about safety: "Napping on a mat is much safer—no one can roll off the bed." Another writes, "I do not like the fact that the number of children you're licensed to [care for] is according to the actual play area when the children use every part of your home." While these providers are not explicitly invoking a professional identity, they are seeing their own experiences and expertise as a valid source of knowledge and standards.

There is also a group of providers who more explicitly oppose state regulation on professional grounds. Their comments reflect a view of the state as outsiders to the childcare system, and they suggest that providers and parents should be the primary regulators for child care. One provider criticizes the regulation body, saying, "I dislike DCFS regulations and regulators who use hindsight judgment and treat us like idiots. I dislike that changes are made and we must conform immediately or face consequences. I believe childcare providers should be licensed. I am all for that however parents have the choice to be in the home environment they prefer. We know our own limitations—these are our homes, families, our businesses." Another provider similarly privileges the expertise of workers over outside regulators, commenting, "We have DCFS rules that I strongly disagree with. I think some of the rules need to be made by parents and providers who actually deal with our children."

Another provider invokes an image of the private sphere of motherhood to contest state regulation of her work, writing, "I dislike all of DCFS rules. Some are put in place for good reasons but the majority of providers are good at what they do. Mothers have been raising children for years; why does this government feel they can tell you how to do it and under what terms?" Another writes simply, "Families and providers alike do not appreciate the state being in control of day-to-day activities."

As the open-ended comments make clear, an opposition to regulation is not synonymous with an opposition to professionalization. Instead, it matters a great deal to providers what they see as the source of regulation. Whether they give primacy to their knowledge as professionals or mothers, many see DCFS as outsiders to the caregiving relationship.

Organizational Involvement

Involvement in professional organizations is considered a key component of professionalization efforts. However, providers may become involved in different types of organizations and for different reasons. These organizations range from national organizations like the NAFCC (and its statewide chapters), with board members, committees, and conferences, to local organizations of providers that organize continuing education opportunities, social events for providers, or group play dates between family day cares during the work day. Due to survey space limitations and the geographic diversity of providers across the state (as well as what would likely be very small numbers participating in particular organizations), I was not able to collect specific information about the organizations to which providers belong, but their narratives describe organizations across this continuum, from highly formal organizations to more informal neighborhood associations.

Just over one-third of the sample report that they are involved in any organization for home day care providers. Providers are mostly likely to participate in organizations close to home; the largest group of providers is involved in local or neighborhood organizations (30 percent), followed by statewide organizations (12 percent), and lastly, by national organizations (8 percent). The survey responses suggest that providers vary in how they assess the value of their organizational involvement. A majority of providers strongly agree that their organization understands their concerns (63 percent) and that the organization's goals are the same as theirs (61 percent). Somewhat fewer (45 percent) strongly agree that they are an important part of the organization.

Providers also gave opinions about the helpfulness of these organizations in dealing with particular issues. Overall, these organizations appear to be most helpful to providers in networking with other providers to discuss similar problems. More than half of providers report that their organization is helpful for talking with providers about child development (56 percent), talking with providers about business issues (55 percent), and being social with other providers (55 percent). They are less likely to suggest that their organizations are helpful with advocacy; less than a third report that their organizations are very helpful for trying to make changes to childcare policies (33 percent) or for dealing with DCFS subsidy or payment (31 percent).

In their open-ended comments, providers support this picture of organizations as forums for them to meet with and receive support from other providers. Several providers note that these organizations are valuable to them because they get the chance to talk with providers about problems they have in common. One comments, "It gives a place for day care providers to compare ideas and concerns. . . . Sometimes it's the only place some of them go to talk to someone." Another notes, "The most helpful is the support from other providers. Experienced providers, educators that have actually done the same job."

Others specifically mention the usefulness of education and training programs offered at their associations, like this provider, who comments, "I enjoy getting together with other local providers for ongoing education and training. I can always learn something new or see a new way of trying things. Sharing ideas and getting help is beneficial. Most training has been good quality." Along with education and training, a number of providers note a practical benefit—that their association offers materials such as toys, books, and other resources for their use.

The providers above who speak of support, education, and resources do seem to be pursuing professional goals via their organizations. These associations are spoken of as valuable resources for professional development. However, many providers also seem to value the social interaction that happens alongside professional interactions, "getting together socially, discussing current issues, providing support, encouragement, and education to fellow providers." One provider presents these groups as a contrast to what some see as an isolating work environment, noting that it is "good to get out of house, see other adults, learn more."

Other providers seem less concerned with the professional and personal resources offered by these organizations and more interested in simply meeting state licensing requirements. They are happy to have a convenient location to get their required training hours for licensure. One notes, "I think our local organization is helpful because it's a way to earn our number of hours needed for educating ourselves on issues of daycare." Another speaks bluntly about state requirements, noting that she attends a group because they are the most convenient provider for training hours, "There's plenty of them but the district I am in the classes are provided 1 hour 45 min drive from my house. Too much travel time and I'd have to take off work to get there in time." However, another respondent expresses annoyance at members who attend only for the in-service hours, noting, "I enjoy my family childcare association but I have found that most of the members are just there for the hours and not the information."

While some providers find these organizations to be useful resources for professional development or social interaction, none of the respondents make comments that suggest that the associations are useful for collective action. One provider specifically says the opposite, noting, "Good for continuing education credits. Good networking. Still not a voice to DCFS or government."

Overall, then, providers appear to be using associations and organizations for day care providers primarily as resources for professional development, although they also see value in the social aspects of these groups. While they find use for themselves as individual providers, there is little evidence that they use these organizations as bases for collective action or advocacy for their profession to the outside world.

The Status of the Professional Project

As one of few studies to examine worker attitudes towards professionalization efforts, this research provides important information about the potential for a professional project for family day care workers. Overall, if there is a professional project for family day care, it is still fragmented and in a fledgling stage. It appears that workers do not take on this professional project as whole—using training, credentials, regulation, and organizations in concert—but rather subscribe to different parts of it for different reasons.

While providers are highly involved in training and desire more opportunities for training, only a small proportion participate in credentialing efforts. This reluctance about credentialing makes sense for this group of workers. In a market where childcare workers receive little to no financial return on investments in education and training, calls for increased training may raise the bar for entry into the profession and simultaneously impose an increased cost to providers with few, if any, benefits (Walker 1992). Professional associations also fill an ambiguous role for these workers. These organizations provide necessary continuing education hours for licensing and a forum for interacting with others in an otherwise isolated occupation. In general, however, providers do not speak of these organizations a location for collective action or advocacy.

The clearest evidence for worker professionalization is in their attitudes toward state regulation. For those who support state regulation, as well as for those who oppose it, individual workers call on professional attitudes. Those who support regulation see it as a way of weeding out unprofessional providers; those who oppose it are showing faith in their preexisting professionalism.

Despite the logistical difficulties and the weak monetary incentives for providers, these data suggest that the tenets of the professionalization project have genuine resonance with these workers. Through the vehicle of professionalization mechanisms, these workers enact their own critiques of the devaluation of their work, viewing themselves as skilled providers who are deserving of autonomy and respect. Whether realized through professionalization or unionization methods, it is this consciousness that provides the foundations for grassroots action.

21

Building a Movement
of Caring Selves

• •

Organizing Direct Care Workers

DEBORAH L. LITTLE

It is 2012 and I am observing training for a pilot senior certified nursing assistants (CNA) program, jointly developed by the Direct Care Alliance (DCA) and a large nursing home corporation in the New York metropolitan area. The DCA is demonstrating the challenges of building alliances with other stakeholders. They have divided the CNAs into three groups representing employers, workers, and seniors. The workers group is requesting higher wages, while the seniors group is asking for more prescription drug coverage. Jose says, "Without decent pay, you get bad workers. Bad workers can lead to bad medication delivery." Maria replies, "But if there are no medications to give, the workers don't matter." Rose, from the workers group, drops her head on the table and moans. "Oh, why is it prescriptions? When I hear that, I want to give up my wage."

Leonila Vega, the executive director of the DCA, interrupts the negotiation and repeats Rose's statement. She says, "This is what workers say. Yes, your heart should be with patient care. But in order for that to matter, you need to have a minimum wage. . . . You can't give away demands at the cost of your own well-being. I have to emphasize this. You've got to watch this nature of self-sacrifice because by sacrificing yourself, you are undermining the thing that you care about, which is patient care." Vega tells me that she witnesses this self-sacrifice every time she uses this exercise. Her observation is all too familiar to those who know direct care workers. According to a DCA fact sheet (2010), direct care workers include "certified nursing assistants, home health aides, personal care assistants, direct support professionals, home care workers, and other similar occupational titles." There are more than 3 million direct care workers assisting more than 13 million elderly, ill, frail, and/or disabled persons in the United States with activities of daily living, healthcare, and rehabilitation services. Direct care jobs are the third (home health aide) and fourth (personal and home care aides) fastest growing occupations in the United States, with demand projected to increase by another 1.6 million workers by 2020 (Paraprofessional Healthcare Institute [PHI] 2013). The majority of direct care workers are nonwhite and fully 31 percent are African American. Twenty percent of these workers are foreign born and 88 percent are women, with an average age of forty-two years (PHI 2012).

As a group, direct care workers are among the lowest-wage workers in the United States. The median hourly wage for all direct care workers averaged $10.59 in 2011, compared with a median wage of $16.57 for all U.S. workers (PHI 2012). For the most part, these caregivers confront unpredictable, often part-time hours, high injury rates, inconsistent training, inadequate healthcare coverage, and heavy reliance on public benefits. Despite these working conditions, many in direct care choose these jobs over other low-wage occupations and cite commitment to their clients as the primary reason for their choice (Howes 2008; Stacey 2011).

Both researchers and organizers recognize the tension direct care workers feel between the emotional and altruistic aspects of their caregiving relationships and the often exploitative working conditions of the labor itself. The workers seek legitimacy for both the skills and the relationality exercised in the work. However, they are caught in a cycle of disrespect. Care work is viewed as unskilled because it draws on women's allegedly innate and natural caring abilities. As low-wage, invisible, and devalued work, the jobs are offered to workers with little economic, political, or social power. When these workers, especially nonwhite or immigrant women, take the jobs, their low market status justifies the low wages (Glenn 2000).

Workers internalize a view of themselves as altruistic within this social and economic context. The value they assign to the relational aspect of their work leads many to place care recipients' interests ahead of their own, particularly if the two are seen as in conflict. Cameron Macdonald and David Merrill (2002) found that childcare workers perceived love and work as being in conflict, making it difficult for them to advocate for better jobs for themselves. Clare Stacey (2011) reports on the caring self that home care aides construct as a work identity, which combines altruism with quality skilled labor. Because workers value the relational aspects of their jobs, they can have difficulty asking for better jobs, wages, and benefits.

How can worker advocates overcome the direct care worker's impulse to sacrifice herself for her clients? How can workers be moved to use their voices for self-advocacy? While attention to skills alone may negate the relationality of the work, focused attention by worker advocates on the emotional labor can reinforce the self-sacrificing aspect of direct care. Within this context, some unions and care worker organizations report that their organizing is successful when they recognize both aspects of care work. Despite these reports, however, we don't know much about the processes by which relationality and skills are linked in their organizing campaigns. This chapter aims to fill this gap by examining the work of the Direct Care Alliance, which trains direct care workers in leadership and advocacy during a program they call the Voices Institute.

I argue that a three-step process can lead direct care workers to become advocates for better jobs for themselves: creating a collective identity, validating the caring self by integrating skill and relationality, and linking quality jobs with quality care. The first step is a common one in advocacy and organizing work. The second step reflects an awareness that care workers do not differentiate between skills and relationality, but see them as fully integrated in quality care work. The third step extends the path of integrating skills and relationality toward a frame that presents good working conditions as essential for the provision of good care. Below I first describe the work of the DCA and my own research methods. I follow that with a discussion of the three-step process of organizing direct care workers.

Organizing Direct Care Workers: The Direct Care Alliance

The Direct Care Alliance was created in 2000 by the Paraprofessional Health Institute (PHI), a national nonprofit engaged in worker training and national advocacy on home care issues. The DCA was organized as a coalition of consumers, workers, and concerned providers advocating for quality jobs as the route to quality care (PHI 2000). Initially, organizational experts did most of the advocacy. In 2007 the DCA moved to incorporate direct care workers themselves into advocacy and convened the first national conference of state worker associations. They started an e-newsletter, *The Direct Care News*, which became the DCA blog, to make the invisible work force of direct care workers visible through news published by the workers themselves. On November 7, 2007, the DCA reported on its blog that it had created the Voices Institute: "For the direct-care services field to truly 'come of age,' direct-care workers must become leaders in their own right. They have a right to speak for themselves, and not only to be spoken for." The flyer for the Voices Institute, posted on the DCA website, advertises that direct care workers, worker association and coalition staff, and other advocates will learn about advocacy, fundraising, organizational development, and message development so that they can build state worker organizations and advocate more effectively for better direct care jobs. The national Voices Institute workshops, which began in 2008, bring participants together for six days; state-level workshops run for two days.

The Voices Institute trains direct care workers from a wide range of care situations. For example, the first institute in 2008 comprised twenty-eight participants, including home health aides, CNAs employed in nursing homes and hospitals, hospice workers, personal assistants for people with disabilities, direct care workers employed in group homes for the developmentally disabled, and an employment specialist for disabled adults. Some had already become activists and were leaders in unions or in organizations of direct care workers. Others were new to grassroots organizing, advocacy, and coalition building work. Approximately one-third had less than ten years' experience in direct care work, while another third had between ten and twenty years, and the remaining third had more than twenty years' experience. Each national institute through 2011 contained a similar mix of workers. This is a choice of the DCA, which recognizes that the diversity of working situations and the isolation of many direct care workers pose organizing challenges. They lack the shared workplace and employer that are usually understood as necessary for worker organizing (Boris and Klein 2008). Many work in the context of ambiguous and nonstandard employment relations which are shaped by public policy and public funding (Rhee and Zabin 2009). Their employment relationships are often triangulated with private or public entities responsible for the work standards and wages and an individual consumer who creates the work environment and defines the relevant tasks of caregiving.

My exploration of the process of connecting the caring self to worker advocacy for quality jobs relies on ethnographic observation of the Voices Institute 2011, informal interviews with all staff and approximately fifteen participants at that institute, DCA records from the 2008 Voices Institute, DCA policy briefs, and blog postings by direct care workers and DCA staff on the DCA website. The DCA is engaged in a form of grassroots organizing, working to build organizations of direct care workers community by community and state by state. While this research looks at one particular advocacy organization, the challenges the DCA encounters are similar to efforts to organize care workers in many arenas. Their strategies for integrating the caring self into movement building provide insights that can be useful to both labor and advocacy organizations.

The DCA uses well-known movement-building tactics to create a collective identity among workers. It also uses empowerment strategies that explicitly validate the caring self by recognizing the altruism and emotional labor of care work and framing the quality of work as a type of professional labor. Finally, it links the desires and capacity of the caring self to perform quality work to a demand for quality jobs.

Creating a Collective Identity

Social movement scholars have identified collective identity as one feature of social movements that helps to explain why individuals come to participate in advocacy and/or activism. Collective identity is defined as "an individual's cognitive, moral, and emotional connection with a broader community, category, practice, or institution" (Polletta and Jasper 2001, 285). Collective identities are shared, positive, and accepted by individuals who choose to become active in movements.

Several approaches were used at the 2011 Voices Institute to create a collective identity among the workers. These included common social movement organizing strategies of identifying shared experience among participants (in work) and framing some aspects of the experiences as a form of injustice (Benford and Snow 2000). Initial icebreakers demonstrated shared experiences. In one exercise, workers were clustered according to birthplace, residence, and workplace. These groupings demonstrated different aspects of shared experience and created groups not formed by preexisting acquaintance. A more powerful exercise involved having workers line up by years of experience in direct care from less than one to more than thirty. The line revealed the tremendous commitment of the workers and introduced relatively inexperienced workers to peers with more experience. As he reviewed the line of participants who had worked between one and thirty-four years, the 2011 facilitator said,

> Now you can sit down with Maria (who has thirty-four years' experience) and I know the stories will inspire us. We have five here with more than thirty years of experience. If you do the math, it's 150 years' experience among them. That's two lifetimes! But who gives acknowledgment to these people? It's important that over the next four days we hear from these voices. . . . Look around the room. More than half have experiences of ten years and more. So we should just pause and honor the years of service and sacrifice that you folks have given to the community and the families. . . . There are about fifteen of you with less than ten years' experience—you are the newbies. . . . This is the movement from one generation to the next. . . . This is why we have the Voices Institute. Because we will be heard. We will speak with one voice.

With this simple icebreaker, the facilitator introduced the core themes used to organize these workers. They are a group with collective experience and stories. They are caring selves who give selflessly ("years of service and sacrifice") and have extensive skills (150 years' experience). They will have a unitary voice in a movement of direct care workers. Throughout the institute, the DCA staff continued to refer to direct caregivers as a group, reframing perceived differences into a broader set of shared work experiences.

While these workers certainly understand the lack of respect and sub-par working conditions many face, most had not situated these realities in an injustice frame. If they blamed anyone, it was greedy employers or an uncaring society. Thus one core focus of the Voices Institute was to introduce a "them" and a target that facilitated inequity and could be challenged. The target was the companionship exemption of the Fair Labor Standards Act (FLSA) and the "them" was the federal government. On the second day, DCA facilitators explained the law to the participants. The FLSA, enacted in 1938 to ensure that most workers would receive a minimum wage, overtime pay, and other protections, excluded domestic workers from coverage. Revisions by the U.S. Department of Labor in 1974 continued to exclude direct care workers assist-ing elderly and disabled persons in their homes on the grounds that they were "companions" rather than workers. Voices Institute participants learned that low wages for home health aides and personal assistants were not idiosyncratic but were, instead, allowed by federal law and regulation.

Government may seem like a curious target for workers who are so depen-dent on public policy for their own working conditions, wages, and benefits. Indeed, the DCA's lobbying work recognizes the government as a stakeholder and potential ally in the struggle for quality jobs and quality care. Yet many social movements challenge governments when they are oppressive or discrimi-natory; the entity that denies rights is also, often, the entity that can and should provide them.

Participants in the Voices Institute learned of the personal injustice experi-enced by Evelyn Coke, a home health aide who had worked more than forty hours a week for twenty years, but had never received minimum wage or over-time pay (Martin 2009). When she sued her employer to overturn the com-panionship exemption, her claim was rejected by the U.S. Supreme Court. This story clearly resonated with the direct care workers at the Voices Institute 2008. For example, Lorenzo's closing speech reported in the DCA blog dated May 22, 2008, explained the consequences of the court decision:

> As a direct result, a colleague of mine, Irene, received a letter from her employer of many years, notifying her that since they were no longer required to pay her overtime, they would stop doing so immediately. Because of the Court's decision, the value of her work was diminished by 33 1/3 percent, although she faithfully put in 50 to 60 hours a week.
>
> I've looked up companion and have found the phrases "helpful friend" and "live-in helper." My friends, it is 2008, and our industry has evolved into so, so much more than that. Dogs and kitties are companions. We are professionals.

In subsequent sessions of the Voices Institute, workers were again profoundly moved by the Evelyn Coke story and the frame it offered for understanding their work situations. The CNAs from the New York area training program referred to at the beginning of this chapter returned to their training and told their peers about this case. They told their unionized coworkers what they had learned about the unfair treatment of many workers in other states who did not have the benefits of unions or legal wage protections. In this report back, the CNAs referred to themselves as "we" with other direct care workers, demonstrating a new group identity.

Integrating the Caring Self

From the outset, the DCA worked to validate the compassionate and altruistic aspect of caregiving rather than ignore it in favor of a skills-based focus, like earlier professionalization efforts. Unions and care worker organizations have reported that successful organizing campaigns recognized both aspects of care work (Boris and Klein 2006; Macdonald and Merrill 2002). Attention to the emotional labor without equal attention to care as skilled work, however, feeds the self-sacrificing aspect of direct care and can lead workers to continue to pay a care penalty evidenced by the performance of unpaid labor (Stone 1999; Tuominen 2000).

Despite the importance of an organizing frame that validates both love and labor in care work, there is very little research on how these frames are crafted in worker organizing. Macdonald and Merrill studied the recruitment of parent allies and argued that childcare providers were successful when they "create[d] a language that articulates the value of the non-quantifiable relational skills of care work; . . . link[ed] the needs and rights of care workers to the needs and rights of care recipients; and . . . advocate[d] for care as a public good and public subsidy for fair wages" (2002, 77). Studies of labor organizing of direct care workers report that unions link quality jobs with quality care, but they rarely explain how the link is made or why it matters (see, for example, Boris and Klein 2006).

Skills are a necessary condition for quality care, the DCA facilitators argued, but they are not sufficient. The message of DCA is that the job is valuable because of both the love and the expertise. The opening lineup of workers on the first evening of the 2011 institute and the enumeration of the lifetimes of skills and experiences showed the participants that their work matters. The focus at that moment was on competence and proficiency. Throughout the week, however, facilitators would invite participants to focus on their relationships with consumers and their families. One afternoon, participants shared storyboards of their careers in care work. These boards, prepared before attending the VI, contained at least one common element; each board revealed worker/consumer engagement, often with photos. The photos of workers and smiling consumers validated participants' caring selves. During one exercise, DCA facilitators asked the workers to connect the skilled tasks with the relationality, affection, and altruism of care work. The exercise, called "these hands," took place during the second day and was a key moment of recognition.

The direct care workers stand in a circle, holding out their hands. One says, "These hands give care." The next says, "These hands give hugs." "These hands rub your back." Around the circle it goes: "These hands give warm baths." "These hands soothe and comfort." "These hands clean up shit." "These hands help you sit and stand." "These hands help you live in the community." "These hands give love." (Author's field notes, Voices Institute May 2011)

While the workers first made general statements like "These hands provide care," their language deepened as more and more workers shared the intimate emotional labor of direct care work. The language reflected tasks like bathing and toileting, yet represented the incredible intimacy and trust of the work.

In fact, the more intimate the task described, the greater the stress was on the necessity and importance of relationality. For example, the May 22, 2008, blog of Roy Gedat on the DCA website quoted a 2008 participant's final speech articulating the connection of skill and care.

> I am much more than a companion, much more than a friend to my consumers. What friend would feel comfortable helping clean you up after you'd had an accident because you're incontinent? What friend would help you with a bath?
>
> Do you know how personal it is helping someone with a bath? You are in their personal space. You are in their comfort zone. You are beyond their comfort zone. . . . There is respect and pride along with joy in the work we do. There is pride and joy in knowing we are helping someone maintain their dignity, their independence.

Workers rejected the idea that they were merely companions for their clients and consumers. While they spoke of the skills needed to perform care tasks, they almost always spoke about the skills in the context of a relationship with a specific client or consumer.

It would seem that workers would easily be drawn to advocacy to overturn the companionship exemption in the Fair Labor Standards Act. Yet this did not happen automatically. The relationships that make direct care work invaluable to both worker and consumer also make it difficult for a direct care worker to seek quality working conditions. Improved wages and benefits to help the worker can seem harmful to a client with minimal resources and appear to make a lie of the relationality claimed and valued by the worker. Thus the challenge for organizers is to demonstrate how poor working conditions undermine the capacity for relationality.

Linking Quality Jobs with Quality Care

Mignon Duffy (2010) suggests that organizers should see the bonds between workers and consumers/clients as a strength rather than a barrier to organizing.

She refers to the PHI's quality care through quality jobs campaign as an example of advocacy that tries to link relationships with working conditions (2010, 136). Unions are also making this link. A quick look at the websites of unions like the Service Employees Industrial Union (SEIU) reveals a strategy connecting worker voice with quality care for consumers and clients.

Macdonald and Merrill (2002) report that one necessary factor in overcoming the tension between love and labor in direct care work is "firmly link[ing] the needs and rights of care workers to the needs and rights of care recipients" (77). My findings are consistent with this claim. In order to overcome the self-sacrificing tendency of direct care workers, the DCA had to interconnect the needs and rights of care workers and care recipients. At Voices Institute 2011, facilitators used a relatively straightforward activity to help workers shift their frame from conflicting to consistent interests. It also demonstrated alignment between workers' expressed needs and the goals of the DCA.

The facilitator invited workers to create a list of issues that affected their jobs. From the room, answers were called out: "Wages." "No health insurance." "No respect." "I want to work full-time, but my agency won't give me the hours." "More training." The facilitator wrote this list on one side of a large sheet of paper. He then asked the caregivers to go into regional subgroups to decide how each issue affected their patients, clients, or consumers.

Each group of workers listed worker impacts—such as high turnover, worker injury, and working sick—that clearly have important implications for consumers as well. When asked to specifically list the consequences of poor working conditions for the consumers, all groups pointed to quality of care generally and patient safety. This was a challenging strategy for the DCA because naming negative outcomes potentially contradicted the skill and relationality of the workers. The participants named commonly referenced outcomes such as consumer well-being, personal choice, continuity of care, abuse, and stress of the consumer and his/her family. They ascribed particularly difficult outcomes, like abuse, to other workers. Their own personal examples focused on the "less than optimum" care that an exploited worker might provide. For example, some workers told stories about being ordered to perform medical tasks for which they had not been trained. Tracy Dudzinski, a 2008 Voices Institute graduate, offered a different example in a February 2, 2013, blog posting:

> On one morning in particular, I remember waking up with a bad cold. I was working with a quadriplegic gentleman, providing all his care. . . . Should I go to work sick and risk getting him sick? If I didn't and lost a day's wages, I would have to choose between gas for my car and food for my family until I got my next paycheck. . . . I finally decided that I would go to work, wearing a mask to try to prevent spreading whatever germs I had and making sure that I washed my hands even more often than usual.

I completed my shift, but was I delivering the best care I could? Of course not. I did what needed to be done, but I didn't do the little extra things that made my care special, like scratching his head, giving him the extra-long shower that he so enjoyed, or reading to him from the daily paper. It made me feel even worse than I was already feeling.

Facilitators explored the negatives of bad working conditions and the positives of good working conditions in ways that connected the workers' feelings about their clients or consumers with the quality of care they were able to provide. In particular, they focused on the potential harms of inadequate training, fatigue from excessive work hours, working sick, and injury. These conditions pose risks to both workers and consumers and they represented outcomes that did not challenge the participants' commitment or core skills.

Connecting to the Caring Self: Does It Work?

The success in connecting quality jobs with quality care is the real test for organizers of direct care workers. Some graduates of the Voices Institute clearly articulate the link, as one wrote simply in his April 6, 2013, blog response: "Workers who live in poverty cannot be expected to care adequately for vulnerable people." However, the effort to link job quality with the quality of care was particularly difficult in discussions of wages. For example, one group of 2011 Voices Institute participants who were strongly allied with the disability community in their home state refused to advocate for an end to the companionship exemption. They, like many families and employers who have opposed including home care workers in the FLSA protections, feared that their low-income consumers would no longer be able to pay for the needed hours of care.

Indeed, researchers have reported that organizing efforts have been particularly successful in states in which unions worked together with organizations for seniors and the disabled to access public funding for wages (Boris and Klein 2006; Mareschal 2006). These types of policy structures, which link pay increases to public funding through Medicaid, respond to workers' and consumers' concerns about a possible trade-off between their own material well-being and the care needs of their clients. While the DCA promotes increased public funding for care work in general terms, it focuses most of its advocacy on laws regarding wages, benefits, and training.

The majority of Voices Institute participants do not immediately pursue advocacy or worker organization activities. However, a number of participants have been extremely active with the DCA. One 2008 graduate served as the national field director of DCA leading both membership development and the Voices Institute for four years. Several graduates have served as DCA board members and 2008 participant Tracy Dudzinski is currently board chair and vice-president of her statewide direct care workers' association.

Many Voices Institute graduates worked steadily beginning in 2009 for an end to the companionship exemption under the FLSA. On December 20, 2011, Dudzinski wrote on the DCA blog about representing the DCA at President Barack Obama's announcement that the Department of Labor would propose a rule to extend FLSA protections to home care workers. During the following year and a half, the DCA and Voices Institute graduates pursued a wide range of advocacy activities to get the rule passed. They wrote op-eds, were featured in local newspaper articles about the impact of the rule, visited their congressional representatives, participated in a National Day of Advocacy for Care Workers, wrote hundreds of comments to the Department of Labor, and testified before the Office of Management and Budget in the final stages of rule passage. They relied on a number of arguments and personal stories, sharing their own experiences of economic hardship, long hours, unpaid work, and reliance on public benefits. Throughout, they demanded the same rights as other wage workers, insisting that justice required it and that their work deserved it. As one worker told her congressional representative, according to the DCA blog dated September 25, 2012:

> I have worked in the home care industry for 10 years and know home care workers deserve dignity, and respect because that's what they give families of this country by providing support for them every day. Home care workers don't want special treatment, they just want minimum wage and overtime pay like all other workers in the labor work force.

On Monday, September 23, 2013, DCA board president Tracy Dudzinski shared the toast she had made in Washington, D.C., on September 17, celebrating final passage of the rule requiring minimum wage and overtime protections for home care workers: "I want to thank all my fellow direct care workers who took up the fight and wrote letters, made calls, signed petitions and rallied the troops to do the same. . . . This rule is a beginning. It is the first step in direct care workers being respected and recognized for the important work that we do."

Continuing Challenges

Direct care workers confront a dominant ideology that represents labor and love as in conflict with each other. These workers often internalize this ideology and develop a workplace identity that links love, in the form of altruism and self-sacrifice, with skilled, but unrewarded, labor. The challenge for organizers of these workers is to overcome the tendency for self-sacrifice and workers' own beliefs in the contradiction between love and labor. It appears that the best way to do this is to integrate skill and relationality in direct care worker organizing. DCA, along with other advocacy and labor organizations, is doing this. Using social movement organizing strategies, they begin by creating a collective identity among workers. They go further, however, in validating the caring self by integrating skill and relationality and then linking quality jobs with quality care. These organizing strategies can lead workers to accept a frame in which quality working conditions are necessary for quality jobs. It can lead them to become advocates to improve their own working conditions.

However, it may be necessary for advocacy organizations to include a demand for public funding for care work in their social movement organizing of direct care workers. Direct care workers reported on the DCA blog that they were continually confronted by fears about the cost of the rule. While they dismissed the challenges of for-profit home care agencies, the concerns of families and people with disabilities were harder to dismiss. Some in the disability community opposed the rule change because one consequence might be increased institutionalization of disabled consumers. Others expressed concern about access to sufficient hours of care, given the overtime rules. Their concerns mirrored those of Voices Institute participants who refused to join DCA in working for the rule change. These potential impacts directly challenge the caring self. Direct care workers will often sacrifice their own interests if those interests conflict with their client's interests. The demand for quality jobs may not be fully accepted by direct care workers if organizing does not also include demands for adequate public funding of care work. If organizers and advocates want to truly validate the caring self they must struggle for reforms that do not pose material or emotional hardship to the clients that workers love.

Dedication

This chapter is dedicated to the memory of Leonila Bautista Vega, 1964–2012, loving and tireless advocate for direct care workers.

22

Healthy Diversity

• •

Promoting a Diverse
Healthcare Work Force Through
Innovative Partnerships

MICHELLE C. HAYNES, MEG A. BOND,

ROBIN A. TOOF, TERESA SHROLL,

AND MICHELLE D. HOLMBERG

Within paid care occupations, women and ethnic/racial minorities are disproportionately likely to occupy lower status and lower wage positions than their white male counterparts (England 2005). Staffing trends within the healthcare system are no exception; while there is some diversity among entry-level healthcare workers, ethnic/racial diversity within the ranks of more credentialed healthcare providers is lacking (Sullivan Commission 2004). Though 21.9 percent of workers in healthcare support occupations (typically unlicensed positions) are African American (U.S. Bureau of Labor Statistics 2012b), African Americans account for only 5.6 percent of employed nurses (U.S. Department of Health and Human Services [DHHS] 2011). Hispanics and Asians also make up only small proportions of the nursing work force, comprising 3.9 percent and 5.8 percent of employed nurses, respectively (U.S. DHHS 2011). Furthermore, only 3.8 percent of physicians in the United States are African American, and 5.3 percent are Hispanic (Boukus, Cassil, and O'Malley 2009).

Underrepresented groups are also exceedingly less likely to hold leadership positions in healthcare facilities; 98 percent of senior managers are white (Betancourt, Green, and Carrillo 2002). The purpose of our research is to investigate strategies that address the ethnic/racial stratification of the healthcare field, with a focus on barriers obstructing the upward mobility of members of diverse groups.

Healthcare settings are a particularly compelling context for considering the stratification of the paid care work force. As in other paid care sectors, addressing ethnic/racial segmentation is grounded in the need to challenge the social and economic inequities perpetuated by these labor markets. Yet integration of workers from diverse ethnic/racial groups into the higher ranks of the healthcare work force not only forwards a critical social justice agenda but improves the overall quality of healthcare delivery for patients and families. The United States continues to grapple with troubling health disparities across ethnic/racial groups (Keppel 2007; Smedley, Stith, and Nelson 2003). Academics, advocacy groups, and policymakers have underscored the compelling evidence that increasing the ethnic and racial diversity of providers at all levels is essential to addressing these disparities because demographic "match" between providers and patients has been shown to improve healthcare outcomes (Smedley, Stith, and Nelson 2003; Sullivan Commission 2004).

A potentially powerful resource for challenging the ways in which ethnic/racial minorities can get "stuck" at the bottom of the care hierarchy is a commitment to promoting the upward mobility of diverse entry-level workers. In this chapter, we focus on community health centers (CHCs), and we draw attention to one of the innovative organizational strategies employed in an attempt to increase the diversity of their work force at all levels, that is, CHC-educational partnerships.

Community Health Centers

CHCs provide a unique setting for exploring efforts to challenge the ethnic/racial stratification of the care work force for several reasons. First, the community health movement emerged in the 1960s as a strong grassroots movement with social justice at its core and embraced the notion of equitable health care for all. Today, over nine thousand CHCs in the United States provide comprehensive primary health care to medically underserved populations without regard for individuals' ability to pay, providing care to over 22 million patients annually (National Association of Community Health Centers [NACHC] 2013). CHCs serve the most economically and socially vulnerable members of society (Lefkowitz 2007), and many low-income communities (particularly those in urban areas) are home to racially and ethnically diverse populations (DeNavas-Walt, Proctor, and Smith 2012). While addressing occupational segregation is not their explicit motivation, their desire to increase the demographic match between providers and patients motivates many CHCs to promote greater diversity at all organizational levels.

CHCs are also distinctive in the depth of their connection to their communities. In addition to caring for the health of the local community, many CHCs are dedicated to employing members of their community. CHCs are federally mandated to have a patient-majority governing board, and their mission includes a commitment to improving living conditions within their low-income communities. Thus another factor that makes these settings distinctive from other healthcare organizations is that they are philosophically committed to addressing inequalities and to capacity building of community members.

Because of their commitment to demographic match between providers and recipients and their broader commitment to community development, CHCs tend to understand that ethnic/racial diversity within all positions from receptionist to physician is integral to their organizational mission. These characteristics make CHCs a compelling setting to investigate strategies employed to fully integrate ethnic/racial diversity in care organizations. Indeed, these unique features may contribute to the special potential CHCs hold for fighting the trends of segmentation that have been documented in more traditional healthcare organizations.

Historically, educational institutions have contributed to the stratification of the healthcare work force. It was not until the late nineteenth century, along with the advent of new technologies and medical discoveries, that medicine became professionalized. Educational institutions have been at the helm of this professionalization, responsible for disseminating knowledge and conferring degrees and licensure in service of standardizing the medical profession. This professionalization has excluded certain individuals from increasing their professional status by creating structural barriers to obtaining required credentialing. Furthermore, as demands for health care have increased, the need to reduce costs further compounded the stratification of the labor market, such that tasks considered more menial have been delegated to lower paid laborers (Duffy 2011). This movement toward professionalization has been mirrored in the nursing sector (Glazer 1991) and has trickled down into lower ranked positions such as community health workers. These historical trends have translated into the healthcare sector we experience today: a rigidly hierarchical system, marked by ethnic/racial segregation, which makes access to specialized training essential to occupational mobility (Duffy 2011).

Our research team has been working with the Massachusetts League of Community Health Centers (MLCHC) to better understand work force diversity efforts of CHCs throughout our state. There are forty-nine community health centers in Massachusetts that provide comprehensive health care to nearly 800,000 state residents at over 280 sites. The first phase of our work involved a survey of all Massachusetts CHCs with follow-up interviews to identify challenges and best practices adopted to promote diversity among their healthcare providers. During this first phase, we confirmed the predicted pattern whereby many Massachusetts CHCs are successful in recruiting and hiring ethnically/racially diverse entry-level staff, but less effective at attracting and retaining diverse individuals in higher-level medical or administrative roles (Bond et al. 2011). The action research revealed a variety of creative strategies aimed at addressing this stratification and pinpointed numerous barriers. One particularly promising strategy emphasized by several CHCs involves partnerships with educational institutions to enhance the upward mobility of existing staff from diverse backgrounds. The guiding motivation behind such partnerships emerges from CHCs' strongly held "grow our own" philosophy, which builds upon their explicit commitment to hiring from their local, diverse communities. These partnerships are the focus of the current chapter.

We uncovered some exemplary educational partnerships designed to address barriers to education for frontline workers during the initial research phase (Bond et al. 2011), and we devoted the second phase reported here to deepening understanding of how such partnerships function. We began this current phase with web-based, archival research to gather publicly available information about the ways in which Massachusetts CHCs partner with formal educational institutions. We augmented this overview by conducting an online survey sent to all Massachusetts CHC executive directors and human resource managers to identify additional educational partnerships. The final, and most intensive, step was to conduct in-depth interviews with key personnel at CHCs that appeared to have well-developed approaches to partnering with formal educational institutions.

Educational Partnership Models: Case Examples

The ways in which CHCs collaborate with formal educational institutions vary widely. Not all approaches build upon a "grow our own" philosophy; some arrangements are designed to attract new individuals to work in community-based healthcare settings. For example, the majority of CHCs host interns and practicum students in nursing, psychology, dental, and pharmaceutical placements. At least two centers are innovative family practice residency sites; one CHC has developed its own family practice residency program in collaboration with local medical schools; and one CHC hosts the only nurse practitioner residency program in the country. These programs serve the critical role of training a new wave of professionals devoted to health care for low-income, vulnerable populations. While most of these programs are not explicitly designed to recruit diverse care workers, CHCs have indicated that such programs often attract highly qualified ethnically/racially and/or linguistically diverse individuals who become invested in continuing to work at CHCs after completing training.

The primary focus of our research has been on partnership models that are explicitly designed to foster the career development of current staff.

As mentioned at the outset of this chapter, the pattern of greater diversity at the bottom of the organizational hierarchy is not uncommon across many types of organizations (Bond and Haynes 2014; Smedley 2009; Yamada 2002); what is unique about CHCs is their strong, explicit commitment to rectify this occupational segregation and work to enable staff from underrepresented ethnic/racial groups to move into higher-level positions. For many healthcare center positions, this type of occupational mobility requires further educational preparation and, for specialized health jobs, includes formal certification or licensure.

The CHCs we studied have adopted approaches that include helping staff with tuition costs (tuition reimbursement and/or loan repayment) and providing incentives for staff to take college-level courses. Some centers help staff accumulate the prerequisites that enable them to be competitive for educational programs like nursing; others provide work time for employees to attend classes. Some CHCs address logistical barriers that can make accessing such education difficult, for example, transportation and child care. One of the programs that we highlight below has invested considerable resources into making college-level courses available on site at the CHC.

All of these approaches are designed to make it easier for current staff to enhance their credentials, which qualifies them to move into better-paid, higher-level positions. Given the ethnic/racial diversity among staff within lower ranks, this approach is a strategic investment that enables CHCs to effectively diversify their corps of healthcare providers. Specific goals may include enhancing a staff member's work in his/her current position, moving from an administrative position into direct care, and advancing into professional health services (including medical, behavioral, social services, dental, pharmaceutical, and so on). Some commonly discussed CHC diversity-related staff development goals include enabling diverse entry-level staff to move into higher-level staff positions and increasing the diversity among clinical providers. We highlight two case examples of CHC-educational partnerships, each embodying one of these two specific goals.

Partnerships to Develop Entry-Level Staff:
East Boston Neighborhood Health Center

East Boston Neighborhood Health Center has established a strong educational partnership with Bunker Hill Community College focused on the development of entry-level staff. Their initially small collaboration has developed into an impressive innovative partnership that involves offering an array of college-credit courses to employees at a CHC-based training center.

In 2005, Bunker Hill offered its first series of courses to East Boston's health center employees. These were short (not full semester), noncredit courses predominately in English as second language (ESL) and other fundamental skills, including business writing and basic medical terminology. The health center contributed one hour of "work time" for one hour of personal time to encourage participation. Given the fast-paced nature of CHC work, it is unfeasible for a staff position to be left uncovered for even one hour per week, and back-up coverage has been cited as a primary constraint for offering development opportunities on work time (Bond et al. 2011). Given the size of the health center (and Bunker Hill's willingness to offer courses several times per year), they increased employee involvement by implementing a rotating schedule where employees could cover for one another while in class. Managers' support for flexible scheduling allowed the program to accommodate the initial enrollees. This positive response increased demand for college-credit courses.

On-site courses provided a number of benefits to CHC employees. In addition to acquiring new skills and promoting general work force development, they provided CHC employees with the opportunity to experience higher education in a nonthreatening way. There was no financial commitment for employees as the cost was covered by the health center, and the noncredit nature of the courses made them less intimidating. Furthermore, success in these foundational courses provided employees who had little or no experience with higher education with the confidence to take courses for credit.

Over time, the partnership developed such that East Boston started hosting additional courses for credit, including computer literacy, medical English, writing skills, mathematics, and medical translation. To enhance enrollments and fulfill their mission to serve the broader community, the health center opened the on-site courses to the community. The leaders of the health center and Bunker Hill made formal commitments to recognizing the health center site as a satellite of Bunker Hill. This expanded audience has been mutually beneficial; East Boston provides work force development opportunities to its workers while Bunker Hill attracts new students. It is clear that increasing numbers of employees are taking advantage of this partnership, though East Boston acknowledges the need for more formal tracking of program participants. Furthermore, Bunker Hill has been able to increase enrollments by offering courses at an off-campus location.

Success Factors

A number of factors enabled this partnership to thrive. Importantly, the initiative was first sparked by the health center's chief executive officer (CEO). Support emanating from the top established a shared value for continuous staff development that has become engrained in the CHC's organizational culture. CHC leadership also played an essential role in garnering support from managers, who are responsible for scheduling backup coverage and who are the most likely to worry that devoting time to education could detract from clinic functioning. Further, the commitment of the CHC's top leadership translated into significant logistical support that ensures the sustainability of the program, including a line item in the CHC budget to help cover tuition costs, staff dedicated to running the training center, a large physical space in which to conduct the classes, and the provision of a shuttle service so that employees can easily travel from all CHC sites to classes offered at the training center.

The fact that the health center CEO brokered the educational partnership agreement with the president of Bunker Hill ensured a parallel commitment and investment of resources on behalf of the community college. Bunker Hill sends representatives to the CHC to process registrations at the start of each semester, and they provide specialized in-person advising for CHC students. They have also trained a few staff at East Boston to be test proctors for their courses, which provides flexibility for CHC employees to take required placement exams in the workplace. Bunker Hill also accommodates incoming CHC students by reserving seats in their classrooms. These steps reinforce reciprocity between the two organizations.

The importance of responsiveness to the lives of staff cannot be overstated when speaking of the successes of this particular program. First, the health center made tuition reimbursement a priority when budgeting. Initially, employees paid tuition upfront, and upon the satisfactory completion of the course (a grade of C or higher), tuition could be reimbursed in full. However, the CHC recognized that upfront payment could be challenging, particularly during September enrollments when many employees' budgets are strained by children's school expenses and upcoming holidays. In response, East Boston established the Back-to-School Incentive program. This is one-time, limited funding that an employee can use to help pay for courses at the start of the term. The health center also arranged for financial advisors to work with CHC employees to file for grants and financial aid.

Both entities have addressed issues that affect the accessibility of further schooling for the CHC workers. A critical aspect of the partnership between East Boston Neighborhood Health Center and Bunker Hill Community College is the strong leadership from both organizations that has translated into concrete supports and creative problem solving to address potential barriers.

Ongoing Challenges

Despite the tremendous success of this program, it has not been without complications. Challenges have emerged around unanticipated side-effects of locating classes on site at the CHC. For example, in some courses, instructors would like to have web access to bring in additional resources. However, some websites like YouTube are restricted by CHC policy. Another similar challenge involved daily administrative details. Coordination between the two sites for new classes and cancellations were at times problematic because of the CHC's limited access to the Bunker Hill computer system. Additionally, the need for front office staff at the training site to address student questions was overlooked in the beginning. These issues were resolved, but initial confusion and uncertainty were considerable. These are also good examples of the level of detailed coordination needed to implement similar partnerships successfully.

Other challenges are related to decisions about the division of responsibilities. These issues highlight infrastructure questions that emanate from the hybrid nature of East Boston's training center and have become apparent as the program has grown. For example, while the CHC took the initiative to purchase and set up computers to be used for instructional purposes, it was unclear who should be responsible for loading specialized software and computer upkeep. Maintaining this bank of computers is not squarely within the priorities of the information technology departments of either institution. For the health center, these computers are lower priority than systems that support medical records; for Bunker Hill, they are off campus. Both IT departments are overtaxed, yet well-maintained computers are critical for teaching. A parallel question has emerged around responsibility for some building maintenance costs for the health center site. For example, because courses are held at night and are now open to the entire community rather than just CHC employees, a security guard needs to be employed to ensure the safety of those in the building. Given their strong relationship, the health center and community college negotiated a solution. When Bunker Hill wanted to add another set of evening courses, they agreed to split the costs.

Program funding is also a perennial challenge. During more prosperous times, East Boston was able to secure grants to sponsor training initiatives, for example, ESL, math classes, certification training in a few areas, and a career coach to work with employees planning their education and professional development. Important initiatives such as these are either eliminated when funding ends or absorbed into general operating costs. The health center has maintained some specialized stipends but enhancing current offerings remains challenging.

Partnership to Support Diversity in Medical Professions: Lawrence Latino Nursing Program

Since 2004, Greater Lawrence Family Health Center (GLFHC), in conjunction with a regional Area Health Education Center (AHEC), partnered primarily with Northern Essex Community College to create the successful Lawrence Latino Nursing Program. The program is designed to provide a pathway for Latino/as to obtain nursing degrees and to increase the number of Latino/a registered nurses employed at the health center. The participants have included medical assistants currently employed at the health center as well as other recruits from the community. Since the program began, approximately thirty individuals have attained their registered nurse (RN) degree, with five to ten new graduates each year.

Greater Lawrence Family Health Center (GLFHC) is located in Lawrence, Massachusetts, home to the largest proportion of Hispanics of any Massachusetts community (GLFHC 2013). Its key collaborator in this program, AHEC, is a statewide organization dedicated to enhancing access to quality health care, promoting work force development, and eliminating health disparities through the provision of training, certification, and outreach. GLFHC is host to one of six AHEC regional offices in the state. There are key staff who straddle both organizations and thus, while technically separate organizations, their work often overlaps.

In 2003, directors of both the health center and the regional AHEC decided they needed to address the nursing shortage at the health center. There was a dearth of Spanish bilingual and bicultural nurses, a necessity given the city's large Latino population. While a number of entry-level staff and other community members expressed interest in pursuing nursing careers, many were the product of under-resourced public school systems that did not provide strong foundations in math and science. Given the highly competitive nature of nursing programs and their attention to foundational courses in the admission process, these prerequisites were a primary missing link. In response, the health center and AHEC reached out to Northern Essex Community College to establish the Lawrence Latino Nursing program.[1] The intent of this partnership was to provide interested candidates with a mechanism to attain the prerequisites needed to apply for nursing school and support them throughout the program.

Prior to placement in the program, Northern Essex Community College conducts a skill gap analysis with each participant. These skill gap analyses are critical for placing individuals into appropriate courses and allow the health center and Northern Essex to work together to ensure the availability of needed courses. The comprehensive program includes prerequisite courses, tutoring, preparation for entrance exams, application review for admission to Northern Essex's nursing program, and mentoring until graduation. The health center provides a medical setting for field placements as well as access to nursing mentors while students complete the program. Moreover, GLFHC medical assistants are offered loans with deferred payments while in school.

Success Factors

A number of factors have contributed to the success of this partnership. The commitment of all of the partnership stakeholders to work with interested candidates before they enter nursing programs has been paramount. Rather than shuffling unprepared students into programs and reactively attending to those who are struggling, the program takes a proactive approach to ensuring student success. Each participant begins with a needs assessment and builds upon existing skill sets to further their preparation. This model delivers students poised for success upon entering nursing programs, with realistic expectations about future courseload demands.

The CEO of the Greater Lawrence Family Health Center, the director of AHEC, and the president of Northern Essex Community College were all strong advocates of the program. Buy-in from organizational leaders gave the program the heft it needed for others in critical positions to move it forward. The alignment of each organization's mission with the commitment to address the needs of the local community facilitated this top-level investment. For instance, the health center has a strong community-based work force. Additionally, AHEC provides the stable infrastructure to manage and lead grant writing efforts to sustain the program. Northern Essex Community College is a Hispanic-serving institution and committed to reserving spaces in programming across the institution for Hispanic students. Moreover, the new president of Northern Essex and the dean of health professions were interested in working with the community and with local agencies to make sure programs would be relevant and accessible to the growing number of adult learners (older than a recent high school graduate, part-time, and returning-to-school students) in the region. Synergistically, these were precisely the types of learners that the health center wanted to develop.

A commitment to working respectfully as partners has also given the program the roots it needed to thrive. Initially, it was challenging for health center and community college representatives to learn the language and culture of the other partnering organization, so staff trained in cultural competency used their skills as cultural brokers to facilitate this process. For example, initially it was not clear to individuals at the health center that the prerequisites did not count toward the nursing degree. Participants needed to be made aware that they were taking additional classes. Communication between Northern Essex's nursing program and the nurses already working at the health center was cited as important to the sustainability of the program. Creating this feedback loop was vital for ensuring that students were able to apply their classroom learning directly to the workplace. Furthermore, it allowed current health center nurses to pass along important information regarding changes to the health center and articulate standards and practices, and vice versa. This has allowed programmatic changes to be made such that both sides are communicating at the practical level of the partnership.

Ongoing Challenges

As with the previous partnership example, funding is an ongoing challenge. The federal funding that enabled initiation of the program was not renewed because they could not produce large numbers of graduates quickly. Because the program works with participants before they enter the nursing program and because many need to go part time, the program took longer to complete than would be true for full-time, previously prepared students. However, the partnership has been able to obtain some funding from the Massachusetts Department of Public Health to continue elements of the program. Cobbling together other funding, while tedious, has been necessary.

Funding was also a barrier for individuals seeking entrance into the program. Paying for courses upfront can be daunting, particularly considering that many participants have families to support. To alleviate this issue, advance loans were offered to students rather than reimbursements. The loan can be repaid by continuing to work for the health center for a predetermined amount of time after graduation. While the health center has been able to retain many of the graduates and hire them into nursing positions, bilingual bicultural nurses are highly marketable and can often find higher wages in hospitals.

Success Factors: Cooperation, Engagement, and Support

The two case examples make clear that health center–educational institution partnerships can provide pathways for healthcare workers striving to move into higher-level positions. They are also potential pathways for CHCs to increase ethnic/racial diversity among providers. However, not all efforts thrive. The two examples in this chapter highlight factors that promote successful partnerships.

First, both examples illustrate the importance of addressing barriers that make accessing further formal education intimidating and/or logistically difficult for current healthcare workers. Our survey revealed constraints in costs of education, including maintaining a full-time job while pursuing further education. Both the time and cost of travel for classes can be a barrier to participation. Family responsibilities limit workers' time to attend class outside of work or to devote to homework. The lack of flexibility means that a degree program may take a very long time. This can be discouraging as well as a strain for workers' families and extended support networks. What is striking in our examples is the commitment on behalf of both the health centers and the educational institutions to approach these sorts of constraints as structural challenges rather than as personal failings or a lack of commitment. The willingness to work together to propose approaches to educational access that go outside of the traditional on-campus college model is key. Both examples showcase awareness of the challenges and the partnership organizations' willingness to address them with innovative solutions.

A second common theme relates to the unique contexts of the community health movement and the community college mandate. Community health centers and community colleges are aligned in their missions to serve their local communities; both are explicit about their priority to make their services accessible and relevant to the community's needs. This shared vision signals that their values are in sync and facilitates collaboration toward shared goals. Further, because both types of institutions often serve ethnically/racially diverse communities (Rosenfeld 2001), the commitment to addressing the needs of the community goes hand-in-hand with a value of diversity.

Alongside the shared values that facilitate collaboration between health center and educational partners, there are important differences in the organizational cultures of health care and higher education. A third lesson is that it is not enough to simply share values at an ideological level; these organizations must be willing to understand the nuances of each other's everyday realities in order to navigate the logistics of the partnership. For example, in addition to adopting a shared understanding of the adult learner working full time, it was important that the educational institutions understood some particulars of the healthcare environment. The challenge of covering shifts for staff who are in class is a unique concern of healthcare settings that can constrain student attendance and potentially frustrate teachers. In addition, the technological requirements of one environment may not suit the other, and thus require a willingness to adapt accordingly, as noted above in the resolution of conflicts about Internet usage and software maintenance. One of our key informants said she employed a cultural competency framework to help facilitate understanding across the different organizational cultures of the college and the health center: "We didn't speak the same language. . . . So the first thing we had to do is find a common language. . . . and because we are trained in cultural competency . . . I saw my role [as] being the cultural broker amongst these groups so that we would make sure that we knew that when we said X, everybody understood that X was X, and not Y or Z. And it wasn't that hard to do, but it really . . . made a difference."

The final theme crossing both examples is the importance of support from the leadership of both entities. The alignment of two organizations to form a true partnership cannot be achieved without such support. Commitment to collaboration often filters down the organizational ladder to permeate all levels. It signals the partnership as a strategic priority, thereby communicating the importance of finding ways to make it work. One interviewee emphasized that "you need that person who's willing to champion [the initiative]." The main proponent may not be the actual college president or health center CEO, but no one will have the power to become a true champion without support from the top. Finally, leadership support is essential for establishing dedicated financial resources, without which these partnerships are unsustainable.

In sum, efforts to reduce ethnic/racial stratification within the healthcare sector still need to bring new professionals from minority backgrounds into all levels of the field. There are people with tremendous potential to enhance the delivery of care already employed within the healthcare sector if provided with accessible educational pathways for advancement. Successful health center–educational institutional partnerships are not easy to implement, but they can succeed with organizational commitment from all partners, flexible and creative approaches to addressing barriers, and a shared belief that the time and money required are worth the return on the investments.

Note

1   The Lawrence Latino Nursing program was started with funding from UMass Medical School as the Health Resources and Services Administration (HRSA) grantee and central office of the statewide AHEC Network.

23

Building Meaningful
Career Lattices

• •

Direct Care Workers
in Long-Term Care

JENNIFER CRAFT MORGAN

AND BRANDY FARRAR

The long-term care services sector in the United States depends greatly on direct care workers (DCWs). In institutional care, for example, it is estimated that 80 to 90 percent of care is provided by DCWs such as nursing assistants. In addition, there has been unprecedented job growth in home- and community-based care, particularly with home care workers and personal care aides. The demand for DCWs (workers who provide direct care in all kinds of long-term care settings such as nursing homes, adult care homes, and home care) is driven, in large part, by the increased proportion of older adults in the U.S. population. People are living longer than ever before and the largest birth cohort in U.S. history, the baby boomer generation, is reaching retirement age. As the healthcare needs of the aging population grow, so does demand for DCWs (for example, nursing assistants, personal care aides, home health aides, and home care aides) in long-term care.

Unfortunately, job growth in long-term care is in entry-level, low-wage, and precarious work (Kalleberg 2011). In the United States, direct care work fits squarely within sociologists' conceptualization of bad jobs (Kalleberg, Reskin, and Hudson 2000). Despite the high intrinsic rewards associated with direct care work (Morgan, Dill, and Kalleberg 2013; Rose 2003), workers in these positions experience low wages, few benefits, and constraints to career advancement. As of May 2011, personal care aides earn a median hourly wage of $9.49. Nursing aides, orderlies, and attendants, the highest-paid direct care occupational category, earn a median hourly wage of $11.63 (U.S. Department of Labor Bureau of Labor Statistics [BLS] 2012e). Fewer DCWs in long-term care (41 percent) than other workers (53 percent) receive employer-based health insurance, and a third of female DCWs live in families whose income is at or below 150 percent of the poverty level (Potter, Churilla, and Smith 2006).

U.S. regulations regarding educational requirements for DCWs vary markedly from state to state and across settings but are generally quite low (Kelly, Morgan, and Jason 2012; Tyler et al. 2010). DCWs typically have no more than a high school education and no or low requirements for continuing education (Smith and Baughman 2007; Squillace et al. 2009). Unlike other sectors where advancement can be achieved through tenure and uncredentialed skill accrual, the heavily credentialized nature of healthcare jobs means that entry-level job holders cannot advance without obtaining credentials such as a certificate or associate's degree.

Direct care workers, like many workers exploring advancement opportunities, face significant challenges to returning to school such as increasing tuition costs, logistical coordination of child care and work schedules to accommodate class and study time, and rusty study skills. These challenges are exacerbated for low-wage workers such as DCWs because they often lack the financial resources, flexibility in work schedules, and educational readiness to cope (see chapter 22). In short, DCWs are often trapped in these "bad jobs" due to structural constraints to career advancement.

It is important to note that direct care work is not considered "bad" in all countries. In other wealthy countries, direct care jobs have higher educational and training thresholds for entry and DCWs enjoy higher job quality than in the United States. For example, nursing assistants in European countries are less likely than in the United States to be low-wage workers (between 0 and 5 percent in the Netherlands, France, and Denmark as compared to 38 percent in the United States). Similarly, nursing assistants in the United States generally have far less training than nursing assistants in other developed countries. Nursing assistants complete approximately six to twelve weeks of training in the United States as compared to thirty-four months of training in Denmark (Appelbaum and Schmitt 2009).

U.S. employers have tended to think of these workers as replaceable and therefore not worth significant investments in education and career ladder development. That these jobs are "bad" in the United States reflects the cultural devaluation of care work and the structure and practices of labor market institutions that organize direct care work. In the United States, the cultural perception is that care work is an extension of the nurturing and reproductive skills that women naturally possess, and therefore undeserving of prestige and financial compensation (Cancian and Oliker 2000). Broader research on work demonstrates that many employers seek to improve organizational and financial performance by deskilling, lowering wages, and restricting development opportunities (Scully-Russ 2005). For example, U.S. hospitals have made greater use of nursing assistants and other low-skill workers as compared to registered nurses (RNs), a practice that is less common in European hospitals. Wages stay low in the United States due to both the organization of work and the availability of low-cost labor. For example, employers keep educational requirements for entry low and minimize the skills that are formally attached to the job descriptions (Tilly 2011). Further, the availability of vulnerable populations, such as women, minorities, and immigrants provide a source of low cost labor.

These "low-road" strategies represent but one end of the continuum of employers' strategies to remain competitive in the global economy. At the other end of the spectrum are workplaces that aim to improve organizational and financial performance by engaging workers, thereby offering increased autonomy, voice, and greater learning and growth opportunities at work (Applebaum et al. 2003; Bernhardt 1999; Folbre 2006b). Examples of these "high road" approaches include employer-hosted or -sponsored education and training programs for low-wage workers linked to career lattices. Career lattices identify the sequencing of positions within or across organizations that represent both lateral and upward job mobility. Career lattices allow workers to understand the structured career pathways within which their jobs are embedded and thus their options for career progression. While these career development opportunities do not directly address the value deficit that depresses wages in direct care work, they are a practical approach to leveraging employer needs to improve job quality for DCWs. In this chapter, we (1) provide insight into what these career development opportunities look like in long-term care, (2) delineate the barriers that undermine more widespread engagement in DCW career development, and (3) describe current legislative, industry, technological, and labor market trends that may give rise to increased employer investments in DCW development. These observations are based on data gathered through three evaluations of innovative projects designed to improve educational and career opportunity for DCWs: the Jobs to Careers: Transforming the Frontlines of Health Care project (http://www.jobs2careers.org), the Pioneer Employer project (http://www.wsha.org/pioneer.cfm), and the North Carolina Personal and Home Care state training grant.

Education and Career Lattices in Long-Term Care

The following four cases provide examples of long-term care employer–educational institution partnerships in which career lattices were implemented to improve outcomes for employers and DCWs.

Career Lattices Implemented alongside Organizational Culture Change

Culture change initiatives in long-term care are becoming increasingly common. These initiatives seek to involve residents and their families in the care process as well as to stabilize staffing by improving morale. Most culture change initiatives are grounded in the concept of person-centered care. Person-centered care changes institutional cultures to prioritize personal preferences and needs of clients rather than determining care processes solely on the needs of organizations and workers. For example, people vary in the times of day they wish to go to sleep or wake up. For purposes of organizational efficiencies, many institutions would set waking times to the start of day shift rather than give clients a choice. Offering clients autonomy over environmental factors like food choice, sleeping schedules, pets, and decorations helps clients feel more at home, feel more in control of their environment, and improve their quality of life. Providers implementing changes that prioritize the value of resident preferences may be more responsive to the needs of DCWs as well.

The career ladder program developed by Southington Care Center, a 130-bed facility specializing in short-term inpatient rehabilitation and rehab nursing care, long-term care, and outpatient rehab services, illustrates this point. Southington Care Center is one of five long-term care facilities that participated in the Certified Nursing Assistant (CNA) Advancement Initiative, a program Capital Workforce Partners developed and implemented in collaboration with four educational institutions as part of the Robert Wood Johnson Foundation's Jobs to Careers: Transforming the Front Lines of Care program. The CNA Advancement Initiative offered a series of seven clinical courses to incumbent DCWs. The courses included issues in aging, dementia and Alzheimer's, rehabilitation, hospice and palliative care, mental health, substance abuse, and medical terminology, and were designed to provide the skills and knowledge to be a successful CNA in long-term care. Workers received half of a credit for each course they completed from a local community college. One of the partnering educational institutions is using these courses to build a long-term care certificate that will transfer as college credit to one of the local state colleges. Southington Care Center integrated these course offerings into a three-step career ladder for its CNAs. Progression up the ladder is tied to completion of courses offered through the CNA Advancement Initiative as well as leadership classes, committee work, and seniority. As workers move through the levels, they receive a small increase in pay.

Implementing the CNA Advancement Initiative alongside culture change laid the necessary foundation for a successful program. The culture change work focused on redefining the supervisor/worker relationship to include mentoring, support, and development of CNAs and involving CNAs more actively in the care team. For example, participating CNAs were allowed to review residents' charts to identify information that might be helpful in their work. In addition, CNAs were instructed to write their own incident reports rather than telling an RN what to write in the report. These small changes helped workers hone their literacy skills and gave them greater responsibility in their jobs. The nursing home's culture change helped create a positive, trustful, and productive dynamic between supervisors and CNAs, which empowered participants to engage more fully in their daily work and in their careers.

There are two major obstacles, however, to widespread dissemination of this type of education and career lattice model: scope of practice constraints and long-term care funding models. Professional nursing bodies (for example, state boards of nursing) are often resistant to infringements on their scope of practice, which makes it difficult to expand the role of CNAs. Further, as nursing home care is largely financed through Medicaid, profit margins are particularly slim, making it difficult for for-profit homes to invest in raises associated with career lattices. Thus, without changes to funding mechanisms, broad-scale replication of this kind of DCW development program will be difficult.

Integrated Delivery Systems Provide Anchoring for Career Lattices

Long-term care facilities that are a part of integrated delivery systems are better equipped to build meaningful career ladders for their workers than independent facilities because they can draw on the resources of the health system. For example, Thompson Health System, an integrated healthcare delivery system located in the Finger Lakes Region of upstate New York, has a not-for-profit residential healthcare facility offering skilled nursing, medical adult day health care, and short-term care. Thompson sponsors CNA training for this continuing care center. The CNA program uses the standardized curriculum for New York State and consists of 130 hours of training (about seventeen class days). After completing the course, participants are eligible to sit for the state certification exam. Participants who pass the exam receive their CNA certification through New York State Department of Health. Thompson Health pays for the CNAs to take the class, the class instructor, the certification exam, and the biannual recertification fees. In return, participants sign a commitment to work at the Continuing Care Center for at least one year. Participating workers receive $8 per hour while they are completing the training, $9 per hour once they pass their state certification exam, and $10 per hour once they have been employed as a CNA in the Continuing Care Center for six months.

After participants are certified as CNAs and have been employed for six months, they are eligible to participate in the Continuing Care Center's four-tier career lattice for CNAs. Advancement is tied to increased education and is rewarded with small bonuses at each step. For example, a CNA I who is interested in progressing to CNA II must complete a ten-module education program and a teaching assignment. The four tiers of the CNA ladder culminate with the geriatric care specialist (GCS) designation. As a GCS, workers have 400 hours of education in addition to the basic CNA training. Geriatric care specialists receive a dollar-per-hour pay increase and have greater responsibility such as involvement in the interview process and auditing. While this wage increase is relatively small in relation to the time investment, this constitutes about a 10 percent increase. More substantial career and wage advancement can occur if CNAs use Thompson's tuition reimbursement benefit to achieve nursing credentials (for example, licensed practical/vocational nurse, registered nurse). Successfully completing these one- and two-year programs can result in increasing wages 100 percent to 200 percent. Thompson offers tuition reimbursement in the amount of $3,000 per year for full-time employees and $1,500 per year for part-time employees to support those enrolled in these programs. Several workers who completed the onsite CNA training did use the Health System's tuition assistance to enroll in a licensed practical nursing or registered nursing program.

Thompson's case is unique in that most long-term care facilities do not have the resources to pay all the costs associated with CNA training (including wages during class time) and to provide a substantial wage increase for additional skills. Further, the availability of tuition assistance to pursue advanced education and access to credentialed positions within the organization is not common in long-term care. These opportunities were possible at the Continuing Education Center due to its association with a company that was committed and well-equipped to invest in career development for its low-wage workers.

Credit, Not Just Continuing Education Units, as Rewards

A core challenge to creating meaningful career development in long-term care is that much of the education and training that community colleges offer for this sector are continuing education courses, rather than college credit. Courses that do result in college credit usually are not "stackable," or applicable toward requirements for a degree program. This is problematic because, as the healthcare system currently stands, living wages are most likely to be secured by employees who have, at minimum, an associate's degree. Thus creating opportunities for workers to build college credit that contributes toward a degree is a necessary component of meaningful career ladders. This is not an easy task, given the rigidity and traditionalism of most academic programs.

Portland Community College (PCC) created a partnership under the Jobs to Careers: Transforming the Front Lines of Care program, in an attempt to bridge the continuing education–college credit divide. Two divisions within PCC—the Division of Workforce Training and Economic Development and the gerontology program—teamed up to develop and offer a series of continuing education training to employees in five assisted living facilities in Oregon.

The Division of Workforce Training and Economic Development is located in PCC's extended learning campus and focuses on delivering work-related continuing education that is responsive to industry needs but not tied to credentials. In contrast, the gerontology program is a traditional academic program housed in the sociology department of PCC. PCC instructors trained assisted living staff to deliver twenty-seven short curriculum modules on caring for the elderly on work time. These modules include topics such as roles and responsibilities, resident service plans, personal care, self-care, and diabetes care. The gerontology program rewarded workers who complete all twenty-seven modules with three hours of college credit.

This case is also notable in that it was successful in creating career lattices that extend beyond the nursing professional jurisdiction. PCC has also developed eight short-term, job-focused certificates. These certificates include a general gerontology certificate, three different activity professional certificates at different levels (assistant, director, and consultant), advanced behavioral and cognitive care, horticultural therapy, and end-of-life care. Each of these specialized certificates meet criteria set by the corresponding professional associations. For example, the three different levels of the activity professional certificates correspond to the categories set by the National Certification Council of Activity Professionals and the advanced behavioral and cognitive care certificate is linked to the National Certification Board of Alzheimer's Care out of the University of Chicago. The credits for these certificates are stackable and can be used toward obtaining an associate degree in applied science.

Aligning course work that typically falls under continuing education training with college credit that transfers into a degree program was a joint effort by the Division of Workforce, Education, and Training and the gerontology program. Without such collaboration, workers would be able accumulate skills and knowledge and have opportunities to enter varied roles in long-term care, but would achieve little in terms of the advanced education necessary to secure living wages in health care. Thus, collaborations between continuing education training departments and traditional academic programs have significant potential to create meaningful career lattices in long-term care.

Widening Pipelines for Entry into Direct Care

The direct care work force has a long history of high turnover rates. One explanation for high DCW turnover, estimated at 75 to 100 percent annually in some states, is lack of understanding of the reality of the jobs (Barry, Kemper, and Brannon 2008). Many people invest valuable resources into training for direct care work, and after they are on the job find that it does not fit with their expectations. The North Carolina Personal Home Care State (PHCAST) training grant, with knowledge of this pattern, developed a four-phase career ladder to assist both new entrants and incumbent workers interested in direct care work. The first phase offers an introduction to what it takes to be a DCW (with examples from all settings), how to get and keep a job, and deciding if DCW is right for the learner through realistic job previewing. At the end of the first phase (sixteen hours of content), the student has both a certificate of completion and lay certification in cardiopulmonary resuscitation (CPR). The second phase (100 hours) emphasizes skills in home management and personal care tasks, such as helping clients with limited assistance activities of daily living, and culminates in a community college certificate (an industry-recognized credential) as a personal home care aide. The third phase is a nurse aide course (120 hours) that focuses on the state-approved nursing delegated tasks such as dressing and undressing and bed baths. The final phase constitutes a next step on the career lattice for nurse aides. This phase (100 hours) enhances skills related to working in a home setting such as person-centered care practices, client and personal safety, and pain management and offers two other specialty courses: geriatric nurse aide specialty and medication aide specialty. The state of North Carolina has worked with the Association of Home and Hospice Care to develop an industry-recognized credential in hopes that employers will reward the achievement of this credential with wage increases or promotions.

The PHCAST example demonstrates two major principles of effective career lattice development. First, the four-phase pathway allows new entrants and incumbent workers both meaningful and manageable steps on the lattice and a comprehensive approach across long-term care settings. DCWs often move from one type of setting to another (for example, nursing home to home care agency) throughout their career. The development of a career lattice that develops a core set of competencies that are applicable across settings should make these transitions easier. Secondly, PHCAST creates credentials that have meaning at all levels of the career lattice, that allow individuals to reach career milestones quickly, and that employers can use to motivate and reward their workers' career development.

These four examples demonstrate that some innovative long-term care organizations are implementing career lattices for DCWs. However, national trends and research continue to demonstrate that the lack of career mobility for DCWs is the norm rather than the exception (see chapter 5; Ribas, Dill, and Cohen 2012). Further, these programs and others like them have struggled to make meaningful inroads toward improving wages, benefits, and career opportunities for DCWs given the sociopolitical contexts within which they were implemented. If the promise of career lattices is to be realized, more widespread involvement of employers and their educational partners along with strategies that address the many overlapping vulnerabilities and structural impediments to advancement is necessary.

The Context Is Ripe for Change

While obstacles to changing the job quality for DCWs abound, particularly in long-term care, the sociopolitical context of health care is ripe for change.

Several national and professional priorities are coming together to provide the potential for positive change for the direct care worker.

The Rise of Accountable Care Organizations

The Affordable Care Act of 2010 and cost containment demonstrations have culminated in increased development of what are now known as accountable care organizations (ACOs). According to the Centers for Medicare and Medicaid Services (2013), "ACOs are groups of doctors, hospitals, and other healthcare providers, who come together voluntarily to give coordinated high quality care to Medicare patients they serve. Coordinated care helps ensure that patients, especially the chronically ill, get the right care at the right time, with the goal of avoiding unnecessary duplication of services and preventing medical errors."

With the influx of many previously uninsured individuals into the healthcare system, these types of organizations are poised to proliferate. In order to contain costs over the longer term, the focus will need to shift to preventive care and increased quality of care and efficiency of care through coordination of care. ACOs, then, might create new and emerging roles for support and transition roles (for example, patient navigators) that DCWs can fill. The rise of ACOs might also result in increased integration across healthcare settings and thus the kinds of structures that allow for stronger career development opportunities like the ones described in the Thompson example.

The Need for Culturally Competent Care

With the focus on preventive health care, the pressure to reach out to underserved communities, reduce health disparities, and improve outcomes with contextualized care will increase. For example, several prominent groups have released formal statements naming cultural competence as integral to high-quality care (American Nurses' Association 1991; U.S. Department of Health and Human Services 2001), and there is a proliferation of research exploring what this means and how to provide it. This focus on cultural competence has placed greater attention on DCWs because of their diversity and the fact that the demographics of the work force often reflect the demographics of the communities they serve. The diversity of the entry-level healthcare work force has the potential to be a strength in this area of care (for example, translation services, outreach to vulnerable community members). Given that the Affordable Care Act, by extending insurance coverage to medically underserved groups, will probably bring even greater numbers of marginalized populations into the healthcare system, demand for the linguistic and cultural proficiency of DCWs will likely continue to rise along with their value to the healthcare system.

The Need for Workers to Support Health Information Technology

Another source of pressure to develop frontline workers relates to recent industry changes. The HITECH Act, for example, provides directives and funding for innovation such as electronic medical records and health information exchanges. In terms of care innovations, there is a rise in pay-for-performance reimbursement models where insurance companies pay healthcare organizations based on the quality of services they provide. These new payment models have spawned numerous quality improvement initiatives led by public and private organizations. Both industry changes have created the need for new skill sets and roles for low-wage workers that require formal education and training. This suggests that technological and care delivery innovations may compel employers to invest in entry-level workers to support these new models of care delivery.

Work Force Development with Nurses

While the economic downturn has created a temporary abatement of many healthcare worker shortages, shortages in mid-level positions, particularly nursing, are another source of pressure for employers to invest in the education of entry-level healthcare workers. Work force aging is likely to hit nursing particularly hard as an older than average and feminized profession. At the same time that age-related nursing work force exits are increasing, the Future of Nursing report (Institute of Medicine 2010) has put pressure on healthcare organizations to increase the education of their nurses. Many registered nurses are educated at the associate's degree level; the report sets a goal to roughly double the proportion of nurses educated at the bachelor's level (BSN) to reach 80 percent by 2020. As strategies are created to fill vacant nursing positions and to move nurses with associate's degrees into bachelor's degree programs, DCWs may be targeted as well. These workers represent a captive and interested pool of workers to feed the nursing pipeline and also may help to meet additional Institute of Medicine goals related to increasing diversity and cultural competency among nurses.

Educational Institutions under Increased Pressure

Educational institutions also have an incentive to get involved in developing incumbent DCWs. U.S. educational institutions, particularly community colleges, are feeling pressure to help individuals achieve short-term credentials that improve employability. Offering various healthcare credentials has been a popular choice given that health care is one of the few growing sectors of the economy. Some states are also implementing pay-for-performance funding schemes for these educational institutions. Pay-for-performance represents a shift from accountability based on quantity (for example, number of students enrolled) to accountability based on quality (for example, completion rates, minority success). This change in the payment and incentive system may align the motivation of community colleges to the needs of vulnerable students.

Next Steps

In order to build career opportunity for DCWs, career lattices that combine lateral and upward pathways must be developed. This effort will inevitably include employers working toward competency-based job descriptions with progressive responsibilities (and higher pay) and educational institutions working to build and match credit-based offerings that serve as threshold requirements along with experience. Employers will need to recognize credentials/training in their development of career opportunities for these workers and in their pay-setting practices. The development of competency-based jobs and articulation of in-house training and credentials/training are critical to increasing job quality (Fitzgerald 2006).

Education and training alone, however, is not likely to yield results for improved extrinsic (pay, benefits, or career opportunity) or intrinsic job quality (social relationships, meaning) or for quality of care for older adults and persons with disabilities. Employers must view these workers as valuable to the success of the organization rather than as replaceable. It will be important to address structural (staffing, reimbursement systems, career lattice development) and cultural contexts (interprofessional collaboration, input to care planning, respect) at the long-term care employer and payer system levels, access-related issues, and credit-bearing policies at educational institutions. The sociopolitical context of health care in the United States suggests that these activities might begin on a broader scale.

As change marches forward in work force development, it will also be important to counteract the cultural devaluation of care work. The scholarly consensus is that the underlying justification for the low quality of direct care jobs is rooted in the fact that society does not value care work nor see it as an activity requiring skill (England 2005). This cultural perspective sets the stage for low wages, lack of respect, and the generally poor working conditions that care workers face. It follows logically that to achieve better working conditions, respect, and material rewards for care workers, there must be a shift in the way that society thinks about care; to remedy the problems of care work, there must be an ideological revaluing of care. From this perspective, the keys to the care revolution are to (1) conceptualize care as a public good, (2) recognize that care requires not only technical skill but creativity and emotional intelligence, (3) give all individuals the right to care and be cared for, and (4) share the responsibility for care (Davies 1995; Glenn 2000; Stone 2000). Value placed on creativity and emotional intelligence could be embedded in new career lattice models. This goes hand in hand with a reevaluation of care practices that emphasize not only the absence of disease for clients but also person-centered care practice that values both the individual and the social relationships in which they are embedded.

The push to conceptualize care as a public good builds upon feminists' longstanding efforts to render visible the activities of nurturant and reproductive labor. Advocates who seek to make the skills involved in care work visible have pushed for care delivery models that explicitly attend to the caring labor involved when treating patients, and document the emotional labor and creativity that care workers often display (Macdonald and Merrill 2002). Those who urge us to think of care as a right argue that, contrary to westernized discourses of rugged individualism, we all need care in some form throughout our lives (Stone 2000; Williams 2010). Accordingly, we should all have access to high-quality care, and those who want to give it should be free to do so without material, status, or psychological penalty (England and Folbre 1999; Glenn 2000). In short, an ideological revaluing of care would shift the way society thinks about care from easy work that women and minorities should be doing for little or no pay to valuable and skillful work that all have a right to give and receive. "Worthy wages" and higher status will follow if this shift were to occur. The diversification of the entire healthcare work force; documenting, rewarding, and prioritizing emotional labor; and finally, seeing long-term care as one part of the continuum of care within integrated and coordinated system may be a few small steps toward the laudable goal of re-envisioning care as a public good.

Epilogue

●●●●●●●●●●●●●●●●●●●●●●●

Making Paid Care Work

MIGNON DUFFY, CLARE L. STACEY,

AND AMY ARMENIA

Our hope in bringing together this body of research is that it will serve to advance both empirical knowledge and theoretical development across a range of academic and policy arenas. We see this book as part of ongoing dialogue about care, and our expectation is that students, scholars, and policymakers will find within these pages different threads of conversation that connect to their specific areas of interest. In these last pages of the book, we highlight a few themes that emerge from the volume as a starting point for further discussion, research, and advocacy.

Autonomy, Collaboration, and Compensation

Leo Tolstoy famously wrote in *Anna Karenina* that "Happy families are all alike; each unhappy family is unhappy in its own way." In their overview of paid care work in the United States, Candace Howes, Carrie Leana, and Kristin Smith make a similar observation about care jobs. They argue that all good care jobs share a set of characteristics: "a significant degree of worker control or autonomy, good collaboration with the others involved in the recipients' care, and compensation that inspires job commitment" (Howes, Leana, and Smith 2012, 89). But, they point out, among the many care jobs that do not meet these criteria, each of them is "bad" in a particular way. The empirical studies in this volume reinforce the importance of some control over work, opportunities for input into the care process, and fair pay to worker satisfaction and ultimately to quality care. And these pages contain vivid examples of the myriad ways in which care jobs fail to measure up to these criteria.

Very few of the workers described in this volume experience high levels of autonomy, collaboration, and compensation. In fact, many are asked to make trade-offs between, say, their own agency in the workplace and their level of pay. For example, home-based work may provide more autonomy to workers but lower levels of compensation. Some workers have the "choice" to take lower levels of compensation because they do not have young children to support or they have a wage-earning partner. Other workers have more constrained choices. In each of the care work jobs discussed in the volume, constraint and choice combine in various ways to produce myriad realities for paid caregivers.

Even apparently similar organizational structures can produce quite different results. For example, the role of third-party agencies emerges as having contradictory effects on worker experiences in different settings. Some of the home care workers studied cited their affiliation with agencies as protection against the isolation that many home-based workers experience. But home-based childcare workers did not report the same sense of connection and collaboration with other similarly situated workers through agency ties, and in fact experienced agency affiliation as significantly lowering their earning potential. Unfortunately, there is no one-size-fits-all solution to the problems that plague the care sector. Fortunately, we do know what the goals should be for improving these jobs.

Care Takes Time

A reoccurring theme throughout the volume is the importance of time. Hospice workers talk about the need to slow down the process of care in order to let dying patients and their families figure out their own wishes. Workers across the occupational spectrum report that the relational aspects of their jobs are some of the most rewarding, and these dimensions of their work get crowded out when time is scarce. It takes time to properly use equipment or call an extra person over to help do a lift correctly to avoid injury. And nursing home workers, home care workers, and childcare workers often find themselves taking their own time to provide what they perceive as better care when enough time is not structured into their schedules. The speed-up of work in the postindustrial economy has been well documented across a range of occupational settings, and care work is certainly not immune from these pressures.

Several chapters in the volume illuminate what happens—to organizations, to providers, to recipients of care—when efficiency and time maximization take priority over the well-being of people. The structural realities of understaffing leave many care workers fighting against the clock, a reality that has deleterious consequences not only for those workers but for those in their care. The time deficit in care work is exacerbated by cultural perceptions that render many aspects of caring labor invisible, unaccounted for in job descriptions and work schedules.

The other aspect of time that emerges in these studies is the particular constraints on workers' control over their own time for those engaged directly in nurturant care. Childcare workers, for example, find that their time is much more constrained than housecleaners. And nursing assistants have inflexible schedules and non-normative work hours that make caring for their own families a challenge. Again, worker control over time is an issue for many jobs in the service sector, but the time crunch that care workers face is unique because they are directly responsible for the well-being of others.

Policy Matters

In an era when government is either a monolithic abstraction or a vilified entity, it is often difficult to make a compelling case for the importance of public policy. The authors in this volume, however, demonstrate how the current policy environment directly impacts workers and their life chances. Some workers (home care aides, for example) have lacked basic worker protections at the same time that others (like family day care providers, for example) are subject to extensive state regulation of their labor. Still others find themselves constrained by public funding structures such as Medicare and Medicaid. Making matters worse, the overall context of shrinking public budgets has had an enormous impact on sectors like elder care and social services, placing workers at risk for exploitation and injury. Public policy can also play a positive role by supporting family caregivers with government funding. What is abundantly clear is that the government plays a significant and necessary role in the care sector: funding as well as regulation decisions impact workers and those they care for.

We have also seen how employers and educational institutions have a role to play in setting the policy context for care workers. Relatively small changes—like making schedules more predictable and creating opportunities for "stackable" credits—can have a meaningful impact on workers' ability to achieve some level of upward mobility. And other changes—like installing assistive devices for patient lifts or changing from carpeted floors to tile—can reduce worker exposure to physical risks of injury. Government and employers have a crucial role to play in creating sustainable jobs in the care sector. That said, governments and businesses respond to pressures from constituents and consumers, respectively. Widespread changes to the policies of care will only come when collective pressure is placed on the change makers to recognize and value caring labor.

Economic Inequality

As many of these pieces make clear, the economic inequality in the labor market as a whole is reproduced and reinforced within the paid care sector. A number of the jobs described in this volume are low paid and offer limited vertical mobility for workers. Benefits such as health insurance or sick pay are spotty, although unionization in some sectors has helped improve working conditions for a subset of caregivers. Education and training are two factors that impact worker mobility, but there are often significant obstacles to moving workers up the career ladder. In the healthcare sector, for example, moving from CNA to RN requires a significant investment of time and money on the part of the worker and the institution for which she or he works. As earlier chapters in the volume show, it takes significant commitment and creativity on the part of the private sector (and in some cases the public sector) to imagine an advancement program—such as "career lattices"—that simultaneously benefits the worker and the employing organization. Such innovations are certainly possible, and will be helped by advocacy groups and service unions that provide both the resources and the rhetoric needed to change working conditions and provide opportunities for advancement.

Professionalizing care workers is not without its limitations, however. As some care workers move up the occupational hierarchy, others remain relegated to the work "at the bottom," which remains undervalued and underpaid. Given the way that race, citizenship, and gender map onto the various strata of the care work sector—with women and racial/ethnic minorities concentrated in lower skilled, non-nurturant work—it is incumbent upon those fighting for the interests of paid caregivers to recognize that a given policy to advance the prospects of care workers must consider implications for the sector as a whole. In an economic context where rewards are unequally distributed, care scholars and policymakers must redouble their efforts to improve conditions for low-skilled workers while also creating opportunities for those who wish to advance and have the resources to do so. It is only through this dual strategy that we can create quality jobs (and quality care) at all levels of this sector.

An Ethic of Care

A number of authors referred either implicitly or explicitly to the "ethic of care" and its role in paid care work. For social workers and others, the feeling of obligation to serving the needs of clients leads to the underreporting of injury and abuse. The expectation of care workers by themselves and by others, including managers, is often that they will sacrifice their own time, health, and family for the needs of those whom they serve. This ethic has created challenges for those working to organize care workers, who worry that advocating for themselves as workers will go against the needs of those for whom they care.

Conceiving of care as a critical part of human infrastructure and as a basic ethical obligation of society transforms this ethic of care from an individual responsibility to a collective imperative. Joan Tronto (2012) argues that care should be integrated as a central concern of our democracy. Part of the goal of this volume is to contribute to creating a broader view of care to replace our currently fragmented approach to care policies and paid care work in the labor force. Building on the ethical dimensions of care work in ways that support rather than undermine workers is a key step to building a strong system of care provision for all.

Documentary filmmaker Gini Reticker (2013) has spoken of her observations of women's roles in regions of the world that are involved in armed conflict. She was struck by how women were perceived as being in the support role—cooking, cleaning, tending to the ill, taking care of children—while the men did the "real" work of fighting in the war. In her view, the women are the ones doing the real work—that is, the work of building a society. As care scholars and others who have an interest in paid care, this is the challenge: to shift the discourse to understand that care work is in fact an end goal in itself, not just the means to get there.

References

Abbott, Andrew. 1988. *The System of Professions: An Essay on the Division of Expert Labor.*
Chicago: University of Chicago Press.

Abel, Emily K. 2002. *Hearts of Wisdom: American Women Caring for Kin, 1850–1940.*
Cambridge, MA: Harvard University Press.

———. 2013. *The Inevitable Hour: A History of Caring for Dying Patients in America.*
Baltimore: Johns Hopkins University Press.

Abel, Emily K., and Margaret K. Nelson, eds. 1990. *Circles of Care: Work and Identity in
Women's Lives.* Albany: State University of New York Press.

Abramovitz, Mimi. 2004. "Saving Capitalism from Itself: Whither the Welfare State?"
New England Journal of Public Policy 20 (Fall/Winter): 21–31.

———. 2005. "The Largely Untold Story of Welfare Reform and the Human Services." *Social
Work* 50(2): 175–86.

Aguiar, Luis L. M. 2001. "Doing Cleaning Work 'Scientifically': The Reorganization of Work
in the Contract Building Cleaning Industry." *Economic and Industrial Democracy* 22 (2):
239–69.

Aguiar, Luis L. M., and Andrew Herod, eds. 2006. *The Dirty Work of Neo-Liberalism: Cleaners
in the Global Economy.* Malden, MA: Wiley-Blackwell.

Aiken, Linda H., Sean P. Clarke, Douglas M. Sloane, Julie Sochalski, and Jeffrey H.
Silber. 2002. "Hospital Nurse Staffing and Patient Mortality, Nurse Burnout, and Job
Dissatisfaction." *Journal of American Medical Association* 288 (16): 1987–93.

Alexopoulos, Evangelos C., Dimitra Tanagra, Ioannis Detorakis, Panagiota Gatsi, Antigoni
Goroyia, Maria Michalopoulou, and Eleni Jelastopulu. 2011. "Knee and Low Back
Complaints in Professional Hospital Nurses: Occurrence, Chronicity, Care Seeking, and
Absenteeism." *Work* 38 (4): 329–35.

American Association of Colleges of Nursing. 2004. *AACN Position Statement on the
Practice Doctorate in Nursing.* http://www.aacn.nche.edu/publications/position/
DNPpositionstatement.pdf.

American Association of Homes and Services for the Aging. 2007. "Aging Services: The Facts."
Accessed March 26. http://www.aahsa.org/aging_services/default.asp.

American Nurses Association. 1991. "ANA Position Statement on Cultural Diversity in
Nursing Practice." *Prairie Rose* 60 (4): 13a–14.

Amott, Teresa, and Julie Matthaei. 1996. *Race, Gender, and Work: A Multi-cultural Economic History of Women in the United States.* Boston: South End Press.

Andersen, Lars L., Thomas Clausen, Roger Persson, and Andreas Holtermann. 2013. "Perceived Physical Exertion during Healthcare Work and Risk of Chronic Pain in Different Body Regions: Prospective Cohort Study." *International Archives of Occupational and Environmental Health* 86 (6): 681–87.

Anderson, Bridget. 2000. *Doing the Dirty Work? The Global Politics of Domestic Labour.* London: Zed Books.

Anderson, Jennifer J., and David T. Felson. 1988. "Factors Associated with Osteoarthritis of the Knee in the First National Health and Nutrition Examination Survey (HANES I): Evidence for an Association with Overweight, Race, and Physical Demands of Work." *American Journal of Epidemiology* 128 (1): 179–89.

Anderson, Nickela, and Karen D. Hughes. 2010. "The Business of Caring: Women's Self-Employment and the Marketization of Care." *Gender, Work, and Organization* 17 (4): 381–405.

Angus, Jan, Pia Kontos, Isabel Dyck, Patricia McKeever, and Blake Poland. 2005. "The Personal Significance of Home: Habitus and the Experience of Receiving Long-Term Home Care." *Sociology of Health and Illness* 27 (2): 161–87.

Appelbaum, Eileen. 2011. "Macroeconomic Policy, Labor Market Institutions, and Employment Outcomes." *Work, Employment, and Society* 25 (4): 596–610.

Appelbaum, Eileen, Peter Berg, Ann Frost, and Gil Preuss. 2003. "The Effects of Work Restructuring on Low-Wage, Low-Skill Workers in US Hospitals." In *Low-Wage America: How Employers Are Reshaping Opportunity in the Workplace,* ed. Eileen Appelbaum, Annette Bernhardt, and Richard J. Murnane, 33–76. New York: Russell Sage Foundation.

Appelbaum, Eileen, and John Schmitt. 2009. "Review Article: Low-Wage Work in High-Income Countries: Labor-Market Institutions and Business Strategy in the US and Europe." *Human Relations* 62 (12): 1907–34.

Arias, Elizabeth. 2007. "United States Life Tables, 2004." *National Vital Statistics Report,* vol. 56, no. 9. Hyattsville, MD: National Center for Health Statistics.

Armenia, Amy. 2009. "More Than Motherhood: Reasons for Becoming a Family Day Care Provider." *Journal of Family Issues* 30 (4): 554–74.

Armstrong, Pat, Hugh Armstrong, and Krista Scott-Dixon. 2008. *Critical to Care: The Invisible Women in Health Services.* Toronto: University of Toronto Press.

Aronson, J., M. Denton, and I. Zeytinoglu. 2004. "Market-Modeled Home Care in Ontario: Deteriorating Working Conditions and Dwindling Community Capacity." *Canadian Public Policy* 30: 111–25.

Aronson, Jane, and Sheila Neysmith. 1996. "'You're Not Just in There to Do the Work': Depersonalizing Policies and the Exploitation of Home Care Workers' Labor." *Gender and Society* 10 (1): 59–77.

Backinger, Cathy L., and George H. Koustenis. 1994. "Analysis of Needlestick Injuries to Health Care Workers Providing Home Care." *American Journal of Infection Control* 22 (5): 300–306.

Badley, Elizabeth M., I. Rasooly, and G. K. Webster. 1994. "Relative Importance of Musculoskeletal Disorders as a Cause of Chronic Health Problems, Disability, and Health Care Utilization: Findings from the 1990 Ontario Health Survey." *Journal of Rheumatology* 21 (3): 505–14.

Baines, Donna. 2004a. "Caring for Nothing: Work Organization and Unwaged Labour in Social Services." *Work, Employment, and Society* 18 (2): 267–95.

———. 2004b. "Pro-Market, Non-Market: The Dual Nature of Organizational Change in Social Services Delivery." *Critical Social Policy* 24 (1): 5–29.

———. 2005. "Criminalizing the Care Work Zone? The Gendered Dynamics of Using Legal and Administrative Strategies to Confront Workplace Violence." *Social Justice* 32 (2): 132–50.

Barbee, Evelyn L. 1993. "Racism in U.S. Nursing." *Medical Anthropology Quarterly* 7 (4): 346–62.

Baron, Sherry L., and Sacoby Wilson. 2011. "Occupational and Environmental Health Equity and Social Justice." In *Occupational and Environmental Health: Recognizing and Preventing Disease and Injury*, 6th ed, ed. Barry S. Levy, David H. Wegman, Sherry L. Baron, and Rosemary K. Sokas, 69–97. Oxford: Oxford University Press.

Barry, Theresa, Peter Kemper, and S. Diane Brannon. 2008. "Measuring Worker Turnover in Long-Term Care: Lessons from the Better Jobs Better Care Demonstration." *Gerontologist* 48 (3): 394–400.

Barth, Michael. 2003. "Social Work Labor Market: A First Look." *Social Work* 48 (1): 9–19.

Bashevkin, Sylvia. 2002. *Women's Work Is Never Done: Comparative Studies in Caregiving, Employment, and Social Policy Reform.* New York: Routledge.

Baughman, Reagan A., and Kristin E. Smith. 2011. "Labor Mobility of the Direct Care Workforce: Implications for the Provision of Long-term Care." *Health Economics* 21(12): 1402–15.

Becker, Amanda. 2013. "Administration to Apply Wage Law to 2 Million Home Care Aides." *Washington Post*, September 18.

Becker, Deborah, Maggie Mulvihill, and Rachel Stine. 2012. "Worried Group Home Workers Seek Protections as Massachusetts Aims to Improve Safety." *New England Center for Investigative Reporting and WBUR* (December 19). http://www.wbur.org/2012/12/19/mass-group-home-safety.

Bell, Alice, and Ivana La Valle. 2003. *Combining Self-Employment and Family Life.* Bristol: Policy Press.

Bell, Carl C., Lynne Mock, and Gary Slutkin. 2002. "The Prevalence of Victimization and Perceptions of Job Neighborhood Safety in a Social Service Agency and the Need for Screening." *Journal of the National Medical Association* 94 (7): 602–8.

Benford, Robert D., and David A. Snow. 2000. "Framing Processes and Social Movements: An Overview and Assessment." *Annual Review of Sociology* 26: 611–39.

Benjamin, A. E. 1993. "An Historical Perspective on Home Care Policy." *The Milbank Quarterly* 71 (1): 129–66.

Bercovitz, Anita, Abigail Moss, Manisha Sengupta, Eunice Y. Park-Lee, Adrienne Jones, and Lauren D. Harris-Kojetin. 2011. "An Overview of Home Health Aides: United States, 2007." *National Health Statistics Report* 34: 1–31.

Berdes, Celia, and John M. Eckert. 2007. "The Language of Caring: Nurse's Aides' Use of Family Metaphors Conveys Affective Caring." *The Gerontologist* 47 (3): 340–49.

Berg, Gretchen, and Susan Farrar. 2000. *IHSS Providers: Characteristics of Caregivers in the In Home Supportive Services Program.* Sacramento: California Department of Social Services.

Bernard, Bruce P. 1997. *Musculoskeletal Disorders and Workplace Factors: A Critical Review of Epidemiologic Evidence for Work-related Musculoskeletal Disorders of the Neck, Upper Extremity, and Low Back.* Cincinnati, OH: U.S. Department of Health and Human Services.

Bernhardt, Annette D. 1999. "The Future of Low-Wage Jobs: Case Studies in the Retail Industry." IEE Working Paper no. 10. *Institute on Education and the Economy* http://citeseerx.ist.psu.edu/viewdoc/download?doi=10.1.1.41.885&rep=rep1&type=pdf.

Betancourt, Joseph. R., Alexander R. Green, and J. Emilio Carrillo. 2002. *Cultural Competence in Healthcare: Emerging Frameworks and Practical Approaches.* Vol. 576. New York: Commonwealth Fund.

Blanchflower, David, and Andrew Oswald. 1999. "Well-being, Insecurity, and the Decline of American Job Satisfaction." Unpublished paper. Accessed August 5, 2003. http://www .dartmouth.edu/~blnchflr/papers/.

Blanchflower, David, Andrew Oswald, and Alois Stuatzer. 2001. "Latent Entrepreneurship across Nations." *European Economic Review* 45 (4–6): 680–91.

Bodenheimer, Thomas, Ellen Chen, and Heather Bennett. 2009. "Confronting the Growing Burden of Chronic Disease: Can the U.S. Health Care Workforce Do the Job?" *Health Affairs* 28: 64–74.

Bolton, Sharon, and Carol Boyd. 2003. "Trolley Dolly or Skilled Emotion Manager? Moving on from Hochschild's *Managed Heart*." *Work, Employment, and Society* 17: 289–308.

Bond, Meg A., and Michelle C. Haynes. 2014. "Workplace Diversity: A Social Ecological Framework and Policy Implications." *Social Issues and Policy Review* 8: 167–201.

Bond, Meg A., Michelle C. Haynes, Robin A. Toof, Michelle D. Holmberg, and Johana R. Quinteros. 2011. *Healthy Diversity: Practices That Support Diverse Staffing in Community Health Centers*. Lowell, MA: University of Massachusetts–Lowell.

Boris, Eileen, and Jennifer Klein. 2006. "Organizing Home Care: Low-Waged Workers in the Welfare State." *Politics and Society* 34: 81–107.

———. 2008. "Labor on the Home Front: Unionizing Home-Based Care Workers." *New Labor Forum* 17 (2): 32–41.

———. 2012. *Caring for America: Home Health Workers in the Shadow of the Welfare State*. New York: Oxford University Press.

Boukus, Ellyn, Alwyn Cassil, and Ann S. O'Malley. 2009. "A Snapshot of US Physicians: Key Findings from the 2008 Heath Tracking Physician Survey." *Center for Studying Health System Change*. Accessed December 29, 2012. http://www.hschange.com/ CONTENT/1078/#top.

Boyer, Jon. 2008. "Ergonomic Exposures, Socioeconomic Status, and Musculoskeletal Disorder Risk Among Healthcare Workers." Sc.D. diss., University of Massachusetts–Lowell.

Boyer, Jon, Monica Galizzi, Manuel Cifuentes, Angelo d'Errico, Rebecca Gore, Laura Punnett, and Craig Slatin. 2009. "Ergonomic and Socioeconomic Risk Factors for Hospital Workers' Compensation Injury Claims." *American Journal of Industrial Medicine* 52 (7): 551–62.

Boyer, Jon, Jia-Hua Lin, and Chien-Chi Chang. 2013. "Description and Analysis of Hand Forces in Medicine Cart Pushing Tasks." *Applied Ergonomics* 44 (4): 48–57.

Brannon, Diane, Jacqueline S. Zinn, Vincent Mor, and Jullet Davis. 2002. "An Exploration of Job, Organizational, and Environmental Factors Associated with High and Low Nursing Assistant Turnover." *Gerontologist* 42: 159–68.

Broersen, J. P., B. C. de Zwart, F. J. van Dijk, T. F. Meijman, and M. van Veldhoven. 1996. "Health Complaints and Working Conditions Experienced in Relation to Work and Age." *Occupational and Environmental Medicine* 53 (1): 51–57.

Brown, Tamara Rose. 2011. *Raising Brooklyn: Nannies, Childcare, and Caribbeans Creating Community*. New York: NYU Press.

Brown University, Center for Gerontology and Health Care Research. 2012. *Facts on Dying: Policy Relevant Data on Care at the End of Life 2004* [cited October 5, 2012]. http://www .chcr.brown.edu/dying/usastatistics.htm#.

Brush, Candida, Nancy M. Carter, Elizabeth Gatewood, Patricia Greene, and Myra Heart, eds. 2006. *Women and Entrepreneurship: Contemporary Classics*. London: Edward Elgar.

Budig, Michelle. 2006a. "Intersections on the Road to Self-Employment: Gender, Family, and Occupational Class." *Social Forces* 84 (4): 2223–39.

———. 2006b. "Gender, Self-Employment, and Earnings: The Interlocking Structures of Family and Professional Status." *Gender and Society* 20 (6): 725–53.

Burnham, Linda, and Nik Theodore. 2012. *Home Economics: The Invisible and Unregulated World of Domestic Work.* National Domestic Workers Alliance: Center for Urban Economic Development, University of Illinois at Chicago.

Butler, Sandra, Sara Wardamasky, and Mark Brennan-Ing. 2012. "Older Women Caring for Older Women: The Rewards and Challenges of the Home Care Aide Job." *Journal of Women and Aging* 24 (3): 194–215.

Cain, Cindy L. 2012. "Emotions and the Research Interview: What Hospice Workers Can Teach Us." *Health Sociology Review* 21 (4): 396–405.

———. 2013. "Consequences of Conflicting Institutional Logics: Inequality and Isomorphism in the Hospice Division of Labor." Preprint, University of Arizona.

Canadian Association of Retired Persons. 2001. *Report on Home Care.* Ottawa: Canadian Association of Retired Persons.

Cancian, Francesca M., and Stacey J. Oliker. 2000. *Caring and Gender.* Thousand Oaks, CA: Pine Forge Press.

Carnoy, Martin, and Henry M. Levin. 1985. *Schooling and Work in the Democratic State.* Stanford, CA: Stanford University Press.

Castle, Nicholas G., John Endberg, Ruth Anderson, and Aiju Men. 2007. "Job Satisfaction of Nurse Aides in Nursing Homes: Intent to Leave and Turnover." *Gerontologist* 47: 193–204.

Centers for Medicare and Medicaid Services. 2013. "Accountable Care Organizations (ACOs): General Information." Accessed December 4. http://innovation.cms.gov/initiatives/aco/.

Chafetz, Janet. 1988. "The Gender Division of Labor and the Reproduction of Female Disadvantage: Towards an Integrated Theory." *Journal of Family Issues* 9 (1): 108–31.

Chambliss, Daniel F. 1996. *Beyond Caring: Hospitals, Nurses, and the Social Organization of Ethics.* Chicago: University of Chicago Press.

Childress, Alice. 1986. *Like One of the Family: Conversations from a Domestic's Life.* Boston: Beacon Press.

Chodorow, Nancy. 1978. *The Reproduction of Mothering.* Berkeley: University of California Press.

Chorn-Dunham, Charlotte, and Bernadette E. Dietz. 2003. "If I'm Not Allowed to Put My Family First: Challenges Experienced by Women Who Are Caregiving for Family Members with Dementia." *Journal of Women and Aging* 15 (1): 55–70.

Clark, Sue Campbell. 2000. "Work/Family Border Theory: A New Theory of Work-Family Balance." *Human Relations* 53 (6): 747–70.

Clarke, John. 2009. "Public Management or Managing the Public? The Frank Stacey Memorial Lecture 2009." Paper presented at the Public Administration Committee Conference, University of Glamorgan, September 8, 2009.

Clawson, Dan, and Naomi Gerstel. 2014. *Unequal Time: Gender, Class, and Family in Employment Schedules.* New York: Russell Sage Foundation.

Cobble, Dorothy Sue. 2010. "More Intimate Unions." In *Intimate Labors,* ed. E. Boris and R. S. Parrenas, 280–95. Stanford, CA: Stanford University Press.

Cognet, Marguerite. 2002. "Les Femmes, les Services et le Don." *Cahiers de Recherche Sociologique* 37: 51–77.

Cohen, Nancy. N.d. "Ten Reasons Why Family Child Care Providers Like Accreditation." Washington, DC: National Association for Family Child Care. Accessed May 28, 2001, http://www.nafcc.orgltenreasons.html.

Colen, Shellee. 1990. "'Housekeeping' for the Green Card: West Indian Household Workers, the State, and Stratified Reproduction in New York." In *At Work in Homes: Household Workers in World Perspective,* ed. Roger Sanjek and Shellee Colen, 89–118. Washington, DC: American Anthropological Association.

———. 1995. "'Like a Mother to Them': Stratified Reproduction and West Indian Childcare Workers and Employers in New York." In *Conceiving New World Order: The Global Politics of Reproduction*, ed. Faye Ginsburg and Rayna Rapp, 78–102. Berkeley: University of California Press.

Collins, Patricia Hill. 2000. *Black Feminist Thought: Knowledge, Consciousness, and the Politics of Empowerment*. New York: Routledge.

———. 2005. *Black Sexual Politics*. New York: Routledge

Committee on the Role of Human Factors in Home Health Care, National Research Council. 2011. *Health Care Comes Home: The Human Factors*. Washington, DC: National Academies Press.

Cowin, Leanne. 2001. "Measuring Nurses' Self Concept." *Western Journal of Nursing Research* 23: 313–15.

Cox, Rachel. 2005. *Making Family Child Care Work: Strategies for Improving the Working Conditions of Family Childcare Providers*. Ottawa: Status of Women Canada.

Cranford, Cynthia, Judy Fudge, Eric Tucker, and Leah Vosko. 2005. *Self-Employed Workers Organize: Law, Policy, and Unions*. Montreal: McGill-Queen's University Press.

Crittenden, Ann. 2001. *The Price of Motherhood: Why the Most Important Job in the World Is Still the Least Valued*. New York: Henry Holt.

Cubbin, Catherine, Felicia B. LeClere, and Gordon S. Smith. 2000. "Socioeconomic Status and the Occurrence of Fatal and Nonfatal Injury in the United States." *American Journal of Public Health* 90 (1): 70–77.

Curbow, Barbara. 1990. "Job Stress in Child Care Workers: A Framework for Research." *Child and Youth Quarterly* 19 (4): 215–31.

Davies, Celia. 1995. "Competence versus Care? Gender and Caring Work Revisited." *Acta Sociologica* 38 (1): 17–31.

Davis, Fred, and Virginia Olesen. 1963. "Initiation into a Women's Profession: Identity Problems in the Status Transitions from Coed to Student Nurse." *Sociometry* 26 (1): 89–101.

Dawson, Steven, and Rick Surpin. 2001. *Direct-Care Health Workers: The Unnecessary Crisis in Long-Term Care*. Aspen, CO: Aspen Institute.

Dellinger, Kirsten. 2004. "Masculinities in 'Safe' and 'Embattled' Organizations: Accounting for Pornographic and Feminist Magazines." *Gender and Society* 18: 545–66.

Delp, Linda, and Katie Quan. 2002. "Homecare Worker Organizing in California: An Analysis of a Successful Strategy." *Labor Studies Journal* 27: 1–23.

Dement, John M., Carol Epling, Truls Østbye, Lisa A. Pompeii, and Debra L. Hunt. 2004. "Blood and Body Fluid Exposure Risks among Health Care Workers: Results from the Duke Health and Safety Surveillance System." *American Journal of Industrial Medicine* 46 (6): 637–48.

DeNavas-Walt, Carmen, Bernadette Proctor, and Jessica C. Smith. 2012. "Income, Poverty, and Health Insurance Coverage in the United States: 2011 Current Population Reports." Washington, DC: US Department of Commerce Economics and Statistics Administration.

Denton, Margaret, Isik Zeytinoglu, Sharon Davies, and Jason Lian. 2002. "Job Stress and Job Dissatisfaction of Home Care Workers in the Context of Health Care Restructuring." *International Journal of Health Services* 32: 327–57.

Department of Early Education and Care. 2013. *Annual Legislative Report FY 2013*. http://www.mass.gov/ edu/docs/eec/2013/fy13eec.pdf.

d'Errico, Angelo, Laura Punnett, Manuel Cifuentes, Jon Boyer, Jamie Tessler, Rebecca Gore, Patrick Scollin, and Craig Slatin. 2007. "Hospital Injury Rates in Relation to Socioeconomic Status and Working Conditions." *Occupational and Environmental Medicine* 64 (5): 325–33.

DeVault, Marjorie L. 1991. *Feeding the Family: The Social Organization of Caring as Gendered Work*. Chicago: University of Chicago Press.

Diamond, Timothy. 1992. *Making Gray Gold: Narratives of Nursing Home Care*. Chicago: University of Chicago Press.

Dill, Bonnie Thornton. 1994. "Fictive Kin, Paper Sons, and Compadrazgo: Women of Color and the Struggle for Family Survival." In *Women of Color in U.S. Society*, ed. Maxine Baca Zinn and Bonnie Thornton Dill, 149–70. Philadelphia: Temple University Press.

Dill, Janette S., Jennifer C. Morgan, and Victor W. Marshall. 2012. "Contingency, Employment Intentions, and Retention of Vulnerable Low-Wage Workers: An Examination of Nursing Assistants in Nursing Homes." *The Gerontologist* 53 (2): 222–34.

Direct Care Alliance (DCA). 2010. "DCA Fact Sheet: Direct Care Workers." Accessed March 13, 2013. http://www.directcarealliance.org/_data/global/images/DCA_VI_description.pdf.

Dodson, Lisa, and Rebekah M. Zincavage. 2007. "'It's Like a Family': Caring Labor, Exploitation, and Race in Nursing Homes." *Gender and Society* 21: 905–28.

Donoghue, Christopher. 2010. "Nursing Home Staff Turnover and Retention." *Journal of Applied Gerontology* 29: 89–106.

Douglass, Anne, and Jody Hiffer Gittell. 2012. "Transforming Professionalism: Relational Bureaucracy and Parent-Teacher Partnerships in Child Care Settings." *Journal of Early Childhood Research* 10 (3): 267–81.

Ducey, Ariel. 2008. *Never Good Enough: Health Care Workers and the False Promise of Job Training*. Ithaca, NY: Cornell University Press.

Dudden, Faye E. 1983. *Serving Women: Household Service in Nineteenth-Century America*. Middletown, CT: Wesleyan University Press.

Duffy, Mignon. 2005. "Reproducing Labor Inequalities: Challenges for Feminists Conceptualizing Care at the Intersections of Gender, Race, and Class." *Gender and Society* 19 (1): 66–82.

———. 2007. "Doing the Dirty Work: Gender, Race, and Reproductive Labor in Historical Perspective." *Gender and Society* 21 (3): 313–36.

———. 2010. "'We Are the Union': Care Work, Unions, and Social Movements." *Humanity and Society* 34 (2): 125–140.

———. 2011. *Making Care Count*. New Brunswick, NJ: Rutgers University Press.

Duffy, Mignon, Randy Albelda, and Clare Hammonds. 2013. "Counting Care Work: The Empirical and Policy Applications of Care Theory." *Social Problems* 60 (2): 145–67.

Duvander, Ann-Zofie, and Linda Haas. 2013. "Sweden Country Note." In *International Review of Leave Policies and Research*, ed. P. Moss. www.leavenetwork.org/lp_and_r_reports/.

Duvander, Ann-Zofie, and Mats Johansson. 2012. "What Are the Effects of Reforms Promoting Fathers' Parental Leave Use?" *Journal of European Social Policy* 22: 319–30.

Dwyer, Rachel. 2013. "The Care Economy? Gender, Economic Restructuring, and Job Polarization in the U.S. Labor Market." *American Sociological Review* 78: 390–416.

Ehrenreich, Barbara. 2002. *Nickel and Dimed: On (Not) Getting By in America*. New York: Metropolitan Books.

Ehrehreich, Barbara, and Deidre English. 1979. *For Her Own Good: 150 Years of Experts' Advice to Women*. Garden City, NY: Anchor Books.

Ehrenreich, Barbara, and Arlie Russell Hochschild, eds. 2002. *Global Woman: Nannies, Maids, and Sex Workers in the New Economy*. New York: Metropolitan Books.

Ekberg, J., R. Eriksson, and G. Friebel. 2013 "Parental Leave—A Policy Evaluation of the Swedish 'Daddy Month' Reform." *Journal of Public Economics* 97: 131–43.

Engels, Friedrich. [1884] 1972. *The Origins of the Family, Private Property, and the State*. New York: International Publishers.

Engkvist, Inga-Lill. 2006. "Evaluation of an Intervention Comprising a No-Lifting Policy in Australian Hospitals." *Applied Ergonomics* 37 (2): 141–48.

England, Kim, and Isabel Dyck. 2011. "Managing the Body Work of Home Care." *Sociology of Health and Illness* 33: 206–19.

England, Paula. 2005. "Emerging Theories of Care Work." *Annual Review of Sociology* 31: 381–99.

England, Paula, Michelle Budig, and Nancy Folbre. 2002. "Wages of Virtue: The Relative Pay of Care Work." *Social Problems* 49 (4): 455–73.

England, Paula, and Nancy Folbre. 1999. "The Cost of Caring." *Annals of the American Academy of Political and Social Science* 561: 39–51.

Erickson, Rebecca, and Clare L. Stacey. 2013. "Attending to Mind and Body: Engaging the Complexity of Emotion Practice Among Caring Professionals." In *Emotional Labor in the 21st Century: Diverse Perspectives on Emotion Regulation at Work*, ed. A. A. Grandey, J. M. Diefendorff, and D. E. Rupp, 175–96. New York: Routledge.

European Commission Directorate-General for Justice. 2013. "Tackling the Gender Pay Gap in the European Union." Luxembourg: EU Publications Office.

Fagermoen, May Solveig. 1998. "Professional Identity: Values Embedded in Meaningful Nursing Practice." *Journal of Advanced Nursing* 25: 434–41.

Family Continuity Inc. 2013. "Governor Signs First Human Service Worker Safety Bill." March eNewsletter. http://www.familycontinuity.org/index.php?name=News&file=article&sid=122.

Faucett, Julia, Taewoon Kang, and Robert Newcomer. 2013. "Personal Service Assistance: Musculoskeletal Disorders and Injuries in Consumer-Directed Home Care." *American Journal of Industrial Medicine* 56 (4): 454–68.

Ferrarini, Tommy, and Ann-Zofie Duvander. 2009. "Swedish Family Policy: Controversial Reform of a Success Story." *Referat Westliche Industrielander*, March 9.

Fine, Michael, and Caroline Glendinning. 2005. "Dependence, Independence, or Inter-dependence? Revisiting the Concepts of 'Care' and 'Dependency.'" *Ageing and Society* 25: 601–21.

Fineman, Martha. 2000. "Cracking the Foundational Myths: Independence, Autonomy, and Self-Sufficiency." *American University Journal of Gender, Social Policy, and the Law* 8: 13–22.

Finnie, Ross, Maud-Catherine Rivard, and Christine Laport. 2002. "Setting Up Shop: Self-Employment amongst Canadian College and University Graduates." Catalogue No. 11F0010MIE, no. 183. Ottawa: Statistics Canada, Business, and Labour Market Analysis Division.

Fisher, Berenice, and Joan Tronto. 1990. "Toward a Feminist Theory of Caring." In *Circles of Care: Work and Identity in Women's Lives*, ed. Emily K. Abel and Margaret K. Nelson, 35–62. Albany: State University of New York Press.

Fisher, Sue. 1995. *Nursing Wounds*. New Brunswick, NJ: Rutgers University Press.

Fitzgerald, Joan. 2006. *Moving Up in the New Economy: Career Ladders for US Workers*. Ithaca, NY: ILR Press.

Fitz Gibbon, Heather M. 2002. "Child Care across Sectors: A Comparison of the Work of Child Care in Three Settings." In *Child Care and Inequality: Rethinking Carework for Children and Youth*, ed. Francesca M. Cancian, 145–58. New York: Routledge.

Flannery, Raymond B., William H. Fisher, and Andrew P. Walker. 2000. "Characteristics of Patient and Staff Victims of Assaults in Community Residences by Previously Non-Violent Psychiatric Inpatients." *Psychiatric Quarterly* 71 (3): 195–203.

Flexner, Abraham. 1915. "Is Social Work a Profession?" Paper presented at the National Conference on Charities and Correction, 584–88.

Folbre, Nancy. 1994. *Who Pays for the Kids? Gender and Structures of Constraint*. New York: Routledge.

———. 2002. *The Invisible Heart: Economics and Family Values*. New York: New Press.

———. 2006a. "Measuring Caring: Gender, Empowerment, and the Care Economy." *Journal of Human Development* 7 (2): 183–99.

———. 2006b. "Demanding Quality: Worker/Consumer Coalitions and 'High Road' Strategies in the Care Sector." *Politics and Society* 34 (1): 11–32.

———, ed. 2012. *For Love and Money.* New York: Russell Sage.

Folbre, Nancy, and Julie A. Nelson. 2000. "For Love or Money—or Both?" *Journal of Economic Perspectives* 14 (4): 123–40.

Folbre, Nancy, and Erik Olin Wright. 2012. "Defining Care." In *For Love and Money: Care Provision in the United States*, ed. Nancy Folbre, 1–20. New York: Russell Sage Foundation.

Foner, Nancy. 1994. *The Caregiving Dilemma: Working in an American Nursing Home.* Berkeley: University of California Press.

Foucault, Michel. 1994. *The Birth of the Clinic: An Archaeology of Medical Perception.* New York: Vintage Books.

Fraser, Nancy. 2000. "After the Family Wage: a Postindustrial Thought Experiment." In *Gender and Citizenship in Transition*, ed. Barbara Hobson, 1–32. New York: Routledge.

Friedman, Mary, and Emily Rhinehart. 1999. "Putting Infection Control Principles into Practice in Home Care." *Nursing Clinics of North America* 34 (2): 463–82.

———. 2000. "Improving Infection Control in Home Care: From Ritual to Science-Based Practice." *Home Healthcare Nurse* 18 (2): 99–105; quiz 06.

Freidson, Eliot. 1970. *Professional Dominance: The Social Structure of Medical Care.* New York: Atherton.

Fudge, Judy. 2006. "Self-Employment, Women, and Precarious Work: The Scope of Labour Protection." In *Precarious Work, Women, and the New Economy*, ed. Judy Fudge and Rosemary Owens, 201–22. Oxford: Hart Publishing.

Gallagher, Dolores, Jonathon Rose, Patricia Rivera, Steven Lovett, and Larry W. Thompson. 1989. "Prevalence of Depression in Family Caregivers." *The Gerontologist* 29 (4): 449–56.

Gallup. 2010. "Nurses Top Honesty and Ethics List for 11th Year." Retrieved http://www.gallup.com/poll/145043/ Nurses-Top-Honesty-Ethics-List-11-Year.aspx.

Garey, Anita Ilta. 1995. "Constructing Motherhood on the Night Shift: 'Working Mothers' as 'Stay-at-Home Moms.'" *Qualitative Sociology* 18: 415–37.

———. 1999. *Weaving Work and Motherhood.* Philadelphia: Temple University Press.

Gass, Thomas E. 2004. *Nobody's Home: Candid Reflections of a Nursing Home Aide.* Ithaca, NY: Cornell University Press.

Geiger-Brown, Jeanne, Carles Muntaner, Kathleen McPhaul, Jane Lipscomb, and Alison Trinkoff. 2007. "Abuse and Violence during Home Care Work as Predictor of Worker Depression." *Home Health Care Services Quarterly* 26 (1): 59–77.

George, Linda K., and Lisa P. Gwyther. 1986. "Caregiver Well-being: A Multidimensional Examination of Family Caregivers of Demented Adults." *The Gerontologist* 26 (2): 253–60.

George, Molly. 2008. "Interactions in Expert Service Work: Understanding Professionalism in Personal Training." *Journal of Contemporary Ethnography* 37: 108–131.

———. 2013. "Seeking Legitimacy: The Professionalization of Life Coaching." *Sociological Inquiry* 83 (2): 179–208.

George, Sheba Mariam. 2005. *When Women Come First: Gender and Class in Transnational Migration.* Berkeley: University of California Press.

Gershon, Robyn R., Maureen Dailey, Lori. A. Magda, Halley E. Riley, Jay Conolly, and Alexis Silver. 2012. "Safety in the Home Healthcare Sector: Development of a New Household Safety Checklist." *Journal of Patient Safety* 8 (2): 51–59.

Gerstel, Naomi. 2011. "Rethinking Families and Community: The Color, Class, and Centrality of Extended Kin Ties." *Sociological Forum* 26: 1–20.

Gerstel, Naomi, and Amy Armenia. 2009. "Giving and Taking Family Leaves: Right or Privilege." *Yale Journal of Law and Feminism* 21: 161–84.

Gerstel, Naomi, and Natalia Sarkisian. 2006. "Marriage: The Good, the Bad, and the Greedy." *Contexts* 5: 16–22.

———. 2008. "The Color of Family Ties: Race, Class, Gender, and Extended Family Involvement." In *American Families: A Multicultural Reader*, ed, S. Coontz, M. Parson, and G. Rayley, 447–53. New York: Routledge.

Gillen, Marion, Irene H. Yen, Laura Trupin, Louise Swig, Reiner Rugulies, Kathleen Mullen, Aurelio Font, David Burian, Greg Ryan, Ira Janowitz, Patricia A. Quinlan, John Frank, and Paul Blanc. 2007. "The Association of Socioeconomic Status and Psychosocial and Physical Workplace Factors with Musculoskeletal Injury in Hospital Workers." *American Journal of Industrial Medicine* 50 (4): 245–60.

Gimlin, Debra. 1996. "Pamela's Place: Power and Negotiation in the Hair Salon." *Gender and Society* 10 (5): 505–26.

Glazer, Nona Y. 1991. "'Between a Rock and a Hard Place': Women's Professional Organizations in Nursing and Class, Racial, and Ethnic Inequalities." *Gender and Society* 5: 351–72.

Glenn, Evelyn N. 1992. "From Servitude to Service Work: Historical Continuities in the Racial Division of Paid Reproductive Labor." *Signs* 18: 1–43.

———. 2000. "Creating a Caring Society." *Contemporary Sociology* 29 (1): 84–94.

———. 2010. *Forced to Care: Coercion and Caregiving.* Cambridge, MA: Harvard University Press.

Goffman, Erving. 1963. *Stigma: Notes on the Management of Spoiled Identity.* Englewood Cliffs, NJ: Prentice-Hall.

Gold, Kathleen, and Jenny Schumann. 2007. "Dangers of Used Sharps in Household Trash: Implications for Home Care." *Home Healthcare Nurse* 25 (9): 602–7; quiz 08–9.

Goldberger, Susan. 2005. *From the Entry Level to Licensed Practical Nurse: Four Case Studies of Career Ladders in Health Care.* Boston: Jobs for the Future.

Goldstein, Lisa. 1998. "More Than Gentle Smiles and Warm Hugs: Applying the Ethic of Care to Early Childhood Education." *Journal of Research in Childhood Education* 12 (2): 244–61.

Gordon, Suzanne. 2006. *Nursing Against the Odds: How Health Care Cost Cutting, Media Stereotypes, and Medical Hubris Undermine Nurses and Patient Care.* Ithaca, NY: ILR Press.

Gornick, Janet C., and Marcia K. Meyers. 2003. *Families That Work: Policies for Reconciling Parenthood and Work.* New York: Russell Sage Foundation.

———. 2009. "Gender Equality: Transforming Family Divisions of Labor." *The Real Utopias Project* vol. 6. London: Verso.

Greater Lawrence Family Health Center. 2013. "GLFHC History." Accessed January 14, 2013. http://glfhc.org/site/about-glfhc/glfhc-history/.

Gruneir, Andrea, Vincent Mor, Sherry Weitzen, Rachael Truchil, Joan Teno, and Jason Roy. 2007. "Where People Die: A Multilevel Approach to Understanding Influences on Site of Death in America." *Medical Care Research and Review* 64 (4): 351–78.

Guberman, Nancy, Éric Gagnon, Denyse Côté, Claude Gilbert, Nicole Thivièrge, and Marielle Tremblay. 2005. "How the Trivialization of the Demands of High-Tech Care in the Home Is Turning Family Members into Para-Medical Personnel." *Journal of Family Issues* 26 (2): 247–72.

Guevara, Anna. 2010. *Marketing Dreams, Manufacturing Heroes: The Transnational Labor Brokering of Filipino Workers.* New Brunswick, NJ: Rutgers University Press.

Hagey, Rebecca, Ushi Choudhry, Sepali Guruge, Jane Turrittin, Enid Collins, and Ruth Lee. 2001. "Immigrant Nurses' Experience of Racism." *Journal of Nursing Studies* 33 (4): 389–94.

Haiduven, Donna, and Shalah Ferrol. 2004. "Sharps Injuries in the Home Health Care Setting: Risks for Home Health Care Workers: Risks for Home Health Care Workers." *American Association of Occupational Health Nurse Journal* 52 (3): 102–8.

Hankivsky, Olena, ed. 2012. "An Intersectionality-Based Policy Analysis Framework." http://www.sfu.ca/iirp/ibpa.html.

Hansen, Karen, and Ilene Philipson. 1990. *Women, Class, and the Feminist Imagination: A Socialist-Feminist Reader.* Philadelphia: Temple University Press.

Hansen-Turton, Tine, Philip Greiner, Mary Allen Miller, and Ann Deinhardt. 2009. *Nurse-Managed Wellness Centers: Developing and Maintaining Your Center.* 1st ed. New York: Springer.

Harrington, Charlene, Christine Kovner, Mathy Mezey, Jeanie Kayser-Jones, Sarah Burger, Martha Mohler, Robert Burke, and David Zimmerman. 2000. "Experts Recommend Minimum Nurse Staffing Standards for Nursing Facilities in the United States." *The Gerontologist* 40 (1): 5–16.

Harrington Meyer, Madonna. 2000. *Care Work: Gender, Labor, and the Welfare State.* New York: Routledge.

Harris, Gardiner. 2011. "With More Doctorates in Health Care, a Fight Over a Title." *New York Times,* October 1.

Harris, Trudier. 1982. *From Mammies to Militants: Domestics in Black American Literature.* Philadelphia: Temple University Press.

Harvey, John H., Terri I. Orbuch, and A. L. Weber. 1990. "A Social Psychological Model of Account-Making in Response to Severe Stress." *Journal of Language and Social Psychology* 9: 191–207.

Hasson, Henna, and Judith E. Arnetz. 2008. "Nursing Staff Competence, Work Strain, Stress, and Satisfaction in Elderly Care: A Comparison of Home-based Care and Nursing Homes." *Journal of Clinical Nursing* 17: 468–81.

Hawkins, Sarah, David Allen, and Rosemary Jenkins. 2005. "The Use of Physical Interventions with People with Intellectual Disabilities and Challenging Behaviour—The Experiences of Service Users and Staff Members." *Journal of Applied Research in Intellectual Disabilities* 18 (1): 19–34.

Hays, Judith C., Anthony N. Galanos, Tahira A. Palmer, Douglas R. McQuoid, and Elizabeth P. Flint. 2001. "Preference for Place of Death in a Continuing Care Retirement Community." *The Gerontologist* 41 (1): 123–28.

Hays, Sharon. 1996. *The Cultural Contradictions of Motherhood.* New Haven: Yale University Press.

He, Wan, and Muenchrath. 2011. *American Community Survey Reports, ACS-17, 90+ in the United States: 2006–2008.* Washington, DC: U.S. Government Printing Office.

Hegewisch, Ariane, Claudia Williams, and Angela Edwards. 2013. *The Gender Wage Gap: 2012.* Washington, DC: Institute for Women's Policy Research. http://www.iwpr.org/publications/pubs/the-gender-wage-gap-2012.

Heistaro, Sami, Erkki Vartiainen, Markku Heliövaara, and Pekka Puska. 1998. "Trends of Back Pain in Eastern Finland, 1972–1992, in Relation to Socioeconomic Status and Behavioral Risk Factors." *American Journal of Epidemiology* 148 (7): 671–82.

Herek, Gregory M. 1999. "AIDS and Stigma." *American Behavioral Scientist* 42: 1106–16.

Hernes, Helga. 1987. *Welfare States and Woman Power.* Oslo: Norwegian University Press.

Hertz, Rosanna, and Faith I. T. Ferguson. 1996. "Childcare Choice and Constraints in the United States: Social Class, Race, and the Influence of Family Views." *Journal of Comparative Family Studies* 27: 249–80.

Himmelweit, Susan. 1999. "Caring Labor." *Annals of the American Academy of Political and Social Science* 561: 52–63.

Hochschild, Arlie. 1983. *The Managed Heart: Commercialization of Human Feeling.* Berkeley: University of California Press.

———. 2003a. *The Commercialization of Intimate Life: Notes from Home and Work.* Berkeley: University of California Press.

———. 2003b. *The Managed Heart: Twentieth Anniversary Edition.* Berkeley: University of California Press.

———. 2012. *The Outsourced Self: What Happens When We Pay Others to Live Our Lives for Us.* New York: Macmillan.

Hodson, Randy. 2000. *Dignity at Work.* Cambridge: Cambridge University Press.

Holmberg, Michelle D., Marian Flum, Cheryl West, Yuan Zhang, Shpend Qamili, and Laura Punnett. 2013. "Nursing Assistants' Dilemma: Caregiver versus Caretaker." *Hospital Topics* 91 (1): 1–8.

Home Care Sector Study Corporation. 2003. "Canadian Home Care Human Resources Study: Synthesis Report." http://www.cacc-acssc.com/english/pdf/homecareresources/final-report.pdf. Human Resources Development Canada.

Hondagneu-Sotelo, Pierrette. 2007. *Domestica: Immigrant Workers Cleaning and Caring in the Shadows of Affluence.* 2nd ed. Berkeley: University of California Press.

Hoogendoorn, Wilhelmina E., Mirielle N. van Poppel, Paulien M. Bongers, Bart W. Koes, and Lex M. Bouter. 1999. "Physical Load during Work and Leisure Time as Risk Factors for Back Pain." *Scandinavian Journal of Work, Environment, and Health* 25 (5): 387–403.

———. 2000. "Systematic Review of Psychosocial Factors at Work and Private Life as Risk Factors for Back Pain." *Spine* 25 (16): 2114–25.

Howell, Joel D. 1991. "Diagnostic Technologies: X-rays, Electrocardiograms, and CAT Scans." *Southern California Law Review* 65 (1): 529–64.

Howes, Candace. 2004. "Upgrading California's Home Care Workforce: The Impact of Political Action and Unionization." Berkeley: Institute for Research on Labor and Employment, University of California.

———. 2008. "Love, Money, or Flexibility: What Motivates People to Work in Consumer-Directed Home Care?" *Gerontologist* 48 (1): 46–59.

Howes, Candace, Carrie Leana, and Kristin Smith. 2012. "Paid Care Work." In *For Love and Money: Care Provision in the United States*, ed. Nancy Folbre, 65–91. New York: Russell Sage Foundation.

Hudson, Christopher. 2007. *Social Work in Massachusetts: A Survey of Employment, Compensation and Working Conditions.* National Association of Social Workers, Massachusetts Chapter. http://www.naswma.org/.

Hughes, Karen D. 2005. *Female Enterprise in the New Economy.* Toronto: University of Toronto Press.

Immigration Policy Center, American Immigration Council. 2009. "Critical Care: Role of Immigrant Workers in U.S. Health Care." http://www.immigrationpolicy.org/sites/default/files/docs/Critical_Care.pdf.

Institute of Medicine. 2001. *Musculoskeletal Disorders and the Workplace: Low Back and Upper Extremeties.* Washington, DC: National Academy Press.

———. 2010. "The Future of Nursing: Leading Change, Advancing Health." http://www.iom.edu/Reports/2010/The-Future-of-Nursing-Leading-Change-Advancing-Health.aspx.

Janowitz, Ira L., Marion Gillen, Greg Ryan, David Rempel, Laura Trupin, Louise Swig, Kathleen Mullen, Reiner Rugulies, and Paul D. Blanc. 2006. "Measuring the Physical Demands of Work in Hospital Settings: Design and Implementation of an Ergonomics Assessment." *Applied Ergonomics* 37 (5): 641–58.

Jayaratne, Srinka, Tom Croxton, and Debra Mattison. 2004. "A National Survey of Violence in the Practice of Social Work." *Families in Society* 85 (4): 445–53.

Jones, Jacqueline. 1985. *Labor of Love, Labor of Sorrow.* New York: Basic Books.

Kalleberg, Arne L. 2011. *Good Jobs, Bad Jobs: The Rise of Polarized and Precarious Employment Systems in the United States, 1970s to 2000s.* New York: Russell Sage Foundation.

Kalleberg, Arne L., Barbara F. Reskin, and Ken Hudson. 2000. "Bad Jobs in America: Standard and Nonstandard Employment Relations and Job Quality in the United States." *American Sociological Review* 65 (2): 256–78.

Karger, Howard Jacob, and David Stoesz. 2010. *American Social Welfare Policy: A Pluralist Approach*. 6th ed. Boston: Pearson.

Katz, Michael B. 1996. *In the Shadow of the Poorhouse: A Social History of Welfare in America*. 10th anniversary ed. New York: Basic Books.

Kelly, Christopher, Jennifer Craft Morgan, and Kendra J. Jason. 2012. "Home Care Workers: Interstate Differences in Training Requirements and Their Implications for Quality." *Journal of Applied Gerontology*. Preprint. doi:10.1177/0733464812437371.

Kemper, Peter, Brigitt Heier, Teta Barry, Diane Brannon, Joe Angelelli, Joe Vasey, and Mindy Anderson-Knott. 2008. "What Do Direct Care Workers Say Would Improve Their Jobs? Differences across Settings." *The Gerontologist* 48 (1): 17–25.

Keppel, Kenneth G. 2007. "Ten Largest Racial and Ethnic Health Disparities in the United States Based on Healthy People 2010 Objectives." *American Journal of Epidemiology* 166 (1): 97–103.

Kessler-Harris, Alice. 1990. *A Woman's Wage: Historical Meanings and Social Consequences*. Lexington: University Press of Kentucky.

Kilbourne, Barbara S., George Farkas, Kurt Beron, Dorothea Weir, and Paula England. 1994. "Returns to Skill, Compensating Differentials, and Gender Bias: Effects of Occupational Characteristics on the Wages of White Women and Men." *American Journal of Sociology* 100: 689–719.

Kittay, Eva. 1999. *Love's Labor: Essays on Women, Equality, and Dependency*. New York: Routledge.

Kontos, Susan. 1992. *Family Day Care: Out of the Shadows and into the Limelight*. Washington, DC: National Association for the Education of Young Children.

Kontos, Susan, Carollee Howes, Marybeth Shinn, and Ellen Galinsky. 1995. *Quality in Family Child Care and Relative Care*. New York: Teachers College Press.

Kontos, Susan, and Andrew J. Stremmel. 1988. "Caregivers' Perceptions of Working Conditions in a Child Care Environment." *Early Childhood Research Quarterly* 3 (1): 77–90.

Krieg, Randall G. 2001. "An Interdisciplinary Look at the Deinstitutionalization of the Mentally Ill." *Social Science Journal* 38 (3): 367–80.

Krisman-Scott, Mary Ann. 2003. "Origins of Hospice in the United States: The Care of the Dying, 1945–1975." *Journal of Hospice and Palliative Nursing* 5 (4): 205–10.

Kunzel, Regina. 1993. *Fallen Women, Problem Girls: Unmarried Mothers and the Professionalization of Social Work, 1890–1945*. New Haven: Yale University Press.

Kurowski, Alicia, Jon Boyer, Scott Fulmer, Rebecca Gore, and Laura Punnett. 2012a. "Changes in Ergonomic Exposures of NAs after the Introduction of a Safe Resident Handling Program in Nursing Homes." *International Journal of Industrial Ergonomics* 42: 525–32.

Kurowski, Alicia, Rebecca Gore, Bryan Buchholz, and Laura Punnett. 2012b. "Differences among Nursing Homes in Outcomes of a Safe Resident Handling Program." *Journal of Healthcare Risk Management* 32 (1): 35–51.

Labor Occupational Health Program, Public Authority for In-house Support Services, National Institute for Occupational Safety and Health, and Service Employees International Union. 2011. "Caring for Yourself While Caring for Others." http://www.lohp.org/docs/projects/homecare/homecareenglish.pdf.

Lagerström, Monica, Tommy Hansson, and Mats Hagberg. 1998. "Work-related Low-Back Problems in Nursing." *Scandinavian Journal of Work, Environment, and Health* 24 (6): 449–64.

Lahiri, Supriya, Saira Latif, and Laura Punnett. 2012. "An Economic Analysis of a Safe Resident Handling Program in Nursing Homes." *American Journal of Industrial Medicine* doi: 10.1002/ajim.22139.

Lamont, Michèle. 2000. *The Dignity of Working Men: Morality and the Boundaries of Race, Class, and Immigration*. New York: Russell Sage Foundation

Lareau, Annete. 2003. *Unequal Childhoods: Class, Race, and Family Life*. Berkeley: University of California Press.

Larson, Magali Sarfatti. 1977. *The Rise of Professionalism*. Berkeley: University of California Press.

Laslett, Barbara, and Johanna Brenner. 1989. "Gender and Social Reproduction: Historical Perspectives." *Annual Review of Sociology* 15: 381–404.

Laurant, Miranda, David Reeves, Rosella Hermens, Jose Braspenning, Richard Grol, and Bonnie Sibbald. 2005. "Substitution of Doctors by Nurses in Primary Care." *Cochrane Database of Systematic Reviews (Online)* (2): CD001271. doi:10.1002/14651858.CD001271 .pub2.

Lee, Jennifer M., Marc F. Botteman, Nicholas Xanthakos, and Lars Nicklasson. 2005. "Needlestick Injuries in the United States: Epidemiologic, Economic, and Quality of Life Issues." *American Association of Occupational Health Nurse Journal* 43 (3): 117–34.

Lefkowitz, Bonnie. 2007. *Community Health Centers: A Movement and the People Who Made It Happen*. New Brunswick, NJ: Rutgers University Press.

Leidner, Robin. 1993. *Fast Food, Fast Talk: Service Work and the Routinization of Everyday Life*. Berkeley: University of California Press.

Lenz, Elizabeth R, Mary O'Neil Mundinger, Robert L Kane, Sarah C. Hopkins, and Susan X. Lin. 2004. "Primary Care Outcomes in Patients Treated by Nurse Practitioners or Physicians: Two-Year Follow-up." *Medical Care Research and Review: MCRR* 61 (3): 332–51.

Levenson, Michael. 2011. "Mental Health Workers Decry Planned Cuts." *Boston Globe*, February 11. http://www.boston.com/news/local/massachusetts/articles/2011/02/11/ mental_health_workers_decry_planned_cuts/.

Lewis, Jane. 2009. *Work-Family Balance, Gender, and Policy*. Cheltenham, Eng.: Edward Elgar.

Lipscomb, Hester, Dana Loomis, Mary Anne McDonald, Robin A. Argue, and Steve Wing. 2006. "A Conceptual Model of Work and Health Disparities in the United States." *International Journal of Health Services* 36 (1): 25–50.

Lipscomb, Jane A., Rosemary Sokas, Kathleen McPhaul, Barbara Scharf, Paxon Barker, Alison Trinkoff, and Carla Storr. 2009. "Occupational Blood Exposure among Unlicensed Home Care Workers and Home Care Registered Nurses: Are They Protected?" *American Journal of Industrial Medicine* 52 (7): 563–70.

Lipscomb, Jane A., Alison Trinkoff, Barbara Brady, and Jeanne Geiger-Brown. 2004. "Health Care System Changes and Reported Musculoskeletal Disorders among Registered Nurses." *American Journal of Public Health* 94 (8): 1431–35.

Lipscomb, Jane A., Alison M. Trinkoff, Jeanne Geiger-Brown, and Barbara Brady. 2002. "Work-Schedule Characteristics and Reported Musculoskeletal Disorders of Registered Nurses." *Scandinavian Journal of Work, Environment, and Health* 28 (6): 394–401.

Lively, Kathryn J. 2001. "Occupational Claims to Professionalism: The Case of Paralegals." *Symbolic Interaction* 24: 343–66.

Lockard, C. Brett, and Michael Wolf. 2012. "Occupational Employment Projections to 2020." *Monthly Labor Review* (January): 84–112.

Lopez, Steven Henry. 2006a. "Culture Change Management in Long-Term Care: A Shop-Floor View." *Politics and Society* 43 (1): 55–79.

———. 2006b. "Emotional Labor and Organized Emotional Care: Conceptualizing Nursing Home Care Work." *Work and Occupations* 33 (2):133–60.

———. 2010. "Workers, Managers, and Customers: Triangles of Power in Work Communities." *Work and Occupations* 37: 251–71.

Lowe, Tony B., and Wynne S. Korr. 2008. "Workplace Safety Policies in Mental Health Settings." *Journal of Workplace Behavioral Health* 22 (4): 29–47.

Macdonald, Cameron. 2010. *Shadow Mothers: Nannies, Au Pairs, and the Micropolitics of Mothering*. Berkeley: University of California Press.

Macdonald, Cameron Lynne, and David A. Merrill. 2002. "'It Shouldn't Have to Be a Trade': Recognition and Redistribution in Care Work Advocacy." *Hypatia* 17 (2): 67–83.

MacDonald, Keith M. 1995. *The Sociology of the Professions*. Thousand Oaks, CA: Sage.

Mäkelä, Matti, Markku Heliövaara, Kai Sievers, Olli Impivaara, Paul Knekt, and Arpo Aromaa. 1991. "Prevalence, Determinants, and Consequences of Chronic Neck Pain in Finland." *American Journal of Epidemiology* 134 (11): 1356–67.

Mareschal, Patrice M. 2006. "Innovation and Adaptation: Contrasting Efforts to Organize Home Care Workers in Four States." *Labor Studies Journal* 31: 25–49.

Markkanen, Pia, Margaret Quinn, Catherine Galligan, Stephanie Chalupka, Letitia Davis, and Angela Laramie. 2007. "There's No Place Like Home: A Qualitative Study of the Working Conditions of Home Health Care Providers." *Journal of Occupational and Environmenatal Medicine* 49 (3): 327–37.

Martin, Douglas. 2009. "Evelyn Coke, Home Care Aide Who Fought Pay Rule, Is Dead at 74." *New York Times*, August 10. http://www.nytimes.com/2009/08/10/nyregion/10coke.html.

McClelland, Jerry. 1986. "Job Satisfaction of Child Care Workers." *Child Care Quarterly* 15 (2): 82–89.

McDonald, Grant, and Frank Sirotech. 2001. "Reporting Client Violence." *Social Work* 46 (2): 107–13.

McManus, Patricia A. 2001. "Women's Participation in Self-Employment in Western Industrialized Nations." *International Journal of Sociology* 31 (2): 70–97.

McPhaul, Kathleen, Jane Lipscomb, and Jeffrey Johnson. 2010. "Assessing Risk for Violence on Home Health Visits." *Home Healthcare Nurse* 28 (5): 278–89.

McPhaul, Kathleen, Matthew London, Kevin Murrett, Kelly Flannery, Jonathan Rosen, and Jane Lipscomb. 2008. "Environmental Evaluation for Workplace Violence in Healthcare and Social Services." *Journal of Safety Research* 39 (2): 237–50.

Melosh, Barbara. 1982. *The Physician's Hand: Nurses and Nursing in the Twentieth Century*. Philadelphia: Temple University Press.

Mendez, Jennifer Bickman. 1998. "Of Mops and Maids: Contradictions and Continuities in Bureaucratized Domestic Work." *Social Problems* 45 (1): 114–35.

Meyer, John, and Carles Muntaner. 1999. "Injuries in Home Health Care Workers: An Analysis of Occupational Morbidity from a State Compensation Database." *American Journal of Industrial Medicine* 35 (3): 295–301.

Michel, Sonya. 1999. *Children's Interests, Mothers' Rights: The Shaping of America's Child Care Policy*. New Haven: Yale University Press.

Minniti, M., P. Arenius, and N. Langowitz. 2005. "Global Entrepreneurship Monitor: 2004 Report on Women and Entrepreneurship." Accessed May 2009. http://www.gemconsortium.org/about.aspx?page=special_topic_women.

Miranda, Helena, Laura Punnett, Rebecca Gore, and Jon Boyer. 2011. "Violence at the Workplace Increases Risk of Musculoskeletal Pain among Nursing Home Workers." *Occupational and Environmental Medicine* 68: 52–57.

Mirchadani, Kiran. 2000. " 'The Best of Both Worlds' and 'Cutting My Own Throat': Contradictory Images of Home-based Work." *Qualitative Sociology* 23: 159–81.

Moen, Phyllis, Erin L. Kelly, and Rachelle Hill. 2011. "Does Enhancing Work-Time Control and Flexibility Reduce Turnover? A Naturally Occurring Experiment." *Social Problems* 58 (1): 69–98.

Mooney, Ann. 2003. "What It Means to Be a Childminder: Work or Love?" In *Family Day Care: International Perspectives on Policy, Practice, and Quality*, ed. A. Mooney, A. and J. Statham, 111–28. London: Jessica Kingsley.

More, Ellen S. 2001. *Restoring the Balance: Women Physicians and the Profession of Medicine*. Cambridge, MA: Harvard University Press.

Morgan, Jennifer C., Janette Dill, and Arne L. Kalleberg. 2013. "The Quality of Healthcare Jobs: Can Intrinsic Rewards Compensate for Low Extrinsic Rewards?" *Work, Employment, and Society* 27: 802–22.

Moroney, Robert. 1998. *Caring and Competent Caregivers*. Athens: University of Georgia Press.

Murray, Charles. 2012. *Coming Apart: The State of White America, 1960–2020*. New York: Crown Forum.

National Association of Community Health Centers. "America's Health Centers: Fact Sheet August 2013." Accessed September 5, 2013. http://www.nachc.com/client/documents/America's_CHCs_0813.pdf.

National Association of Social Workers. 2008. "Fact Sheet: Social Work Profession." http://www.socialworkers.org/pressroom/features/general/profession.asp.

National Hospice and Palliative Care Organization. 2002. "Hospice and Palliative Care Code of Ethics." Alexandria, VA.

———. 2012. "NHPCO Facts and Figures: Hospice Care in America." Alexandria, VA.

National Institute for Occupational Safety and Health. 2010. "NIOSH Hazard Review: Occupational Hazards in Home Healthcare." National Institute for Occupational Safety and Health.

National Institute of Occupational Safety and Health, Centers for Disease Control and Prevention. 2009. "Healthcare and Social Assistance Advancing Priorities through Research and Partnerships." DHHS (NIOSH) Publication No. 2009-149.

———. 2012. "Prevention through Design." http://www.cdc.gov/niosh/topics/ptd/.

National Occupational Research Agenda (NORA). 2009. "State of the Sector: Identification of Research Opportunities for the Next Decade of NORA." Developed by the NORA Healthcare and Social Assistance Sector Council. http://www.cdc.gov/niosh/docs/2009–139/.

National Public Radio. 2011. *All Things Considered*: "Pynoos Discusses Senior Housing." Radio program. Recorded 2011.

Neal, Rusty. 1994. "Public Homes: Subcontracting and the Experience of Cleaning." In *Maid in the Market: Women's Paid Domestic Labour*, ed. W. Giles and S. Arat-Koc, 65–79. Halifax, Canada: Fernwood Publishing.

Nelson, Audrey, John Lloyd, Nancy Menzel, and Clifford Gross. 2003. "Preventing Nursing Back Injuries." *American Association of Occupational Health Nurses* 51 (3): 126–34.

Nelson, Margaret J. 1990. *Negotiated Care: The Experience of Family Day Care Providers*. Philadelphia: Temple University Press.

———. 1994. "Family Day Care Providers: Dilemmas of Daily Practice." In *Mothering: Ideology, Experience, and Agency*, ed. Evelyn Nakano Glenn, Grace Change, and Linda Rennie Forcey, 181–209. New York: Routledge.

Nelson, Sioban, and Suzanne Gordon. 2006. "Moving Beyond the Virtue Script: Creating a Knowledge-Based Identity for Nurses." In *The Complexities of Care: Nursing Reconsidered*, ed. Sioban Nelson and Suzanne Gordon, 13–29. Ithaca, NY: Cornell University Press.

Newhill, Christina. 1996. "Prevalence and Risk Factors for Client Violence towards Social Workers." *Families in Society* 77: 488–95.

———. 2003. *Client Violence in Social Work Practice: Prevention, Intervention, and Research*. New York: Guilford Press.

Noble, Sharon. 2011. "Social Services, Part XVII. Services and Trade, Chapter: 97. Health Care Facilities and Services." In *Encyclopedia of Occupational Health*, ed. Annalee Yassi. Geneva: International Labor Organization.

Noordegraaf, Mirko. 2007. "From 'Pure' to 'Hybrid' Professionalism: Present-day Professionalism in Ambiguous Public Domains." *Administration and Society* 39 (6): 761–85.

O'Brien-Pallas, Linda. 2004. *Building the Future: An Integrated Strategy for Nursing Human Resources in Canada. Survey of Employers: Health Care Organizations' Senior Nurse*. Ottawa: The Nursing Corporation.

Ohlen, J., and K. Segesten. 1998. "The Professional Identity of the Nurse: Concept Analysis and Development." *Journal of Advanced Nursing* 28: 720–27.

Omolade, Barbara. 1994. *The Rising Song of African American Women*. New York: Routledge.

Ong, Paul, and Tania Azores. 1994. "The Migration and Incorporation of Philippines Nurses." In *The New Asia Immigration in Los Angeles and Global Restructuring*, ed. Paul Ong, Edna Bonacich, and Lucie Cheng, 164–95. Philadelphia: Temple University Press.

Ontario Community Support Association (OCSA). 2000. "The Effect of the Managed Competition Model on Home Care in Ontario: Emerging Issues and Recommendations." Briefing note. http://www.ocsa.on.ca/PDF/brief-Managed_care.PDF.

Orbuch, Terri L. 1997. "People's Accounts Count: The Sociology of Accounts." *Annual Review of Sociology* 23: 455–78.

Organization for Economic Cooperation and Development (OECD). 2000. "The Partial Renaissance of Self-Employment." In *OECD Employment Outlook*. Paris: OECD.

———. 2010. "International Migration of Health Workers: Improving International Co-operation to Address the Global Health Workforce Crisis." Accessed May 5, 2010. http://www.oecd.org/dataoecd/8/1/44783473.pdf.

Page, Ann, ed. 2004. *Keeping Patients Safe: Transforming the Work Environment of Nurses*. Washington, DC: National Academies Press.

Palmer, Elyane, and Joan Eveline. 2012. "Sustaining Low Pay in Aged Care Work." *Gender, Work, and Organization* 19 (3): 254–75.

Paraprofessional Healthcare Institute (PHI). 2000. "The Launch of the Direct Care Alliance: A Report on the Conference Proceedings." Accessed December 15, 2012. http://phinational.org/research-reports/launch-direct-care-alliance-proceedings-june-2000-conference.

———. 2012. "America's Direct Care Workforce. PHI Facts 3." Accessed March 13, 2013. http://phinational.org/sites/phinational.org/files/phi-facts-3.pdf.

———. 2013. "Occupational Projections for Direct Care Workers 2008–2018. PHI Facts 1. February 2013 Update." Accessed March 13, 2013. http://phinational.org/sites/phinational.org/files/phi_factsheet1update_singles_2.pdf.

Parks, Jennifer A. 2003. *No Place Like Home? Feminist Ethics and Home Health Care*. Bloomington: Indiana University Press.

Parrenas, Rhacel Salazar. 2001. *Servants of Globalization: Women, Migration, and Domestic Work*. Stanford, CA: Stanford University Press.

Pew Report. 2010 "The Decline of Marriage and the Rise of New Families." November. http://pewresearch.org/.

Philipson, Irene. 1993. *On the Shoulders of Women: The Feminization of Psychotherapy*. New York: Guilford Press.

Pines, A., K. Skulkeo, E. Pollak, E. Peritz, and J. Steif. 1985. "Rates of Sickness Absenteeism among Employees of a Modern Hospital: The Role of Demographic and Occupational Factors." *British Journal of Industrial Medicine* 42 (5): 326–35.

Polletta, Francesca and James M. Jasper. 2001. "Collective Identity and Social Movements." *Annual Review of Sociology* 27: 283–305.

Potter, Sharyn J., Allison Churilla, and Kristin Smith. 2006. "An Examination of Full-Time Employment in the Direct-Care Workforce." *Journal of Applied Gerontology* 25 (5): 356–74.

Presser, Harriet. 2003. *Working in a 24/7 Economy*. New York: Russell Sage Foundation.

Preston, Jo Anne. 1993 "Domestic Ideology, School Reformers, and Female Teachers: Schoolteaching Becomes Women's Work in Nineteenth-Century New England." *New England Quarterly* 66 (4): 531–51.

Quadagno, Jill. 1996. *The Color of Welfare: How Racism Undermined the War on Poverty*. New York: Oxford University Press.

Quinn, Margaret, Pia Markkanen, Catherine Galligan, David Kriebel, Stephanie Chalupka, Hyun Kim, Rebecca Gore, Susan Sama, Angela Laramie, and Letitia Davis. 2009. "Sharps Injuries and Other Blood and Body Fluid Exposures among Home Health Care Nurses and Aides." *American Journal of Public Health* 99 (3): S710–17.

Raghuram, Parvati, and Eleonore Kofman 2004. "Out Of Asia: Skilling, Re-skilling, and Deskilling of Female Immigrants." *Women's Studies International Forum* 27 (2): 95–100.

Rakovski, Carter, and Kim Price-Glynn. 2010. "Nursing Assistants, Caring Labor, and Intersectionality." *Sociology of Health and Illness* 32 (3): 400–414.

———. 2012. "Intersectional Identities and Worker Experiences in Home Health Care: The National Home Health Aide Survey." *Research in the Sociology of Health Care* 30: 261–80.

Rauhala, Auvo, Mika Kivimaki, Lisbeth Fagerstrom, Marko Elovainio, Marianna Virtanen, Jussi Vahtera, Anna-Kasia Rainio, Kati Ojaniemi, and Juha Kinnunen, Juha. 2007. "What Degree of Work Overload Is Likely to Cause Increased Sickness Absenteeism among Nurses? Evidence from the RAFAELA Patient Classification System." *Journal of Advanced Nursing* 57 (3): 286–95.

Ray, Rebecca, Janet C. Gornick, and John Schmitt. 2010. "Who Cares? Assessing Generosity and Gender Equality in Parental Leave Policy Designs in 21 Countries." *Journal of European Social Policy* 20 (3): 196–216.

Rees, Gareth, and Sarah Fielder. 1992. "The Services Economy, Subcontracting and the New Employment Relations: Contract Catering and Cleaning." *Work, Employment, and Society* 6 (3): 347–68.

Reese, Ellen. 2011. *They Say Cut Back, We Say Fight Back!: Welfare Activism in an Era of Retrenchment.* New York: Russell Sage Foundation.

Reskin, Barbara F., and Patricia A. Roos. 1990. *Job Queues, Gender Queues: Explaining Women's Inroads into Male Occupations.* Philadelphia: Temple University Press.

Reticker, Gini. 2013. Untitled speech presented at Women in Public Service Conference Celebration Dinner, University of Massachusetts–Lowell, Lowell, MA, June 4.

Reverby, Susan. 1987. "A Caring Dilemma: Womanhood and Nursing in Historical Perspective." *Nursing Research* 36 (1): 5–11.

Rey, Lucy D. 1996. "What Social Workers Need to Know about Client Violence." *Families in Society* 77: 33–39.

Rhee, Nari, and Carol Zabin. 2009. "Aggregating Dispersed Workers: Union Organizing in the 'Care Industries.'" *Geoforum* 40: 969–79.

Ribas, Vanesa, Janette S. Dill, and Philip N. Cohen. 2012. "Mobility for Care Workers: Job Changes and Wages for Nurse Aides." *Social Science and Medicine* 75 (12): 2183–90.

Richardi, Kristina, Luc Schuster, and Nancy Wagman. 2011. *Quality, Cost, and Purpose: Comparisons of Government and Private Sector Payments for Similar Services.* Boston: MassBudget.

Ringstad, Robin. 2005. "Conflict in the Workplace: Social Workers as Victims and Perpetrators." *Social Work* 50 (4): 305–13.

———. 2009. "CPS: Client Violence and Clients Victims." *Child Welfare* 88 (3): 127–44.

Rivas, Lynn M. 2003. "Invisible Labours: Caring for the Independent Person." In *Global Woman: Nannies, Maids, and Sex Workers in the New Economy*, ed. Barbara Ehrenreich and Arlie Russell Hochschild, 70–84. London: Granta Books.

Rollins, Judith. 1985. *Between Women: Domestics and Their Employers.* Philadelphia: Temple University Press.

Romero, Mary. 1992. *Maid in the U.S.A.* New York: Routledge.

———. 2001. "Unraveling Privilege: Workers' Children and the Hidden Costs of Paid Care." *Chicago-Kent Law Review* 76: 1651–72.

Roschelle, Anne R. 1997. *No More Kin: Exploring Race, Class, and Gender in Family Networks.* Thousand Oaks, CA: Sage.

Rose, Michael. 2003. "Good Deal, Bad Deal: Job Satisfaction in Occupations." *Work, Employment, and Society* 17 (3): 503–30.

Rosenfeld, Stuart A. 2001. "Rural Community Colleges: Creating Institutional Hybrids for the New Economy." *Rural America* 16 (2): 2–8.

Rury, John L. 1989. "Who Became Teachers? The Social Characteristics of Teachers in American History." In *American Teachers: Histories of a Profession at Work*, ed. Donald Warren, 9–49. New York: Macmillan.

Sacks, Karen Brodkin. 1990. "Does It Pay to Care?" In *Circles of Care*, ed. Emily Abel and Margaret J. Nelson, 188–206. Albany: State University of New York Press.

Sarkisian, Natalia, and Naomi Gerstel. 2005. "Kin Support among Blacks and Whites: Race and Family Organization." *American Sociological Review* 69: 812–37.

———. 2012. *Nuclear Family Values, Extended Family Lives: The Power of Race, Class, and Gender.* New York: Routledge.

Sassen, Saskia. 2002. "Global Cities and Survival Circuits." In *Global Woman: Nannies, Maids, and Sex Workers in the New Economy*, ed. Barbara Ehrenreich and Arlie Hochschild, 254–74. New York: Metropolitan Books.

Schindel, Jennifer, Edward O'Neal, Brian Iammartino, Kim Solomon, David Cherner, and Janine Santimauro. 2006. *Workers Who Care: A Graphical Profile of the Frontline Health and Health Care Workforce.* Princeton, NJ: Robert Wood Johnson Foundation.

Scott, Marvin B., and Stanford M. Lyman. 1968. "Accounts." *American Sociological Review* 33: 46–62.

Scully-Russ, Ellen. 2005. "Agency versus Structure: Path Dependency and Choice in Low- Wage Labor Markets." *Human Resource Development Review* 4 (3): 254–78.

Seavey, Dorie, and Abby Marquand. 2011. "Caring in America. A Comprehensive Analysis of the Nation's Fastest Growing Jobs: Home Health and Personal Care Aides." New York: Paraprofessional Healthcare Institute.

Seifert, Ann M., and Karen Messing. 2006. "Cleaning Up after Globalization: An Ergonomic Analysis of Work Activity of Hotel Cleaners." *Antipode* 38 (3): 557–78.

Sharkey, Shirlee, Lesley Larsen, and Barb Mildon. 2003. "An Overview of Home Care in Canada: Its Past, Present, and Potential." *Home Health Care Management and Practice* 15 (5): 382–90.

Sharma, Ursula, and Paula Black. 2001. "Look Good, Feel Better: Beauty Therapy as Emotional Labour." *Sociology* 35: 913–31.

Sherman, Martin F., Robyn R. Gershon, Stephanie M. Samar, Julie M. Pearson, Allison N. Canton, and Mark R. Damsky. 2008. "Safety Factors Predictive of Job Satisfaction and Job Retention among Home Healthcare Aides." *Journal of Occupational and Environmental Medicine* 50 (12): 1430–41.

Sherman, Rachel. 2007. *Class Acts: Service and Inequality in Luxury Hotels.* Berkeley: University of California Press.

———. 2010. "Time Is Our Commodity." *Work and Occupations* 37 (1): 81–114.

———. 2011. "The Production of Distinctions: Class, Gender, and Taste Work in the Lifestyle Management Industry." *Qualitative Sociology* 34 (1): 201–19.

Shields, Glenn, and Judy Kiser. 2003. "Violence and Aggression Directed toward Human Service Workers: An Exploratory Study." *Families in Society* 84 (1): 13–20.

Shotter, John. 1984. *Social Accountability and Selfhood.* Oxford: Oxford University Press.

Simon, Michael, Angelika Kummerling, and Hans-Martin Hasselhorn. 2004. "Work-Home Conflict in the European Nursing Profession." *International Journal of Occupational and Environmental Health* 10 (4): 384–91.

Sitzman, Kathleen L., Marjorie A. Pett, and Donald S. Bloswick. 2002. "An Exploratory Study of Motor Vehicle Use in Home Visiting Nurses." *Home Healthcare Nurse* 20 (12): 784–92, quiz 93.

Smedley, Brian D. 2009. *Addressing Racial and Ethnic Healthcare Disparities: A Multi-level Approach.* Washington, DC: Health Policy Institute, Joint Center for Political and Economic Studies.

Smedley, Brian D., Adrienne Y. Stith, and Alan R. Nelson, eds. 2003. *Unequal Treatment: Confronting Racial and Ethnic Disparities in Healthcare.* Washington, DC: National Academies Press.

Smith, Kristin, and Reagan Baughman. 2007. "Caring for America's Aging Population: A Profile of the Direct-Care Workforce." *Monthly Labor Review* 130: 20–26.

Smith, Peggie R. 2006. "Laboring for Child-Care: A Consideration of New Approaches to Represent Low-Income Service Workers." *University of Pennsylvania Journal of Labor and Employment Law* 8: 583.

Smith, Wendy A., and Mary C. White. 1993. "Home Health Care: Occupational Health Issues." *AAOHN Journal* 41 (4): 180–85.

Smith Maguire, Jennifer. 2008. "The Personal Is Professional: Personal Trainers as a Case Study of Cultural Intermediaries." *International Journal of Cultural Studies* 11: 211–29.

Sofie, Jennifer, Basia Belza, and Heather Young. 2003. "Health and Safety Risk at a Skilled Nursing Facility: Nursing Assistants' Perceptions." *Journal of Gerontological Nursing* 29 (2) 13–21.

Solari, Cinzia. 2006. "Professionals and Saints: How Immigrant Careworkers Negotiate Gender Identities at Work." *Gender and Society* 20 (3): 301–31.

Soss, Joe, Richard Fording, and Stephen Schram. 2011. "The Organization of Discipline: From Performance Management to Perversity and Punishment." *Journal of Public Administration Theory and Research* 21: 1203–32.

Spector, Paul. 1997. *Job Satisfaction: Application, Assessment, Causes, and Consequences.* Thousand Oaks, CA: Sage.

Spencer, Sarah, Susan Martin, Ivy L. Bourgeault, and Eamon O'Shea. 2010. *The Role of Migrant Care Workers in Ageing Societies: Report on Research Findings in the U.K., Ireland, the U.S., and Canada.* IOM Migration Research Series No. 41. http://publications.iom.int/bookstore/free/MRS41.pdf.

Spitzer, Denise, S. Bitar, and M. Kalbach. 2002. *In the Shadows: Live-In Caregivers in Alberta.* Edmonton: Changing Together: A Centre for Immigrant Women.

Squillace, Marie R., Robin E. Remsbur, Lauren D. Harris-Kojetin, Anita Bercovitz, Emily Rosenoff, and Beth Han. 2009. "The National Nursing Assistant Survey: Improving the Evidence Base for Policy Initiatives to Strengthen the Certified Nursing Assistant Workforce." *The Gerontologist* 49 (2): 185–97.

Stacey, Clare L. 2005. "Finding Dignity in Dirty Work: The Constraints and Rewards of Low-Wage Home Care Labour." *Sociology of Health and Illness* 27 (6): 831–54.

———. 2011. *The Caring Self: The Work Experiences of Home Care Aides.* Ithaca, NY: Cornell University Press.

———. 2012. "For Love and Money: The Experiences of Paid Family Caregivers." *Qualitative Sociology* 35 (1): 47–64.

Stack, Carol. 1974. *All My Kin: Strategies for Survival in a Black Community.* New York: Harper and Row.

Starr, Paul. 1984. *The Social Transformation of American Medicine: The Rise of a Sovereign Profession and the Making of a Vast Industry.* New York: Basic Books.

Statistics Canada. 1997. *Labour Force Update: The Self-Employed.* Ottawa: Statistics Canada.

Statistics Sweden. 2012. http://www.sbc.se.

Steinberg, Ronnie J. 1990. "Social Construction of Skill: Gender, Power, and Comparable Worth." *Work and Occupations* 17 (4): 449–82.

Stone, Deborah. 1999. "Care and Trembling." *The American Prospect* 43: 61–67.

———. 2000. "Caring by the Book." In *Care Work: Gender, Labor, and the Welfare State*, ed. Madonna Herrington Meyer, 89–111. New York: Routledge.

———. 2005. "For Love nor Money: The Commodification of Care." In *Rethinking Commodification: Cases and Readings in Law and Culture*, ed. Martha M. Ertmann and Joan C. Williams, 271–90. New York: New York University Press.

Strauss, Anselm, and Juliet Corbin. 1998. *Basics of Qualitative Research Techniques and Procedures for Developing Grounded Theory*. 2nd ed. London: Sage Publications

Strazdins, Lyndall, and Gabriele Bammer. 2004. "Women, Work, and Musculoskeletal Health." *Social Sciences and Medicine* 58 (6): 997–1005.

Strober, Myra, Suzanne Gerlach-Downie, and Kenneth E. Yeager. 1995. "Child Care Centers as Workplaces." *Feminist Economics* 1 (1): 93–119.

Sullivan Commission on Diversity in the Healthcare Workforce. 2004. *Missing Persons: Minorities in the Health Professions: A Report of the Sullivan Commission on Diversity in the Healthcare Workforce.* Battle Creek, MI: W. K. Kellogg Foundation.

Swarz, Teresa. 2009. "Intergenerational Family Relations in Adulthood: Patterns, Variations, and Implications in the Contemporary United States." *Annual Review of Sociology* 35: 191–212.

Swedish Social Insurance Agency. 2003. "Social Insurance in Sweden 2003: Family Assets— Time and Money." Stockholm: Social Insurance Agency.

Swidler, Ann. 1986. "Culture in Action: Symbols and Strategies." *American Sociological Review* 51: 273–86.

Thistle, Susan. 2006. *From Marriage to the Market: The Transformation of Women's Lives and Work.* Berkeley: University of California Press.

Thurow, Lester C. 1969. *Poverty and Discrimination.* Washington, DC: Brookings Institution.

Tilly, Chris. 2011. "The Impact of the Economic Crisis on International Migration: A Review." *Work, Employment and Society* 25 (4): 675–92.

Trinkoff, Alison M., Jane A. Lipscomb, Jeanne Geiger-Brown, and Barbara Brady. 2002. "Musculoskeletal Problems of the Neck, Shoulder, and Back and Functional Consequences in Nurses." *American Journal of Industrial Medicine* 41 (3): 170–78.

Trinkoff, Alison M., Jane A. Lipscomb, Jeanne Geiger-Brown, Carla L. Storr, and Barbara A. Brady. 2003. "Perceived Physical Demands and Reported Musculoskeletal Problems in Registered Nurses." *American Journal of Preventative Medicine* 24 (3): 270–75.

Tronto, Joan C. 1993. *Moral Boundaries: A Political Argument for an Ethic of Care.* New York: Routledge.

———. 2012. *Caring Democracy: Markets, Equality, and Justice.* New York: New York University Press.

Trotter, LaTonya. 2013. "Professional Actors, Organizational Actors: Reconfiguring Medical Work Through the Nurse Practitioner." Unpublished manuscript.

Tuominen, Mary. 2000. "The Conflicts of Caring: Gender, Race, Ethnicity, and Individualism in Family Child-Care Work." In *Care Work: Gender, Class, and the Welfare State*, ed. Madonna Harrington Meyer, 112–135. New York: Routledge.

———. 2002. "'Where Teachers Can Make a Livable Wage': Organizing to Address Gender and Racial Inequalities in Paid Child Care Work." In *Child Care and Inequality: Rethinking Carework for Children and Youth*, ed. Francesca M. Cancian, Demie Kurz, Andrew S. London, Rebecca Reviere, and Mary C. Tuominen, 193–206. New York: Routledge.

———. 2003. *We Are Not Babysitters: Family Child Care Providers Redefine Work and Care.* New Brunswick, NJ: Rutgers University Press.

Twigg, Julia, Carol Wolkowitz, Laura Cohen, and Sarah Nettleton. 2011. "Conceptualising Body Work in Health and Social Care." *Sociology of Health and Illness* 33: 171–88.

Tyler, D. A., H. Y. Jung, Z. Feng, and V. Mor. 2010. "Prevalence of Nursing Assistant Training and Certification Programs within Nursing Homes, 1997–2007." *The Gerontologist* 50(4): 550–55.

Ungerson, Clare. 2005. "Gender, Labour Markets and Care Work in Five European Funding Regimes." In *Care and Social Integration in European Societies*, ed. B. Pfau-Effinger and B. Geissler, 49–72. Bristol, Eng.: Policy Press.

U.S. Department of Health and Human Services. 2011. "The Registered Nurse Population: Findings from the 2008 National Sample Survey of Registered Nurses." Accessed December 29, 2012. http://bhpr.hrsa.gov/healthworkforce/rnsurveys/rnsurveyfinal.pdf.

U.S. Department of Health and Human Services. Office of Minority Health. 2001. *National Standards for Culturally and Linguistically Appropriate Services in Healthcare: Final Report.* Washington, DC: U.S. Dept. of Health and Human Services, Office of Minority Health.

———. 2005. "Lost-Worktime Injuries and Illnesses: Characteristics and Resulting Days away from Work, 2003." USDL 05–521.Washington, DC: U.S. Dept. of Health and Human Services, Office of Minority Health.

U.S. Department of Labor. Bureau of Labor Statistics. 2006. "Survey of Workplace Violence Prevention, 2005."

———. 2010a. "Nonfatal Occupational Injuries and Illnesses Requiring Days away from Work." http://www.bls.gov/news.release/osh2.t01.htm.

———. 2010b. "Women in the Labor Force: A Databook, 2010 Edition." Annual Social and Economic Supplements, 1988–2009, Current Population Survey.

———. 2012a. "Employment Projections: Fastest Growing Occupations." 2012. http://www.bls.gov/emp/ ep_table_103.htm.

———. 2012b. "Employment Projections: Industries with the Fastest Growing and Most Rapidly Declining Wage and Salary Employment." http://www.bls.gov/emp/ep_table_203.htm.

———. 2012c. "Nonfatal Occupational Injuries and Illnesses Requiring Days Away from Work, 2011." Retrieved January 9, 2013. http://www.bls.gov/news.release/pdf/osh2.pdf.

———. 2012e. "Occupational Outlook Handbook, 2012–13 Edition, Home Health and Personal Care Aides." http://www.bls.gov/ooh/healthcare/home-health-and-personal-care-aides.htm.

———. 2013. *Occupational Outlook Handbook, 2012–2013 Edition, Registered Nurses.* Retrieved June 15, 2013. http://www.bls.gov/ooh/Healthcare/Registered-nurses.htm.

U.S. Department of Labor Occupational Safety and Health Administration (OSHA). 2012. *Safety and Health Topics: Workplace Violence.* http://www.osha.gov/SLTC/workplaceviolence/

Uttal, Lynet. 1996. "Custodial Care, Surrogate Care, and Coordinated Care: Employed Mothers and the Meaning of Child Care." *Gender and Society* 10: 291–311.

———. 2002. *Making Care Work: Employed Mothers in the New Childcare Market.* New Brunswick, NJ: Rutgers University Press.

Uttal, Lynet, and Mary Tuominen. 1999. "Tenuous Relationships: Exploitation, Emotion, and Racial Ethic Significance in Paid Child Care Work." *Gender and Society* 13: 758–80.

Village, J., M. Frazer, M. Cohen, A. Leyland, I. Park, and A. Yassi. 2005. "Electromyography as a Measure of Peak and Cumulative Workload in Intermediate Care and Its Relationship to Musculoskeletal Injury: An Exploratory Ergonomic Study." *Applied Ergonomics* 36 (5): 609–18.

Waehrer, Geetha, J. Paul Leigh, and Ted R. Miller. 2005. "Costs of Occupational Injury and Illness within the Health Services Sector." *International Journal of Health Services* 35 (2): 343–59.

Waerness, Kari. 1978. "The Invisible Welfare State: Women's Work at Home." *Acta Sociologica.* Special Congress Supplement: The Nordic Welfare State.

———. 1996. "The Rationality of Caring." In *Caregiving: Readings in Knowledge, Practice, Ethics, and Politics*, ed. S. Gordon, P. E. Benner, and N. Noddings, 231–54. Philadelphia: University of Pennsylvania Press.

Wåhlstrom, Jens, Christina Ostman, and Ola Leijon. 2012. "The Effect of Flooring on Musculoskeletal Symptoms in the Lower Extremities and Low Back among Female Nursing Assistants." *Ergonomics* 55 (2): 248–55.

Walker, James R. 1992. "New Evidence on the Supply of Child Care: A Statistical Portrait of Family Providers and an Analysis of Their Fees." *Journal of Human Resources* 27: 40–69.

Wang, Wendy, Kim Parker, and Paul Taylor. 2013. *Breadwinner Moms.* Pew Research Center May 29. www.pewresearch.org.

Ware, John E., Mark Kosinski, and Susan D. Keller. 1995. *SF-12: How to Score the SF-12 Physical and Mental Health Summary Scales.* 2nd ed. Boston: The Health Institute, New England Medical Center.

Waters, Thomas R., Audrey Nelson, and Caren Proctor. 2007. "Patient Handling Tasks with High Risk for Musculoskeletal Disorders in Critical Care." *Critical Care Nursing Clinics of North America* 19 (2): 131–43.

Waters, Thomas R.,Vern Putz-Anderson, and Arun Garg. 1994. *Applications Manual for the Revised NIOSH Lifting Equation.* Cincinnati, OH: National Institute for Occupational Safety and Health, Centers for Disease Control and Prevention.

Weeden, Kim. 2002. "Why Do Some Occupations Pay More Than Others? Social Closure and Earnings Inequality in the United States." *American Journal of Sociology* 108 (1): 55–101.

Westlund, Jennie. 2007. "Increased Parental Choice Can Lead to Reduced Gender Inequality." *NIKK Magazine* 2.

Wexler, Sherry. 1997. "Work/Family Policy Stratification: The Examples of Family Support and Family Leave." *Qualitative Sociology* 20 (2): 311–22.

Wharton, Amy. 1999. "The Psychosocial Consequences of Emotional Labor." *Annals of the American Academy of Political and Social Science* 561 (1): 158–76.

———. 2009. "The Sociology of Emotional Labor." *Annual Review of Sociology* 35: 147–65.

Whittington, Frank J. 2011. "Denying and Defying Death: The Culture of Dying in 21st Century America." *The Gerontologist* 51 (4): 571–79.

Wilburn, Susan Q. 2004. "Needlestick and Sharps Injury Prevention." *Online Journal of Issues in Nursing* 9 (3). September 30.

Williams, Joan. 2010. *Reshaping the Work-Family Debate: Why Men and Class Matter.* Cambridge, MA: Harvard University Press.

Winstanley, Sue, and Lisa Hales. 2008. "Prevalence of Aggression towards Residential Social Workers: Do Qualifications and Experience Make a Difference?" *Child Youth Care Forum* 37: 103–10.

Wipfli, Brad, Ryan Olson, Robert Wright, Layla Garrigues, and Joanne Lees. 2012. "Characterizing Hazards and Injuries among Home Care Workers." *Home Healthcare Nurse* 30 (7): 387–93.

Witz, Anne. 1990. "Patriarchy and Professions: The Gendered Politics of Occupational Closure." *Sociology* 24 (4): 675–90.

Wolf, Carin, and Niklas Löfgren. 2007. "Welcome to the Swedish Social Insurance Agency." Presentation to Social Insurance Agency, Stockholm.

Wolkowitz, Carol. 2006. *Bodies at Work.* Thousand Oaks, CA: Sage.

Wrigley, Julia. 1995. *Other People's Children.* New York: Basic Books.

Yamada, Yoshiko. 2002. "Profile of Home Care Aides, Nursing Home Aides, and Hospital Aides: Historical Changes and Data Recommendations." *Gerontologist* 42 (2): 199–206.

Yassi, Annalee, Marcy Cohen, Yuri Cvitkovich, Il Hyoek Park, Pamela A. Ratner, Aleck S. Ostry, Judy Village, and Nancy Polla. 2004. "Factors Associated with Staff Injuries in Intermediate Care Facilities in British Columbia, Canada." *Nursing Research* 53 (2): 87–98.

Yeates, Nicola. 2009. *Globalizing Care Economies and Migrant Workers: Explorations in Global Care Chains.* London: Palgrave Macmillan.

Zelizer, Viviana A. 1985. *Pricing the Priceless Child: The Changing Social Value of Children.* New York: Basic Books.

———. 2005. *The Purchase of Intimacy.* Princeton, NJ: Princeton University Press.

Zelnick, Jennifer R., Elspeth Slayter, Beth Flanzbaum, Nanci Ginty Butler, Beryl Domingo, Judith Perlstein, and Carol Trust. 2013. "Part of the Job? Workplace Violence in Massachusetts Social Service Agencies." *Health Social Work* 38 (2): 75–85.

Zerubavel, Eviatar. 1979. *Patterns of Time in Hospital Life: A Sociological Perspective.* Chicago: University of Chicago Press.

Zhang, Yuan, Laura Punnett, Rebecca Gore, and CPH-NEW Research Team. 2012. "Relationships among Employees' Working Conditions, Mental Health, and Intention to Leave in Nursing Homes." *Journal of Applied Gerontology* DOI: 10.1177/0733464812443085.

Zimmerman, Mary K. 2013. "Theorizing Inequality: Comparative Policy Regimes, Gender, and Everyday Lives." *Sociological Quarterly* 54 (1): 66–80.

Zimmerman, Mary K, Jacquelyn Litt, and Christine Bose. 2006. *Global Dimensions of Gender and Carework.* Stanford, CA: Stanford University Press.

Notes on Contributors

Nickela Anderson holds an MA in sociology from the University of Alberta. Her contribution to this collection was supported by a Faculty of Arts Summer Student Research Award. Anderson continues to be interested in research methodology and methods. She currently works as a research analyst for the Safety Codes Council of Alberta.

Amy Armenia, PhD, is an associate professor of sociology at Rollins College in Winter Park, Florida. Her dissertation research explored professionalization and unionization campaigns for family daycare workers and involved field research with movement organizations and a large-scale survey of home day-care workers. She has also conducted research on unpaid care, including work on family leave taking and employer compliance with the Family and Medical Leave Act.

Lindsey L. Ayers is a doctoral student in the Department of Sociology at Kent State University. She earned a BA in anthropology from Douglass College of Rutgers University and an MA in sociology from Kent State University. Her dissertation examines the extent to which concepts and relationships central to identity theory can explain stigmatized identity processes. Her research interests include identity and the self, stigma, and emotion.

Meg A. Bond is a professor of psychology and the director of the Center for Women and Work at the University of Massachusetts–Lowell. Her past publications have addressed sexual harassment, collaboration among diverse constituencies, and empowerment of underrepresented groups in community and organizational settings. Her book *Workplace Chemistry: Promoting Diversity through Organizational Change* (2007) chronicles a long-term organizational change project focused on issues of gender and race/ethnicity. Bond is a former president of the Society for Community Research and Action (SCRA) and currently serves on the American Psychological Association Board for the Advancement of Psychology in the Public Interest.

Ivy Bourgeault, PhD, is a professor of health sciences at the University of Ottawa and the Canadian Institutes of Health Research Chair in Health Human Resource Policy. Bourgeault has garnered an international reputation for her research on health professions, health policy, and women's health. She has published in national and international journals and edited volumes on midwifery and maternity care, primary care delivery, advanced practice nursing, qualitative health research methods, and complementary and alternative medicine.

Jon Boyer, ScD, practices environmental health and safety risk management at a teaching hospital in Boston. Trained in industrial hygiene, ergonomics, occupational epidemiology, and work environment policy, his interests include sociotechnical systems theory to translate research into sustainable engineering solutions for employee and patient health and safety. He has authored journal articles on biomechanics, ergonomic risks of patient handling, exposure assessment methods, musculoskeletal epidemiology, and socioeconomic risk factors for healthcare worker health and safety.

Cindy L. Cain, PhD, is a postdoctoral research associate at the Health Policy and Management Division of the School of Public Health at the University of Minnesota. Her research focuses on emotional experiences in end-of-life care, team dynamics in the administration of care, and institutional logics that structure caring work and workers' sense of self.

Dan Clawson is the author of *The Next Upsurge: Labor and the New Social Movements* and teaches sociology at the University of Massachusetts–Amherst.

Janette S. Dill is an assistant professor in the sociology department at the University of Akron in Akron, Ohio. Her current research focuses on job quality in a changing economy, particularly in the healthcare sector.

Lisa Dodson is a research professor in the sociology department at Boston College and visiting scholar at the Institute for Child, Youth, and Family Policy, Brandeis University. Her work focuses on race, class, and gender; low-wage work and family care; and two-generation social mobility. She is the author of numerous scholarly and policy papers on low-income family life. Her most recent book, *The Moral Underground: How Ordinary People Subvert an Unfair Economy* (2010), explores uncovered cross-class concerns, conflicts, and alliances in response to growing economic inequality and family care crises.

Mignon Duffy, PhD, is an associate professor of sociology and the associate director of the Center for Women and Work at the University of Massachusetts–Lowell. Duffy's research focuses on the theoretical, empirical, and policy implications of understanding paid care as a sector. Her 2011 book, *Making Care Count: A Century of Gender, Race, and Paid Care Work*, provides a comprehensive history of the evolution of paid care.

Brandy Farrar is a researcher at the American Institutes for Research in Washington, DC. Her research involves evaluating the effectiveness, viability, and impact of innovative programs designed to improve quality, access, and capacity of healthcare services. Trained as a social psychologist, Farrar's work explores the interplay of individual, institutional, and cultural processes in shaping the education, training, status, rewards, and quality of care associated with occupations at all levels and sectors in the healthcare industry.

Naomi Gerstel, PhD, is Distinguished University Professor in the Department of Sociology at the University of Massachusetts–Amherst. Her current research with Dan Clawson, supported by the National Science Foundation, the Sloan Foundation, PERI, and the Russell Sage Foundation, examines the processes producing the hours and schedules faced by paid care workers (see their 2014 book, *Unequal Time: Gender, Class, and Family in Employment Schedules*). Her prior research on paid and unpaid care has been published in numerous peer-reviewed journals. She is the recipient of several honors, including a Russell Sage Foundation Visiting Scholar Award, the Rosabeth Kanter Award, and the Robin Williams Award.

Clare Hammonds is a professor of practice at University of Massachusetts–Amherst. Her dissertation compares unionization efforts among childcare workers and personal care attendants. Hammonds worked as a research assistant measuring the scope of paid care work for the project *Counting on Care: Human Infrastructure in Massachusetts* and has published work on emotional labor among intensive care unit nurses. She received a BS in Industrial and Labor relations from Cornell University and an MS in Labor Studies from the University of Massachusetts–Amherst.

Michelle C. Haynes, PhD, is an associate professor of psychology and an associate at the Center for Women and Work at the University of Massachusetts–Lowell. Her research examines workplace diversity issues with a particular focus on how stereotyping contributes to obstacles individuals face in their climb up the organizational hierarchy. She is particularly interested in how organizations can cultivate and benefit from diverse workforces. She is also the co-founder and coordinator of the Workplace Diversity Graduate Certificate at the University of Massachusetts–Lowell.

Michelle D. Holmberg, MA, focuses her work on empowering marginalized groups, both in terms of workforce representation and in access to important resources like broadband Internet. Her research has examined attitudes toward minority groups, with a focus on lesbian, gay, bisexual, and transgender (LGBT) rights and issues.

Karen D. Hughes is a professor in the Department of Sociology and the Department of Strategic Management and Organization at the University of Alberta. She holds a PhD from the University of Cambridge. She is the author of four books, including *Female Enterprise in the New Economy* and *Work, Industry, and Canadian Society*, and has published numerous articles on issues related to women's employment and entrepreneurship, gender diversity and inclusion, and work-family balance and caregiving. She currently serves on the editorial board of the journal *Gender in Management.*

Alicia Kurowski, ScD, is a postdoctoral research fellow in the Department of Work Environment at the University of Massachusetts–Lowell. She earned a BS in industrial engineering at Northeastern University and an MS and ScD in occupational ergonomics at the University of Massachusetts–Lowell. Her doctoral dissertation examined the ergonomic exposures and physical workload of nursing assistants in nursing homes following a safe resident handling program. Her research interests also include occupational health, injury epidemiology, and return-to-work and disability research.

Deborah L. Little, PhD, is an associate professor of sociology at Adelphi University. She is an ethnographer who studies struggles to define and control the provision of care. Little has published articles on the conflicts between clients and workers over the meaning of good mothering in welfare reform programs and on the challenges of constructing disability identity in the face of medicalized definitions of impairment. She is currently studying tensions between care theory and disability theory as they each seek give voice to participants in care relationships.

Cameron Lynne Macdonald, PhD, a founding member of the Carework Network, teaches medical sociology, health policy, and research methods at Harvard University. Her research explores caregiving in public and private contexts. Her book *Shadow Mothers: Nannies, Au Pairs, and the Micropolitics of Mothering* analyzes how factors like ethnicity, social class, and mothering ideologies influence the negotiation of the division of mothering labor between working mothers and their childcare providers. Her most recent work on "healthcare offloading" explores how unpaid, untrained family members cope with the complex medical care they must provide at home.

Pia Markkanen, ScD, is a research professor in the Department of Work Environment at the University of Massachusetts–Lowell. Dr. Markkanen has been a co-investigator on the National Institute for Occupational Safety and Health (NIOSH)–funded Safe Home Care Project, which investigates a wide range of OSH hazards and promising practices among home care aide occupations in Massachusetts, as well as for Project SHARRP (Safe Home Care and Risk Reduction for Providers), which evaluated sharps injury and other blood exposure risks among home health care nurses and home health aides.

Jennifer Craft Morgan, PhD, is on the faculty of the Gerontology Institute at Georgia State University. Her research interest is in workforce studies within healthcare organizations. She has led five major funded projects evaluating the impact of career ladder, continuing education, and financial incentive workforce development programs on healthcare worker outcomes, quality of care outcomes, and perceived return on investment for healthcare organizations and educational partners. Her work seeks to tie research, education, and service together by focusing on the translation of lessons learned to help stakeholders build evidence-based solutions to pressing problems.

Kim Price-Glynn, PhD, is an associate professor of sociology and urban and community studies at the University of Connecticut. She was the inaugural recipient of the University of Connecticut College of Liberal Arts and Sciences Faculty Achievement Award for Excellence in Teaching in the Social Sciences. Her research examines labor, health, and caregiving in diverse organizational settings like nursing homes and strip clubs. Her book, *Strip Club: Gender, Power, and Sex Work*, was published in 2010.

Laura Punnett, ScD, is a professor of occupational ergonomics and epidemiology in the Department of Work Environment, University of Massachusetts–Lowell, as well as a senior associate of the UML Center for Women and Work. Her research focuses on work-related musculoskeletal disorders, the contribution of work environment to socioeconomic disparities and gender differences in health, and the effectiveness of workplace ergonomics and health and safety programs. Punnett is co-director of the Center to Promote Health in the New England Workplace (CPH-NEW), where she directs the evaluation of safe resident handling and employee health programs in a large chain of skilled nursing facilities.

Margaret Quinn, ScD, CIH, is a professor in the Department of Work Environment at the University of Massachusetts–Lowell. Her research focuses on creating healthy environments at work, home, and in communities. She directs the Sustainable Hospitals Program to conduct research and provide technical expertise to members of the healthcare community to implement environmentally sound, healthy, and safe materials, products, and work practices. She has been the principal investigator of two NIOSH-funded projects: Safe Home Care Project, which assesses a range of occupational safety outcomes in home care, and Project SHARRP, which evaluates the risks of sharps injuries and other blood and body fluid exposures among home healthcare workers.

Carter Rakovski, PhD, is an associate professor of sociology at California State University. Her research areas are work and gender, especially healthcare and caring labor. In addition, she studies employment among women with chronic conditions and is a researcher at the Fibromyalgia and Chronic Pain Center at CSUF. Her work has been published in a range of journals including the *Sociology of Health and Illness, Work, Employment and Society, Medical Care,* and the *Journal of Accounting Research.*

Susan Sama, ScD, RN, is a research professor in the Department of Work Environment at the University of Massachusetts–Lowell. She worked as a senior epidemiologist at the Washington State Department of Labor and Industries in the Safety and Health Assessment and Research for Prevention (SHARP) Program in Olympia, Washington. She is also part of a multidisciplinary occupational health research team that conducts a variety of epidemiological investigations. Dr. Sama provides epidemiological support for the Reliant Medical Group Research Department in Worcester, Massachusetts.

Rachel Sherman teaches sociology at the New School for Social Research. Her interests include social class, culture, and the production and consumption of services. She is the author of *Class Acts: Service and Inequality in Luxury Hotels.* Her current research is on elites in New York City.

Fumilayo Showers recently completed her PhD from the Sociology Department at the Maxwell School of Citizenship and Public Affairs of Syracuse University, and she is now an assistant professor of sociology at Central Connecticut State University. Her research interests include globalization, care work, gender, and international migration. Her current research examines the labor market incorporation of West African immigrant women as nurses, focusing on the Washington, DC, metropolitan area.

Teresa Shroll, BA, is a graduate student in the Community Social Psychology program at the University of Massachusetts–Lowell working with community leaders to improve senior citizens' access to community services. She worked through the Emerging Scholars program at the Center for Women and Work as part the Healthy Diversity Team, investigating strategies used by community health centers to educate and promote their culturally diverse entry-level employees. She volunteers at the Chelmsford Crossing assisted living home, committed to improving the lives of our seniors.

Clare L. Stacey is an associate professor of sociology at Kent State University. Her book *The Caring Self* (2011) explores the work experiences of home care aides in the United States. Research and teaching interests include death and dying, care work in health contexts, and doctor-patient interaction. Her new work examines how patient and provider cultures converge in the context of end-of-life care.

Robin A. Toof, EdD, is co-director of the University of Massachusetts–Lowell Center for Community Research and Engagement and the director of the Service-Learning and Community Co-Op Resource Office. She has worked in the field of research and evaluation, community partnerships, program management, and facilitation for over twenty years. She also has facilitated numerous team building, training, and strategic planning workshops for corporate, nonprofit, college, and youth work teams and has taught graduate courses in grant writing, program evaluation, and working with groups.

LaTonya J. Trotter is an assistant professor in the Department of Sociology at Vanderbilt University. Trotter is a sociologist of medicine whose research explores how shifts in the organization of medical work create and dismantle forms of meaning, value, and sociality. Her current work focuses on nurse practitioners. Through ethnographic attention to workplace interactions, she explores how the nurse practitioner's work, expertise, and value is crafted through routine interactions with physicians, patients, administrators, and others who work in primary care settings.

Jennifer Zelnick, ScD, MSW, is associate professor and chair of the Social Welfare Policy Sequence at the Touro College Graduate School of Social Work. She is the author of *Who Is Nursing Them? It Is Us*, a study of needlestick injuries among South African public sector nurses in the context of post-apartheid economic globalization. Currently she is involved with an investigation of the connections between gender, stigma, and occupational risk of infectious disease among South African health care workers, a series of studies on workplace violence and stress among social workers in the United States, and a collaboration with South African social work faculty comparing social welfare policy and practice in the global South and North.

Mary K. Zimmerman is Joy McCann Professor of Women in Medicine and Science, University of Kansas School of Medicine, and a professor of sociology and of health policy and management at the University of Kansas. Her research centers on care work in the context of comparative social policies and health care systems and focuses on issues of gender equity and women's health. Her most recent book is *Global Dimensions of Gender and Carework* (2006).

Rebekah M. Zincavage is a doctoral candidate for a joint PhD in sociology and social policy at Brandeis University, where she teaches courses on family, inequality, and health policy. Her current research examines care work among adult siblings and is focused on the intersections of mental health policy and family life.

Index

wages for paid care, 10–11, 56, 226; for
administrative workers, 61; care workers at
risk of poverty, 29, 35–36, 63, 181–182, 184,
276; for childcare workers, 11, 44, 47–48,
52, 241; for direct care workers, 36–37, 56,
60, 252, 276–277; economic inequality,
290; for frontline workers, 55–57, 60–63,
66n2; of home care workers, 11, 28, 102; of
long-term healthcare workers, 56, 62–63,
276; of nurses, 11, 44, 133; for nursing
assistants, 11, 181–182, 194–195, 251; of
self-employed workers, 47–49, 51, 241;
stratification within paid care jobs, 11; for
teachers, 11, 237–238; unionization and,
237; wage penalty for nurturant care
workers, 44, 133
welfare reform, 15, 20, 22, 114–116
Williams, Joan, 214
Witz, Anne, 242
women: as administrative workers, 61;
associated with nursing, 132–133, 145–146;
as builders of society, 291; charity work of,
23; as childcare providers, 241; devaluation
of women's work, 132–133; as direct care
workers, 35–36, 60, 252, 277; as domestic
servants, 16; dual earner/dual carer model
and, 215; experiences of immigrant nurses,
143–152; as frontline healthcare workers,
54, 56, 64; gender inequality, 7, 55, 132,
220, 242; history of mothering, 22; as
home-care workers, 20; in lesser-skilled
occupations, 19, 263, 290; as majority
of care workers, 133, 189; as nursing
assistants, 181; parental insurance and, 220;

parental leave (Swedish) and, 214–222;
as primary breadwinners, 213;
professionalization of medicine and, 18,
242; in psychology, 24; self-employment
and, 44–45, 52; teaching as female
occupation, 21–22; wage gap, 10, 132;
welfare reform and, 15
working conditions, 11, 38, 187, 285; of
childcare workers, 45–46, 52; consequences
of poor, 259–260, 285; of direct care workers,
252, 256, 258–260; efforts to improve, 12, 41,
103, 225, 229, 240, 244, 259, 262, 290;
emotional work and, 174; home care
contrasted with facility-based care, 33–35,
38, 41; of home care workers, 20, 94–96,
103; older adult care workers, 118–120, 123,
125; professionalization and, 242; of
self-employed workers, 43–47, 53;
workplace injuries and, 83–89, 103, 105
work schedules, 185–186, 226; as barrier to
advancement, 226; home-based care and,
68, 70–71, 75–77; job satisfaction and, 43;
of nursing assistants, 183–186; quality of
care and, 288–289; workers' lack of control
over, 86, 123

Yaeger, Brenda Lee, 116n1

Zelizer, Viviana, 21, 190–191, 202, 211–212
Zelnick, Jennifer, 323–324; chapter by,
79–80, 104–116
Zimmerman, Mary K., 324; chapter by, 213–223
Zincavage, Rebekah, 324; chapter by, 177–178,
191–200